JOHNSON COUNTY PUBLIC LIBRARY

3 2938 00530 8328

#44426879

W9-BUU-828

940.40973 M
Mead, Gary
The doughboys

WHITE RIVER LIBRARY

Johnson County Public Library
401 South State Street
Franklin, IN 46131

WITHDRAWN

THE DOUGHBOYS

THE DOUGHBOYS

AMERICA AND THE FIRST WORLD WAR

GARY MEAD

THE OVERLOOK PRESS

WOODSTOCK & NEW YORK

White River Library
Johnson County Public Library
1664 Library Boulevard
Greenwood, IN 46142

For Freya and Theodora

First published in the United States in 2000 by
The Overlook Press, Peter Mayer Publishers, Inc.
Lewis Hollow Road
Woodstock, New York 12498
www.overlookpress.com

Copyright © 2000 by Gary Mead

All Rights reserved. No part of this publication may be reproduced or
transmitted in any form or by any means, electronic or mechanical, including
photocopy, recording, or any information storage and retrieval system now known
or to be invented without permission in writing from the publisher, except by
a reviewer who wishes to quote brief passages in connection with a review
written for inclusion in a magazine, newspaper, or broadcast.

Library of Congress Cataloging-in-Publication Data

Mead, Gary.
The Doughboys : America and the First World War / Gary Mead.
p. cm.
Originally published: London : Allen Lane, 2000.
Includes bibliographical references and index.
1. World War, 1914-1918—United States.
2. World War, 1914-1918—Campaigns—Western Front.   I. Title
D570 M43 2000 ✓ 940.4'0973—dc21   00-055751

Manufactured in the United States of America
FIRST EDITION
1 3 5 7 9 8 6 4 2
ISBN 1-58567-061-8

Contents

CONTENTS

List of Figures and Maps

Introduction and Acknowledgements

This book is not a comprehensive history of the years 1917 to 1920, nor even of US–European relations during that period, but a version of some of the key events of that period seen from the US perspective. It tries to redress the balance of history by reinstating the vital importance of the American contribution to the defeat of the Central Powers in November 1918. For many, the suggestion that it was the United States that ensured a victory may come as a surprise. A fog of historical forgetfulness fell, for different reasons, upon the Americans, the British and the French alike, fairly soon after the war ended in 1918. Dispelling that fog will take much more than a single book, but this, along with other recent works, is perhaps a start.*

The huge book-publishing industry which has grown up around the US Civil War probably generates annual revenues bigger than those of some of the world's smaller nations. Almost all aspects of the campaigns American soldiers participated in during the Second World War, in Korea, and in Vietnam, have been microscopically scrutinized. But who remembers the two million Americans shipped to France in 1917–18, never mind the two million more who joined up but never even crossed the Atlantic? Yet many of their individual stories are fascinating, while the more general account of how they got to France, what they found there and how they responded to the complexities of a European war has a significance far beyond the Great War itself. If we want to understand America's continuing role in Europe we need to grasp how and why America became involved in the First World War before that story recedes further into oblivion. We are now almost as distant from the Great War as some of its participants were from the struggle to defeat Napoleon Bonaparte.

---

* The bibliography refers the reader to a number of recent publications.

The reason why such history is vital is because, as many have said before, it helps us to understand the present and the future. This was the first time a US military force fought on European soil, the first time the United States took upon itself a kind of policing role there, an uncomfortable role with which it has had to struggle ever since. The latest manifestation of this ambivalence – a theoretical commitment to act as Europe's policeman while loathing the inevitable frustration that entails – can be seen just as clearly today in the disasters following the collapse of the former Yugoslavia. Individuals and nations understandably resent ingratitude; if we seek reasons why the United States has been on occasion a relatively reluctant saviour of European civilization, an understanding of what happened in the Great War is vital. The rescue of Europe from a military, social and human disaster, then as now, incurred little but ingratitude. The intervention in April 1917, when the war was already almost three years old, was undertaken by President Woodrow Wilson at a time when there was no obvious immediate threat to US interests; when there was no compelling need to go to war; and in the absence of any overwhelming conviction among the American general public that such a step was imperative. In other words, America went to war in April 1917 because its president believed that it was morally the right thing to do. The United States had, he implied, an ethical duty to act as Europe's policeman, to step in and break up this ghastly brawl and make sure that such a murderous struggle could never happen again.

In Europe that moral idealism dribbled away like mercury during the Great War as the soldiers and politicians began to grasp that the issues were not as black-and-white as they had been led to believe, and that the concepts 'enemy' and 'ally' were less rigid than they might have hoped.

Without the doughboys* the Allies (Britain and France) would not have defeated the Central Powers (Germany and Austro-Hungary) in November 1918, and possibly never would have done so. This book hopes to establish that without the American Expeditionary Force (AEF) and the blood, sweat and tears of the American troops who

---

* Slang term for the US soldier of the day; see Chapter 4 for an exploration of the etymology.

came to France the Allies would have been in a very sorry state indeed by 1919. It re-examines the always prickly, often turbulent, relationship between the Americans and the Allies, and concludes that the mutual misunderstandings of 1917–19 sit uncomfortably with the notion that there has always been a 'special relationship' between Britain and the United States. If such a relationship existed in the First World War it was at the very least suffused with ambivalence, largely as a result of the many clashes experienced on the Western Front – clashes not with the German armies but between the British, French and US military leaderships.

The troubled relations of the Allies and the United States on the battlefield created the basis for the myth that the final victory was due almost entirely to the heroic efforts of the British and French armies from mid-1918 until 11 November that year. Those Allied soldiers showed tremendous courage and determination, but their efforts in the summer of 1918 would once more have failed to convert temporary breakthrough into lasting success without the presence of the AEF. This has been almost entirely obliterated in the European and American popular memory of the Great War.

How has this relative neglect come about? In the Great War almost nothing is simple; perhaps we should not expect a straightforward, rational explanation of how the importance of the AEF has come to be so seriously overlooked. Part of the answer must be the tremendous antipathy between the Americans and their supposed allies, which rapidly developed during the war and became the dominant response during its aftermath. The relationship between the Allies and their Associate (as Woodrow Wilson insisted on describing the United States, once he had declared war) was truly a case of familiarity breeding mutual contempt. The British and French wanted the Americans to join in the war against Germany, but only on their own terms – and those terms did not include giving away much glory in the event of a final victory.

Another explanation may be the relatively small number of deaths in battle suffered by the AEF. In this war of vast numbers, the death of tens, rather than hundreds, of thousands might seem to weigh less in the balance. The physical proximity of the battlefields to the British and French participants has also done much to keep alive in Britain and France the memory of what it was like to be there. By contrast, the geographical distance from the United States may have discouraged American veterans from returning (and thus breathing life into their past experiences) in the early years following the end of the war. On top of the physical distance has been grafted an emotional disengagement, as later, more immediately gut-wrenching conflicts (the Second World War, Korea, Vietnam) have come to dominate American domestic consciousness.

It is equally possible that, just as few individuals are fortunate enough to be able to look back on their adolescence with much pride, nations may forget the emotional blunderings of their youth. While the Civil War forged the birth of a nation, the First World War took the adolescent United States by the scruff of its neck and crushed its last remaining juvenile idealism; the United States grew up, for good and ill, in the final twenty months of the First World War. In the immediate aftermath of the Great War, particularly following the collapse of Woodrow Wilson's aspirations for the League of Nations, many Americans questioned the sacrifice America had made in order to extricate Europe from its mess. Wilson's utopianism, which persisted against the mass of contrary evidence in believing that the warring European nations would eventually see reason, rapidly passed into disfavour once it became clear that his calls for a lasting and equitable peace had fallen on stony ground. Soldiers returned from France with grim stories of the avarice, arrogance and incompetence of their former allies – and their own difficulties in finding work further embittered them. When they were back home, many doughboys heartily wished to forget the truculent, snobbish, and ultimately ungrateful British and French allies they left behind. Large numbers of them had undergone a physically terrifying and damaging experience; many more had found the Western Front psychologically brutalizing. In the 1920s many influential Americans came to regard the whole affair as a mistake, an adolescent adventure which in retrospect was rather embarrassing.

It can be argued too that the widespread amnesia concerning the AEF and the US contribution in general has arisen largely because Americans long ago surrendered the debate. For most of the Americans who fought in Europe in the Great War the experience was so embittering, and became so entwined with the belief that it helped bring about economic depression, that American popular consciousness increasingly concluded that participation was from the outset an error, that the practicalities of it were badly handled, and that ultimately all that sacrifice did nothing for US domestic interests.

The sheer magnitude of the US war effort in 1917–18 wreaked enormous havoc and left lasting scars on the country. Under Woodrow Wilson the United States managed to stay neutral for almost three years, but when America finally joined the Allies against the Central Powers the overwhelming majority of its population threw its weight behind the war effort. Prodigious quantities of men and money were ploughed into the battle against Germany. In less than twenty months more than three million American men joined the armed forces, many of them eager volunteers. This stupendous effort was directly responsible for bringing the war to an end far earlier than any British or French politician or general considered possible at the start of 1918.

This fast and – although accompanied by some horrendous logistical chaos – relatively well-organized effort to convert the United States from a civil to a military power was achieved at considerable social as well as economic cost. The drastic curtailment of civil liberties, the introduction of the draft, the federal government's indifference to widespread anti-German xenophobic violence and its fierce punishment of anti-war dissent – all were fundamental blows to the painstakingly constructed democratic fabric of the nation, of which Wilson had so often depicted himself as its greatest defender. The right of the individual to think and speak openly and without fear, surely the core principle to which most Americans would point if asked what their democracy was founded on, was seriously undermined. Of course such rights in 1917 were largely extended only to whites, so to speak of the United States as being an entirely democratic nation at that time is misleading. One of several cruel ironies of the US involvement was that while many American whites opposed to joining in the war soon began to doubt that they lived in a benign democracy, most American blacks started with high hopes that the 'freedom' being fought for would include them too.

This book focuses on the individual doughboy experience, and tries to place that experience in the larger context of the Allied–US relationship during the war itself. It is not a general history of the final days of the war, and makes only the briefest of references to the battles going on elsewhere on the Western Front, in sectors other than those held by the AEF. Military, not political, history is its subject matter, and though some political, economic and social history is necessary in order to understand more clearly the AEF and its impact, the delineation of that context is kept to a minimum. Nor is this book a foray into fiction, along the lines of 'counter-factual' history, the imagining of what might have been. It takes for granted that France and Britain were morally and politically correct to oppose German aggression, even if the conduct of the war by most of their politicians and senior military commanders often left much to be desired.

This vast panoply of human catastrophe, of individual courage amid mass mania, is a powerful story, one which has been largely submerged beneath the unquestioned assumption that the doughboys arrived late and did little, a mistaken view which as late as 1996 was being served up to non-specialist audiences: 'The Americans played an important, but not a decisive role in the final phase of the war.'*

What follows is an attempt to challenge such damnation by faint praise.

I am greatly indebted to the vast array of previous hands who have tilled the Western Front soil and produced invaluable texts; the bibliography identifies those I found most useful but makes no pretence to be a definitive guide, which would in itself be another book. I have quoted extensively from the diaries, letters and memoirs of the doughboys who have neither fame nor often much glory, simply because these are

---

* Winter and Baggett, p. 296. Such offhand dismissals of the AEF have gained ground in recent years: 'Partly because of deep institutional unpreparedness, and partly because of [General John] Pershing's personal insistence on the status of a "cobelligerent" rather than an "ally", the Americans failed to play any truly effective part in the war before September [1918]' (Griffith, p. 90). It was President Woodrow Wilson, not Pershing, who insisted the United States should be considered an 'Associate' and not an 'Ally', because the United States did not join the Triple Entente, the alliance signed between Britain, France and Russia. Pershing insisted on following the orders given him by Wilson, i.e. to form an independent US army in France. Griffith is far from being alone in castigating Pershing for following the orders given him by his commander-in-chief, Wilson.

the type of soldiers who interest me most of all. I do not claim their experiences to be particularly unusual; I hope rather that they are fairly representative. Although I am aware that the US marines have long been called 'leathernecks' (from the leather stock they were forced to wear round the neck to keep the head erect – part of their uniform between 1775 and 1875), and that the marine brigade which served so magnificently with the 2nd Division deserves special mention, I have for simplicity's sake used the general term 'doughboys' to apply to all troops of the AEF.

A small number of people and institutions deserve special thanks. This book would have been impossible without the kindness, loyalty, hard work and faith of my agent, Christopher Sinclair-Stevenson, and at Penguin Simon Winder and his colleague Ellah Allfrey. They are consummate professionals in an age where such high standards have all but disappeared. Considerable gratitude also goes to J. D. F. Jones, Katy Calder, Anne Kjelling, Martin Marix-Evans, the librarians at the Imperial War Museum in London, and all the staff at the Army Military History Institute at Carlisle Barracks in Pennsylvania, USA, especially Dr Richard Sommers and David Keogh. Thanks also to Brana Radovic, himself no mean military historian, for the comprehensive maps and graphics.

I would also like to thank the staff at The Overlook Press, who have done a fine job with the US edition; thanks especially to Peter Mayer, whose kind decision it was to see that the book gets in the hands of those potential readers whose grandfathers and great-grandfathers fought, and died, in France all those years ago.

My biggest gratitude, however, is to my wife Jane and our daughters Freya and Theodora. They each in their different ways made huge sacrifices. Their patience and toleration of prolonged absences were above and beyond the call of duty.

I take full responsibility for the final result.

A note on the text. The presence of square brackets enclosing an ellipsis indicates where I have excised material from the quoted source, solely for the purposes of brevity. In most cases I have left original spelling, except where it would interfere with the clarity of sense.

I

No More Sleeping Treason

'Good Lord! You're not going to send soldiers over there, are you?'
Thomas S. Martin, chairman of the
Senate Finance Committee, 6 April 1917[1]

A little after 8.30 p.m. on Monday, 2 April 1917 President Woodrow Wilson asked the US Congress to support his declaration of war on Germany. Wilson delivered his speech with his usual careful, slightly nasal enunciation; his audience was spellbound, the silence being interrupted only by a loud and eerie crash as a soldier standing guard dropped his rifle. 'The world,' Wilson told Congress, 'must be made safe for democracy.'[2] By 11 November 1918 it was evident that part of the price paid by the United States to ensure the safety of democracy in Europe was the weakening of its defences at home.

When Wilson sat down, Congress erupted with the kind of hysterical passion not seen since the wild scenes in Berlin, London and Paris in August 1914. Rather than ask themselves why Wilson's remarkable volte-face would be of greater benefit to democracy than his previous obstinate refusal to be forced into belligerency, almost as one the politicians jumped to their feet, shouting, applauding, crying and hugging one another. Some roared their opposition, but they were drowned amid the clamour for Wilson and war. Those like Theodore Roosevelt, who had been a bitter opponent of Wilson's neutrality, naturally praised his decision:

'The President's message is a great state paper which will rank in history with the great state papers of which Americans in future years will be proud. It now rests with the people of the country to see that we put into practice the policy that the President has outlined and that we strike hard, as soon and as efficiently as possible, in an aggressive war against the government of Germany.'[3]

Two days later the Senate convened at 10 a.m. to debate the presidential request. Many senators relished the opportunity to speak in a debate which they knew would mark a new epoch in US foreign affairs. The Senate droned on and the session did not rise until 11.15 p.m., though there was little opposition to Wilson's declaration. Only five spoke against war, including three Progressive Republicans: Robert La Follette of Wisconsin (a state with a large German-speaking population), George Norris of Nebraska, Asle Jorgenson Gronna of North Dakota; and two Democrats: James K. Vardaman of Mississippi and William J. Stone of Missouri. Norris, convinced the United States was being dragged into the conflict in order to ensure the Allies were able to repay their US-denominated debts and further boost the profits of US munitions manufacturers, declared: 'We are going into war upon the command of gold!' La Follette, a former presidential candidate, had a reputation as an honest, incorruptible and stubborn pacifist. Despite attempts to shout him down and yelled accusations that he was a pro-German traitor, La Follette spoke eloquently for three hours and gave Wilson a sombre warning:

'The poor, sir, who are the ones called upon to rot in the trenches, have no organized power, have no press to voice their will upon this question of peace or war, but, oh, Mr President, at some time they will be heard!'[4]

La Follette's oratorical skills were wasted. The Senate voted 82 to 6 in favour of war; of eight absentees, each one sent word they would have voted for war. As La Follette left the floor he was handed a noose, an undignified and tasteless gesture which set the tone for the manner in which America was to handle those who spoke out against war. On 5 April the House of Representatives followed the lead of the Senate and voted for war by 373 to 50. There was not only to be no turning back; there was to be no room for dissent, either. The editorial of the *Los Angeles Times* on 6 April 1917, when Congress formally declared war on Germany, did what newspapers do best; it voiced the *Zeitgeist*'s lowest common denominator:

The American people now freely forgive Woodrow Wilson for his inconsiderate, unconsidered, and sometimes dangerous actions and utterances in the past. [He] unthoughtfully, and unwisely, and unpatriotically put life into the sleeping treason that would avoid the righteous sacrifices of war.[5]

The editorial writer of the *Los Angeles Times* was relatively sober in his response to the changed course of government policy, but was nevertheless guilty of heavy-handed misrepresentation. For one thing, few of Wilson's utterances, and even fewer of his actions, were unconsidered. His adamant stance against involving the United States on either side in the European war, despite much provocation by both belligerent groups, was genuinely motivated by a deeply felt revulsion against bloodshed. In reluctantly setting course for war, Wilson was not jettisoning his most precious ambition, the achievement of a lasting and equable world peace. Instead he hoped to use the conflict to herd the Allies and the Central Powers more rapidly and firmly towards precisely the same goal.

This seemed a dramatic reversal of Wilson's previous policy, and yet he had quietly gone far towards committing himself to the Allied cause just over a year before. Colonel (an honorific title) Edward M. House, Wilson's closest political confidant, who had a roving informal ambassadorial brief to seek ways of achieving peace in Europe, had drawn up on 22 February 1916 with Sir Edward Grey, the British Foreign Secretary, the House–Grey Memorandum. This committed Wilson to calling for a conference to end the war when he was given an indication by Britain and France that they thought the time was right. Under its terms, if Britain and France accepted the invitation to come to the peace table and the Germans refused, the United States would 'probably' join the war on the side of the Allies. An additional point stated that the United States would 'probably' join the Allies if the conference met and Germany refused to accept a 'reasonable' settlement. House was already emotionally committed to the Allied cause; it was Wilson who inserted the two instances of 'probably'.[6] By April 1917 America was in any case operating a twin-track policy towards the war in Europe – the official government line was strict neutrality, but unofficially the Allies had come to depend for their survival upon American credit and munitions supplies. Wilson frequently protested that the United States regarded all the belligerents equally, but from 1914 a blind eye was turned to the rapid intertwining of US industry and finance with the cause of the Allies. The United States rapidly became the Allies' most important supplier of munitions, particularly explosives, a development which might have played into the hands of German propaganda but for the fact that in December 1914 the German Foreign Ministry had instructed Count Johann von Bernstorff, the German ambassador in Washington, to hand a memorandum to the US government expressly stating that Berlin recognized the legality of munitions exports.[7] This form of neutrality, financial profit without human cost, was good for American business. By the time America joined the war its munitions factories were churning out a million pounds of smokeless explosive powder a day, all of it destined for Allied artillery:

Instead of plunging at once into the conflict, we had some two years – discounting the preliminary depression – in which we sold munitions at high profits and received a general stimulus to our own production through the diffused and cumulative effects, with the result that we were able to consume more and at the same time to save enormously more; building up without felt abstinence the greater part of the productive plant for munition-making which was of actual service in fighting the War.[8]

By the end of 1916 Britain was obtaining 40 per cent of its military supplies from America.[9] Such trade was entirely legitimate under American law and many US business empires were founded on feeding the Allied war machine. Other American businessmen were less happy, as their customers in Germany, Scandinavia and the rest of continental Europe were put beyond their reach by the interference of Royal Navy ships in controlling, inspecting and impounding any of the world's merchant shipping suspected of carrying 'contraband'. Britain organized its purchase of US arms and supplies through the leading US finance house of J. P. Morgan,[10] appointing it in January 1915 the sole purchasing agent, as well as its US financial agent for the War Office and the Admiralty. This was a politically charged choice by the British government; the firm of J. P. Morgan was staunchly Republican and deeply resented by Wilson's Democratic administration, particularly as Wilson had made clear during his election campaign his dislike of large financial corporates. J. P. Morgan Jnr., who ran the firm (J. P. Morgan Snr. had died in 1913), was a fervent anglophile, spending six months of each year in England and socializing with the English aristocracy. The Morgan name – including Morgan Grenfell in London and Morgan Harjes et Cie in France – quickly came to dominate Allied purchasing and the business of raising loans for the Allied war effort. Under a commercial agreement signed on 15 January 1915 by the British War Office and Admiralty and J. P. Morgan, Morgan promised to 'use their best endeavours to secure for His Majesty's Government the most favourable terms as to quality price delivery discounts and rebates and also to aid and stimulate by all means at their disposal sources of supply for the articles required'.

In exchange, the house of Morgan got a 2 per cent commission on the net price of all items purchased up to £10 million, and 1 per cent on any goods above that; the amount of commission thus earned by J. P. Morgan has been put at some £30 million altogether, in excess of £1 billion in 1998 terms. Morgan Grenfell in London and J. P. Morgan in the United States even had a private code for their telegraphic correspondence, which – unlike that of the War Office and the Admiralty – was not required to go through the Foreign Office, such was the importance accorded to the business of purchasing supplies.[11] Thus while Wilson did his utmost to preserve America's position of neutrality, much American business was completely partisan, though that did not necessarily imply anything more than good business sense:

> To allege that J. P. Morgan & Co. brought the United States into the World War to save their investments (which for the most part they passed on anyway, of course) is to take a very romantic view of such affairs. All they did was simply to facilitate – in accordance with their own sympathies, their own interests and business philosophies – the erection of the machinery which made us a vital part of the World War. Our neutrality was at an end. After that, our actual military participation was largely a question of chance.[12]

By April 1917 Washington hosted three permanent British missions: one from the Ministry of Munitions, with 1,600 staff, purchasing military supplies for both Britain and France; representatives from the

Board of Trade; and the Wheat Export Company, representing the Royal Commission on Wheat Supplies (which in fact controlled purchases not just of wheat but all types of grain and pulses).[13] By 1916 the Wheat Export Company was purchasing supplies not just for Britain but also for France and Italy. Inspectors from the US section of the Ministry of Munitions

were in every [US] factory which had a contract with Britain, its agent rode the trains carrying the munitions to port in order to prevent thievery and sabotage, and its agents watched the loading of the munitions on board the ships to prevent time bombs being placed aboard. Its relations with Morgan's were amicable. Its success as an organization lay in its simultaneous efficiency and unobtrusiveness; even when Anglo-American relations were most strained, neither the Administration nor the Congress singled it out for attack.[14]

At a moment of crisis in Anglo-American relationships in late 1916 the Treasury revealed that of the £5 million daily costs to Britain of running the war, £2 million was spent in the United States.[15] By January 1917 the intensity of the relationship had reached the critical point 'where Britain no longer had control over her external financial affairs, but was at the mercy of events and the American government'.[16]

The financial situation for Britain was then indeed desperate. Its spending in America on vital munitions and other military and civil supplies was running at the equivalent of $75 million a week in the first months of 1917. By April 1917 its credit facilities in the United States were almost exhausted; at the current rate it had an estimated three weeks before all means of American finance dried up. There was still £114 million in gold sitting in the vaults of the Bank of England, but that was it. Without further American credit (and there was little willingness by US banks to lend any more), Britain's war effort would have rapidly ground to a halt, leaving little option but to sue for a negotiated peace, watch its armies fall apart for lack of weapons, shells and foodstuffs – and perhaps face the humiliating prospect of seeing President Woodrow Wilson finally be able to achieve his ambition of dictating a settlement to the belligerents.[17]

While some American businessmen made handsome profits from the Allies, others were bitterly antagonistic towards the British, as a result of the Royal Navy's policy of search and confiscation of any contraband cargoes aboard neutral merchant vessels deemed to be headed for Germany and its allies. On 18 July 1916 the British government, much to the disgust of American businessmen and politicians, published a blacklist of 87 US and 350 Latin American companies alleged to be trading with the Central Powers. It made little difference to US businessmen and politicians that the vast majority of these companies were outside the United States; since the Monroe Doctrine (in 1823) the United States had regarded South America as within its sphere of influence. Many resented the fact that through a variety of neat devices, including the establishment in neutral European countries of 'shell' companies, the British controlled every aspect of transatlantic trade:

[. . .] at both ends of the Atlantic passage, American trade with the Central Powers was subject before the end of 1914 to a 'voluntary' system of British supervision as astonishing in its extent as it was probably abhorrent both to domestic and international law. One hesitates to think of the storm of popular outrage which would have resulted had the Germans been in a position to exert one tenth of the interference [. . .] practiced by the Allies [. . .] already cotton cargoes en route to Europe were being solemnly unloaded at New York and X-rayed, bale by bale, at the American shipper's expense and under the eyes of British officials, lest they might carry concealed contraband. American manufacturers and exporters were being formed into the first of the trade associations which, acting in effect as the agents of a foreign power in American industry, were rigidly to enforce every order from Downing Street, and to act – despite anti-trust laws – in complete restraint of trade with the Central Powers.[18]

Yet the British blockade of Germany – which required all neutral merchant vessels to enter the North Sea only by way of the Straits of Dover, thus making the detaining, inspection and confiscation of suspect cargoes so much simpler – was rendered more effective than it might have been by the relative passivity of the US government. Ships which went by alternative routes were informed that they did so at their own peril as they were full of mines; but in reality this was a veiled warning to neutral merchant ships, including those of the United States, not to challenge the dominance of the Royal Navy. Thanks to the influence of pro-British diplomatic and political figures such as Colonel House and Walter Hines Page, the US ambassador to the Court of St James, this violation of the laws of the sea evoked from the federal government hardly a ripple of protest to London, even though the State Department was bombarded with letters of protest from cotton and other basic-commodity producers, complaining about British interference; each of these was taken up, investigated, presented to the British for comment . . . and then usually filibustered out of existence. If the complaint was pursued to the bitter end, the British caved in and bought the withheld cargo at the prevailing market price.

Wilson had fought long and hard to preserve his country's neutrality, but when the time for action arrived he threw his whole weight behind both the war and the peace efforts:

I advise that the Congress declare the recent course of the Imperial German Government to be in fact nothing less than war against the Government and people of the United States; that it formally accept the status of belligerent which has thus been thrust upon it, and that it take immediate steps not only to put the country in a more thorough state of defense but also to exert all its power and employ all its resources to bring the Government of the German Empire to terms and end the war.

What this will involve is clear [. . .] It will involve the organization and mobilization of all the material resources of the country to supply the materials of war and serve the incidental needs of the nation in the most abundant and yet the most economical and efficient way possible.[19]

While the declaration of war on Germany delighted an influential minority of anglophiles and satisfied the *amour propre* of the patriotically inclined majority, it was nevertheless something of a surprise for most Americans, who had imagined that their president was irrevocably wedded to neutrality, no matter the degree of insult endured. The popular view, encouraged by his political aides, was that Wilson had campaigned for re-election in November 1916 on the slogan 'he kept us out of the war'. Yet this phrase never actually passed Wilson's own lips; he was far too astute to commit himself irrevocably to peace, knowing that one day he might have to take America into war. Wilson inhabited what he undoubtedly felt was the moral high ground, a region he clearly demarcated from that occupied by his fellow international statesmen. Another way of looking at it is that his high-minded idealism was out of touch with the realities of what had *de facto* spread from being a European into a global conflict. Though in public Wilson vowed nothing but peace, in private he had often acknowledged the possibility of war. On 22 January 1917 he had addressed the Senate and insisted his goal was

'peace without victory [...] Victory would mean peace forced upon the loser, a victor's terms imposed upon the vanquished. It would be accepted in humiliation, under duress, at an intolerable sacrifice, and would leave a sting, a resentment, a bitter memory upon which terms of peace would rest, not permanently, but only as upon quicksand. Only a peace between equals can last, only a peace the very principle of which is equality and a common participation in a common benefit. The right state of mind, the right feeling between nations, is as necessary for a lasting peace as is the just settlement of vexed questions of territory or of racial and national allegiance.'[20]

At such a distance it is hard to know what to make of this. To some extent the speech was an elaboration of Wilson's objective (set forth by him in May 1916) of establishing a league of nations to ensure that such wars would never happen again. It came also after a note from him of 18 December 1916, which called for peace negotiations to start. At this time Wilson hoped that the relative weakness of both the Allies and Germany after years of debilitating conflict might have induced in them a readiness to talk terms. Yet on the other hand it was quite clear at the time that among the combatants on the Western Front there was no interest whatsoever in achieving a 'peace between equals' but only victory, and the spoils of victory. To preach morality and reason to those engaged in a bitter life-and-death struggle was either saintly or silly; it was not particularly sagacious. For Wilson, whose mind was framed by the nineteenth-century Liberal virtues of peace and free commerce, war was both immoral *and* stupid. Since August 1914 he had deftly performed a high-wire act by preserving America's position as the most important neutral power. His earnest desire to be a peace-broker on the international stage neatly coincided with US self-interest; Wilson's neutrality inadvertently permitted American munitions-makers to expand their activities and reap immense profits by supplying the Allies. By nature an ascetic, academically-inclined character – the only US president (so far) to have gained a Ph.D. – Wilson's natural emotional chilliness had been cast into deep-freeze by the death of his first wife just as war broke out in August 1914. Her demise badly scarred him and sapped his otherwise formidable grasp on international affairs, just at the moment when his powers of ratiocination and appetite for patient negotiation might have been useful.

But although the silent majority of Americans probably longed for nothing more than a continuation of their country's neutrality, by April 1917 their patience had been sorely tried by the German prosecution of the war. For more than two years American citizens had been the inadvertent victims of German efforts to starve the Allies into submission. Drowned by U-boat torpedoes, their factories subject to incendiary attacks and their sensibilities disgusted by alleged German atrocities, even-handed judgement as to which side bore the heaviest guilt for the slaughter had become gradually more difficult. The sinking of the liner *Lusitania* in May 1915 had been for many Americans a symbolic turning-point. A young regular army officer, George Patton, wrote to his father after that incident: 'I think that we ought to declare war if Germany failes [*sic*] as she should to pay heed to our foolish talk. If Wilson had as much blood in him as the liver of a louse is commonly thought to contain he would do this.'[21] The widely held assumption after the *Lusitania* was that if Wilson would not be spurred into action by such an outrage, then nothing would budge him.

Just as the nation was taken by surprise on 2 April 1917, so too were the authorities responsible for putting the declaration into action. Not until a month had passed after Wilson addressed Congress did Major-General John Pershing receive a cable (on 3 May) hinting at what his future role might be. Even then it did not come from the War Department or even the President but from Pershing's father-in-law, Senator F. E. Warren. The telegram asked Pershing to 'wire me to-day whether and how much you speak, read and write French'. Pershing replied (with, as he admitted later, little regard for the strict truth) that he had 'spent several months in France in nineteen eight studying language. Spoke quite fluently; could read and write very well at that time. Can easily reacquire satisfactory working knowledge.' It transpired that Warren had been casually sounded out by the Secretary of War, Newton D. Baker,[22] as to whether Pershing might be suitable for the job of commander-in-chief of an expeditionary force to France. Another week passed before Pershing was ordered to present himself in Washington.

Almost simultaneously with Warren's cable Pershing received one from Major-General Hugh Scott, the elderly chief-of-staff of the army. As with most of the top figures of the US regular army, Scott's combat experience (of campaigns to suppress Native American uprisings) bore little relevance to what was going on in France. Scott instructed Pershing to select four regiments of infantry and one of artillery to serve in France. In consultation with his own chief-of-staff, Colonel M. H. Barnum, Pershing chose the 16th, 18th, 26th and 28th infantry regiments and the 6th field artillery regiment; these were eventually to form the 1st Division, its insignia – a large red numeral 1 – giving it the nickname the 'Big Red One'. In Washington on 10 May, Scott told Pershing he would command a division to be sent to France. A lifelong professional soldier, Pershing was nevertheless shocked to discover just how ill-prepared the armed forces were:

It had been apparent to everybody for months that we were likely to be forced into the war, and a state of war had actually existed for several weeks, yet scarcely a start had been made to prepare for our participation. The War Department seemed to be suffering from a kind of inertia, for which perhaps it was not altogether responsible.[23]

An unreadiness to fight had long been used by Wilson to demonstrate to both the Allies and the Central Powers that any attempt to drag the United States into the conflict would be futile. Wilson's lack of interest in military affairs was, however, to prove hugely liberating for Pershing, who enjoyed more independence and executive power than commanding generals of either the Allies or Central Powers. Pershing also, crucially, had a completely free hand to organize his own General Staff, the nerve centre from which the future success or failure of the American Expeditionary Force (AEF) would flow.

Though caught off-guard, the United States moved hastily to

compensate for its years of neutrality. So too did the Allies, whose demands of America after 2 April flowed thick and fast. Washington was soon awash with visiting Allied missions. The most important British mission arrived in Washington on 22 April 1917, led by Arthur Balfour, while the French mission, led by the former prime minister René Viviani, arrived soon after. The sending of separate missions in itself speaks volumes. Even at this late stage in the war the British and French were still fighting a relatively uncoordinated campaign in France, and preferred to compete for separate attention. Once in Washington, the two missions naturally did not bother to unify their lobbying:

The French only asked for all the money in the world. The British mission [. . .] was more pragmatic in its requests. It formally asked that America ship to England 500,000 boys in their shirt tails, where they would be issued British uniforms and Enfield rifles and given seven weeks' training in trench warfare. They would then be given seven days' orientation in France before being sent into battle as riflemen [. . .] The proposed period of training was the same the British gave their own sons before shipping them off to death or mutilation in France.[24]

This first British mission (and several more in 1917) did not simply ask for men; it too pleaded poverty and asked, if not for all the money in the world, then certainly a considerable portion of it. One concrete result of this high-level political pressure was the passage by Congress of the Loan Act on 24 April, authorizing the addition of $5 billion to the US national debt in the form of bonds at $3\frac{1}{2}$ per cent interest; $2 billion was earmarked for the Treasury for war costs and $3 billion for the Allies, as loans. There were to be thirty more such loan acts before the Armistice, each sold to the banks who then sold them on to the public. These loans quickly became known as 'Liberty Loans'. Before the war, fewer than 350,000 Americans were in the habit of regularly buying bonds; by the time the books of the first Liberty Loan were closed on 15 June 1917 more than four million subscribers had offered to take up $3.035 billions of Liberty Bonds.[25]

If greater credit was readily forthcoming, the physical means with which to beat the Germans – men and weapons – were not. The declaration of war was, in purely military terms, little more than a noble gesture. The US regular army was on a par with that of Chile, Denmark or the Netherlands; all four nations then shared equal seventeenth place in the world's league table of army size. Plans for rapid growth were set in motion, but in the first months after the declaration of war too much had to be done in too little time. According to Fox Conner, then a junior officer with Pershing's general staff:

We declared war on April 6, 1917, without any definite plan as to our participation or contribution. No commander had been selected nor was there any nucleus of a staff. There was not even an adequate plan for the expansion of the War Department itself. Looking back we can find only one definite decision. This was the method to be employed in raising men.[26]

Among the many open questions which faced the US administration immediately following the declaration of war was whether it should, or could, send anything more than a token military force to France. Many on both sides of the Atlantic – including the German High Command – took it for granted that America's biggest contribution to the Allies would be an expansion of its supply of credit and munitions. Some US government departments certainly seemed to lack any sense of urgency. On 5 April the regular army's Chief of Ordnance submitted a request to the War Department for $3 billion, to cover initial arms purchases for a 1 million-strong army. His request was denied – because he had failed to itemize the demand: 'Ultimately, Congress appropriated the full $3 billion initially requested, but it took until 5 June, 1917, to do so. An additional request for $3.7 billion to arm the second million men inducted did not pass until 6 October, 1917.'[27]

Yet some of the Allies' initial expectations and hopes of the US military contribution were relatively small. Some British and French commanders were still confident of being able to secure an outright battlefield victory without a great contribution from the US army. As Wilson was preparing to declare war on Germany the French were promising a final, breakthrough offensive under General Robert Nivelle, while the chief of the British Imperial General Staff, General Sir William Robertson, believed early in 1917 that American troops would be of little consequence in the final outcome:

From all accounts Germany is in a very bad state and we frequently hear that Austria and Bulgaria would like to throw in their hands. We cannot pay too much attention to this, but it serves to show which way the wind is blowing. I do not think that it will make much difference whether America comes in or not. What we want to do is to beat the German Armies, until we do that we shall not win the war. America will not help us much in that respect.[28]

Robertson was entirely correct in one assertion; until the German armies were humbled there would be no end to the war. But he was wrong in his belief that America would play a nugatory role in securing the eventual victory. German intelligence sources in the United States – who often enough at this early stage had merely to scour the daily press for their most useful insights – had long before the declaration of war presumed the Americans would arrive in France too late and in insufficient numbers to cause significant trouble, or to prevent the untrammelled German U-boat campaign from bringing about a swift collapse in British and French resistance. On 26 May 1917 German intelligence reports permitted the German Supreme Command to conclude:

According to the experience of the British [. . .] about ten months will be necessary for the raising, equipping, and training of larger formations. The claims made on shipping in order to supply the Entente exclude the possibility of the transport of larger numbers of men, all the more, so long as submarine warfare remains effective [. . .] The transport of American recruits to Europe, demanded by the press, and the formation of parts of the new American Army in France is therefore improbable. The Regular Army will have to give up its best men and instructional staff for the new formations and is therefore not available for the present in large numbers. Until the winter, therefore, we need not reckon with the appearance of considerable forces from the United States at the front. Nevertheless, it is possible that for political reasons a weak expeditionary corps of from one to two divisions of the Regular Army may be transferred to France in the course of the summer.[29]

This timetable proved almost exactly correct. German intelligence knew that US strategic military plans drawn up before the declaration of war were entirely defensive in scope, considering possible seaborne invasions by Japan, Germany and even Britain. Given such scenarios American military thinking placed emphasis on coastal defence and a strong navy, with a small regular army and the National Guard a second line of defence. In the most belligerent plans drawn up by the War Department for a war with Germany – War Plan 'Black' – the US fleet, based in Guantanamo, Cuba, and Culebra, Puerto Rico, would confront the German fleet 500 miles out at sea and prevent the landing of any troops. There were no contingency plans which envisaged shipping thousands, let alone millions, of troops across the Atlantic.[30]

Allied complacency, however, soon fell apart after America entered the war. In May, soon after his appointment as commander-in-chief, Pershing was informed of mounting French and British requests for American reinforcements. But these reinforcements were not for an American army as such. The French 'really wanted us to send small, untrained units for incorporation in their divisions. Their views were clearly set forth in a memorandum by the French General Staff.' The French did not want US army senior officers either, just enlisted men and officers up to the rank of captain, to serve in French combat units and in other capacities. These 'auxiliary troops' (as the French referred to them) would be used to plug the gaps in French divisions, depleted by years of wasteful attrition. As well as combat troops the French mission asked for '50,000 trained men for service on their railways, in the shops, and with their medical units'.[31] British demands became no less peremptory. Major-General G. T. M. Bridges, the military representative with the British mission in Washington, outlined the position in a letter in May 1917 to Major-General Hugh Scott:

If you ask me how your force could most quickly make itself felt in Europe, I would say by sending 500,000 untrained men at once to our depots in England to be trained there, and drafted into our armies in France. This is the view alike of our Commander-in-Chief in France and the Chief of the Imperial General Staff (Sir Douglas Haig and Sir William Robertson), their reasons being that we are short of men, the war is at a critical stage, when we may yet be able to turn the scale and force a decision during the summer, and *every day* [original italics] counts. Our recruits are put into the field after 9 weeks' training in England, and 9 days in France, and give a good account of themselves. With your intelligent men under our system and instruction this would be found ample. In no other way could those 500,000 men make their presence felt before what we call the fighting season is over for the year.[32]

The conflict between the Allies and Pershing and his General Staff as to who would ultimately control the AEF was to plague the Allied–US relationship until the end of the war. As the situation on the Western Front grew more desperate, so the demands of the British and French of their US counterparts became increasingly arrogant. The cracks began to appear very soon after Wilson addressed Congress.

On 16 April 1917 General Robert Nivelle, a fluent English-speaker who enjoyed the high esteem of Lloyd George, launched the latest mighty French offensive, an attack between the river Oise and the Montagne de Reims, aiming to cross the Chemin des Dames, the ancient road that sliced across much of mid-France and on which a great deal of blood had been spilt since 1914. Nivelle had promised much – 'We can break through the German front at will' – but like so many before it the attack was almost immediately bogged down.

More than 1.2 million French troops went over the top heavily loaded, slowly trudging behind an artillery barrage. Many were mown down even before seeing the enemy: 'When the French attacked on 16 April, 1917, they fell in rows. The infantry could not follow "the insane pace of the barrage". Well-sited machine-gun nests and strongpoints blasted the attackers from all sides, including the rear.'[33]

Tanks were used by the French, but their foolish design – petrol tanks placed at the front – rendered them little more than gigantic, lumbering Molotov cocktails. Within the first few days of the attack the bodies of 40,000 dead Frenchmen littered the plains of Laon. Despite the obvious pointlessness of pursuing the offensive Nivelle sustained the battle over the next few weeks; by 20 April the French had suffered about 120,000 casualties.

For many French soldiers this repetition of earlier General Staff blunders was the final straw. Across sixteen French army corps some 750,000 men mutinied, demanding improved food and conditions and more regular leave; some of these troops had not seen their families since the start of the war. On 15 May Nivelle was replaced by General Henri-Philippe Pétain, whose first task was not so much the defeat of German armies as the rescue of French ones from complete collapse. According to General Peyton March, who was to become chief-of-staff at the War Department in Washington, Pétain achieved this by giving

leaves of absence to 350,000 soldiers, who recovered their morale in the quiet of their homes [. . .] He personally restored the morale of his armies, worn to the bone by the tremendous struggle of the preceding three years, in which they had lost in deaths alone approximately 1,500,000 men. None of this was allowed to become known to the people of America. But I knew, and so did [Newton D.] Baker.[34]

Thus the prevailing strategic situation soon after the United States joined the war did not inspire confidence in an ultimate Allied victory. The precarious position was carefully delineated by Major-General Fox Conner, who sailed with Pershing to France on the *Baltic* as a lieutenant-colonel and ended the war a brigadier:[35]

The end of Russia appeared closer. Mutinies which were to involve more than one hundred French regiments had broken out. The campaign of 'Defeatism' was well under way in France. Backbiting between the Allies [i.e. the British and French] was considerably greater than the irreducible minimum which apparently must always be expected.[36]

The National Security League, a pro-Allies Republican-dominated organization, which had acquired some 100,000 members following its inaugural rally in New York City on 1 December 1914, saturated the nation in propaganda pamphlets once war broke out. One was called *Fifteen Little War Stories*; no. 3 contained this:

Of the 320,000 Canadians first to serve, only 2,000 are alive unscathed after three years' warfare. When the offer came to be relieved and sent home, these survivors of a hundred battles preferred to 'keep on doing our bit!'

That's patriotism.

A 1-in-16 chance of getting out without being killed or wounded may have struck thoughtful doughboys as more like pretty poor odds than patriotism.

2

Hearts and Minds

I wanted to see peace. I at least tried to bring it about. Most men
did not even try.   Henry Ford[1]

Nothing will bring American sympathy along with us so much as
' American blood shed in the field.   Winston Churchill[2]

Long before the doughboys fired a shot in anger they had been subjected
to the crossfire of the Allied and Central Powers' conflicting propaganda
campaigns fought inside the United States. While many Americans
remained inclined to neutrality in April 1917, the hearts and minds
of many others had been swayed by some highly resourceful Allied
propaganda. One of the key elements in this cloak-and-dagger war to
seduce America was the atrocity story. As Lieutenant Charles Donnelly
of the AEF's 32nd Division shepherded his artillerymen off the ship
and onto a troop train at the quayside at Brest in March 1918, he was
disturbed by a shocking sight:

One Belgian youngster, about twelve, made a good thing by exciting the
pity of the Americans by showing his wounds, which he said were from
German atrocities. He had an inch-long scar in his tongue, caused, he said,
by a German soldier piercing it with a bayonet. On his back was a mass of
scar tissue and blackened skin, about six inches across, which must have been
caused by a severe burn. There had been so much publicity in the States about
German atrocities, real or alleged, that most of us accepted the Belgian stories
as truth at the time, and I believe that many of them were; war is something
which brings out the best and worst of men.[3]

It is difficult to imagine how a bayonet could be thrust into a tongue without also damaging jaw or face – unless the Belgian boy obligingly stuck out his tongue for a German soldier to stab it.

Stories of German atrocities perpetrated upon innocent Belgian civilians were as old as the war itself, and most were as improbable as this one. Day three of the war – 6 August – saw the appearance of one of the first. The *New York Herald* carried a story with a Brussels dateline: 'The Germans fired on stretchers containing wounded being cared for by the Red Cross at Vise, a small town near the Dutch frontier.'

British control of the means of transatlantic communication got on the right track from the outset, when on 5 August 1914 the British cable ship *Telconia* sailed close to the German naval base at Emden and cut Germany's deep-sea cables, snapping this important communications thread between Germany and North America. A further advantage for the British was the fact that US newspapers and press associations – and their readers – had long been accustomed to having the whole of Europe covered by London-based reporters:

The dean of the American correspondents in London, Mr Edward Price Bell of the Chicago *Daily News*, had arrived fresh from college to remain there for the rest of his active life, and it was naturally impossible for the others not to reflect the atmosphere by which they were daily surrounded. The whole arrangement was simply a matter of convenience, economy and the absence of any very lively American interest in European affairs; the result was, however, that the American view of Europe was normally and unavoidably colored very deeply by the British attitude.[4]

At the start of the war some US reporters made a strenuous effort to cover the story objectively. Some ninety American journalists travelled to France as war correspondents from August 1914, but as the trench stalemate took a firmer grip, and the Allies realized that they had very little good news to tell, it finally became impossible for journalists to move freely anywhere near the front lines. The French refused access to both French correspondents and neutral correspondents to the front lines; if found there they were arrested and put in jail. The British only permitted journalists near the front line in tightly controlled guided tours. If a journalist from a neutral nation accredited to the British side then covered the war from the German side, and was later captured by the British, he was liable to be summarily shot as a suspected spy. Under these circumstances neutral journalists usually found themselves inevitably reduced to reporting only one side of the conflict.

Before this clamp-down occurred five US reporters travelled from Brussels and spent several days at the front in August 1914, even accidentally finding themselves behind German lines. One of the party, Irvin S. Cobb of the *Sunday Evening Post*, eagerly asked every refugee he found for some hard evidence of German cruelty:

Every one of them had a tale to tell of German atrocities on noncombatants; but not once did we find an avowed eye-witness to such things. Always our informant had heard of the torturing or the maiming or the murdering, but never had he personally seen it. It had always happened in another town – never in his own town.[5]

Cobb certainly found plenty of evidence of an invading army, one with little time for the niceties of bargaining over food or horses. He was also told by German officers that the penalty for Belgian civilians who shot at German troops was death by firing squad; Cobb witnessed evidence of such sentences. But where there was no resistance there was no house-burning, or any signs of wanton pillage. Even in Louvain, where Cobb spent three days before it was put to the torch, there was no German pillage in the first few days, when there was little initial resistance by the Belgian populace:

Young Belgian girls began smiling at [German] soldiers swinging by and the soldiers grinned back and waved their arms [. . .] This phase of the plastic Flemish temperament made us marvel. When I was told, a fortnight afterward, how these same people rose in the night to strike at these their enemies, and how, in so doing, they brought about the ruination of their city and the summary execution of some hundreds of themselves, I marvelled all the more.[6]

Cobb's portrayal of the invading German army did its best to counteract stereotypical images which had begun to gain ground in the United States in the previous few years:[7]

We in America are accustomed to think of the Germans as an obese race, swinging big paunches in front of them; but in that army the only fat men we saw were the officers, and not so many of them. On occasion, some colonel, beefy as a brisket and with rolls of fat on the back of his close-shaved neck, would be seen bouncing by, balancing his tired stomach on his saddle pommel; but, without exception, the men in the ranks were trained down and fine drawn. They bent forward under the weight of their knapsacks and blanket rolls; and their middles were bulky with cartridge belts, and bulging pockets covered their flanks.

Inside the shapeless uniforms, however, their limbs swung with athletic freedom, and even at the fag-end of a hard day's marching, with perhaps several hours of marching yet ahead of them, they carried their heavy guns as though those guns were toys. Their fair sunburned faces were lined with sweat marks and masked under dust, and doubtless some were desperately weary; but I did not see a straggler. To date I presume I have seen upward of a million of these German soldiers on the march, and I have yet to see a straggler.[8]

With a degree of exasperation Cobb bluntly concluded that in his personal experience there were no atrocities:

As for Uhlans spearing babies on their lances, and officers sabring their own men, and soldiers murdering and mutilating and torturing at will – I saw nothing. I knew of these tales only from having read them in the dispatches sent from the Continent to England, and from there cabled to American papers.[9]

Thanks to reporters such as Cobb, American public opinion was at the start of the war solidly against being sucked into what seemed an insane conflict. The stance of newspaper and magazine editors, dependent as they always were upon giving the public what it wants, was a fair litmus test of general attitudes. On 14 November 1914 the American periodical *Literary Digest* published an opinion poll of the country's newspaper editors in which 242 out of 367 described themselves as favouring neither the Allies nor the Central Powers.[10] This desire to stay out of the war did not alter significantly until 1917 and it is not hard to see why. Many of America's new citizens – from Ireland, Poland, Russia, Italy, Greece, Ukraine and various Slavic countries – had flocked to the United States, a rapidly growing country, largely because they wanted to shun the poverty and political repression of the very countries now engaged in a bitter struggle for European dominance. In 1900 almost 40 per cent of the white population of the United States had either been born in Europe or had at least one European-born parent. Moreover America had a large German *émigré* population whose sympathies over the war were naturally with Germany.

When war broke out in August 1914 Woodrow Wilson – a high-minded politician but a politician all the same – was acutely aware of how little spirit there was in the American nation to take part in a conflict 3,000 miles away. He took swift steps to ring-fence America and its citizens from being drawn into the war. In a presidential proclamation of 4 August 1914 Wilson forbade American citizens from enlisting in any of the armies involved in the conflict, or indeed from doing anything which might help either side. This decree was, however, widely flouted. On 19 August 1914 Wilson declared to Congress that the United States should be neutral in deed as well as in name, saying 'we must be impartial in thought as well as action'.

Both the Allies and the Central Powers put considerable money and time into trying to break down the stubborn neutrality of the United States. The process by which the Allies achieved relatively greater success in this struggle was composed of one part cunning, one part innate disposition, and two parts diplomatic ineptitude. Like a house whose foundations have been nibbled away by termites, America seemed immovably neutral right up until the last moment. Germany's first use of poison gas, and the German execution by firing squad of the British nurse Edith Cavell in October 1915 for the 'crime' of helping Allied prisoners to escape, were portrayed by the British (and seen by many Americans) as especially despicable acts, while U-boat sinkings of myriads of unarmed (and unwarned) merchant ships, in the process killing American men, women and children, were easily depicted as barbaric outrages. Proved and suspected German sabotage of American factories, seaports and transport routes – such as the arrest on 2 February 1915 of a German-born US resident, Werner Horn, who was attempting to blow up the railway bridge linking the US and Canada at Vanceboro, Maine – seemed to threaten domestic security. There were at least eighty-eight suspicious accidents and acts of proven sabotage between 1 January 1915 and 11 January 1917, affecting US vessels at sea, warehouses and factories. One of the worst was the explosion on 30 July 1916 at the Lehigh Valley Railroad's Black Tom Island ship-loading terminal, on the New Jersey side of the Hudson River, close to the lower end of Manhattan. The Black Tom terminal was an important loading centre for munitions being shipped to the Allies. On Saturday 29 July supposed German agents placed time-fused incendiary bombs on several munitions barges at the terminal. Massive blasts occurred on the afternoon of 30 July, wrecking the terminal and destroying munitions with an estimated value of $20 million. Miraculously only three people died, though the explosions shattered windows all across lower Manhattan. Against such pressure President Wilson fought hard to preserve America's neutrality, though in one key area his government early on appeared implicitly to favour the Allies when, in August 1914, the United States immediately conceded that all belligerents had the right to search neutral merchant vessels (including American) in order to prevent delivery of so-called 'contraband' exports to the enemy.[11] As the British ruled the seas above the waves (while Germany attempted to dominate below) this acceptance of one of the flimsy 'laws' of the sea then prevailing inevitably played into Britain's hands.

The war at sea was ultimately to drag America into the European conflagration. In 1915, for a moment, many Americans understandably thought their president might have declared war on Germany following the sinking of the 31,550-ton passenger ship *Lusitania*, a British-owned Cunard liner. In 1914 Admiral von Pohl, chief-of-staff of Germany's Admiralty, vociferously advocated the use of submarines against enemy merchant shipping, but there were technical and moral difficulties which complicated what might have appeared a straightforward military decision. Informal but widely accepted 'rules' at the time governed the way in which a naval vessel could attack an enemy's unarmed merchant ship. Essentially these stipulated that surface vessels must give fair warning of an attack, to prevent the unnecessary loss of life of those unable to defend themselves. In return, merchant ships were expected not to carry artillery or other means of defending themselves. This chivalric code quickly broke down when it became evident that the war would not be swiftly over. Merchant ships began to disguise themselves, and to carry cannon and machine-guns. When a naval captain spotted an enemy merchant ship on the horizon, he knew that it could be a fatal mistake simply to steam up to it and ask for its surrender; what appeared to be an innocuous tarpaulin on the fore deck could very well conceal a powerful gun. This dilemma was even worse for U-boat captains. The only method by which they could avoid a mistake was to surface and carry out a close inspection. That could be very risky, particularly for a U-boat which was normally very much slower than the slowest of merchant ships. The U-boat could play by the rules of the game, surface and then find itself the target of a surprise attack from a merchant ship which actually turned out to be heavily armed. British merchant ships also frequently used neutral flags in an effort further to deceive U-boat commanders. In November 1914 the British publicly declared the whole of the North Sea was henceforth a war zone. Neutral ships traversing it would be required to stick to certain passages controlled by the Royal Navy. In other words, Britain imposed a blockade against Germany, though it did not call it that.

Germany retaliated on 4 February 1915 by decreeing the waters around the British Isles a war zone in which, from 18 February, every enemy merchant ship would be sunk on sight, with no guarantee that crews and passengers would be rescued; the proclamation warned neutral ships not to enter the war zone.[12]

These blockades caused no end of nuisance for American shipping and exporters, who found their efforts to deliver goods to European customers subject to increasing bureaucratic interference by the British. The US government was perpetually swamped by angry letters of protest from American corporations. Controversy still continues today as to which side was more morally blameworthy over blockades, interference with neutral shipping, and infringements of the so-called 'laws' of the sea. The simple truth is that both Britain and Germany did all they could to perpetrate extreme damage on one another, and wherever necessary lied and cheated to disguise their own culpability. The rules of maritime blockade in 1914 were contained in the Declaration of London, a treaty which Britain had signed in 1909 but, crucially, had never ratified. This Declaration defined three types of contraband:

- 'Absolute contraband': this consisted of articles useful only for military purposes. In times of war, these could be stopped and impounded in all circumstances.
- 'Conditional contraband': this meant articles which had potentially both military and civilian uses. Such material could, according to the Declaration, be confiscated only if consigned to an enemy destination.
- 'Non-contraband': this described products which were deemed to have civilian use only; these could not be withheld under any circumstances.

The British never obeyed the Declaration of London for the simple reason that it would have seriously curtailed its ability to interfere with Germany's sea trade:

Conditional contraband could have flowed freely into Germany through the contiguous neutrals: and many of the most important of her military needs (rubber, hides, cotton, wool, and metallic ores) would have gone direct and without interference. The blockade would have been entirely ineffective and would not have been worth the expense. It gradually became apparent that the distinctions in the Declaration were inapplicable to a war in which the whole effort of the combatant nations was engaged. 'In this war,' as Ludendorff has said, 'it was impossible to distinguish where the sphere of the army and navy began and that of the people ended.' First raw materials and then food were, therefore, brought within the orbit of the blockade, and by 1916 all distinction as to use or intermediate destination had practically disappeared.[13]

In 1914 the US government asked Britain to accept the Declaration of London, but to have done so would have meant allowing the unrestricted importation of such commodities as copper and cotton (both vital for production of cartridges and shells), rubber (essential for tyres), leather hides (vital for boots and infantry packs), agricultural nitrates (easily converted into explosives), and paper (without which no maps could be drawn or orders written down). Sir Edward Grey politely but firmly declined to agree and Washington backed down after weeks of fruitless negotiation.[14]

It was against this background that the *Lusitania* was attacked, though she was far from being either the first or last sent to the bottom by a German torpedo; 8,208 other Allied ships were sunk in the course of the war, the first to go being the 866-ton *Glitra* in 1914. The *Lusitania* was a big prize. At 790 feet long, with four distinctive smokestacks, she was a large ship for the time. Normally capable of a top speed of 27 knots, on her final voyage she could only manage 21 knots, having only forty-one able-bodied seamen instead of the full complement of seventy-seven; the demands of the trenches meant labour was scarce everywhere, even on such an important vessel as this. This reduced crew could keep only nineteen of her twenty-five boilers fed, but her reduced maximum speed was still 6 knots faster than the fastest U-boat of the time.

The *Lusitania* has achieved a place in the wider collective imagination, and controversy still rages over her status. There has traditionally been a close connection between Britain's merchant fleet and the Royal Navy. The *Lusitania*, together with her sister ship *Mauretania*, had been partly commissioned from Cunard by the British government (which heavily subsidized the deal) in 1905, on the basis that in time of war they could be converted to armed cruisers, fitted out with two quick-firing 6-inch guns.[15] However, as *Lusitania* was carrying civilian passengers on her scheduled, publicized voyage when she was attacked on Friday, 7 May 1915, she obviously had a strong claim to be regarded on this occasion as purely a merchant vessel. She had on board absolute contraband, in the form of 1,250 boxes of light-artillery ammunition and eighteen boxes of percussion fuses, but the mere presence of this did not entitle a U-boat to sink her without first giving warning, under the prevailing rules of engagement.[16]

Just two days before she was attacked Colonel House, in London on yet another diplomatic mission, had cabled President Wilson concerning an attack by a German U-boat on the US tanker *Gulflight*, off the west coast of Ireland. *Gulflight* did not sink, but her master died of heart failure the morning after the attack, and two sailors were drowned. With uncanny foresight House declared:

I believe that a sharp note indicating your determination to demand full reparation, would be sufficient in this instance. I am afraid a more serious breach may at any time occur, for they [the Germans] seem to have no regard for the consequences.

On 7 May House drove to Kew with Sir Edward Grey. He recalled their conversation:

We spoke of the probability of an ocean liner being sunk, and I told him if this were done, a flame of indignation would sweep across America, which would in itself probably carry us into the war.

That same day House was at Buckingham Palace, in audience with King George V. House recorded:

We fell to talking, strangely enough, of the probability of Germany sinking a trans-Atlantic liner. He said, 'Suppose they should sink the *Lusitania* with American passengers on board [...]'[17]

On the morning of 7 May the weather off the coast of southern Ireland was very foggy, though sunshine burst through later. In the early afternoon the *Lusitania* was steaming ten miles off the west coast of Ireland when, without warning, she was torpedoed. One passenger, Robert Rankin, gave a description of the scene in a telegraphed message:

At exactly 2.10 p.m. one of our group of four sighted submarine low black ridge about quarter mile starboard bow. Lusitania going slow all morning, had been blowing foghorn till about 10 a.m. and was still steaming about 15 knots. Torpedo left submarine almost instantly and traveled rapidly toward boat, leaving white trail. Struck ship not far from a line below bridge and through boiler room. Explosion tore upward through deck destroying part of forward lifeboat. A boiler exploded immediately. No second torpedo. Boat listed immediately and began to fill through open ports and hole caused by explosion. Ship sank 2.33 by watch of passenger who jumped sea. Torpedo fired without warning whilst most of passengers were below at food.[18]

On board the ship as it began to list to starboard, people began tying on lifebelts and lowering lifeboats, though on the bridge Captain William T. Turner was shouting

in stentorian tones not to lower away the boats, ordering all passengers and sailors to get out of them, saying that there was no danger and that the ship would float. A woman passenger beside me called out to Captain Turner in a perfectly calm and clear voice, 'Captain, what do you wish us to do?' 'Stay right where you are, Madam, she's all right.' Then the woman asked him, 'Where do you get your information?' – and he replied in rather a severe and commanding voice, 'From the engine room, Madam.'[19]

Stationed at his periscope, 32-year-old Captain Walther Schwieger, the lieutenant-commander of the U-20, had been on the lookout for fresh targets, having sunk three ships since 5 May. He recorded in his ship's log the effect on the *Lusitania* of his single torpedo:

Shot hits starboard side right behind bridge. An unusually heavy detonation follows with a very strong explosion cloud. High in air over first smokestack. Added to the explosion of the torpedo there must have been a second explosion. (Boiler or coal or powder.) The superstructure over the point struck and the high bridge are rent asunder, fire breaks out and smoke envelops the high bridge.[20]

Schwieger watched the ship glide beneath the waves; he could see the gold lettering spelling *Lusitania* on its stern. Of the 1,257 passengers – 159 of them American citizens – and 702 crew, 1,198 died, including 124 of the American,[21] drowned in some sixty fathoms of water. Some of America's leading socialites went down with the ship, including Alfred Gwynne Vanderbilt, whose personal wealth was put at the time at $42 million; he was off to France to offer his services to the Red Cross.[22] Charles Frohman, the leading Broadway impresario of the day, also died. Frohman had reportedly the day before sailing wished to make a jotting in a red pocketbook he always carried with him; he opened it to find it had no more spare pages.[23] Some of those who had planned to make the voyage had taken note of German advertisements warning against boarding the ship, placed in New York's morning newspapers on 1 May, the sailing date; the actress Ellen Terry cancelled her reservation, as did Isadora Duncan's dance troupe.[24] Such threats were fairly common at the time. The German press also boasted that the *Transylvania*, the next ship to leave New York after *Lusitania*, would be sunk – though it was not.

The *Lusitania* sank eighteen minutes after being struck by the torpedo, according to Captain Turner, a rapidity which surprised many; the *Titanic* had stayed afloat for some 150 minutes after having her hull ripped open for almost a third of its length, while the *Tuscania*, the first troopship carrying doughboys to be sunk, also off the coast of Ireland, on 5 February 1918, took five hours to die. Given the *Lusitania* had 175 separate watertight compartments a single torpedo should, in theory, have failed to have such a swiftly devastating effect. The most likely reason for such a rapid plunge to the bottom is that the torpedo created a fire among some combustible materials, which set off a massive explosion in the ammunition store. Schwieger dived and headed for home, recording in his log the position of the sunken liner: 'off the Old Head of Kinsale, lighthouse bearing 358 degrees true, fourteen sea miles off in 90 metres of water. The shore and lighthouse are clearly seen.'[25]

Captain Turner survived.[26] Photographs were taken of all the recovered dead to facilitate identification at a later stage of those bodies not identified at the time, and then the majority of them were buried in three large pits. Wesley Frost, US consul in County Cork, had a very busy war, dealing with the hundreds of cases of Americans drowned when their ships were sunk by German U-boats. On this occasion the redoubtable Frost was almost overwhelmed. He took it upon himself to hire a professor from the University College Medical School to embalm the 'identified American dead of importance [including Frohman and Vanderbilt] – now thirteen in all. The expense is £20 each, but in a number of cases the payment is guaranteed, and probably no expense will ultimately fall on the Department [of State].'[27]

The sinking of the *Lusitania* created in the minds of many Americans, in ways that a barrage of Allied propaganda had failed to do, a clear image of the 'beastly Hun' who cared nothing for innocent women and children; the death of 94 of the 129 children on board wrought a savage detestation of everything German. US newspapers were almost united in their reaction. Said the *Times-Dispatch* of Richmond, Virginia, on 8 May:

Germany must surely have gone mad. The torpedoing and sinking of the *Lusitania* evinces a disregard of the opinions of the world in general and of this country in particular – only compatible with the assumption that blood lust has toppled reason from its throne.

The *Memphis Commercial Appeal* called for immediate action:

The United States should notify Germany that the loss of American life and passenger ships by torpedoing without taking off passengers will be regarded as an act of war and demand an answer. If an answer is not satisfactory Congress should be called in extra session to consider a declaration of war.[28]

Theodore Roosevelt called upon the government not merely to assert the rights of American ships to sail, of the United States to send ammunition to France and Britain, and of American citizens to travel unmolested on the merchant ships of belligerent nations, but to enforce those rights. In his view the sinking 'represents not merely piracy, but piracy on a vaster scale of murder than old-time pirates ever practiced'.[29]

But although widely seen in America as a cowardly act, some influential Americans publicly prayed it would not be used as a *casus belli*. Thomas Edison put the matter bluntly: 'How can we help by going to war? We haven't any troops, we haven't any ammunition, we are an unorganized mob.'[30]

From his perspective in the trenches, the poet Alan Seeger thought those who had decided to sail in such an obvious target had been irresponsible:

I cannot understand the American state of mind, nor why Americans have the temerity to venture into a declared war-zone, much less let their wives and children go there, when anyone with a grain of sense might have foreseen what has happened. They might just as well come over here and go out Maying in front of our barbed wire.[31]

This was not so very different from the view of the *Frankfurter Zeitung* of Sunday, 9 May:

What have we done? A German war vessel has sunk the *Lusitania* off the coast of Ireland. A mighty asset which lay on the enemy's side of the scale is destroyed. Property to the value of many millions is annihilated, and an immeasurable store of moral power and self-confidence of a people whose whole life is centred in the prosperity of its shipping and commerce sank to the bottom with the proud vessel [. . .] They mocked at us when we gave warning. Let them turn to those who committed the *crime* of allowing passengers to travel on a war vessel.

Displaying a remarkable insensitivity to the effect on US public opinion, the Germans struck a commemorative medal recording the *Lusitania*'s sinking. Designed by Karl Goetz, a well-known coin and medallion designer, the $2\frac{1}{4}$-inch diameter iron coin weighed $1\frac{1}{2}$ ounces. On its obverse was a depiction of the sinking of the *Lusitania*, showing it as a warship carrying aircraft and carrying the inscription *Keine Bannware* – 'No Contraband'. On its reverse the inscription *Geschaft über alles*, 'Business above all', stood above a scene showing a smiling skeleton at the New York booking office of the Cunard line, with queues of people ignoring an official of the German embassy warning them to stay away.[32] The British minted their own, depicting the sinking as a brutal act.

On 10 May Wilson used the opportunity of a speech in Philadelphia to think through his reaction to this incident. It was a speech which unquestionably permitted the more aggressive wing of the German military hierarchy to believe that the United States would never retaliate for unannounced attacks on merchant ships. Wilson later suggested that the following remark was made off-the-cuff, but it was to haunt him:

'There is such a thing as a man being too proud to fight. There is such a thing as a nation being so right that it does not need to convince others by force that it is right.'[33]

This did not fit squarely with what House and others, who took a much more pro-Allied line, hoped for. House cabled Wilson:

America has come to the parting of the ways, when she must determine whether she stands for civilized or uncivilized warfare. We can no longer remain neutral spectators. Our action in this crisis will determine the part we will play when peace is made, and how far we may influence a settlement for the lasting good of humanity. We are being weighed in the balance, and our position amongst nations is being assessed by mankind.[34]

The British ambassador to Washington, Cecil Spring-Rice, poked fun at Wilson in a way he could be virtually certain would leak to the wider world. He sent the Republican Senator Henry Cabot Lodge, long an advocate of a more belligerent American stance towards Germany, a piece of doggerel depicting a schoolmasterly Wilson finger-wagging at the Kaiser:

I told you not to do it: I said that it was wrong
I meant and you knew it: my words were kind but strong [. . .]
You knew that I was frowning and sharpening my pens,
Yet you would persist in drowning my fellow citizens.
About a hundred were destroyed;
I was exceedingly annoyed [. . .]
Excuse the observation, I wouldn't hurt your feelings,
But really, Kaiser, the excuse,
It simply was the very deuce.[35]

But despite Wilson's obvious determination to avoid war the sinking of the *Lusitania* initiated a lengthy exchange of sharply-worded notes between Washington and Berlin. On 13 May William Jennings Bryan, then US Secretary of State, sent a 31-page telegram (written by Wilson) to ambassador Gerard in Berlin, asking him to deliver a statement to the German Minister of Foreign Affairs, Gottlieb von Jagow. Bryan pointed out that the *Lusitania* was merely the last and most extreme of a series of violations:

The sinking of the British passenger steamer *Falaba* by a German submarine on March 28, through which Leon C. Thrasher, an American citizen, was drowned; the attack on April 28 on the American vessel *Cushing* by a German aeroplane; the torpedoing on May 1 of the American vessel *Gulflight* by a German submarine, as a result of which two or more American citizens met their death; and, finally, the torpedoing and sinking of the steamship *Lusitania*, constitute a series of events which the Government of the United States has observed with growing concern, distress, and amazement.[36]

The tanker *Gulflight* was the first American flag-carrier to be torpedoed, off the Scilly Isles, though it did not sink. Bryan grasped the essence of the dilemma facing the German High Command:

Manifestly submarines can not be used against merchantmen, as the last few weeks have shown, without an inevitable violation of many sacred principles of justice and humanity.

He called upon the Germans to respect the 'sacred freedom of the seas' even though the seas by this time clearly were neither sacred nor free. In the end there was to be no declaration of war, no ultimatum, no demand, only a statement that the US government 'confidently expects' a disavowal of such acts, reparation 'so far as reparation is possible for injuries which are without measure' and a promise that the German government will not do it again.[37]

Gerard's response was swift. On 15 May he replied that he had delivered Bryan's note to von Jagow personally:

[. . .] he asked that he might read it himself as he understands written better than spoken English. While reading it he laughed and said, 'Right of free travel on the seas, why not right of free travel on land in war territory?' [. . .] he was sure Germany would never give up this method of submarine warfare.[38]

In Washington the German ambassador, Count Bernstorff, was less confident that the federal government would not be eventually provoked into war. He cabled Berlin on 16 May, warning that if there was another sinking of a passenger liner with more American deaths, then he was convinced Wilson would declare war, adding that as a result of the *Lusitania* incident 'our propaganda here has collapsed completely'.[39]

While Bryan's warning to the German government contained no hint of a declaration of war – or even a suggestion of breaking diplomatic relations, as was counselled by ambassador Walter Hines Page in London – it nevertheless shook some key figures in the German High Command, in particular General Erich von Falkenhayn, chief of the General Staff, who insisted the demands contained in Bryan's note must be complied with. Falkenhayn's view was that America should be kept out of the war, not least to encourage other neutral powers to stay out. Italy joined the Allies against the Central Powers on 23 May 1915. What would Bulgaria, Romania, or the Netherlands do if the United States, the leading neutral power, joined in?

The German Foreign Ministry took until 28 May to reply formally to the US protest letter. It pointed out that the German government had already expressed regret over the loss of lives of a neutral nation, but given that the ship had carried contraband in the form of ammunition, that it had concealed artillery below deck, that it was a registered reserve cruiser for the Royal Navy and had on her previous voyage carried Canadian troops for the British army in France, it was considered that the *Lusitania* was a military vessel and thus a legitimate target for unannounced attack. The British denied these charges, but in truth the German case was a strong one. Yet fear of a US entry into the war inspired a command from the Kaiser on 1 June to all U-boat commanders, instructing them that they had 'a solemn duty [. . .] not to attack unless they [had] the well-founded conviction that the ship in question [was] an enemy ship. In cases of doubt it [was] better to let an enemy freighter escape than to sink a neutral ship.'[40]

On 9 June Robert Lansing – who had been promoted from his position as State Department counsellor to acting Secretary of State following the 7 June resignation of the pacifist William Jennings Bryan, who felt this second *Lusitania* note would bring war closer – applied greater pressure. Lansing telegraphed Gerard in Berlin, instructing him to deliver a note to von Jagow. The note was a model of diplomatic reasoning, and firmly reminded the German government that it was illegal to sink an unarmed merchant ship without warning and without providing for the safety of those on board, and that it was 'irrelevant' if it was carrying contraband. Lansing denied the accusation that the ship did not have merchant status and asked the German government for 'convincing evidence'[41] of this allegation. He reminded the Germans that the US authorities had a duty to ensure that the *Lusitania* was not ready for offensive action when it left America, and added that 'it performed that duty and enforced its statutes with scrupulous vigilance through its regularly constituted officials. It is able, therefore, to assure the Imperial German Government that it has been misinformed.'[42] Lansing reiterated the request of the note of 15 May, that the German government give assurances that it would respect American lives and American ships, no matter where they might be.

Misinformed or not, there was a degree of disingenuousness about the State Department's high-mindedness over the *Lusitania* incident. As a Royal Navy registered reserve armed cruiser the *Lusitania* was not a shining example of unthreatening virtue, but something rather more ambiguous. Not only was it as close to being a Royal Navy vessel as possible without actually being so, it had also previously violated one of the cardinal rules of the sea. Sailing from Liverpool on 16 January 1915 the ship's captain had feared a torpedo attack, so he hoisted the Stars and Stripes in the hope that any marauding U-boat would think it an American ship and thus steer clear. News of this illegal use of the American flag soon reached the front pages of American newspapers and drew the inevitable (and justifiable) German protest. The sinking of the *Lusitania* arguably put paid for ever to the by then artificial rules of engagement, which had nobly sought but failed to protect the innocent. If blame lies anywhere it is with the British Admiralty, which by muddling the merchant with the military, and by failing to keep the civilian status of passenger liners strictly sacrosanct, gave the desperate Germans little choice but to extend U-boat attacks on all vessels.

A third note was sent by Wilson, under Lansing's signature, to the Germans on 21 July. Its conciliatory tone made clear that Wilson had no intention of going to war. While it informed the German government that a repetition of such an incident would 'constitute an unpardonable offense against the sovereignty of the neutral nation affected' it nevertheless reversed the assertion of the first note, which had suggested that it was impossible to conduct submarine warfare against merchant shipping in a legal fashion. This retreat came after a secret imperial order dated 6 June was sent to all U-boat commanders ordering them not to torpedo any large passenger ships until further notice.

The post-sinking rumblings dragged on into August. To complicate the issue still further, on 19 August the U-24, commanded by Lieutenant Schneider, torpedoed and sank the British 16,500-ton White Star liner the *Arabic*, just a few miles from the spot where the *Lusitania* had gone down, drowning forty-four passengers, including two US citizens. This fresh attack provoked another storm of newspaper-led American hysteria against Berlin. Coming so close upon the as yet unresolved *Lusitania* crisis the incident induced considerable alarm among civilian political circles in Berlin, where the Chancellor, Bethmann Hollweg, managed to persuade the Kaiser on 27 August to inform the United States that he had ordered a cessation of attacks without prior warning upon enemy liners.[43] On 28 August Count Bernstorff was instructed to hand a letter to Lansing containing this crucial passage:

Liners will not be sunk by our submarines without warning and without safety to the lives of non-combatants, provided that the liners do not try to escape or offer resistance.

This gesture towards protecting the rights of civilians and citizens of neutral powers, followed by an order by Admiral von Holtzendorff, the newly-installed Chief of the Admiralty, on 18 September 1915 that U-boat activities against merchant shipping round the British Isles for the immediate future should be restricted to the North Sea (thus eliminating much of the risk that American citizens would be caught in any attack as the vast majority of them were sailing across the Atlantic), considerably placated those in the Wilson administration who had been pressing for tougher action. Bernstorff went further than he was instructed, by authorizing Lansing to publish the German declaration that no liners would be torpedoed without warning, and by formally repudiating the action of the commander of U-24 in his surprise attack upon the *Arabic*.

*

The propaganda struggle to wean the United States from its neutrality was fought largely through the printed word, and individual voices of relative reason were sometimes drowned by sensationalist clamour. The British were rather more adroit at exploiting opportunities than the Germans, never more so than in the wake of the sinking of the *Lusitania*. Of the millions of words written with the aim of persuading the Americans of the rightness of the Allied cause, few were as high-minded and thoroughly misleading as those contained in the Bryce Report, which was rushed out a few days after the sinking of the *Lusitania*. Brought into being by the British government in December 1914, the Bryce Commission's brief was to investigate allegations of German atrocities in the attack on Belgium. For the price of one penny the *Report of the Committee on Alleged German Outrages* – to give it its full title – was available to anyone who cared to read it. It contained 1,200 anonymous depositions, said to have been taken from Belgian refugees, as well as extracts from thirty-seven captured and supposedly authentic diaries of German officers and enlisted men. Its 300-page appendix contained dozens of grisly case histories of alleged execution, torture, rape and mutilation of Belgian women and children.[44] To no one's surprise it found the Germans guilty of systematic abuse of civilians and concluded:

It is proved

i. That there were in many parts of Belgium deliberate and systematically organized massacres of the civil population, accompanied by many isolated murders and other outrages.

ii. That in the conduct of the war generally innocent civilians, both men and women, were murdered in large numbers, women violated, and children murdered.

iii. That looting, house burning, and the wanton destruction of property were ordered and countenanced by the officers of the German Army, that elaborate provisions had been made for systematic incendiarism at the very outbreak of the war, and that the burnings and destruction were frequent where no military necessity could be alleged, being indeed part of a system of general terrorization.

iv. That the rules and usages of war were frequently broken, particularly by the using of civilians, including women and children, as a shield for advancing forces exposed to fire, to a less degree by killing the wounded and prisoners, and in the frequent abuse of the Red Cross and the White Flag.

[. . .] Murder, lust, and pillage prevailed over many parts of Belgium on a scale unparalleled in any war between civilized nations during the last three centuries.[45]

The lurid nature of the Bryce Report gained it widespread coverage in the United States, while the fact that its chairman, James Bryce, had been a popular and respected British ambassador in Washington from 1907 to 1913 gave it considerable credence. The résumé of US press coverage compiled by the British Foreign Office noted smugly: 'Even in papers hostile to the Allies, there is not the slightest attempt to impugn the correctness of the facts alleged. Lord Bryce's prestige puts scepticism out of the question, and many leading articles begin on this note.'[46]

There is now little doubt that the Bryce Report was an exceptionally clever piece of propaganda; it may not have told outright lies, but merely failed to discount hearsay and gossip. Clarence Darrow, the famously independent-minded American lawyer, visited France in 1915 to see for himself just how far the atrocities had gone. He believed the Bryce Report initially but became increasingly sceptical; he could find no one who had actually suffered or witnessed an abuse by a German soldier. When Darrow returned to America he offered the handsome reward of $1,000 to anyone who could prove a single French or Belgian child had had their hands chopped off by a German soldier, a common enough atrocity story at the time. His money was safe.[47]

The British also made considerable use of what today we call junk mail. Junk seems an entirely appropriate word to use in relation to Sir Gilbert Parker, the Conservative and Imperialist Member of Parliament for Gravesend, who in 1914 was appointed head of the American section of Britain's War Propaganda Bureau. A Canadian by birth, the 52-year-old Parker was a master of what his *Times* obituary described as 'voluminous melodrama [. . .] In all he wrote 36 books, of which several were dramatized and in that form enjoyed popular success; but he never cured himself of turgidity in his style nor of morbid interest in torture, mental and physical.'[48]

With his interest in the fabrication of wild tales based upon no research or facts and his capacity for churning out vast quantities of words at the drop of a top hat, the appointment of Parker to this role was inspired. His job was made easier by the British Foreign Office's intelligent determination to avoid the mistake of the Germans, which was to subject the United States to a tidal wave of overt propaganda. Instead, the Foreign Office correctly decided that the best form of propaganda was that which encouraged Americans first to absorb and then to regurgitate the British view of the war. This was Parker's mission, and he set about it with gusto, compiling a list – ultimately containing 260,000 names and addresses – of influential Americans, including lawyers, academics, businessmen, scientists, editors, bankers and politicians. He regularly updated them on the British view of the war, while his office fed stories and news items to more than 500 US newspapers. Sir Gilbert did not bludgeon his audience; he encouraged it to pull up a leather armchair by the fireside of a hushed London gentlemen's club. His materials were restrained and even academic in tone, and were accompanied by egregiously flattering covering letters. A typical one read:

I am well aware that American enterprise has made available reprints of the official papers relating to the present European war; but the original British prints of these publications may not be accessible to those persons of influence who can study them for a true history of the conflict. I am venturing to send to you under another cover several of these official documents. I am sure that you will not consider this an impertinence but will realize that Britishers are deeply anxious that their cause may be judged from authoritative evidence. In common with the great majority of Americans, you have, no doubt, made up your own mind as to what country should be held responsible for this tragedy, but these papers may be found useful for reference, and because they contain the incontrovertible facts, I feel you will probably welcome them in this form.

My long and intimate association with the United States through my writings gives me confidence to approach you, and I trust you will not think me intrusive or misunderstand my motive.[49]

Parker was ably assisted by senior British journalists such as Wickham Steed, foreign editor of *The Times*, who regularly briefed US journalists based in London and ensured they had access to the highest levels of secret (and of course manipulated) British sources; the journalists were wined, dined, entertained and courted at the British taxpayer's expense. Some US journalists based in London and Paris tried to maintain an open mind, but the tight control exercised by the British and French over access to the front and to the cable telegraph (the sole means of rapid communication, as wireless telegraphy was in its infancy; 95 per cent of British government propaganda travelled by cable) did much to ensure that many American newspaper editors and readers had their views of the war heavily filtered by Allied watchdogs. All dispatches leaving London went through the rigorous hands of the British censorship office. Controlling and steering the flow of information across the Atlantic was as important a battle as many fought in Flanders, and this censorship extended to denying access to certain hostile US correspondents, particularly those from the press group owned and controlled by Randolph Hearst, whose newspapers took a strongly pro-German, anti-British line up to the moment America joined the war. London-based correspondents of Hearst's empire had an official embargo placed on them during 1916–17, following their critical coverage of British affairs during the Easter Rising in Dublin, the battle of Jutland and German air raids on Britain.[50] Germany lacked the kind of widespread news service Britain was able to secure; the British government paid Reuters £120,000 a year to provide an additional service, called Agence Service Reuter, to cable official propaganda.[51] In addition to all this the British government recruited eminent writers such as John Buchan, Arthur Conan Doyle, H. G. Wells and Thomas Hardy to commission, write and sanctify official propaganda.

Germany fought hard to influence American opinion but its propaganda travelled relatively slowly across the Atlantic, by ships' couriers or by circuitous cable routes via third- and sometimes fourth-party communications. The German Information Service – established in New York City in August 1914 and financed by the German Foreign Office – was intended to counteract Allied propaganda by influencing American popular opinion through newspapers. It subsidized a weekly paper called *The Fatherland*, the first edition of which hit the streets on 10 August 1914. *The Fatherland* was owned and edited by George Sylvester Viereck, who although born in Munich to a German father and American mother was brought to live in the United States in 1895, when he was eleven. Adopting a completely pro-German line, *The Fatherland*'s circulation grew to an impressive 100,000, by far the biggest of the several hundred German newspapers and periodicals then being published in America. The US government also allowed two German-language radio stations to remain in operation in the early stages of the war.

Against both British and German propagandists, average American citizens were, if they chose, more than able to defend themselves by a variety of means, not least of which was by paying attention to the plethora of pacifist groups that preached a vigorous opposition to the European war. The US pacifist movement was vociferous though frequently riddled with factional disputes, and its ideas were sometimes brought into disrepute by the very people who claimed to back it most strongly. One of the most muddle-headed and eccentric opponents to US participation in the war was also one of the wealthiest. Henry Ford – anti-Semite, teetotaller, bully and industrial genius – was replete with paradox. The arch-capitalist himself, he publicly and frequently accused 'the Jews', Wall Street financiers and fellow capitalists of having started the war. He was immensely tight-fisted, yet his Ford Motor Company gave him such vast personal wealth that one year he paid $79 million in federal taxes. At the outset of the war in Europe he demanded, 'Do you want to know the cause of war? It is capitalism, greed, the dirty hunger for dollars. Take away the capitalists and you will sweep war from the earth.'[52]

In November 1915 Ford was so shocked by what he read of the slaughter on the Western Front that he said he would devote his personal fortune to ending the conflict. He commissioned a 'peace ship' (the *Oscar II*) to sail to Europe with a complement of American and international pacifists. What they would do on arrival in Scandinavia was not clear, but they hoped it would usher in peace. When *Punch* magazine mocked Ford's venture it knew it was on safe ground and that it voiced, as usual, widely held opinion:

Mr Henry Ford's voyage to Europe on the *Oscar II* with a strangely assorted group of Pacifists does more credit to his heart than his head, and the conflicting elements in his party have earned for his ship the name of 'The Tug of Peace'. Anyhow, England is taking no risks on the strength of these irregular 'overtures'.[53]

When Ford later published his autobiography (*My Life and Work*) he devoted less than twenty lines of its 200 pages to the peace ship, but at the time nothing preoccupied him more. In the 22 August 1915 issue of the *Detroit Free Press*, Ford said he hated war because 'war is murder, desolation and destruction, causeless, unjustifiable, cruel and heartless to those of the human race who do not want it, the countless millions, the workers'.[54] Two years later his factories were churning out tanks, steel helmets and automobiles for the war effort.

Louis Lochner, secretary of the Chicago Peace Society (one of a number of US pacifist movements) recalled how Ford had first encouraged the hopes of American pacifists, only to drop them on a whim when they no longer suited his interests. Ford had promised to donate $200,000 to the International Committee of Women for Permanent Peace, organized by two of the leading figures in the international peace movement of the time, Jane Addams (from the United States) and Rosika Schwimmer (of Hungary); but he never sent the cheque. Together with Schwimmer, Lochner met Ford at his home in Dearborn, Michigan, on 19 November 1915; the aim of the meeting was to persuade Ford to fund the establishment of a neutral commission in Europe, with a mandate to lobby for the promotion of peace. After a lunch during which Ford lectured his guests on how the poor had only themselves to blame for their poverty, they were treated to the delights of listening to Ford's only child, the 22-year-old Edsel, performing a drum solo to the accompaniment of a phonograph.

On 20 November they all travelled to New York City, where Ford made a number of flamboyant statements to the press:

'We're going to try to get the boys out of the trenches by Christmas. I've chartered a ship and some of us are going to Europe' [. . .] No details, no method of procedure, no intimation as to what ship had been engaged, who was to man it, when it was to leave – just these two statements.[55]

The Danish-registered *Oscar II* sailed for Christiana in Norway on 4 December 1915, loaded with 54 US reporters, 3 movie cameramen, 83 delegates, 18 students and 50 administrative staff. Its departure was accompanied by a great hullabaloo, and the press had a field day at Ford's expense. Several dignitaries had been invited to join the expedition – including ex-Secretary of State William Jennings Bryan – but without exception they declined, probably sensing that it would swiftly collapse into farce. There was precious little sympathy for Ford among British political leaders. In the House of Commons one MP asked if the delegates might not have a right of asylum in Britain, 'and cannot we certify them?'[56] By the time *Oscar II* arrived in Christiana on 15 December many of the delegates were at each other's throats and Ford was intensely regretting his involvement with such a disordered, uncontrollable group. He developed a diplomatic cold, declined to meet any of the Norwegian press, refused to leave his hotel room and, together with his bodyguard and one delegate, sneaked out of his hotel at 4 a.m. on Thursday, 23 December. He boarded a train to Bergen and thence proceeded back to the United States by ship, amid rather fewer fanfares. What the *Spectator* dubbed the SOF (Ship of Fools) then toured Sweden and the Netherlands without Ford. It left in its wake numerous speeches and committees. Lochner meanwhile persisted in his fruitless cause, commenting only that Ford had 'been tried in the balance and found wanting'.[57]

Ford emerged from his expedition looking rather foolish, but the case of neutrality was not greatly damaged. Of more concern in late 1915 was the growing suspicion in America that the country was becoming increasingly subject to terrorist activity by German-financed spies. British Naval Intelligence codebreakers had already, in September 1915, exposed a network of German saboteurs. Papers carried by J. F. J. Archibald, a US citizen, were seized when he arrived in a Dutch vessel on the south coast of England at Falmouth. These documents implicated Constantin Dumba, the Austro-Hungarian ambassador to Washington, in a plot to sabotage US munitions plants. They were passed by British intelligence to the London correspondent of the *New York World*, which published the story. Dumba was forced to leave the United States in October, closely followed by Captain K. Boy-Ed, the German naval attaché, and Captain Franz von Papen, the military attaché and future German chancellor. British intelligence was adroit when it came to dirty tricks, too. In late 1916 the British press obtained and disseminated a perfectly harmless photograph of the German ambassador to Washington, Count Johann von Bernstorff, good-humouredly posing with a bathing beauty on either side. While totally innocuous, it seemed to show Bernstorff to be a frivolous character. Norman Thwaites, the *Times* correspondent in Washington, thought this a devastating coup: 'As a piece of anti-enemy propaganda, I have no hesitation in saying that this incident was more effective than pages of editorial matter which the British were alleged to inspire in the United States.'[58]

But all these propaganda efforts would have gone for nothing had it not been for Germany's U-boat warfare against unarmed neutral vessels, which greatly angered President Wilson. As Wilson said when he asked Congress to support his declaration of war:

Property can be paid for; the lives of peaceful and innocent people can not be. The present German submarine warfare against commerce is a warfare against mankind.

It is a war against all nations. American ships have been sunk, American lives taken, in ways which it has stirred us very deeply to learn of, but the ships and people of other neutral and friendly nations have been sunk and overwhelmed in the waters in the same way. There has been no discrimination. The challenge is to all mankind.[59]

3

Easeful Death

'Their language English, their literature English, their traditions
English and quite unknown to themselves their aspirations English.
We shall be d—d fools if we don't exploit this for the peace of
the world and the dominance of our race!'

Admiral Sir John Fisher, First Sea Lord,
speaking of the United States in 1910

'There is many a boy here today who looks on war as all glory,
but, boys, it is all hell.'   General Sherman, speaking at

Colombus, Ohio, on 11 August 1880

In September 1915 Theodore Roosevelt confidently consigned the
brightest and the best to what he no doubt imagined was a noble and
glorious cause:

Every young man just leaving college – from Harvard, from Yale, from
Princeton, from Michigan, Wisconsin or California, from Virginia to Sewanee,
in short, from every college in the country – ought to feel it incumbent on
him at this time either to try to render some assistance to those who are
battling for the right on behalf of Belgium, or else to try to fit himself to help
his own country if in the future she is attacked as wantonly as Belgium has
been attacked. The United States has played a most ignoble part for the last
thirteen months. Our Government has declined to keep its plighted faith, has
declined to take action for justice and right, as it was pledged to take action
under the Hague Conventions. At the same time, it has refused to protect its
own citizens; and it has refused even to prepare for its own defense.[1]

Roosevelt's tub-thumping on behalf of the Allies struck home with some youthful Americans. By late 1915 the British government was increasingly confident that, despite US irritation with the British naval blockade and the interruption to free trade, it could depend upon American sympathies to lie much more with the Allies than the Central Powers. A crucial, though unquantifiable, ingredient was the intangible influence exercised by the significant numbers of young men who, partly out of a romantic attachment to the vision of France as the cradle of republicanism and liberty, went to serve in both combatant and non-combatant roles with the Allies. For the *jeunesse dorée* of America the smell of war drifted slowly but surely across the Atlantic, seeping under the doors of their college dormitories. The natural wanderlust of late adolescence and a sense of collegiate comradeship enticed an estimated 25,000 Americans to fight in France on the side of the British and French, most in the Foreign Legion, but some in the Lafayette Escadrille, a volunteer air squadron staffed entirely by Americans, before the United States declared war.[2] The years 1915 and 1916 saw Germany begin to lose an important battle – not on the fields of Flanders but in the waters of the Atlantic, on the threshold of every newspaper-reading American home, and in the dormitories of America's Ivy League colleges.

In May 1916 seven Americans formed the Lafayette Escadrille Americaine, though its name was truncated in December that year after the Germans protested against this open breach of US neutrality. The brainchild of Norman Prince, a Harvard graduate and the polo-playing son of a wealthy Boston banking family, owners of an estate in Gascony, Prince joined the French air service in 1914 and gained permission to form a volunteer squadron in December 1915. The Lafayette Escadrille attracted some of the most colourful of American volunteers, including Raoul Lufbery, whose French parents had brought him up in America. Before long their 'death-or-glory' escapades were so well publicized that a stream of would-be volunteers arrived on their doorstep in France.[3]

Many volunteers published accounts of their service with the Allies, memoirs invariably tinged with affection, such as this by James Norman Hall, an American who enlisted in the British army in August 1914:

French soldiers are conscious of the romantic possibilities offered them by the so-called 'divine accident of war'. They go forth and fight for Glorious France, France the Unconquerable! Tommy shoulders his rifle and departs for the four corners of the world on a 'bloomin' fine little 'oliday!'[4]

By the time he left 'Kitchener's Mob' at the end of 1915, Hall had fully embraced the British cause:

In England, before I knew [the British soldier] for the man he is, I said, 'How am I to endure living with him?' And now I am thinking, how am I to endure living without him; without the inspiration of his splendid courage; without the visible example of his unselfish devotion to his fellows? [...] Tommy is sick of the war – dead sick of it. He is weary of the interminable procession of comfortless nights and days. He is weary of the sight of maimed and bleeding men – of the awful suspense of waiting for death [...] It is men of this stamp who have the fortunes of England in their keeping. And they are called, 'The Boys of the Bulldog Breed'.[5]

The 'Bulldog Breed' mythology, which these kinds of records helped to create, promoted the image of the blunt, honest, straight-talking and utterly dependable British soldier, and did much to persuade young Americans into viewing the war through British eyes.

Perhaps the most famous American volunteer in the French Foreign Legion was the young poet Alan Seeger, who died in the early evening of 4 July 1916 in an attack near the village of Belloy-en-Santerre.[6] Seeger's parents both came from old New England families; his privileged upbringing on Staten Island and then in Mexico prepared him for the most enviable destination for a young American man in 1908 – Harvard. He left for Paris in 1912 where for two years, supported by his parents, he did nothing very much except write some pretty bad poetry which no one would publish. Three weeks after the start of the war he joined the Foreign Legion, where he found a spiritual home and the impetus to write some poems which have lived. His war diary and selected letters were published to considerable acclaim in the United States in early 1917. Passages such as this, written in 1914, seemed almost designed to set young blood racing:

[. . .] imagine how thrilling it will be to-morrow and the following days, marching toward the front with the noise of battle growing continually louder before us [. . .] The whole regiment is going, four battalions, about 4,000 men. You have no idea how beautiful it is to see the troops undulating along the road in front of one in colonnes par quatre as far as the eye can see, with the captains and lieutenants on horseback at the head of their companies.[7]

The delight of Seeger and other early volunteers in the sights, sounds and smells of the battlefield, even late in the war, runs directly counter to today's received opinion that, even at the time, front-line soldiers regarded the war as merely a filthy absurdity. At the front for the first time in November 1914 Seeger found conditions were already abominable, but he did not reject the war:

It is a miserable life to be condemned to, shivering in these wretched holes, in the cold and the dirt and semi-darkness. It is impossible to cross the open spaces in daylight, so that we can only get food by going to the kitchens before dawn and after sundown. The increasing cold will make this kind of existence almost insupportable, with its accompaniments of vermin and dysentery. Could we only attack or be attacked![8]

His last diary entry, of 28 June 1916, reads:

We go up to the attack to-morrow. This will probably be the biggest thing yet. We have the honour of marching in the first wave [. . .] I am glad to be going in the first wave. If you are in this thing at all it is best to be in it to the limit. And this is the supreme experience.[9]

There is no shred of irony in Seeger's use of the phrase 'the supreme experience'. He here expresses a quasi-mystical longing to transcend the diurnal banalities of existence. This is one vital element of Romanticism, and Seeger's most famous poem, 'I have a rendezvous with Death . . .', unmistakably alludes to the line 'I have been half in love with easeful Death' in Keats's 'Ode to a Nightingale'. The contemporary popular view of the First World War is uncomfortable with the notion that some intelligent young men actually *enjoyed* it. For many young men the Great War was of course an appalling experience, but it was

49

also terribly compelling, the most profound episode of their lives, something about which they felt extremely ambiguous. British and French romantic soldier-intellectuals found it difficult by mid-1916 to sustain the type of melancholia which is Seeger's dominant poetic mood. But for young Americans in 1917 it was still new, and Seeger spoke to them, even after his death, of beauty, truth – and a glorious death:

> *Resurgam*
> Exiled afar from youth and happy love,
> If Death should ravish my fond spirit hence
> I have no doubt but, like a homing dove,
> It would return to its dear residence,
> And through a thousand stars find out the road
> Back into earthly flesh that was its loved abode.[10]

The thought expressed here is, to say the least, rather opaque; but the feeling is strikingly obvious. Marching, uniforms, the sense of fighting for a just cause, the sheer *foreignness* of it all appealed to a certain privileged, highly-educated, semi-aristocratic class of American society, where the voluntary shouldering of others' burdens was undertaken as a kind of *noblesse oblige*.

For the glamour and adventure of war on the Western Front young Americans often turned to published articles by members of the American Field Service (AFS) in France, which had within its ranks many who were keen to get into print. The Allies were glad to have them too, not least because most of the recruits were such fine, strapping lads: 'Of the foreign volunteers who are enlisting with the French Army, 57 per cent of the Russians were rejected medically, 32 per cent of the Poles, 11 per cent of the Italians, 4 per cent of the British, and no Americans.'[11]

The AFS started as the voluntary ambulance arm of the American Hospital in Paris. It owed its existence and fame to A. Piatt Andrew, a former US Treasury assistant secretary and Harvard economics professor, a man perfectly placed to recruit the flower of upper-class American manhood for a foreign adventure. The AFS was an Ivy League in exile, taking its drivers from among only the top-notch US universities. In 1915 the AFS became firmly tied to the Allies by agreeing to have its ambulances attached to French line divisions. It was finally merged with the US army on 30 August 1917; by the end of the war 127 AFS drivers and former drivers (some transferred to the AEF) had been killed in action, out of a total of about 2,500.[12] The other volunteer US ambulance service was the Norton-Harjes Ambulance Corps, created by merging the Harjes Formation of the American Red Cross (established by A. Herman Harjes, a French banker) and the American Volunteer Motor Ambulance Corps, organized in 1914 by Richard Norton, son of Harvard's Charles Eliot Norton; Norton-Harjes suffered no fatalities among its drivers.

Ernest Hemingway and John Dos Passos both served as volunteer ambulance drivers, Hemingway in Italy with the Red Cross and Dos Passos in France with Norton-Harjes. A number of other figures who later gained literary fame or importance were volunteers in France, including Robert Service (whose *Rhymes of a Red Cross Man* derived from his experience) and e.e. cummings. The *Atlantic Monthly* published the accounts of his ambulance service by Charles Nordhoff (co-author with Charles Norman Hall of *Mutiny on the Bounty*), while Hall served in the Lafayette Escadrille. Gertrude Stein wrote about her First World War experiences as a driver for the American Fund for French Wounded in *The Autobiography of Alice B. Toklas*. The poet and literary critic Malcolm Cowley joined the AFS, as did the playwright and screenwriter Sidney Howard, a 1925 Pulitzer Prize winner. Edmund Wilson served as a stretcher-bearer in the US army. William Faulkner joined the Canadian air force; T. S. Eliot tried to enlist in the US navy after America declared war but was rejected as physically unfit. Edith Wharton, who was in Paris when war broke out in August 1914, established and funded the American Hostel for Refugees, giving housing, employment, education and medical assistance to refugees. She also set up the Children of Flanders Rescue Committee, which sustained 600 children and 200 old people, mainly Flemish refugees from German-occupied Belgium.

It is impossible to assess the propaganda value to the Allies of the ephemeral writings by AFS drivers and other non-combatant American volunteers which were published in the United States during the early days of the war. But much of it was precisely the kind the British

Foreign Office had decreed was ideal – not material pumped out by obviously biased British commentators or analysts, but written from the heart by Americans who clearly knew what they were talking about. The best Allied propaganda was of the type written by Preston Lockwood, about his AFS section based in that part of Alsace-Lorraine which the French managed to recapture after the war had started:

Alsace has been for forty years German territory. For forty years young Alsatians have been forced to learn German in the schools, to serve in the German army, to be links in the civil and military chains which bound them to the Kaiser's empire. A few days ago I took the photograph of an Alsatian girl standing in the doorway of her home, which she said she was going to send through Switzerland to her brother in the German army 'somewhere in Russia'. But French hearts doubtless beat under many a German uniform, and those of us who have lived in Alsace are confident that re-annexation by France will not be a slow or a difficult process. Alsace has been tied to France by something which forty busy years have not found a way to change. The armies of the [French] Republic have been received with an open hand and an open heart. I know of a fine field hospital organized and staffed entirely by Alsatian ladies happy to be nursing wounded French soldiers. I know of Alsatian boys, at the outbreak of the war not yet old enough to have commenced their German military training, who are today volunteer, and only volunteer, French soldiers.[13]

Some volunteer drivers resorted to poetry:

Un Blessé à Montauville
'Un blessé à Montauville – urgent!'
Calls the sallow-faced telephoniste.
The night is as black as hell's pit,
There's snow on the wind in the East.

There's snow on the wind, there's rain on the wind,
The cold's like a rat at your bones;
You crank your car till your soul caves in,
But the engine only moans.

[. . .]

Christ! Do you hear that shrapnel tune
Twang through the frightened air?
The Boches are shelling on Montauville –
They're waiting for you up there!

'Un blessé – urgent? Hold your lantern up
While I turn the damned machine!
Easy, just lift him easy now!
Why, the fellow's face is green!'

'Oui, ça ne dure pas longtemps, tu sais.'
'Here, cover him up – he'd cold!
Shove the stretcher – it's stuck! That's it – he's in!'
Poor chap, not twenty years old.

[. . .]

'Il est mort, m'sieu!' 'So the poor chap's dead?'
Just there, then, on the road
You were driving a hearse in the hell-black night,
With Death and a boy for your load.

O dump him down in that yawning shed,
A man at his head and feet;
Take off his ticket, his clothes, his kit,
And give him his winding-sheet.

It's just another poilu that's dead;
You've hauled them every day
Till your soul has ceased to wonder and weep
At war's wild, wanton play.

He died in the winter dark, alone,
In a stinking ambulance,
With God knows what upon his lips –
But on his heart was France!¹⁴

Bad poetry; but possibly useful propaganda.

While Wilson's declaration was, in a formal sense, a complete rever-sal of government policy up to that time, the intellectual, financial and emotional ground had shifted to the point where he felt he could declare war and bring the American nation with him in such a momen-tous decision. By April 1917 the Germans had clearly proved they could not or would not keep their word about unrestricted submarine warfare. Having promised not to attack unarmed liners without prior warning after the *Lusitania* affair, German U-boats were once again killing American civilians who imagined themselves able to cross the Atlantic in safety.

The German High Command was preoccupied throughout 1916 by internal wrangling over whether or not to use its submarine weapon in an unrestricted fashion. The row over the *Lusitania* had been handled badly by Germany; hardliners such as Grand Admiral von Tirpitz and General von Falkenhayn, both of whom wished to see an urgent resumption of unrestricted U-boat warfare in the belief that this would more quickly bring Britain to starvation and surrender, felt that much valuable ground had been unnecessarily conceded. Opposing them was the German Chancellor, Bethmann Hollweg, who on 4 March 1916 succeeded in imposing his will against unlimited U-boat war. His opposition derived not from intrinsic humanity but because

he considered the chances of success to be very uncertain; because he had not given up the hope of an acceptable peace by negotiation, and because he was of the opinion that the proposed radical intensification of German naval warfare would eliminate all possibilities of a compromise.[15]

Tirpitz resigned in protest and was succeeded by Admiral Edouard von Capelle, former Under-Secretary of State for Naval Affairs, who opposed unrestricted U-boat attacks on merchant shipping. On 13 March 1916 a new order was issued to all U-boats, instructing them that while all enemy merchant ships in the war zone around the British Isles were to be torpedoed without warning, outside that zone only *armed* enemy merchant vessels could be attacked without warning; enemy passenger ships were always to be given prior warning, wherever they were.

This clarification did not prevent a spate of U-boat attacks which angered Washington. On 16 March the British steamer *Berwindvale*, carrying four Americans, was sunk off Bantry, Ireland, *en route* to the United States. A French passenger ship, the *Sussex*, was badly holed in the English Channel on the afternoon of 24 March 1916, leaving eighty dead and several US citizens wounded. Also on 24 March the Dominion Line steamer *Englishman*, a horse transport carrying several Americans to Portland, Maine, had two warning shots fired across her bows from U-19, twenty miles west of Islay; she refused to stop and tried to outrun the submarine, which forced her to a halt by further gunfire and, after lifeboats were lowered, sank her with a torpedo. On 27 March the liner *Manchester Engineer*, carrying American civilian passengers, was torpedoed without warning off Waterford. On 28 March the British steamer *Eagle Point* was torpedoed and sank after surrendering to a U-boat 130 miles south of Queenstown in Ireland, the lifeboats – carrying several Americans – being left in heavy seas and gales.

On 6 April 1916 the hard-pressed consul, Wesley Frost, cabled Robert Lansing at the US State Department with an account of good treatment offered by one U-boat crew to sailors aboard *The Pet*, a small fishing vessel. But he added:

On the other hand, the instances in which any consideration is shown appear to be diminishing. The attack on the *Berwindvale* seems to have been unwarrantably merciless. To-day a new case has arisen, in which no American citizens are involved, that of the *Zent*, an Elder and Fife fruit steamship outward bound, which was sunk without the faintest warning at 10 p.m. last night 30 miles south of the Fastnet Rock. This ship went down within two minutes, it is said, and there are only 8 survivors out of a crew of about 50 men.

It is difficult, if not impossible, to deduce from actual submarine attacks the principles which the commanders are under instructions to heed, to my mind: but there is an unmistakable tendency towards ruthlessness in the recent group of submarine attacks in the waters bounding this consular district.[16]

Amid this welter of torpedoings, sinkings, anxiety and death, Wilson felt he must act more firmly. He pinned his next rebuke, sent to Berlin on 18 April, on the most serious and flagrant recent attack, that on the *Sussex*. Wilson, who preferred to talk softly and carry a big stick, now adopted a tone of resignation tinged with threat. His barely restrained anger was not helped by initial German denials (later withdrawn following conclusive forensic evidence gathered by US investigators) that the *Sussex* had been torpedoed, arguing instead that she had struck a mine, laid by the British. Wilson had no time for this squirming:

[. . .] again and again no warning has been given, no escape even to the ship's boats allowed to those on board. Great liners like the *Lusitania* and *Arabic*[17] and mere passenger boats like the *Sussex* have been attacked without a moment's warning [. . .] The roll of Americans who have lost their lives upon ships thus attacked and destroyed has grown month by month until the ominous toll has mounted into the hundreds.

The Government of the United States has been very patient [. . .] It has become painfully evident to it [the Government of the United States] that the position which it took at the very outset is inevitable, namely, the use of submarines for the destruction of an enemy's commerce is, of necessity, because of the very character of the vessels employed and the very methods of attack which their employment of course involves, utterly incompatible with the principles of humanity, the long-established and incontrovertible rights of neutrals, and the sacred immunities of non-combatants.

If it is still the purpose of the Imperial Government to prosecute relentless and indiscriminate warfare against vessels of commerce by the use of submarines without regard to what the Government of the United States must consider the sacred and indisputable rules of international law and universally recognized dictates of humanity, the Government of the United States is at last forced to the conclusion that there is but one course it can pursue. Unless the Imperial Government should now immediately declare and effect an abandonment of its present methods of submarine warfare against passenger and freight-carrying vessels, the Government of the United States can have no other choice but to sever diplomatic relations with the German Empire altogether.[18]

A crisis meeting between Bethmann Hollweg, Holtzendorff (chief-of-staff of the Admiralty) and Falkenhayn on 26 April to agree a response to this latest diplomatic development was inconclusive. Falkenhayn demanded unrestricted submarine warfare, a view which he apparently managed to persuade the Kaiser to support, as Wilhelm informed Hollweg on 30 April that he expected nothing to result from continued diplomatic relations with the United States – except being deprived of the means of winning the war by use of the U-boat.[19] But pressure from von Capelle, among others, brought the Kaiser to accept Hollweg's view that it was essential to placate the Americans. Falkenhayn tendered his resignation, but was persuaded to stay on by the Kaiser; he did so and continued to press for totally unrestricted U-boat warfare.

On 4 May 1916 the Germany Foreign Ministry sent a conciliatory note to Washington, suspending all U-boat operations but only on condition that America would press Britain to lift its blockade, and that it would be able to show some results on this matter within two months. This demand was doomed from the outset, as Britain by now understandably felt America to be an ally in all but name. Meanwhile Falkenhayn had become so confident of victory on the Western Front that on 28 May 1916 he informed Bethmann Hollweg Germany would defeat the Entente by the end of the winter of 1916–17 – even *without* a return to submarine warfare.

By the autumn of 1916 there was little lingering hope among the German High Command that the United States would be able to bring the Allies to the negotiating table. Their earlier optimism that a swift victory could be achieved on the battlefield was also fading. Romania joined the Entente against the Central Powers on 27 August 1916, to which the Kaiser responded by sacking Falkenhayn, holding him responsible for the failure to break through on the Western Front. As the stalemate dragged on the thoughts of the German Admiralty began to return to the possibilities of submarine warfare. At a conference on submarine warfare at Pless on 31 August, Holtzendorff called for a policy of unrestricted U-boat combat. He reasoned that the time was ripe for an all-out killer blow: in Germany good harvests meant less domestic pressure, and America could not be more hostile than it already was. Even if the United States declared war, its shipping tonnage was puny and its army risibly small. There was also at the back of the minds of all present the fact that America was soon to have a presidential election, with the possibility of a much more belligerent president than Wilson being returned to office. It was high time Germany stopped fighting with one hand tied behind its back. The conference decided that Generals Hindenburg and Ludendorff – who wished to make a detailed assessment of the condition of the Western Front, having just taken over from Falkenhayn – should be given the right to decide when the submarine question should be re-examined. The issue remained unresolved until 4 October when, in a meeting between the Kaiser and Holtzendorff, it was decided to postpone making any changes in the current policy; the Kaiser wished to await developments in Russia and also to give the Americans more time to come up with a peace plan of sufficient persuasiveness for the Entente.[20]

Yet despite this official 'suspension' of U-boat warfare there was a spate of submarine attacks – most without warning – on unarmed merchant vessels which carried American citizens during September–December,[21] leading to the death and injury of a number of Americans and increasing the pressure on Wilson to do something to prevent what the US press shriekingly referred to as barbarism.

The US administration had clear early warning as to the thinking within the German High Command. On 16 October 1916 Leo Allen Bergholz, the diligent American Consul-General at Dresden, passed on to Robert Lansing, Secretary of State, a vital piece of intelligence from 'an army officer connected with the Ministry of War at Dresden, whom I have known for over two years'.[22] This source told Bergholz during a three-hour conversation that

in the first months of 1917 Germany contemplated an unrestricted use of submarine warfare; that she had been building submarines at the rate of two a week and hoped by a sudden attack with an overwhelming number of them to break through the barriers which protected the fleets of France and Italy in the hope of bringing about peace.

Bergholz's spy was well-informed, and confirmed messages relayed by James Gerard, Washington's ambassador in Berlin, that outright U-boat warfare might be resumed if the United States could not influence the Allies to come to the negotiating table. The mood within the German Admiralty and the High Command had already turned away from hope that America might be able to bring pressure to bear on the Entente. While Germany at this time had less than half the 222 submarines a pre-war study thought necessary to conduct an effective blockade around the British Isles,[23] it was nevertheless managing to sink ships at an alarming rate: 162,744 tons had gone under in August; 230,460 tons in September; and 353,660 tons in October.[24]

Then, out of the blue, came a peculiar speech to the Reichstag by Bethmann Hollweg on 12 December 1916. On the one hand Hollweg simply declared Germany and its allies already considered themselves the victors;[25] almost as an afterthought he said they were now ready to listen to approaches from the Allies. Hollweg smugly said the defeat of Romania (which had been accomplished with relative ease, the shattered Romanian army losing as many as 400,000 men and having to retreat to Moldavia and sacrifice Bucharest) had merely added to the supplies of food and oil[26] in German hands; he declared himself 'resolved for battle, ready for peace'.

His peace 'offer' was ignored. On 18 December 1916 President Wilson sent to US ambassadors in the belligerent nations a letter setting out his own stall, inviting all belligerents to come to the peace table. This too fell on stony ground; the right-wing German press, with notable *chutzpah*, described it (on 23 December) as a desperate effort by the Americans to save the British from disaster. As so often with Wilson's peace overtures, it was not clear precisely what he hoped to achieve:

> The President is not proposing peace; he is not even offering mediation. He is merely proposing that soundings be taken in order that we may learn, the neutral nations with the belligerent, how near the haven of peace may be for which all mankind longs with an intense and increasing longing.[27]

Well, not *all* mankind. On 8 December Hindenburg saw the Kaiser and called for unrestricted U-boat warfare to commence at the end of January 1917. On 22 December von Holtzendorff asserted in a letter to Hindenburg that his submariners could sink 600,000 tons of Allied shipping a month and that within five months Britain would sue for peace, so long as unrestricted U-boat warfare began not later than 1 February 1917. Holtzendorff acknowledged that this would probably bring America into the war, and argued that everything must be done to prevent such an outcome; but he warned that a ruthless use of

U-boats probably represented Germany's last hope of achieving a decisive victory:

[. . .] an unrestricted war, started at the proper time, will bring about peace before the harvesting period of the 1917 summer, that is, before 1 August; the break with America must be accepted; we have no choice but to do so. In spite of the danger of a breach with America, unrestricted submarine war, started soon, is the proper, and indeed the only way to end the war with victory.[28]

The hardening of German attitudes over unrestricted U-boat warfare was clearly prompted by the country's deteriorating domestic situation. Joseph Clark Grew, counsellor at the US embassy in Berlin, considered the domestic crisis Germany faced in November 1916.[29] Despite good harvests generally, the food situation was rapidly deteriorating in some urban areas:

It is an open secret that this food question is becoming alarming to those in a position to know the exact conditions. The authorities are becoming nervous over the growing dissatisfaction of the people in the decrease of the supply of foodstuffs and the difficulty of finding even the amounts which their food cards [rations] call for. Riotous demonstrations of the working people have occurred in Kiel and other places, which necessitated the calling out of the marines and soldiers to enforce order, and though nothing of this appears in the press, it is probable that the unrest is widespread.

Grew quoted from a much more detailed report he had received from the US Consul-General at Dresden on 4 November:

There is virtually no meat, butter, eggs, or sugar to be had and very few vegetables and very little milk, and the little there is, is sold at least between a hundred and two hundred per cent above the prices before the war [. . .] Each inhabitant is allowed an egg a week which costs $0.12 and which in normal times could be had for $0.0125. We are supposed to receive 9 ounces of meat a week, but in fact we get about the half. If one is rich one can buy geese, costing from $7.50 to $10 each, ducks from $3.73 to $6.25 each, and hens at $2.50 each. In *ante bellum* times geese sold for $2 to $2.50

each, ducks for $0.75 to $1.25, and chickens for $0.50 to $0.75 each [. . .]

The result of all this is that there is, if not actual starvation, at least woeful distress among the poor, want among the middle class, and a great deal of grumbling among the rich who can still live on geese, ducks and game and who, it must be frankly stated, seemed to be favored by the Government as no meat cards are required for these luxuries.

In this context it was inevitable that Berlin would decide to stake all on the one weapon which gave hope of a decisive breakthrough – the U-boat. Hindenburg threw the army's weight behind Holtzendorff; the naval and army leadership met on 8 January 1917 to confirm their agreement. The last remaining dissenting government voice, Bethmann Hollweg's, was outmanoeuvred at a session of the Crown Council at Pless on 9 January 1917.

Germany warned that from 1 February 1917 all ships, no matter which flag they sailed under, should stay away from all European coastal areas or face the possibility of U-boat attack. This provoked Wilson to break off diplomatic relations with Germany. From a possibility, war with Germany had now become a probability.

An enterprising American reporter called Floyd Gibbons, of the *Chicago Tribune*, spotted in this development an opportunity for a good story. He booked himself onto the first available ship sailing from New York to Liverpool, the 18,000-ton *Laconia*. Like several other Cunard liners the *Laconia* had been in and out of uniform since the start of the war, first as an armed merchant cruiser in 1914, based at Simonstown in South Africa, from where she acted as the headquarters ship for the British campaign to capture German East Africa. She was handed back to Cunard, becoming a 'civilian' ship once more, in July 1916. On 17 February 1917 she left New York – with Gibbons on board – under the command of Captain W. R. D. Irvine.

On the evening of 25 February after dinner, when the *Laconia* was sailing off the coast of Ireland, Gibbons stood in the ballroom chatting over drinks. Gibbons introduced a new topic into the conversation:

'What do you say are our chances of being torpedoed?' I asked.

'Well,' drawled the deliberative Mr Henry Chetham, a London solicitor, 'I should say four thousand to one.'

Lucien J. Jerome, of the British diplomatic service, returning with an Ecuadorian valet from South America, interjected: 'Considering the zone and the class of this ship, I should put it down at two hundred and fifty to one that we don't meet a sub.'

At this moment the ship gave a sudden lurch sideways and forward. There was a muffled noise like the slamming of some large door at a good distance away. The slightness of the shock and the meekness of the report compared with my imagination were disappointing. Every man in the room was on his feet in an instant.

'We're hit!' shouted Mr Chetham.

'That's what we've been waiting for,' said Mr Jerome.

'What a lousy torpedo!' said Mr Kirby in typical New Yorkese. 'It must have been a fizzer.'

I looked at my watch. It was 10.30 p.m.

In the flurry of activity to launch lifeboats, Gibbons recorded only one incidence of hysteria, on the part of a certain French-Polish actress by the name of Miss Titsie Siklosi. On the whole there was good order among the passengers and crew, and Gibbons certainly had a good story. Moments later he had an even better story, one which would guarantee him front-page world headlines.

As the survivors watched from their lifeboats the *Laconia* slip beneath the waves, some 150 miles west of Fastnet, a black hulk arose nearby; the U-boat responsible for the sinking was surfacing. A bizarre conversation then ensued between an officer on the U-boat's conning tower and the *Laconia*'s chief steward:

'Vot ship was dot?' the correct words in throaty English with the German accent came from the dark hulk, according to Chief Steward Ballyn's statement to me later.

'The *Laconia*,' Ballyn answered.

'Vot?'

'The *Laconia*, Cunard line,' responded the steward.

'Vot did she veigh?' was the next question from the submarine.

'Eighteen thousand tons.'

'Any passengers?'

'Seventy-three,' replied Ballyn, 'men, women, and children, some of them in this boat. She had over two hundred in the crew.'

'Did she carry cargo?'

'Yes.'

'Vell, you'll be all right. The patrol will pick you up soon,' and without further sound, save for the almost silent fixing of the conning tower lid, the submarine moved off.

Gibbons and the others then spent some six hours adrift before being rescued and taken to Ireland where, once more, the redoubtable Wesley Frost dispensed help and collected eye-witness accounts. Gibbons immediately wired his piece to the United States, where it was instantly picked up and syndicated nationwide. His article – 'The Sinking of the *Laconia*' – was to have a profound effect upon American opinion:

The Cunard liner *Laconia*, 18,000 tons burden, carrying seventy-three passengers – men, women, and children – of whom six were American citizens – manned by a mixed crew of two hundred and sixteen, bound from New York to Liverpool, and loaded with foodstuffs, cotton, and war material, was torpedoed without warning by a German submarine last night off the Irish coast. The vessel sank in about forty minutes.

Two American citizens, mother and daughter, listed from Chicago, and former residents there, are among the dead.

They were Mrs Mary E. Hoy and Miss Elizabeth Hoy. I have talked with a seaman who was in the same lifeboat with the two Chicago women and he has told me that he saw their lifeless bodies washing out of the sinking lifeboat.

The American survivors are Mrs F. E. Harris, of Philadelphia, who was the last woman to leave the *Laconia*; the Rev. Father Wareing, of St Joseph's Seminary, Baltimore; Arthur T. Kirby, of New York, and myself.[30]

An almost forgotten footnote, the sinking of the *Laconia* was yet another provocation. It is intriguing that while the *Lusitania* – which did *not* bring America into the bloodiest war yet seen – is probably a familiar name to most Americans and Europeans, the *Laconia* – which helped do so – is not. Perhaps it has dropped into relative obscurity because, after all, the *Laconia* represented only 3.5 per cent of the total 540,000 tons of ships sent to the bottom by U-boats in February *alone*; a further 593,841 tons were sunk in March, meaning that more than 500 ships disappeared as a result of torpedoes in the first two months of the unrestricted U-boat campaign.[31] But perhaps it is merely that two dead Americans – mother and daughter, who died of exposure in the lifeboats – command less attention than the 128 who perished on the *Lusitania*.

Coming so soon after the torpedoing of the *Laconia*, the newspaper headlines in the United States on 1 March – GERMANY SEEKS AN ALLIANCE AGAINST US; ASKS JAPAN AND MEXICO TO JOIN HER; FULL TEXT OF PROPOSALS MADE PUBLIC – were another devastating slap in the face. Arthur Zimmerman, Germany's foreign minister, sent to Count Bernstorff in Washington on 16 January 1917[32] a telegram instructing the German minister in Mexico City to offer Mexico the US territories of Texas, New Mexico and Arizona, in exchange for Mexican entry on the side of Germany in the anticipated war against the United States. The coded telegram was fairly rapidly deciphered by British naval intelligence but not passed on to the US government until late February. President Wilson knew of the telegram on 24 February and it was swiftly leaked to US newspapers, which published splash headlines on 1 March. The telegram was regarded as devastatingly treacherous, not least because one of the three ways it was sent to the German embassy in Washington was via the American State Department Cable Office, the use of which had been extended by Washington to Germany as a goodwill gesture after the British cut Germany's transatlantic cables. The view of Germany by most Americans as utterly perfidious was now complete.

On 4 March Wilson entered his second term as US president, conscious that his policy of pursuing peace and neutrality, upon which he had been re-elected, was a complete failure. Despite all his efforts, Zimmerman's note was an authentic indication that America was going to be dragged into this European conflagration, whether it wished for it or not. In his inaugural address Wilson called for 'an America united in feeling, in purpose, in its vision of duty, of opportunity, and of service'.[33]

That call would soon be put to the test, as a succession of American merchant ships were sunk by U-boats. On 12 March the US steamer *Algonquin*, carrying foodstuffs, copper, tin, acids and formaldehyde bound for London, was shelled by U-38 without warning, the American flag clearly painted on the ship's sides doing nothing to prevent its sinking.[34] The *Vigilancia*, bound for Le Havre from New York, was torpedoed without warning and sank in seven minutes on 16 March; fifteen of its multinational crew, including six Americans, drowned. On 17 March the *City of Memphis*, another US merchant vessel, owned by the Ocean Steamship Company, had a warning shot fired across it at 3.55 p.m. The ship stopped and was fired on again before its captain, I. P. Borum, gave the order to abandon ship and the U-boat sank it at 4.40 p.m. On the afternoon of 18 March the *Illinois* was shelled without warning and sank about twenty miles north of Alderney. Even President Wilson's patience had run out. In a Cabinet meeting on 20 March every one of his ministers, including those who had previously been ardent supporters of a pacifist line, voted for war. Now it would be peace through victory.

4

Enter the Doughboys

The only complaint one would make about them is that they don't take sufficient care; they're too apt to get themselves killed.

Teilhard de Chardin[1]

[American] soldiers were first known as doughboys. Later we became known as dog-faces. Where we got the doughboys name was always a mystery to us. Dogface was more patently understood. It was said we were so called because we wore dog tags, slept in pup tents, growled at everything we ate and tried to f*** every female we saw.

Sergeant Earl R. Poorbaugh, 26th Infantry, 1st Division[2]

It is far from clear why the 4 million officers and men who served in the United States army in 1917–20 came to be known as 'doughboys', a sobriquet which has not been favoured by the passage of time. In 1918 the word carried connotations of battlefield heroism, grit, toughness, and physical endurance; today it's the brand name of oven-ready bread mix. French and British soldiers were initially at a loss to know what to call their new comrades but they soon hit on the nickname 'Sammie', after Uncle Sam. That failed to catch on; 'doughboys' stuck, partly because the promoters and defenders of the myths surrounding the American soldier in France – not least the journalists who ran the official US army magazine *Stars and Stripes* – waged a strong campaign on its behalf. But the struggle between 'Sammie' and 'doughboy' lasted a long time. As late as 29 March 1918 *Stars and Stripes* found it necessary to run an editorial firmly rejecting 'Sammie':

A Sammie may be defined as an American soldier as he appears in an English newspaper or French cinema flash. It is a name he did not invent, does not like, never uses and will not recognize. When he sees it in the papers from home, it makes him sick. The American doughboy has had his baptism of fire, but he has not yet been christened [. . .]

When, in the fullness of time, the American army has been welded by shock and suffering into a single fighting force [. . .] the American soldier will find his name [. . .] He does not know what that name will be. He simply knows it won't be 'Sammie'.

Where did 'doughboy' come from? Did it perhaps refer to the fact that even the lowest rank of AEF soldier – who got $30 a month, a stack of cash in France at that time when 1 franc was worth about $0.20, and when French soldiers were paid ten times less – felt loaded with 'dough'? Some argue it was invented by the US cavalry, who contemptuously christened their foot-slogging dust-covered compatriots 'dobies' from the adobe huts they inhabited during the campaign against Pancho Villa in Mexico. A spirited debate over the derivation of 'doughboy' was conducted in the 'Ask Grandpa' column of *Stars and Stripes* at late as 1919, when A. E. Sanderson asked 'Grandpa' why an infantryman was called a doughboy. Replied Grandpa:

The word 'doughboy' originated in the Philippines. After a long march over extremely dusty roads the infantrymen came into camp covered with dust. The long hikes brought out the perspiration, and the perspiration mixed with the dust formed a substance resembling dough; therefore, their lucky brothers, the mounted soldiers, called them 'doughboys'.[3]

Other learned contributors to this *Stars and Stripes* debate argued that Grandpa had got his etymology right but his history wrong. It was during the Indian wars that infantry became known as doughboys. Then someone who signed himself 'Old Regular Army Man, 22 Years' Service' entered the dispute:

The word dates back to the time when the Infantry wore spherical buttons on their blouses. Doughboys at that time were a kind of dumpling that they

67

put in a soup. Being about the size of the blouse buttons, the term was applied to the Infantry on account of the buttons they wore. The Cavalry at that time wore flat buttons on their blouses; hence the term 'doughboy' applied only to the Infantrymen.

By the 19 April 1918 issue of *Stars and Stripes* the 'doughboys vs. Sammie' debate had reached a climax. The editors, with backing from Pershing, then felt confident enough to lay down the law:

More and more in the training camps and in the trenches, over there and over here, the name 'doughboy' is attaching itself to every living man who wears the olive drab. Time was when it applied only to enlisted infantrymen. Time was when there was a suggestion of good-natured derision in it. But of late, with the original doughboys in the very vanguard of the AEF, the name appears insensibly to have taken on a new accent of respect. Infantrymen and artillerymen, medical department boys and signal corps sharks, officers and men alike, all of them are called doughboys and some of them are rather proud of it.

Their nickname may have been peculiar but there is no disputing the courage displayed by many doughboys. Even Lloyd George, surely the First World War's greatest humbug, who in his memoirs sneered at the US military and political wartime leadership, praised their valour:

The American soldiers were superb. That is a fact which is acknowledged, not only by their friends and British comrades, but by their enemies as well.

There were no braver or more fearless men in any army, but the organization at home and behind the lines was not worthy of the reputation which American business men have deservedly won for smartness, promptitude and efficiency.[4]

When he failed to get his own way with the US army in France, Lloyd George became a bitter and petulant opponent of General Pershing and his senior officers. Some of Lloyd George's criticisms of the organization of America's war effort were justified; many were not. In his denigration of the way in which America went to war in 1917–18 this instinctively mendacious character laid the foundation of a bitterly negative view of America's participation in the war: because 'Pershing wanted to fight his own battle and win his own victories with his own Army'[5] the implication was that Pershing had been guilty of dangerous, irresponsible egotism, which undermined an otherwise united and successful Allied war effort. There is no truth in this damaging accusation but it has largely passed into received opinion.[6]

Had Lloyd George focused his criticisms on the pre-war condition of the US regular army, which was to form the core of the 'doughboy army', he would have been on firmer ground. It was, by the standards of the armies then fighting in Europe, fairly unimpressive in terms of size and training. In April 1917 the regular army was led by elderly men who had made their mark as fighters against the Indians; the army's chief-of-staff, General Hugh Scott, and his deputy, Major-General Tasker H. Bliss, were close to retirement. Both were intellectually gifted and had faithfully served successive federal governments, but they were out of touch with the sort of technology and tactics then deployed on the Western Front. Few of their 5,000 or so officers and some 120,000 other ranks had ever fired a shot in anger. The United States could also count on the National Guard, which in 1917 consisted of about 80,000 (often ill-trained and poorly equipped) officers and men, many of them having joined to assist their aspirations for social advancement.[7] To corral this odd assortment of soldiers Scott and Bliss had at their fingertips a General Staff of just fifty-one officers; the long-standing civilian suspicion and resentment of the army meant that by law only nineteen of these officers were permitted to be stationed in Washington DC. Against that, in August 1914 the British General Staff comprised 232 officers, the French 644 and the German 650.

The urgent need to conscript and train many more soldiers became a priority after the failure of the Nivelle offensive. Yet there was at the start not even much of an infrastructure simply to process the planned mass recruiting: the US army in April 1917 had only 126 commissioned officers and 1,077 enlisted men on general recruiting detail, manning 189 recruiting stations across the country.[8] President Wilson was determined there would be no room for the type of misguided romantic adventurism of a volunteer force which had proved so unreliable in the Civil War and other more recent US engagements.

Besides, the British and French experience of depending upon volunteers rather than imposing conscription had caused enormous disruption to key industries such as mining or shipbuilding, as workers vital for the war effort left their jobs and disappeared into the mud of the Western Front. The senior officers of the US regular army were also determined that this would be a professionally conducted war; or at least, which was not necessarily the same thing, a war which they and not the civilians or the National Guard controlled. US regular army officers also saw that a good large-scale war would free long-paralysed promotion prospects. Captains could see themselves becoming colonels; colonels could even entertain the possibility of becoming generals.

Thus the Selective Service Act – the draft – was overwhelmingly backed by the US Congress[9] and signed into law by President Wilson on 19 May 1917. In principle the Act was remarkably egalitarian:

There would be no bounties, no substitutes, and no purchased exemptions. All male citizens and resident aliens, from age 21 to 30 (later extended to 18 to 35), had to register with the local boards that actually administered the draft [...] Between May 1917 and the Armistice, conscription was the principal means of raising men for the military services. While the draft directly supplied over two-thirds of military personnel during the war, indirectly it also spurred voluntary enlistments. Local boards registered nearly 24 million men, inducted almost 3 million, and forced millions of others into vital war industries.[10]

Tuesday, 5 June 1917 saw 9,660,000 young men present themselves for registration. Apart from a few skirmishes in the backwoods of Montana, Arkansas, Texas and other far-flung parts of the country, there was barely a whisper of opposition. Each registrant was required to complete a form giving name, address, age, distinguishing physical features and reason for claiming exemption, if any. In exchange, they received a green card as proof of having fulfilled the legal requirement to register. About 800,000 men were deferred on the basis that their occupation was essential for the civilian war effort. On 20 July a national lottery was held to select from the registrants the first batch of 687,000 who would actually join the army. A blindfolded Secretary of War, Newton Baker, was brought before a public meeting in the Senate Office, where he drew from a glass bowl a black capsule which contained the number 258 (all the registrants had been tallied on grouped lists, the biggest local draft board having a list of 10,500 names). Other numbers followed, each one signifying a new batch of recruits. There were to be two more registrations. Those staged on 5 June and 24 August 1918 dealt with those who had attained the age of twenty-one since the first registration; the third and final was on 12 September 1918, taking in men aged from eighteen to forty-five.

Altogether 24,234,021 men (from a total male population in April 1917 of some 54 million) were registered and 2,810,296 were inducted by the 4,650 local draft boards.[11] Of every 100 men who served, 10 were National Guardsmen, 13 were from the original regular army, and 77 belonged to the newly-created National Army, or would have done if the three services had not been consolidated on 7 August 1918. The biggest recruiting centre was the most populous state, that of New York, which sent 9.79 per cent (367,864 men) of the total; at the other end of the spectrum Alaska mustered just 2,102 recruits, 0.06 per cent of the total. The Middle West states (Wyoming, Kansas, Oklahoma, Iowa and others), with their high level of agricultural rather than industrial work, produced the fittest and toughest recruits; from these states 70 to 80 per cent of those inducted passed both physical examinations:

[. . .] the country boys made better [physical] records than those from the cities; the white registrants better than the colored; and native-born better records than those of alien birth. These differences are so considerable that 100,000 country boys would furnish for the military service 4,790 more soldiers than would an equal number of city boys. Similarly, 100,000 whites would furnish 1,240 more soldiers than would an equal number of colored. Finally, 100,000 native-born would yield 3,500 more soldiers than would a like number of foreign-born.[12]

The overwhelming majority of those called to serve did so gladly. But there were anomalies, including a puzzlingly higher rate of rejection of white than black candidates in the Class 1 registration: 30.29 per cent and 25.40 per cent respectively. This alarmed the white officers of the US regular army; it offended their innate belief that white Americans were physically superior. The explanation is that enlistment boards initially tended to have much lower expectations (and thus adopted far lower standards) for black recruits, a policy which was ditched following a heated memo from Pershing:

Colored stevedore troops arriving with tuberculosis, old fractures, extreme flat feet, hernia, venereal diseases all existing prior to enlistment, not able to stand hardship of climate and travel, larger proportion of sick than among white troops. Recommend elimination of unfit by rigid physical examination before embarking.[13]

While it was relatively easy to raise a large mass of conscripted troops, the real weakness of the AEF throughout its brief existence was, in manpower terms, its lack of capable, experienced and competent middle-ranking commissioned officers. To some extent the shortage of junior officers was eased by the existence of the pre-war Military Training Camps Association (MTCA), the so-called Plattsburgh training camps. These were formed on the initiative of General Leonard Wood, who had initially nurtured the hope that as the regular army's most senior serving officer he, and not Pershing, would be asked to lead the AEF. But General Wood lacked Pershing's diplomatic charm and could not bite his tongue when necessary; in August 1914 Wood blunderingly voiced the view that Woodrow Wilson's response to the outbreak of war was pusillanimous by publicly referring to the President as 'a rabbit'. Presidents do not forget this kind of insult; this and the fact that Wood was in very poor physical shape gave Wilson the perfect excuse for preferring the more junior, fitter and pliant Pershing. The aspirant officers drawn to Wood's month-long military training offered at his Plattsburgh camp in the summer of 1915 were all from the patriotically inclined middle and upper classes, the type of person whose support for the war was essential if it were to be successful. By 1916 Congress had voted $2 million to help fund Wood's camps; after the declaration of war the Plattsburgh camps provided the basis for a nationwide series of officer training camps, where potential commissioned officers were over ninety days tested, assessed and, unless completely helpless, sent on to join units. Many ordinary private soldiers, including thousands of long-standing regular army troops, were later to complain bitterly of the so-called '90-day wonders' who were put in charge of them.

The first 43,000 officer candidates were admitted to OTCs on 16 May 1917 to undergo training by existing officers and NCOs of the US regular army. Less than half the original cadre of regular army officers were ever to find their way to France – the rest spent the war in the United States, training new officers. Although the calibre of its graduates sometimes left much to be desired, at least the MTCA system provided the basis for the speedy recruitment and processing of large numbers of officer candidates: 'Connections between the War Department and the MTCA not only produced tangible results, but also assured support for the military by a significant segment of upper-middle-class American society.'[14]

If we were to try to describe the quintessential doughboy we would probably end up with a white man in his early twenties, having little education and no previous military experience. If he was lucky, he received six months' training in the United States and then two months' in France. Many of those recruited in the second half of 1918 had much less training and some who were flung into battle had never fired a rifle before. Many were relatively recent immigrants with naturalized status, and spoke or read very little English. From town and country, salon and factory, farm and schoolroom, they came in an apparently endless stream. Of all the other participants in this war only Russia had been able to call upon such a vast reservoir of manpower. The American writer James B. Wharton attempted to capture the range of ethnic backgrounds of the doughboy army in his 1929 novel *Squad*:

Ole Andreson, a Swedish-American rancher from the Texas Panhandle. Stanley G. Allen, American, a high school youth from San Francisco. James Marzulak, Serb, a miner from Coal Valley, Pennsylvania. Harvey Whittaker, American, from Oklahoma City, Oklahoma. Emmanuel Waglith, Jewish proprietor of a shoe store in the Bronx, New York. Giuseppe Novelli, from 'Little Italy', South Eight Street, Philadelphia. Michael O'Connors, itinerant Irish-American worker.

Hugh Gray, American graduate of Center High School, Columbus, Ohio.[15]

Wharton's novel is full of the clichés of disillusioned 1920s anti-war fiction, but at least it tries to convey the doughboy army's genuine diversity of religious, social and ethnic backgrounds. In another post-war fictional account, *Company K*, William March carefully constructed his own hard-bitten view of the experiences from 113 short tales purporting to come from individuals in the same company. Like much of the post-war fiction which sought to comprehend the meaning of the Western Front, March's novella distils the experience of the AEF into a bleak overall picture, where cowardice, the murdering of prisoners, lust after prostitutes, and the incompetence of junior officers mingle with the chilling fear, mud, death and gruesome daily grind. Yet the reality is that most doughboys did not hear a shot fired in anger. The average doughboy who saw any battlefield action at all was under fire for a total of just seven days; on the other hand, some divisions were in action for several months continuously.

German interrogators of the very few AEF prisoners taken – put at 2,163 in total[16] – frequently remarked on the sheer heterogeneity of their 'American' opponents. There was even a large sprinkling of Native Americans, including fourteen Choctaw Indian men employed as field telephone operators who used their language as a form of code in the front line.[17] Speaking in Choctaw, a language which utterly confused the Germans, these members of the 142nd Infantry Regiment of the 36th Division (which arrived in France on 30 July 1918) happily chatted away to one another in their own language over their field telephones, thwarting all German attempts to decode their communications. Their contribution to the final victory was only recognized as late as 3 November 1989, when the then Choctaw chief, Hollis E. Roberts, was presented with the insignia of the Chevalier de l'Ordre National du Mérite by the French government on behalf of the surviving family members.

This heterogeneous army was a natural consequence of the relatively liberal immigration policy of the United States in the decades preceding the war. Between 1880 and 1910 America acquired vast numbers of immigrants, primarily Europeans seeking to improve their economic prospects. Before 1880, the United Kingdom, Germany, France, Belgium, Holland, Switzerland, Denmark, Sweden and Norway accounted for the majority of emigrants, and in 1880–90 more than 80 per cent of US immigrants came from those countries. After 1900, 75 per cent of them came from the Austro-Hungarian empire, Russia, the Balkans, the Mediterranean and Portugal. Net arrivals grew from 308,000 in 1900 to 815,000 in 1913.[18] Almost the only bar to immigration was the possession of an Oriental or Asian appearance. The background of some of the doughboys who, just a few years before, had lived in very different societies was thus often highly colourful. Captain Raymond Austin, an artilleryman in the AEF's 1st Division, described the background of his 'striker', the servant to which every US officer was entitled (and who was also known more graphically as a 'dog robber'):

His name is Vladimir Krasowski – a Novgorod Russian (near Petrograd). A real Russian, no Pole or Jew. He's 6ft. 2in. tall but doesn't look it, very blond. His father is or was a railway official of some sort in Russia. Walter (he adopted that first name after coming to the States) was in a private school in Petrograd where he got mixed up in some sort of student socialistic club. He tells me that the President of it had a fuss with his (the President's) girl who told them and they all had to skip the country. He has a bullet in his leg that some Cossack gave him. His father gave him some money and he came to America via Germany. He has an uncle in Chicago, head of some Russian Catholic school [. . .] He is naturalized now. He can repair clothes like a real tailor and press them, etc. and is a wizard with boots. I'm going to bring him home with me to drive my new car – 'après la guerre'.[19]

Ethnic diversity there may have been; racial integration there was not, despite much jingoistic propaganda pumped out by all manner of pro-war lobbying organizations:

Black men, yellow men, white men, from all quarters of the globe, are fighting side by side to free the world from the Hun peril.

That's the patriotism of equality![20]

Not quite. One aspect neither March nor Wharton, nor many other contemporary writers of the time, touched upon was the fact that the AEF had large numbers of black Americans, many of whom were proud to be part of what they frequently assumed was a fight on behalf of democracy not just in Europe but everywhere, including the United

States. The regular army, as American society generally, was ferociously bigoted and practised total segregation. No black Americans were permitted to serve alongside whites in the same unit, and in the handful of black regiments which (after a hard struggle) managed to get to France, the majority of the officers were white. Few white doughboys would ever have seen any black Americans in France, save perhaps the black stevedores employed to unload the transports arriving at French ports. Most black doughboys quickly had their illusions shattered. In the middle of July 1918 Private Sidney Wilson, of the 368th Infantry Regiment, decided to get a few things off his chest. He wrote an anonymous letter to the chairman of the board which had drafted him into the army from his home in Memphis, Tennessee:

Dear Sir,

It afoads to the soldier boys wich you have sint so far away from home a great deal of pledger to write you a few lines to let you know that you low-down Mother Fuckers can put a gun in our hands but who is able to take it out? We may go to France but I want to let you know that it will not be over with untill we straiten up this state. We feel like we have nothing to do with this war, so if you all thinks it, just wait until Uncle Sam puts a gun in the niggers hands and you will be sorry of it, because we have colored luetinan up here, and thay is planning against this country everday. So all we wants now is the amanation, then you all can look out, for we is coming.[21]

There was on the part of most whites a real failure to understand or even imagine the humiliation felt by most black doughboys. After the war was over there was published a popular collection of humorous wartime items culled from many places, including the *Stars and Stripes*, the AEF's sometimes brilliant weekly newspaper, which produced some of the war's finest cartoons and illustrations. One was the following:

After the Armistice
Boastful Mose

After the Armistice, two dusky soldiers, whose presence in the AEF was positively necessary to the successful conclusion of the war, were expostulating on what they were going to do when they got back home. 'Rastus,' said Mose, 'do you know what I'se gwin to do when I get back to de States?'

'No, what's yo gwin to do, Mose?' said Rastus.

Mose: I'se gwin to buy me a white suit of clothes, white shoes, white shirt and tie, and I'se gwin to tend de white folks' church, and sit by the white women.

Rastus: Does yo now what I'se gwin ter do?

Mose: No, what's yo gwin to do, Rastus?

Rastus: I'se gwin to buy me a black suit of clothes, black shoes, black shirt and tie, and black gloves, and attend yo funeral.[22]

This kind of stuff was commonplace in *Stars and Stripes*, which simply tried to give its readership what it thought was wanted. But it did not go entirely unchallenged. The editor of *Stars and Stripes*, Guy T. Viskniskki, received a letter dated 19 November 1918 from 1st Lieutenant Charles L. Holmes, who protested against the 'ridicule [. . .] degrading remarks [and the] prejudicial propaganda' against black American soldiers; it was, said Holmes, a waste of 'good type and paper. [. . .] try to find out really what the Negro is doing and has done, then, give the man who has done a man's work the credit for being a man'.

Viskniskki was unmoved. He replied to Holmes: 'The trouble is you are altogether too sensitive in this matter. You cannot expect to put the colored man above other Americans, and that is what you are doing when you object to war dialect stories. In my opinion your viewpoint is entirely warped and your criticism has no foundation in fact.'[23]

There was no question that, at the time, Viskniskki spoke for majority white opinion; jokes about 'darkies' and 'Rastus' were simply 'dialect stories'. Black Americans saw such humour for what it was – a degrading humiliation. From this distance it is probably impossible to establish whether Viskniskki and his helpers – who included Private Harold Wallace Ross, who went on to found the *New Yorker*, and Alexander Woollcott, the drama critic of the *New York Times* – were deceiving themselves or whether they genuinely believed that such material was innocuous. They certainly reflected what the vast bulk of white soldiers thought and said.

Marginalized, despised, poorly led and inadequately trained, only two black combat divisions were raised and sent to France, the 92nd and 93rd. Only the 92nd saw service alongside white American divisions. Most of those black Americans who enlisted were shepherded towards the Service of Supply (SOS), the logistics branch of the AEF, where they were generally shovelled into the worst kinds of brutalizing labour. The SOS provided an essential support for the combat divisions, building roads, raising encampments, digging trenches and so on – but it was not a glamorous posting. The four infantry regiments of the 93rd Division were assigned to four French divisions, the French army having fewer prejudices about skin-colour. To French generals, accustomed to having black colonial troops in the same division as white men, when blood was spilt it was all the same colour. Once with the French divisions the segregated black regiments ate French rations, were clad in French uniforms and equipped with French weapons, including the unreliable, slow-firing and inaccurate Lebel rifle, the loading of which 'could be heard for 100 yards'.[24]

Pershing made excuses about the segregation practised in the army he commanded, stating that these black regiments 'were anxious to serve with our armies, and I made application for the organization and shipment of the rest of the division, but to no purpose and these regiments remained with the French to the end'.[25] This is a distortion; Pershing held sway over where his divisions went, and had he chosen to exercise his power in this instance no one would have stood against him. The truth is that neither he nor his General Staff wanted black regiments serving in combat roles in the AEF alongside white soldiers. The 93rd's four regiments – the 369th, 370th, 371st and 372nd – came from New York City, Connecticut, Illinois, Maryland, Massachusetts, Ohio, Tennessee, Arkansas and South Carolina. These four black regiments were never equipped by Pershing with their own artillery, engineers, signallers, or supply trains; they were thus beggars, dependent on the generosity of their French allies. The 369th, from Harlem, had a splendid reputation as a well-trained outfit, with a fierce pride in its origins as the New York 15th National Guard; it had both white and black officers from the outset, the former mainly Ivy Leaguers, the latter intellectuals from black colleges. They happily dubbed themselves the '15th Heavy Foot'. The regiment's colonel was a leading New York socialite, William Hayward. He formed it from scratch and persuaded Jim Europe, the most famous bandleader of the time, to join and create for the 15th the best band in the AEF. Jim Europe said recruiting the best players would cost money, but that did not unduly perturb the wealthy and well-connected Hayward, who asked forty of his wealthiest friends to write cheques for a $10,000 fund. One, Daniel Reid, whose fortune was based on tin, wrote a cheque for the whole $10,000, saying, 'That's a damn sight easier than writing a lot of letters.'

Black or white, the new soldiers had little or no military experience and what they found in France was a revelation for all, a shock for many. Probably many enlisted for the same or similar reasons as those given by Arthur Ellwood Yensen, though few would be as brutally honest: 'For the excitement and adventure of it. Even at that age [Yensen was eighteen when he joined up on 13 October 1917] I thought wars were silly, but if they were going to have one I wanted to see it.'

He was quickly disillusioned: 'I thought the army was full of heroes and I was bitterly disappointed to find most of those in authority over me were so domineering, tyrannical, unreasonable and tried so hard to continually humiliate me.'[26]

Yensen trained at Fort Leavenworth, a tough institution at the best of times, where he was assigned to the 7th Engineers Train of the 5th Division, a regular army division which arrived in France on 1 May 1918.

Ralph T. Moan, born in the small town of East Machias, Maine, was nineteen years old in April 1917. A chauffeur by trade, Moan volunteered and became a corporal in Company K, 103rd Infantry, part of the 26th Division (National Guard, recruited from New England), which arrived in France on Sunday, 28 October 1917. The 26th was to be in the thick of some of the fiercest fighting in 1918. A fit and hardy youngster, Moan was picked for one of the more dangerous front-line jobs, that of a runner, a vital but highly dangerous function as the runner would normally only be required to be above ground at precisely the worst moment, during an artillery bombardment which had cut field telephone lines. Like many bright and quick-witted doughboys, Moan[27] understandably felt that he was about to embark upon such an extraordinary experience that he would keep an account of all that he saw and heard. But by 30 March 1918 – significantly, some time before the 26th first went into action – Moan was suffering the initial symptoms of combat fatigue: 'Have decided to cut this diary out right now, for no man wishes after seeing what we have seen to recall them but rather wishes to forget. From now on all we see is HELL.'[28]

Malcolm Aitken, twenty-three in April 1917, gave up his studies at agricultural college to enlist at San José, California, just before Christmas 1917. As many young Americans before and since, Aitken fell in love with the razor-sharp turnout of a couple of marine recruiting officers. Attached to the 67th (Company D) of the 5th Marines, Aitken sailed for France at 11 p.m. on the USS *Henderson* on Saturday, 27 April 1918, after having recovered from a bout of mumps; one month later his unit, as part of the 2nd Division, was in the thick of the fighting at Belleau Wood, one of 1918's most bitter battles, and where the AEF took centre stage. It was the first of several engagements in which Aitken fought, but he too survived the war. When he returned to the United States he was a 'shadow of my former self, physically and perhaps mentally'. His parents were 'at [their] wits' end' and did not know how to deal with him. His experience, he laconically noted, 'put me in shape physically (teeth; amoebic dysentery; mental reaction to combat; nightmares etc.)'. It took him two years to find 'my spot' as a schoolteacher, and settle to marriage, in 1922.[29]

Other doughboys not only survived but thrived under the stress of combat, using the experience to great effect in their later professional life. The teetotal, non-smoking Harry Amos Bullis, twenty-seven years old and 6 feet 2 inches, left Hastings, Nebraska, to serve first as a sergeant, then lieutenant and finally as a captain in France for eighteen months. His personal motto could almost have stood for the AEF as a whole: 'Drive straight ahead with a positive mental attitude.' This soldierly posture obviously stood him in good stead in later life. By the time he died in 1946 Bullis had climbed through the ranks to become president of General Mills, one of America's corporate giants.[30]

Some who were to become doughboys first experienced combat under another national flag. Oliver Cromwell Carmichael, a Rhodes Scholar at Oxford University in 1914, found himself on holiday in

Munich in August 1914, far from his native Alabama. From Munich he took a 36-hour train journey to Belgium where he joined Herbert Hoover, then masterminding relief work for Belgian civilians. Carmichael then joined the British army in 1915 and was sent to East Africa, where his experience in organizing emergency food aid was put to good use – he was placed in charge of a field canteen. He then returned to Princeton to continue his studies but, on America joining the war, he volunteered to train as an officer in the AEF. He first served as a 1st lieutenant with the 321st Infantry, 81st Division (which arrived in France on 16 August 1918), and his fluent French and German were soon put to use interrogating German prisoners-of-war. He eventually rose to become chancellor of Vanderbilt University.[31]

Raymond Thornton Chandler may perhaps be considered an honorary doughboy. He was born into a family of Quakers in Chicago in July 1888. When he was only nine, the future author of *The Big Sleep* and other *noir* thrillers had been taken by his mother to Britain, following her divorce from Chandler's father. But unlike his fellow thriller-writer, Dashiell Hammett – who joined up but was too ill to serve in France – Chandler saw plenty of action on the Western Front. He enlisted in the Canadian forces on the outbreak of war in 1914, gained two medals for valour, and was a pilot in the Royal Flying Corps by the end.

Chandler's novels made him a household name, which cannot be said of another American pulp-fiction thriller-writer, Philadelphia-born Baynard Hardwick Kendrich. Kendrich was another American who could not wait for Wilson's declaration of war but immediately joined the Canadian army in August 1914. If his novels are forgotten, his name should live on for being the first American to volunteer to fight on behalf of the Allies. He saw action with the Canadian 1st Battalion in France, was wounded and transferred to the Medical Corps, with which he went to the Salonika front. Wounded again in 1916, he was not finally demobbed until 1918.

Chandler and Kendrich were just two Americans who volunteered for the Canadian army. Some half-Americans were already there, including Raymond Massey, the future film star. Massey might be said to be a retrospective doughboy, as he became a US citizen in 1944.[32] Born in Toronto to an American mother and Canadian father,

Massey joined the Canadian army when war broke out and served as a lieutenant in the field artillery. Wounded at Ypres in 1916, he then served with the British military mission to the United States as a gunnery instructor at Yale and Princeton. Massey was one of the poor souls who found themselves embroiled in a largely forgotten and today almost completely inexplicable conflict in Siberia in 1918 and 1919 as part of the Allies' expeditionary forces, where he amused himself (and others) by organizing a minstrel show in the officers' mess.

Almost 1,300 Americans joined the Canadian Expeditionary Force as part of the 97th Infantry Battalion, which began recruiting in late 1915 in the Toronto area. Through a series of scandals – including numerous desertions back across the US–Canada border, and unfounded accusations of embezzlement against the battalion's colonel – the 97th was broken up before it left for France. By January 1917 most of the remnants were fighting in France as part of the Royal Canadian Regiment, participating in the storming of Vimy Ridge on Easter Monday, 1917.

Some doughboys found their true home in the army. Graves Blanchard Erskine, from Louisiana, was training for medical practice when war broke out. In his spare time the twenty-year-old was a sergeant trumpeter in the National Guard. He could not wait for his unit to be called into action so joined the marines as a 2nd lieutenant, entering France as part of the 6th Marine Regiment. He was in action at St-Mihiel, Belleau Wood and Soissons, and was eventually wounded at Marbache. After 1918 he stayed in the regular army and rose through the ranks, ending as a major-general in command of the marines at Iwo Jima in the Second World War.[33] Other Second World War US commanders who fought on the Western Front in 1918 were George C. Marshall (infantry), Douglas MacArthur (infantry), and George Patton (tanks). Two future presidents joined up. Harry S. Truman served in France as an artilleryman, while Dwight D. Eisenhower had to wait until the Second World War to see active service. Eisenhower was deeply disappointed at not getting to France in 1917–18, though he gained a Distinguished Service Medal back home where he commanded the fledgling tank training facility at Camp Colt, which in 1918 was reactivated as an army base at Gettysburg. The lack of equipment when he started was so serious that he mounted small

3-pound naval guns on the back of flatbed trucks and had his recruits fire from these mobile platforms in the vicinity of Big Round Top, a prominent spot in the Gettysburg battlefield.

The AEF also had some splendid long-forgotten heroes, such as Jay Catherwood Hormel, later known as 'the Spam Man'. Born in Austin, Minnesota, Hormel was the son of a meat retailer who established a business – George Hormel & Co. – packing pork. It rapidly grew to become the largest independent meat packer in America. Jay followed in his father's footsteps, eventually improving the business considerably by developing the gourmet's delight known as luncheon meat, which he branded as Spam. On 5 September 1917 Hormel, then just twenty-five, became the first enlisted man to join the 351st Infantry, part of the 88th (National Army) Division, which took its recruits not just from Minnesota but also from Iowa, Illinois and North Dakota. Despite being formed relatively early, the 88th did not arrive in France until quite late, between 17 August and 9 September 1918. Hormel's military career was impressive: in just nine days after his enlistment he was made a corporal; eleven days later he was promoted to sergeant-major; and two weeks after that he became a 2nd lieutenant. In November 1917 someone spotted his true talent and assigned him to the 301st Ice Plant Company. One of the most troublesome issues of the US participation in the war was a perennial pressure on shipping space across the Atlantic. Hormel's single biggest contribution to the war effort was to save 40 per cent of the shipping space occupied by meat sent from America to the AEF in France. Like all great ideas, Hormel's was simplicity itself – bone the beef and compact it before it was frozen and loaded onto the ships. But there were no medals for those who simply helped Pershing get his divisions across to France more rapidly. Had a stray whizz-bang alighted upon Hormel before his scheme was put into practice, who knows, the war might have had a different outcome; but then we would never have had Spam.[34]

Another participant came into his own very late in the war. Captain Edwin P. Hubble found the army had no means of working out the mathematical complications of elevation, distance, muzzle-velocity and so forth for the four 14-inch naval guns brought from the United States and trained upon Sedan from behind the US lines in the final days of the war. Hubble – later to win a Nobel Prize and have one of the most important space exploration missions named after him – solved the problems, and the guns began firing more accurately.

There were of course many authentic combat heroes, including Lance-Corporal William H. Metcalf, the only American to win the Victoria Cross, the highest British award for valour. Born in Waige, Walsh County, Maine, Metcalf served with the 16th Battalion in the Canadian army. In September 1918, 23-year-old Metcalf directed a tank while under intense machine-gun fire, and although wounded he continued the advance and survived to tell the tale.[35]

Some had already achieved American hero status even before the war started. John M. T. Finney, fifty-four in 1917, was a chief consultant surgeon for the AEF and later became founder and first president of the American College of Surgeons. But many sports fans recalled him as the only person ever to play football for both Princeton and Harvard. He was on the Princeton team in his senior year and played for the Harvard squad during his first year at Harvard medical school; the rule restricting eligibility to undergraduates had yet to be introduced.

Others were already well-known faces, such as the actor Harry Kendall, who in 1914 was a leading man in motion pictures at the Vitagraph studios in Hollywood, playing opposite such vamps as Norma Talmadge. According to his own account, Kendall 'grew tired' of living 'in the enervating atmosphere of powerful lights, unpleasant heat and the more or less mechanical occupation of having my photograph taken endlessly, so I thought that perhaps "The Show" over in Europe might be bigger and more interesting'. He sailed to Liverpool and joined the British army. 'Under heavy shellfire,' he said, 'it was safest to fall down flat.'[35]

Some Americans never polished a single brass button but served in useful ways back home. The thriller-writer Rex Todhunter Stout was a Quaker who perhaps would have protested against being drafted; but he never had to face that dilemma. By the time the war started Stout, then thirty-one, was occupying a vital sinecure. Good with figures, he had been a relative failure until in 1912 he invented a system for school financing, which he called the Educational Thrift Service. He managed to sell his system to more than 400 towns and cities.

When war broke out he turned over his accounting scheme to the government. It was used for the sale of War Savings stamps, and he stayed on as its manager.[37]

Some were already famous. Orville Wright, inventor of the first practical aeroplane, was commissioned as a major in the Signal Corps Aviation Service at the venerable age of forty-five. Some were to become famous. William Bernard Ziff – chairman and founder of what became one of the world's biggest publishers of computing magazines, Ziff-Davis Publishing – was only nineteen when he took one of the riskiest roles on the Western Front, as a balloonist with the 202nd Aero Observation Squadron. Some never found fame at all, but simply did their duty; as a nineteen-year-old Charles H. Donnelly joined up as a private in Battery A of the Field Artillery of the Michigan National Guard on 14 May 1915, and later saw plenty of action in France. The AEF also had its fair share of cynics, who, as Arthur Yensen recorded, may have joined up along with his brother Walt 'because we believed we could soon rise to fame and glory'.[38]

Yensen quickly discovered there was no fame and precious little glory as a waggon-driver, or 'muleskinner' in the argot of the day, on the Western Front in 1918. As part of the 5th Division, which landed in France between 12 March and 19 June 1918, Yensen was shelled, sniped at, starved and finally ignored, one of the forlorn forgotten doughboys who, miserable and in despair, remained behind in Germany as part of the army of occupation until the middle of 1919, months after the war had come to an end; by that time most of the AEF had returned home to fanfares and accolades. When Yensen stepped off the quayside in New York at the end of July 1919, his unit 'patiently listened to a speech on keeping our war-risk insurance, then one on venereal diseases; but when a recruiting officer got up to talk on re-enlistment, we booed him off the platform'.[39]

Yensen had joined up in the expectation that his talents as an illustrator and cartoonist would find him work as an official war artist; in typical army fashion his hands wielded nothing more useful than a pair of reins for much of the war, though he did make some powerfully satirical sketches for himself.

Yensen certainly ended up a rather eccentric character, but even stranger were two Americans who fought in the Foreign Legion along-side the Swiss-Scottish author Blaise Cendrars. They were

Buywater (killed at Vimy Ridge) and Wilson (killed in the cemetery at Souchez): two North American citizens who came to join us at Hangest-en-Santerre, two old men, Buywater seventy-two years old and Wilson sixty-nine, both of them surgeons from Chicago; both of them refusing absolutely to fire a rifle because it went against their conscience; both belonging to I know not what sect of Mennonites or Seventh Day Adventists, who, to honour Christ's garment without a seam, forbid their followers to wear buttons on their clothing – and our two fanatics conscientiously cut all the buttons off their uniforms; both of them bombarding their consul in Paris with complaints and recriminations accusing the sergeants in the French army of interfering with the liberty of free American citizens and forbidding them the practice and rites of their religious convictions; and when you asked these two stubborn men why they had joined up, Buywater, who had brought his friend along with him, replied, speaking through his nose like all Yankees: 'If I joined up, it wasn't for the sake of France, nor against Germany, it was for the mud-baths. The trenches are very healthy for the body.' And when it was their turn for sentry duty, they ran to the loop-hole, undressed, *unlaced* themselves in haste (their clothes were held together by a whole network of bits of string) and mounted guard in their birthday suits, with their cartridge-belts next to their bare flesh and their rifles in sheaths; crouching down, they wallowed and paddled with joy in the nauseating mud, and eyeing us, the young, with contempt [. . .] as they had plenty of money, the two old monkeys paid their comrades to give up their guard duty so that they could put in supplementary hours at the loop-hole![40]

Whatever their background and military experience, the doughboys were like an injection of adrenalin into the bloodstream of the cadaverous Allied armies. They swept in with a lusty arrogance not seen on the Western Front battlefields since 1914. Contemporary assessments by the French military were, on the whole, highly complimentary about the doughboys' physique and morale, if not their military skills. In a confidential document written in March 1918, General Ragueneau, chief of the French military mission with the AEF, attempted to describe what he called 'the mentality of Americans':[41]

The first American troops to be organized as units, are sturdy, eager, and well-disciplined, and have made rapid progress. Their officers, who are constantly subjected to a rigorous process of selection by elimination, already possess distinct qualities of character and leadership. The technical knowledge and the practical experience, which they lack, they can only acquire by degree [. . .] It must be said that the American is free from the born stiffness of the Englishman, and many American officers are now on terms of lasting and sincere friendship with a considerable number of our own officers.

What particularly surprised the British and French was the dough-boys' willingness to fight, to take the initiative in combat, and to develop as aggressive a posture as possible against the Germans. After more than three years of fruitless attrition, where advances were normally measured in yards, casualties in hundreds of thousands, and where, as Marc Ferro eloquently explained, 'from 1914 onwards the grave preserved life',[42] it was perhaps high time that the stagnant ambitions of getting either a flesh wound (to be sent home to safety), or being placed in a *bon secteur* where the shelling was by timetable and mutual agreement only, were replaced by energy, initiative and individualism. Equally, the doughboys were initially roundly criticized by some senior generals of the Allied armies and their political leaders, condemned for being either naive and inexperienced, or brash and over-confident. But the first few tens of thousands of doughboys had an enormous responsibility placed on their shoulders; nothing less than the saving of France was expected of them, when several million French troops had been unable to achieve the same thing. Those unrealistically high expectations were sometimes disappointed; but what the dough-boys never failed to deliver was an almost insatiable appetite for closing with the enemy.

In that respect they resembled the Australians, New Zealanders and Canadians, whose own morale never seemed to dip below magnificent. Like these irrepressible Commonwealth troops, the doughboys sus-tained their morale by being able to laugh at themselves and their situation. They defied the perpetual presence of death by taking nothing very seriously, and this easy-come, easy-go attitude was perfectly mirrored by *Stars and Stripes*. The magazine ran a regular column entitled 'Free Advice for Lovelorn Lads', by 'Miss Information'. It took the form of replies to anonymous or disguised requests for advice. One read:

Yes, if she sent you a book of war poetry, you have a perfectly good excuse for breaking with her. That is the most heartless thing a woman could possibly do. I blush for my sex to think that one member of it could stoop to such baseness. Forget her – and the poetry too.[43]

The girl back home was important, not least because she (and other members of the family) could alleviate the monotony of life at the front, by writing letters, keeping 'home' in the mind – and sending parcels, possibly the biggest morale-booster in all armies. The 'Christmas Catalog' of 1917 published by the Philadelphia-based retail firm John Wanamaker warned, 'we cannot guarantee delivery, our responsibility ceasing when the parcels are handed to the foreign Post Offices or other forwarding agencies', and – of course – 'prices are subject to change without notice'. Twenty dollars provided a very satisfactory Christmas hamper for the doughboy of your heart in 1917, sufficient for 100 Sweet Caporal cigarettes ($1); a one-and-a-half-pound jar of honey ($1.25); one and three-quarter pounds of 'fancy lunch biscuits' ($0.65); a pound of chocolate ($1.50); half a pound of Parasitox, 'a remedy for insects' ($0.40); a Gillette safety razor ($6.50) plus a dozen blades ($1.50); five bars of toilet soap ($1); two toothbrushes ($1); two tubes of toothpaste ($1); and two sticks of shaving soap ($0.80). The tense moments before jump-off for the non-smoker could be alleviated, perhaps, by chewing gum, at 15 cents a packet. That Christmas there was a restriction on the amount of candy which could be sent abroad, to five pounds per person per week, of which only one pound in every five could be chocolate.[44] Doughboys' service apparel and equipment was rather spartan, but for $50 they could obtain via mail order from the States a leather-lined coat, guaranteed to be 'absolutely waterproof, fleece storm warm', while another useful item, trench waders – rubber thigh-boots with leather soles – cost $20.

The doughboys' general good humour not only helped sustain their morale and those of the Allied armies; it also benefited the civilians they lived alongside. In comparison with other nationalities few soldiers of the AEF were found guilty either of serious civilian crimes or of serious military offences. As commander-in-chief of the AEF Pershing was required to confirm all sentences of death, and had to pass judgement on just forty-four criminal cases carrying the ultimate penalty. Only eleven, for murder or rape, were actually carried out. President Wilson was the final arbiter for the death penalty for military crimes. Four cases of execution were recommended by Pershing; Wilson, a humane man, approved none. These are astonishingly small figures, given the eventual size of the AEF in France. By the time of the Meuse–Argonne offensive of September–November 1918 (jointly carried out by the AEF and the French, and the AEF's final battle), the AEF's First Army alone reached 896,000 men, the largest single army mustered by the United States up to that time; Grant's army in 1864 was about 120,000 strong, while Sherman's in the same year was some 80,000 and Lee's was perhaps 70,000.[45]

One thing the doughboys achieved which not even the grudging accolade of Lloyd George could damage: their presence guaranteed eventual victory. In 1919 Western Europe owed its freedom to the largest conscript force in US history.[46]

5

To France

It has always been my dream that the two English-speaking nations should some day be united in a great cause, and today my dream is realized. Together we are fighting for the greatest cause for which peoples could fight. The Anglo-Saxon race must save civilization.

King George V[1]

'Do you think they will send Americans down here?' asked the adjutant.

'Oh, absolutely. Americans twice as large as myself, healthy, with clean hearts, sleep at night, never been wounded, never been blown up, never had their heads caved in, never been scared, don't drink, faithful to the girls they left behind them, many of them never had crabs, wonderful chaps. You'll see.'

Ernest Hemingway[2]

Pershing's appointment as commander-in-chief of the American Expeditionary Force did not mean that he became a frequent visitor to the White House. In fact Pershing met Wilson only once between the outbreak of war and Wilson's visit to France after the Armistice in November 1918. Wilson called for Pershing to visit him at the White House shortly before he sailed for France. The meeting was understandably stiff, as both were weighed down by the sense of occasion and the burden of their respective responsibilities:

Mr Wilson spoke of my recent expedition into Mexico and inquired about my acquaintance with France. I had naturally thought that he would say something about the part our Army should play in the war in cooperation with the Allied armies, but he said nothing [...]

Upon leaving, I said, 'Mr President, I appreciate the honor you have conferred upon me by the assignment you have given me and realize the responsibilities it entails, but you can count upon the best that is in me.' His reply was, 'General, you were chosen entirely upon your record and I have every confidence that you will succeed; you shall have my full support.'[3]

Pershing sailed for France with not one but two sets of orders, both dated 26 May. One was signed by Newton D. Baker on behalf of Wilson, the other by General Tasker Bliss, as acting chief-of-staff, though it had been drafted by Pershing and Major James Harbord. Crucially, both sets of orders instructed Pershing that he was to maintain a separate, distinct and uniquely American army, under his command. In preserving the AEF as an independent force Pershing did no more than obey his orders. Baker added one more instruction – to make sure he returned home. On 28 May 1917 the *Baltic* sailed from New York late in the afternoon of a foggy, cold and rainy day. Aboard was the first small contingent of the AEF – 190 officers and men, most of them hand-picked by Pershing. Initially 'depressed'[4] at the enormous burden of his responsibility, Pershing paid careful attention to the selection of his General Staff; this small band of officers and men would greatly colour the whole course of events. Pershing needed reliable, physically tough, intellectually strong, utterly loyal and totally dedicated men. The relatively small size of the regular army meant that Pershing was not spoilt for choice. The most important officer after him would be his chief-of-staff and for this vital role he selected Major Harbord. They had known one another since December 1898, when they shared a tent for two weeks at the 10th Cavalry Regiment's camp at Huntsville, Alabama.[5]

Two months after the American declaration of war the arrival of such a puny contingent was slightly disappointing to the British and especially the French, not least because the latest grand attack on the Germans, the Nivelle offensive, had fizzled out with nothing gained except the almost complete destruction within the ranks of the French army of the will to fight. The French mutiny threatened to hand the Germans an easy victory before the Americans had even fired a shot. General Pétain took over at the head of the French army and made it clear that the Allies would not be able to count upon any fresh French attacks for the rest of the year.

The failure of the Nivelle offensive [. . .] brought a sobering note of reality to French operations. In 1917, Pétain abandoned hopes for a breakthrough in favor of 'attacks with limited objectives, unleashed suddenly on a front wide enough to make full use of the numbers and various types of existing artillery' [. . .] Pétain had inaugurated a real war of attrition relying upon materiel rather than manpower.[6]

In the wake of the Nivelle disaster French expectations of the Americans, particularly in terms of equipment, became astonishingly fanciful. At the end of May 1917 Alexandre Ribot, then France's prime minister, demanded of the US War Department the following:

The formation of a flying corps of 4,500 airplanes – personnel and materiel included – to be sent to the French front during the campaign of 1918. The total number of pilots, including reserve, should be 5,000 and 50,000 mechanics.

2,000 airplanes should be constructed each month as well as 4,000 engines, by the American factories. That is to say, that during the first six months of 1918, 16,500 planes (of the latest type) and 30,000 engines will have to be built.[7]

This was breathtakingly unrealistic. Pershing pointed out that at the time of Ribot's demand the US Air Service Section of the Signal Corps had 65 officers and 1,000 men, that only 35 officers could fly a plane, and 'none of them could have met the requirements of modern battle conditions'.[8] He regarded Ribot's request as 'a most convincing confession of the plight of the Allied armies'.[9] America's lack of trained air combat personnel was matched by the inadequacy of its equipment:

We could boast some 55 training planes in various conditions of usefulness, all entirely without war equipment and valueless for service at the front. Of these 55 planes, it is amusing now to recall that the National Advisory Committee for Aeronautics, which was then conducting a scientific study of the problem of flight, advised that 51 were obsolete and the other 4 obsolescent.

We could not have put a single squadron in the field, although it was estimated later that we should eventually need at least 300 squadrons, each to be composed on the average of some 24 officers, 180 men and 18 airplanes, besides a large reserve of planes for replacements.[10]

General Peyton March, appointed army chief-of-staff in Washington on 4 March 1918, was – characteristically – much more robust in his assessment of Ribot's demand. March thought it patently absurd, not just because the United States had nothing like the men and equipment which the French assumed it possessed, but because it revealed that Ribot and his kind had, incredibly enough, succumbed to a form of monstrous idiocy about the war. In March's opinion the three-year stalemate on the Western Front had convincingly demonstrated the fallacy of believing that victory came through attrition, quantity and size, rather than through quality, imagination and planning. In any case, March pointed out that Ribot was asking America to supply, within less than one year, more than 'all the planes in Europe owned by France, England, Italy, and by our enemies – Germany and Austria [. . .] Their demand for 16,500 planes and 30,000 engines to be built during the first six months of 1918 turned a very serious matter into a farce.'[11]

Ribot expected American industry – which had yet to switch from peacetime to military production – to be able to produce 750 planes a month more than the German Supreme Command called for from German factories, which were devoted to little else but the war effort. Throughout the whole course of the war Germany had managed to construct just 47,637 airplanes, of more than 150 types.[12] It was necessary to damp down unrealistic expectations, as Dennis Nolan, soon to become head of G-2, Intelligence, quickly discovered after landing in France:

My own troubles began in earnest upon my arrival in Paris [where initially he gave two news briefings a day]. Most of the American writers had been there during the entire course of the war and had a thousand questions to ask as to what we proposed to do and when we were going to do it. They were all quite filled with the French propaganda that we were to furnish huge airplanes and were quickly to end the war by bombing German cities and forcing the German Air Service out of the battle, and all of them were very disappointed when they found out how lamentably lacking we were in any air preparation.[13]

The unrealistic expectations of the French were matched by the almost complete ignorance of the AEF General Staff. Although the war had been raging since August 1914 the US War Department had made no systematic attempt to educate senior army officers in the new methods of warfare that had evolved. For the US regular army in April 1917, the cavalry was still the most important formation, while the most familiar enemies were the ill-equipped and poorly led armies of Cuba, Mexico and the Philippines. But if largely unaware of the realities of the combat which was to face them, at least they had a clear mandate from their commander-in-chief, President Wilson, who gave Pershing complete control over military operations in France, and commanded him to create a distinct and separate US army:

In military operations against the Imperial German Government, you are directed to cooperate with the forces of the other countries employed against that enemy; but in so doing the underlying idea must be kept in view that the forces of the United States are a separate and distinct component of the combined forces, the identity of which must be preserved. This fundamental rule is subject to such minor exceptions in particular circumstances as your judgement may approve. The decision as to when your command, or any of its parts, is ready for action is confided to you, and you will exercise full discretion in determining the manner of cooperation. But, until the forces of the United States are in your judgement sufficiently strong to warrant operations as an independent command, it is understood that you will cooperate as a component of whatever army you may be assigned to by the French Government.[14]

The frequent clashes which were to plague the relationship with the Allies were due in large part to the British and French military authorities choosing to focus only on the final phrase of the last sentence of this command.

Blind optimism as to what the Americans would quickly provide and do was of course not only a French characteristic; British leaders suffered the same misconception. After arriving in London in June 1917 Pershing was invited to a royal reception at Buckingham Palace on the evening of Saturday, 9 June. King George V was extremely anxious about the course of the war and to Pershing expressed his hope that

we 'would send over a large number of destroyers'. As to aviation, he had heard through the dispatches the extravagant claims of certain boastful Americans and he asked me whether we really expected soon to have 50,000 airplanes in the field. I had to acknowledge that such reports were extremely exaggerated and that we should not be sending over any planes for some time to come.[15]

This vast gulf between expectation and capacity was to be found in every aspect of the American military–industrial complex. America had what was widely recognized to be the best rifle of the day, the Springfield 1903, but it was produced in only two factories, the Springfield Armory in Springfield, Massachusetts, and the Rock Island Arsenal at Rock Island, Illinois. By 1917 the latter had ceased production of the Springfield. Some US regular army units were armed with the Krag-Jorgensen rifle, which was regarded as obsolete. On the eve of its entry into the war the United States had about 600,000 Springfields and 160,000 Krags, and 40,000 sawn-off shotguns, the latter being handy for close-order combat in trenches and dense forest.[16]

Nor was America able to provide much artillery. Following various 'shell crises' in France and Britain in 1914 and 1915, the Allies had learned the importance of stockpiling artillery ammunition; while British troops had been starved of shells in that period (using respectively in those two years 500,000 and 6 million), by 1916 the British army had more than 45 million shells, increasing to above 76 million in 1917 and more than 67 million in 1918.[17] America, on the other hand, entered the war with an artillery shell stockpile sufficient for nine hours, a paltry amount in the context of the Western Front. In April 1917 just one German army group on the Western Front, amounting to 140,000 men, fired each day as many as seven trainloads of heavy shells, requiring 26,000 horses to haul them from the rear echelon railhead to the front lines.[18] On 21 March 1918, when the German artillery started firing on British positions preparatory to the start of the spring offensive, more than 6,000 guns fired in excess of 9 million shells for four days and nights without cease. But the US regular army had so few cannon in April 1917 that it had little use for shell stockpiles.

While crossing the Atlantic Pershing settled down with his skeleton General Staff to try to formulate estimates for precisely what would be needed to maintain an army of 500,000 men in the field. They came up with the figure of an initial requirement of 2,524 artillery pieces of various calibres, a highly optimistic guesstimate given that they were also aware that US foundries would be able to supply just 80 cannon in September 1917, 40 more in October, and none thereafter until June 1918.[19] By the end of the war the AEF mustered 2,106 75mm field guns (the vast majority of them bought from the French), 1,485 heavy artillery pieces (purchased from both the British and the French), and 1,761,000 rifles; but that sort of strength took many months to build up.[20] The lack of sufficient artillery was to prove a serious problem for the AEF throughout the war. In late July 1917 Pershing visited the British GHQ in France, accompanied by his chief-of-staff, now Colonel Harbord, Colonel Benjamin Alvord, and the young Captain George Patton. They learned from the head of the BEF's artillery, Major-General Birch, that the British at that time possessed 3,712 field guns and howitzers, and 2,258 guns of other calibres – one artillery piece for every twenty-five yards of the BEF's eighty miles of front line.[21]

Shortages of another increasingly important weapon, the tank, were also to blight the AEF's assaults. In 1918 no full-scale battle on the Western Front was complete without a contingent of tanks. Although highly primitive, the tank often proved useful when used in significant numbers in massed formation. As developed by the British during the war the tank had its origins, ironically enough, in the caterpillar-tracked steam tractors built by the Holt Company of the United States, invented to cope with soft delta farmland. In February 1915 Winston Churchill, then First Lord of the Admiralty, chaired a committee which observed a trial of a Holt tractor; the upshot of that was the development of what became the familiar lozenge-shaped beast which first drove

German troops into panic at Cambrai in 1917. In 1917 Britain produced 1,110 tanks; in 1918, another 1,359.[22] But although it possessed the progenitor of the tank, the AEF was to fight without any US-produced versions and depended entirely upon French armour.[23]

Nor did the AEF ever have sufficient motorized transport, and there were perpetual crises concerning lack of horse and mule transport.[24] The nation which had invented cheap, mass-produced combustion-engined vehicles (the Model T Ford first went on sale in 1908 and by 1915 more than 1 million had been churned out) could not ever provide enough trucks and buses for its troops. In 1917 US motor-vehicle manufacturers produced 1,749,791 civilian passenger autos and 128,157 trucks. President Wilson's government arrogated to itself a vast number of highly restrictive, authoritarian powers which, it argued, were essential for the war effort; but not until spring 1918 did the War Industries Board, established by the government to impose control over manufacturing production deemed vital for the war, manage to persuade the auto manufacturers to divert the bulk of its production towards vehicles urgently needed in France. By then it was too late to recover much of the lost ground.[25]

As for the dominating trench warfare weapon, the machine-gun, the American situation was potentially disastrous. Congress had appropriated $12 million for the purchase of machine-guns in 1916, but the War Department had dithered for a year; when he took command Pershing had just 1,500 machine-guns, 1,000 fewer than the French army had in August 1914. In 1917 the British army had almost 80,000 machine-guns; in 1918 more than 120,000.[26] The AEF's guns were also of four different types, complicating unnecessarily both supply and maintenance.

Artillery, tanks, machine-guns – all were hopelessly lacking. The same was true of more esoteric means of destruction. Flame-throwers had been introduced by the Germans at Malancourt forest in February 1915; poison gas (again by the Germans) at Langemarck on 22 April 1915; trench mortars in early 1917. America possessed none of these essential items either before or during the war; when they were used either by or on behalf of the AEF, such weapons were purchased from either British or French sources.[27]

The difficulties encountered in attempting to catch up with the Allies' vast experience in modern warfare are symbolized in the bureaucratic and disorganized fashion the United States dealt with one of the Western Front's most terrifying, though it needs to be added, least effective weapons: poison gas. In April 1917 the US regular army had not a single gas mask or drop of poison gas. The Medical Corps directed defensive gas production, while offensive production was controlled by the Ordnance Department. Gas alarm devices were the responsibility of the Signal Corps. The Engineers Corps was in charge of the 30th Regiment (Gas and Flame), as well as field training. The Research Section was in the hands of the Bureau of Mines, a civilian organization, and a Chemical Service Section was formed to deal with overseas problems. On top of all this the Director of the Gas Warfare Service back in the United States, Major-General William Sibert, had not sought the post but had it imposed on him by Pershing, who had sacked him from command of the 1st Division in France. Sibert was expected to coordinate all these diverse activities, yet was given no authority to control policy, research or production. The War Department commissioned the office of the Surgeon General to deliver 1.1 million gas masks by 30 June 1918, an enormous task from a standing start.[28] The Bureau of Mines offered to deliver the first 25,000 gas masks, but these proved completely inadequate under battlefield conditions, and the AEF had to beg, borrow or steal gas masks from the British and French throughout the war. The US army's gas service remained a relative backwater for ambitious officers.[29]

Painfully aware of the Allies' high hopes of the AEF and the slim chance of meeting them with alacrity, an anxious and impatient General Pershing arrived in Liverpool at 9.30 a.m. on 8 June 1917, where the Americans were greeted by a guard of honour from the 3rd Battalion, Royal Welch Fusiliers. 'Not the least picturesque member of the detachment was the thoroughly groomed, ribbon-bedecked goat, the regimental mascot, which strode up and down with an air of considerable importance,' noted Pershing.[30] A brief press conference and session of public hand-shaking followed before they boarded the royal coach of a train bound for London. There they were greeted by British and American dignitaries, including Lord Derby, Secretary of State for War; Field Marshal Sir John French; Lieutenant-General Sir Francis Lloyd; Brigadier-General Lord Brooke; Walter Hines Page, the intensely anglophile US ambassador to London; and Admiral William Sims, in charge of the US navy in Europe. Apart from the politeness of the social round, Pershing enjoyed a rather less gracious encounter with General Sir William Robertson, Chief of the Imperial General Staff. Robertson was an unusual British army product; he had enlisted as a private and clambered his way to the top by offending no one and ensuring that he reflected the views of superior officers who could promote him. Robertson had only one ambition for the embryonic AEF, to make it serve as part of the British forces:

Like all the British officials, he was much in favor of having our army serve with or near their forces [. . .] I emphasized our lack of tonnage and told him that we must have additional shipping if we were to bring over an army worth while, but his reaction to this was not encouraging. He said he thought it was entirely out of the question for the British to provide us with any shipping since they were already in sore straits to find vessels for their own national necessities.[31]

Pershing met the same response a few days later from Lloyd George. On 12 June the British prime minister

went right to the point and inquired as to when our troops would be organized and trained and the numbers we expected to send over [. . .] when I stressed our need of assistance to transport our troops he did not seem to be particularly interested and gave little hope that the British would be able to furnish us any shipping whatever.[32]

Pershing and Lloyd George took an early and strong dislike to each other; privately, Pershing referred to him as 'that son-of-a-bitch'.

On 13 June Pershing and his General Staff sailed across the English Channel on the steamer *Invicta*, landing at Boulogne at 10 a.m. and reaching Paris late that afternoon. Among the several thousand hysterically cheering French citizens who thronged the streets to see the Americans was an official delegation, led by Paul Painlevé, Minister of War, Marshal Joffre, Major-General Ferdinand Foch and William G. Sharp, the American ambassador. The contrast between public hopes and private anxieties could not have been more sharply focused.

'The Americans are here!' shouted the crowds. 'I hope you have not arrived too late,' said William Sharp.[33] 'The General without an army,' commented the German press next day.

Pershing established his temporary base at the Hôtel Crillon in Paris, and spent the first few days grappling with what seemed to be an imminent collapse of the French forces. Neither the Allies nor the Germans could have drawn much comfort from 1916; Germany suffered 500,000 casualties during the battle of the Somme and 282,000 during Verdun, as well as 350,000 on the Russian front.[34] British and French losses were equally vast; the French lost some 350,000 dead at Verdun, while total British casualties for the year were at least 450,000. By mid-1917 the morale of the French army was smashed, and there were growing fears that the British army was beginning to run out of manpower, not least because Lloyd George was preventing the shipping of any more men to France until his generals came up with a convincingly successful strategy. The French and British accused one another of failing to put their backs into the fight, while both were united in their contempt for Italian and Belgian efforts. The Germans, meanwhile, had seen the collapse of the Russians, with the result that Germany in 1918 could divert dozens of divisions to the Western Front.

Some of the AEF's General Staff were shocked at just how poor French morale was. On 19 June 1917 Captain Hugh Drum, aged thirty-eight, wrote to his wife an account of an inspection trip he had made across France. He found

few people who are not in mourning. The common dress on the street is black. We only see old men or boys, the women are doing the work of the men and indeed are worthy of praise. I have never seen such a staunch class of women. I tell you all this as preliminary to saying that I am glad we are in this war. My heart has gone out to these people. They need and deserve our help.[35]

Yet if French military and civilian morale was low, materially speaking the French appeared rather better off than some of the newly-arrived American reinforcements had expected. General Robert Lee Bullard recalled that

To me, who had been accustomed from my childhood to stories and memories of the hardships and poverty that resulted in the Southern States from the four years' War of Secession, the apparent condition of the French seemed very far from bad. I had expected to find rags and hunger. Instead I found good clothes and by no means empty stomachs. Soldiers and civilians alike looked well kept and well fed. Of course, the Government was supervising the use of meat, bread, and sugar, but there was apparently enough, especially for the economical, careful, saving French.[36]

If France's home front was not an outright disaster, its military capabilities were certainly precarious. The rot in the French army was stopped by the timely dismissal of Nivelle and his replacement by General Henri Pétain, who by handling the mutinous French troops with a combination of toughness and sensitivity, managed to bring the army round.

Following the mutinies, 3,427 sentences were decreed, 10 per cent of the mutineers; of these 554 were condemned to death, and 49 actually executed. This is lower than the anti-militarist tradition would have it, although it is still large enough, the more so as the men who were really responsible, those who had blundered into the offensive [. . .] were not themselves molested or sentenced in any way. Throughout, Pétain's role seems clear – he wanted a repression at once limited and merciless.[37]

Pétain made it clear that there would be no more futile attacks, and probably no more attacks at all for a long time. But if the French were too exhausted and the British too under-strength to attack, then who would winkle the Germans out of their impressive defences? All eyes turned to the AEF.

Pétain and Pershing met for the first time on 16 June at the French GHQ at Compiègne. The two shared many characteristics. Both were instinctively pragmatic, were blunt speakers and extremely stubborn. They grew to like and admire one another, and after the war Pershing publicly said Pétain was 'the greatest general of the war'.[38] By 26 June they had agreed that the AEF, when strong enough, would hold a sector of the front in Lorraine to the east of the Argonne forest. This was for several reasons the most logical point to place the Americans.

It was a relatively quiet sector, long regarded by both French and Germans as a spot to place battle-weary divisions in need of a rest. At the far southern end of the Western Front, it meant the politically highly-charged responsibility of defending Paris from any renewed German thrust would not directly fall on the AEF. Nor would they be called upon to defend the Channel ports, to which the British were determined to keep an easy access in case of the need for a rapid retreat. In logistical terms it also made sense to put the AEF on the east wing. The Channel ports were already choked with supplies to the British, and the AEF would soon place onerous demands on French ports and railways. It would best be served by developing independent supply lines. St Nazaire, Bassens and La Pallice – three deep-water ports on the French Atlantic coast – would be ideal for supplying the AEF's heavier shipping, while three other, shallower-draught, ports – Bordeaux, Pauillac and Nantes – would be used for lighter vessels. Most doughboys stepped ashore at Brest.

Pershing was delighted to have the Argonne for another reason; a successful offensive here could quickly bring the AEF's divisions onto German soil. Pershing and his staff were desperately keen to prove they had as much fighting spirit and combat skills as anyone else, and to carry the war into Germany itself would be a tremendous coup, one which would help President Wilson's often reiterated desire of bringing the war to a swift conclusion. On the *Baltic* the AEF's General Staff had drawn up a proposal to launch an offensive in precisely this region, with the main thrust being the elimination of the St-Mihiel salient, a carbuncle which had irritatingly obtruded into French territory since 1914. From the Argonne region the AEF was theoretically within striking distance of a German-held strategically vital railway line, running north-west from Thionville, a crucial supply link for the Germans. Just two days' hard marching in front of the Lorraine battle lines – about forty miles in some places – were the important Saar coalfields and the equally vital iron mines of Longwy-Briey, the loss of either of which could cripple the German war effort.

Pershing's ambition to run his own army, occupying its own stretch of the front line and taking its own initiatives, was, however, not completely shared by the Allies. For them, the AEF represented above all a manpower reservoir, the chance to rebuild their own depleted divisions. While the AEF would indeed be accorded its own stretch of the front line, for the Allied military leaders this carried no implication of independence of action. The prime function of the doughboy divisions arriving in France would initially – and perhaps open-endedly – to be amalgamated with the Allied divisions, serving under British and French commanders. Pershing, however, had no intention of permitting any such amalgamation. The bitter clash over this issue soured US relations with Britain and France throughout the rest of the war. Was Pershing right or wrong to stand his ground on this issue? Some historians have suggested that, given the lack of training and equipment, as well as the shortage of experienced junior officers and NCOs, Pershing's refusal to accept amalgamation unnecessarily delayed the defeat of Germany. This view argues that if Pershing placed them in the ranks of the British and French, the doughboys would have been trained more quickly, entered the trenches earlier, and pushed the Germans back faster. This line of reasoning ignores certain other vital factors. There were several difficulties, not the least of which was national status – a United States army could hardly be expected to fight as a subsidiary of the army of another nation. Moreover, the AEF was sent to France not simply to defeat German soldiers but to bolster America's claim to a front-row seat at any peace talks:

[. . .] a policy of amalgamation might have obscured the American contribution to victory, whereas the effort of an independent American army was more discernible, more obvious [. . .] Pershing and his staff thought amalgamation would disperse American strength [. . .] The psychological impact of a separate American army, positive for the Allies, especially the French, and negative for the Germans, is difficult to gauge. But there is reason to believe that an independent expeditionary force had more of an effect on both sides than amalgamated reinforcements would have had. Neither the Allies nor the Germans anticipated the speed and impact of the American build-up in France, nor the ability of US forces once on the battlefield.[39]

In any case there was little to amalgamate in the early days. Captain Drum confided to his diary on 16–19 June, just a few days before the arrival of the first contingent of doughboys, that the 1st Division would inevitably disappoint the French:

It is too bad that our troops will have to train before going into the fight for so long a time. They can hardly be ready even the first of them before Jan 1918. But the great expansion we are undergoing is the cause of it all. These first troops have $\frac{2}{3}$ recruits and & $\frac{1}{2}$ the co. cmdrs have had less than six years service. The NCOs 60% of them were left in the States training to be officers. So soon we will hear demands for action and will not be ready.

My hours are hard & tedious. I get up at 7:00 am. Work every night until 11 or 12 pm. Take a short time off for meals. No mail. Sometimes quite lonely.[40]

The first contingent of doughboys, some 14,000 soldiers – the core of what was to become the famous 1st Division – set foot in France at St Nazaire on 28 June 1917. Their passage across the Atlantic, aboard three transports accompanied by three destroyers and the cruiser *Charleston*, had been largely uneventful, apart from a few submarine scares:

On the second or third day out the whole little squadron had target practice at a simulated submarine periscope. Some two hundred shots in all were fired, but the simulated periscope escaped all damage. This was not very reassuring [. . .][41]

But it had been rough in other senses, as Corporal Clarence Mahan recalled:

We were packed in the ship like sardines in a can. Regiment strength was 250 to a Company, and a regiment was made up of 12 Infantry Companies [. . .] The carpenters made bunks four high. The bottom man was almost on the floor while the top man was practically against the ceiling. I drew the second bunk from the floor [. . .] For the noon meal the first day out we had ham and beans. They were cooked just right like my mother cooked them so they tasted wonderful to me. I ate all of mine with relish. It was a lovely day so I went up on deck and stood at the rail looking down at the swirling waters. Suddenly a stream of ham and beans gushed out of my mouth.[42]

These troops were all drawn from regular army regiments and were thus in a technical sense 'professional', but they were far from that in reality. Mahan, twenty-three, was by trade a mechanic and had only joined the army after the start of the war. The survivors of this division were eventually to bask in the glory of having fought in most of the AEF's important engagements, but there were few seasoned veterans among them when they first landed in France. More than half the company commanders had less than six months' experience, and two-thirds of the rank-and-file were raw recruits, often ill-disciplined, sometimes rowdy and not yet properly trained. General Bullard later acknowledged that it was an ignorant and incomplete force which arrived that foggy morning in France:

The troops, both officers and men, still knew little of the real purpose for their appearing in France. Most of them expected to join in the fighting at the front without delay. So little real comprehension had any of us of the conditions we were facing! It was to be months before any of us would see the front. We had not upon landing, we later found out to our chagrin, anything but a willingness to fight. We lacked not only the training, but the organization; and even for the infantry, the body of the army, we lacked the kind of arms with which we were later to face the enemy.[43]

The greatest asset of this first wave of the AEF was its boisterous goodwill, invaluable in a country so devastated by the war. Time would improve their mettle and vastly extend their combat skill to a level almost matching their initial self-estimation. Among the officers who were to rise to eminence from the 1st Division were Peyton March, Charles Summerall (a future division and corps commander), Bullard himself, Hanson Ely (later to lead the 5th Division), Frank Parker (who ended up as commander of the 1st Division), and George Marshall, who later took over responsibility for Operations of the American First Army and in the Second World War was the US army's chief-of-staff.

Marshall too recognized the rawness of these first elements of the 1st Division:

Most of the men were recruits and many were issued their arms after boarding the train in Texas en route to Hoboken [whence they were to be shipped to France]. The personnel of the division was not impressive. Many of the men were undersized and a number spoke English with difficulty.[44]

But in one vital respect the 1st Division had a great advantage over all the divisions formed later: it had the pick of the crop of lieutenants, the rank of commissioned officer closest to the rank-and-file and upon whose shoulders rested the traditionally most testing task of leadership, that of getting scared, poorly concentrated, exhausted and grousing men to give every last bit of themselves in combat:

In the matter of Lieutenants [. . .] we were especially fortunate. Each of the [US] training camps had been called upon to select the best 15 or 20 candidates for immediate overseas service. This meant out of the 2,500 [lieutenants] in each camp the First Division received the 20 best. I have never seen more splendid-looking men and it makes me very sad to realize that most of them were left in France.[45]

Immediate anxieties were momentarily put aside in the jubilation with which Parisians greeted the arrival of the first contingent of combat doughboys during the 3 July gala welcome for the 16th Infantry Regiment, as the city's guests of honour. These doughboys' first night in Paris was literally lousy; some of them were billeted in infested barracks dating from the Napoleonic era. Fleabites notwithstanding, on 4 July the 16th Infantry's regimental band struck up alongside a French military band in Les Invalides, welcoming Pershing, Joffre, President Poincaré and others. As part of the ceremonies,

A lion cub was presented to the American army as a mascot, by the City of Paris. Private Smalley, of Company G, was designated to be its keeper. It was taken by us to Gondrecourt and kept there until it became ill and died in September. Perhaps the fall weather or overfeeding were factors in its death. Anyway, we could not have kept it very long.[46]

Pershing wooed the hearts of the French by kneeling to kiss the sword of Napoleon Bonaparte, and the 16th Infantry swaggered on a five-mile march through the city *en route* to the cemetery containing the tomb of Lafayette. There Pershing – perhaps conscious of his execrable French – delegated one of his aides, Captain Stanton, to speak. Stanton captured the spirit of the occasion by crying, with a flourishing salute, 'Nous voilà, Lafayette!' The myth immediately grew, fostered by accompanying French officers, that it was Pershing who uttered these famous words. Pershing clearly later wished he had:

> Many have attributed this striking utterance to me and I have often wished that it could have been mine. But I have no recollection of saying anything so splendid. I am sure that those words were spoken by Colonel Stanton and to him must go the credit for coining so happy and felicitous a phrase.[47]

The 16th Infantry marched on and all too soon the flag-waving, flower-tossing, band-playing celebrations were over; reality swiftly set in as that evening the doughboys clambered aboard railway carriages on the outside of which was daubed a slogan which none of them ever forgot or forgave: *'Chevaux 8, Hommes 40'*.

By the middle of July the 1st Division was in a training area with its HQ at Gondrecourt, close to the St-Mihiel salient. The doughboys were here to be given intensive training by some elite French soldiers, but Bullard was depressed and not a little confused at the contradictory nature of these tutors in the arts of Western Front combat. On 18 July he witnessed a review of a French division: 'It was a fine, fine sight. Everything was cocky and snappy. They were in full uniform, though just from the front, and horses and men were beautifully kept.'

Yet a few days later he feared that the French were sadly lacking in the offensive spirit, which he and others in the AEF thought was the only really necessary component to defeat the Germans:

> The French count on nothing else than purely trench warfare. Plainly they show that they consider their part of the offensive of this war as done. Without saying, they seem to feel that they have done their part, and expect others to carry on the war when any carrying on is to be done.[48]

Meanwhile, Pershing got down to the urgent business of forming clear lines of communication and control. On 5 July he finally confirmed the structure of his General Staff. There were to be five branches. Administration, G-1, dealt with supplies, transport, storage and re-placements of both men and animals. Intelligence, G-2, handled such matters as map-making and propaganda and the collection and analysis of information concerning the enemy. Operations, G-3, had responsibility for strategy and tactics. Coordination, G-4, controlled the distribution of men, supplies and other items. Training, G-5, was the branch which dealt not only with training but also fifteen other minor departments (such as the Air Service or Gas Warfare Service), being part of a Technical section.

The officers in command of each of these units all knew and respected one another and were devoted to Pershing. Colonel James Logan was put in command of G-1; Colonel Dennis Nolan took over as head of G-2; Lieutenant-Colonel John McAuley Palmer was given G-3, but through illness was soon replaced by Colonel Fox Conner, who possessed the rare and highly useful skill of fluent French; Lieutenant Colonel William Connor was given charge of G-4, to be replaced later by Colonel George Van Horn Moseley; Lieutenant-Colonel Paul Malone was in command of G-5.

Now that the scope of the General Staff was confirmed it was possible for the War Department to probe it to see how best it might be assisted by Washington. The future course of the AEF was thus debated on 7–8 July in France by Pershing's General Staff and a Washington-sponsored mission, sent by Newton Baker and under Colonel Chauncey B. Baker. Its brief was to make an independent report on the AEF's organization, training, operations, administration and supply. The Baker mission and the General Staff agreed on most things except for artillery; Colonel Charles P. Summerall (as part of the Baker mission) argued vehemently that the AEF's divisions, as currently laid out on paper, would be severely under-strength in artillery, a view which Fox Conner equally vociferously opposed. Conner paid for this later, for Pershing so admired Summerall's refusal to be cowed at this meeting that when Summerall returned to the United States Pershing sent for him and promoted him at every opportunity until he finally took command of the all-important 1st Division – from where he consistently blocked the promotion of Fox Conner. The discussions concluded on 10 July with a set of recommendations called the General Organization Project (or GOP), which specified an army in the field totalling 1 million men, to be in France by 1918, organized in twenty combat divisions, with the possibility of expanding this figure to reach 3 million in all by the end of 1919, a total of 100 divisions. But in mid-1917, with a crisis in merchant shipping, getting even 100,000 across the

Atlantic seemed a tall order. Britain had the world's biggest merchant fleet, and to it fell the task of getting the doughboys to France – though only at a price which the United States was not prepared to pay.

6

Black Jack

Pershing is the man for this great emergency. He has an immense faculty for disposing of things. He is not only a great soldier, but he has great common sense and tremendous energy.

Charles Gates Dawes[1]

Of Cadet Pershing, one memory more. He was a hop-goer, what cadets called a 'spoony' man. He loved the society of women. That, too, like other early characteristics, seems to have held on with him.

Major-General Robert Lee Bullard[2]

'"Old Black Jack", as we call General Pershing, is a large man with small, trim arms and legs, and an underslung jaw that would defy an aerial bomb. He has a thin, crescent-shaped mouth which turns down like a bull-dog's and makes him look as if he had never smiled in his life. His eyes, while kindly and snapping with intelligence, are sharp as a hawk's, giving the impression that he can see round a corner.'[3]

The man chosen to lead the AEF had every appearance of tough restraint, but that stiff neck, rigid back and braced body disguised a welter of private emotions and passions. Brusque and stubborn, Pershing cultivated an image of himself as a tartar, who neither needed nor cared for material or physical comforts.

He loved the Sam Browne belt, a British invention worn by officers across the chest and back and round the waist. Pershing thought it looked snappy and instructed that it should be worn by all officers in the AEF. He particularly appreciated its quality of requiring the wearer to straighten the back and stiffen the shoulders.[4] Of all the uncomfortable uniforms of the First World War none were quite as poorly designed as those worn by the AEF's commissioned officers, who particularly resented the stiff, high collars. The jackets lacked useful pockets into which to stuff the ephemera of trench life; Pershing insisted that pockets would spoil the neat line. He was determined his officers would look and act the part; perhaps this was to conceal a fear that the substance might be lacking, or simply a result of the belief that spit and polish builds character, and character is what is most useful in a fight. He relished discipline and toughness and most admired those among his senior officers who imposed strict control over subordinates.[5] He rarely smiled in public. In April 1917, at the age of fifty-seven, he could be forgiven for concluding that despite his relatively successful military career, his personal life was blighted by tragedy. His wife Frankie and all three daughters had died in a fire in San Francisco on the night of 26 August 1915 while Pershing was absent, leading the 8th Brigade on the Mexican border. Only his young son, Warren, was left.

While the public persona purported to be entirely wrapped up in his professional existence, Pershing was privately a very different character, passionate, emotional, and given to considerable internal doubt and anxiety. Charles Dawes, a key figure in Pershing's inner circle in France, recalled driving in Paris *en route* to supper at the Ritz on Sunday 2 September 1917. Dawes had also suffered personal loss:

Neither of us was saying anything, but I was thinking of my lost boy and of John's loss and looking out of the window, and he was doing the same thing on the other side of the automobile. We both turned at the same time and each was in tears. All John said was, 'Even this war can't keep it out of my mind.'[6]

Nor was Pershing's passion exclusively retrospective. Within a few weeks of arriving in France he had acquired an attractive mistress thirty-four years younger than himself, an artist of Romanian extraction. When Pershing left for France he had left behind in the United States another woman who believed herself engaged to marry him, Anne ('Nita') Patton, the thirty-year-old sister of Captain George Patton (who travelled with Pershing to France aboard the *Baltic*). Patton had successfully served under Pershing in the punitive expedition against Mexico, so he had a good claim on Pershing's attention; but the general's love for his sister would not have been a disadvantage.

Pershing was a strongly sexual being, never at a loss for female company. His intensely physical and emotional relationship with Micheline Resco, who had taken French citizenship, began when Resco was twenty-three. They met in the summer of 1917 in Paris; by the time Pershing relocated his GHQ to Chaumont in September to be closer to the front the AEF aspired to occupy, he and Resco, a successful portrait painter of public figures such as Marshal Foch and King Faisal I of Iraq, were lovers.[7] Their privacy was facilitated by Pershing being able to visit Paris frequently, where he stayed at 73 rue de Varenne, a large mansion owned by Ogden Mills, a wealthy American citizen who happily lent the accommodation to Pershing for the duration of the war. After the war was over Resco visited Pershing in the United States and he spent six months of each year in France with her, but although the relationship was to all intents and purposes a common-law marriage, Pershing evidently preferred the sexual freedom of remaining technically single. But he clearly loved her enough to ensure that she was financially secure: 'Although there may have been other women from time to time, Micheline clearly occupied the prime place in Pershing's life. He sent her a regular monthly check, named her as beneficiary on a $25,000 life insurance policy in 1926, and established a life income trust for her in 1938.'[8]

When war again erupted between France and Germany in 1940, Resco and her mother came to stay in America; she visited Pershing daily in the Walter Reed hospital in Washington DC, where he had moved in May 1941, when he was eighty years old. On 2 September 1946 Micheline Resco and John Pershing were quietly married in the hospital, twenty-nine years after they had first become lovers, and two years before Pershing died.[9]

But what was good enough for the general was denied the ordinary doughboy. Consorting with women in France was strongly discouraged in the AEF, not least because Pershing was obsessively concerned that his troops should not contract venereal disease. One of his standard questions when visiting a unit would be to ask the officer in charge how many VD cases he had; one was too many. Even on the voyage across the Atlantic in May–June 1917 Pershing sacrificed battlefield strategy planning time to have his General Staff listen to several lectures by Dr Hugh Young, an expert on VD brought along by Pershing as part of the General Staff:

When Dr Young later reported that British prostitutes sought out foreign troops because they had more money, Pershing cabled the War Department to withhold a portion of each soldier's pay. What a man didn't have, he couldn't spend on a prostitute.[10]

Pershing, however, was not so naive as to think that withholding a portion of a doughboy's pay would make him think twice about succumbing to physical urges. He tried to ensure that the ban on using prostitutes was enforced by the AEF's military police, and – when possible – French judicial authorities. Care was also taken to prevent fraternization between doughboys and locals; this was often achieved by billeting the doughboys in areas outside towns and villages, as Griffith L. Adams, of the 105th Machine Gun Battalion (part of the 27th Division and serving with the British army in July 1918) complained in a letter home:

I have been trying to get some small trinkets to send home but so far have been unable. We are always located outside of any town and we are kept busy so much, that when evening comes, our bunk looks the best of any place for miles around [. . .] The French and Belgium [sic] people are not very clean but are extremely congenial; and oblidging [sic] when we have just been paid.[11]

Even when in rest camps doughboys were given little time to themselves; almost every hour was filled with organized games, training or drill. On 25 June 1918 2nd Lieutenant John D. Clark, of the 15th Field Artillery (2nd Division) complained to his diary: 'Our week's maneuvres [. . .] northwest of Paris, amounted to the usual early morning reveilles, inspections and other troublesome details in vogue at AEF "rest" camps.'[12]

Pershing's aim of minimizing the number of VD cases in the AEF was obviously sensible, if only because he could ill afford any weakening of his embryonic army. But his interest in the subject bordered on the obsessive. It was rumoured by some of his critics that his fascination derived from his having twice contracted gonorrhoea in the Philippines. Pershing's way of trying to control VD clearly involved a degree of hypocrisy. Rather than accept the inevitable – as did the French military authorities – and try to control and monitor brothels and the possibility of disease, Pershing preached chastity while failing to practise it.[13] Those soldiers who did contract VD were given extremely painful medical treatment which, it was suspected, was partly intended as punishment and deterrent. Many doughboys with sexually transmitted diseases in any case acquired them outside Pershing's jurisdiction, back in the States, before they set out for France. On the fringe of every US training camp there sprang up the inevitable brothels. A fairly typical example was outside Fort Sam Houston in Texas:

One entire district of San Antonio, perhaps ten blocks square, was a 'red light' district. The madames, by mutual agreement, permitted no alcohol sales anywhere in the area. At each exit from the area there were prophylactic stations where the men were supposed to give the names and addresses where they may have been exposed to VD, and at the same time were given prophylactic treatment which was supposed to prevent it.

If a soldier was found with VD he was hospitalized until cured, then court-martialled for having wilfully contracted VD. Usual sentence by Summary Court was three months' confinement at hard labor; loss of two-thirds of pay for this period, and help in service to make up the time spent in the hospital and under confinement.[14]

The complexities of Pershing's character worked on more levels than the sexual. While determinedly if not ruthlessly ambitious, he nevertheless could inspire tremendous devotion and loyalty, characteristics which he valued highly in his subordinates. Major Harbord had enlisted as a private in the army in 1889 and was, according to Pershing, 'the ablest officer I know'.[15] For Pershing that meant a combination of energy, obedience, professional competence and, above all, loyalty. Equally, Harbord believed there was no question that in 1917 Pershing was the best candidate for the job of commander-in-chief:

He was at the height of his physical and professional vigour. He had great personal charm though not all the AEF were privileged to feel it. He was an exceedingly temperate man, not a drinker, and seldom smoked. He appeared to have no routine for exercise, though in France he seemed always in fine physical condition. A good rider and a fast walker, he was physically and mentally alert. He was the personification of neatness and a model of military smartness. I have seen him show some temper but never saw him lose control of himself. Caution and canniness were strong traits of his character. He was very impersonal in his military decisions: quiet, definite, but willing to hear explanations. He had a contempt for haziness and indefiniteness in his subordinates. When he had made up his mind it was not easy to get him to change it, but it was tenacity and firmness and not obstinacy, and it could be changed. Patience was not his most conspicuous trait, but he had it in great degree when necessary. He never 'spilled the beans'.[16]

This last trait – an absolutely unswerving devotion to professional diplomacy – probably did as much to get Pershing the job as anything in his military background. In 1936 Dennis Nolan, Pershing's intelligence chief, recalled another key aspect of Pershing's nature:

The General was great on asking questions. He had no false pride of 'Now we know it all' but he let the other French Generals and staffs tell him things and he would question them during that summer and fall before our troops came, question after question. He was not satisfied with just handing them a copy of their orders. He always wanted to know what are troops doing and he would go right down to talk to Colonels, Majors and Captains, how about this, especially fellows who had had a lot of experience in command of companies in the battle and been wounded four or five times [. . .] I think myself that the General was the best-informed all-round man that we had over there in our Army [. . .] because he talked not only to the higher commanders but to everybody. He met people we didn't reach and he also went even lower than we did [. . .] Pershing was relatively a young man with a marvelous physique who could work eighteen hours a day and he did as a rule.[17]

There is no doubt though that Pershing's relative success in charge of the AEF owed almost everything to his exceptional good fortune in being surrounded by first-class organizers and thinkers, such as

Nolan, both on his General Staff and among the first few key combat divisions in France. He was also lucky in that the small size of the pre-war US army meant he knew personally most of the AEF's senior officers; of the forty-two divisions which served under him in France, fourteen at one time or another were commanded by classmates of his 1886 graduating year at West Point, while sixteen others were under the command of officers he had known as cadets there.[18]

Pershing possessed another vital strength: he was prepared immediately to sack any officer who was obviously not up to the onerous task of shifting vast masses of men and materials to a strict timetable, and to get those men to give their all once engaged in fighting. Sometimes this quality – which filtered down through the senior ranks, so that as Pershing kicked those below him, they in turn kicked their juniors harder still – led to excessive and unfair decisions to 'Blooey' an officer. This term derived from the French town of Blois, on the Loire. Here the AEF established a Classification Depot for misfits from the fighting troops, for all officers below the rank of major-general; major-generals who were deemed unable to cut the mustard (such as Major-General Clarence Edwards, who commanded the 26th Division, a National Guard unit, until 25 October 1918) were simply booted all the way back to the United States.[19]

Pershing's military career prior to leading the AEF was about as glittering as any US regular army officer could have hoped for at the time. His relative success owed much to the good fortune of being in the right place at the right time, and to having made what would have then been called a good marriage, to a politically well-connected woman. Born in 1860 in Laclede, Missouri, the eldest of nine children, his grandfather had left Alsace-Lorraine (the family name originally was Poersching or Pförschin) for Pennsylvania, where he took up farming. At the age of twenty-two Pershing beat off strong competition to gain a place at West Point, which he attended from 1882 to 1886. He became president of his class, though academically he was not outstanding, being placed thirtieth in his class of seventy-seven. During 1886–91 he served in Mexico and South Dakota, and taught military science at the University of Nebraska from 1891 to 1895, studying for a law degree at the same time. He returned to West Point as an instructor in 1897–8, when his disciplinarianism made him deeply unpopular with cadets. They nicknamed him 'Black Jack', intended as an insulting reference to his having once commanded the 10th Cavalry, an elite black unit. Black Americans were permitted to attend the incorrigibly racist and snobbish West Point, but the brave few who did were utterly cold-shouldered.

A US army career in those days was usually a dismal poverty-stricken affair. Most officers spent a lifetime waiting to reach the giddy heights of a captaincy. Poor promotion and pay prospects meant brighter officers, such as Pershing, would often leave when interest died or was killed by the financial demands of a wife and family. Pershing, however, struck lucky. In 1897 he managed to rub shoulders with Theodore Roosevelt, then police commissioner of New York City. They immediately began a lifelong friendship, and Roosevelt did much to assist Pershing's previously languishing career. Further luck arrived in 1905 in the form of Helen Frances Warren, daughter of the influential Wyoming Republican senator Francis E. Warren. Pershing's marriage to 'Frankie' that year meant his career immediately got onto a faster track. First he was given a plum diplomatic posting as a military attaché in Tokyo in 1905, where he gained an insight into large-scale warfare in 1905–6, acting as an observer on the Japanese side in Manchuria during the Russo-Japanese War. He followed this in 1906 by controversially vaulting over the heads of 862 more senior officers to gain promotion from captain to brigadier-general. Among those he magically passed were a great number of officers he would later command in France.[20] Was this pure nepotism? Few doubted so at the time. His father-in-law was chairman of the Senate Military Affairs Committee, and all such promotions had to be ratified by this commit-tee. As president, Theodore Roosevelt of course lent his backing to this advancement of his protégé. Some envious rival officers who lacked Pershing's powerful mentors tried later to besmirch Pershing's reputation by leaking allegations to Philippine and US newspapers that Pershing had fathered illegitimate children in the Philippines – a story which cropped up from time to time throughout the rest of his career.[21]

In 1915 Pershing led the punitive expedition into Mexico, command-ing 15,000 regular army troops and backed up by some 156,000 National Guardsmen protecting the US–Mexico border against the bandit Francisco (Pancho) Villa. This politically ill-considered foray, initiated by Wilson, was conducted by Pershing with skill and courage. He led his troops 400 miles into Mexican territory, wounding Villa and scattering his bandits before being ordered to pull back to within 150 miles of the border in June 1916. The expedition was withdrawn in February 1917, whereupon Pershing was appointed to command the Southern Department, with his HQ at Fort Sam Houston, Texas. By April 1917 Pershing was certainly the leading contender for command of the AEF in terms of combat experience; but chasing bandits on horseback across semi-desert plains was rather different from wading through mud and barbed wire to assault concrete emplacements manned by hard-bitten German machine-gunners.

General Bullard, an outspoken regular army officer who quickly rose to command the AEF's 1st Division and was on the first transport of doughboys to France, was not, initially, an admirer of Pershing. They had overlapped at West Point and although they were not on intimate terms, the two obviously knew each other well. Bullard recalled Pershing's physique and bearing at West Point, then as now not a place for cissies:

Of regular but not handsome features and of robust, strong body, broad-shouldered and well developed; almost or quite six feet tall; plainly of the estate of man while most of those about him were still boys; with keen searching gray eyes and intent look, Pershing inspired confidence but not affection. Personal magnetism seemed lacking. He won followers and admirers, but not personal worshippers. Plain in word, sane and direct in action, he applied himself to all duty and all work with a manifest purpose, not only of succeeding in what he attempted, but of surpassing, guiding, and directing his fellows in what was before them. His exercise of authority, was then and always has been since, of a nature peculiarly impersonal, dispassionate, hard and firm. This quality did not in him, as in many, give offence; the man was too impersonal, too given over to pure business and duty. His manner carried to the mind of those under him the suggestion, nay, the conviction, of unquestioned right to obedience.[22]

As at West Point, so too in France. Pershing's natural taciturn-ity, plus widespread suspicions that his political connections had hauled him up the ranks so fast, inevitably meant he was some-thing of an isolated figure. Bullard later arrived at a grudging albeit genuine admiration for Pershing, yet could not bring him-self after the war to give more than this cold assessment of his character:

ambitious, fit, intent upon his purpose, vigorous, firm, thoughtful, discreet, impersonal and dispassionate in requiring obedience, creating and holding confidence by this very efficiency, but nowhere arousing enthusiasm except upon success; not a personal leader; admirable but not magnetic.[23]

Pershing drove himself hard and expected everyone else in the AEF to do the same. His careful preservation of the privacy of his relationship with Micheline Resco, and his frequent fourteen-hour, seven-day work-ing weeks, were not only inspired by the exigencies of fighting a war, nor even by possible accusations of moral impropriety. He was also mindful that many in the United States wanted to see him slip.

One general especially wanted to see him fail. Pershing was appointed commander of the AEF over the heads of five more senior major-generals – Leonard Wood, J. Franklin Bell, Thomas H. Barry, Hugh L. Scott and Tasker H. Bliss. The choice was narrowed as Barry and Bell were ill, while Bliss and Scott were close to retirement. But many Americans and not a few Europeans were astonished to learn that Wood had been denied the top job. Wood himself was livid that he should be displaced by such a relative junior; he remained an enemy of Pershing's throughout the war, doing his utmost to undermine his credibility to the politicians in Washington. But for Wilson, Pershing had one essential quality – unswerving, tight-lipped loyalty to his civilian superior. Wood, a former chief-of-staff and ex-Indian fighter, whose main claim to fame was that he once covered 136 miles of desert in twenty-four hours while trailing Geronimo, was as loose-tongued a man as ever walked the earth. While Pershing was the lucky recipient of political favours, Wood much preferred to try to dispense and control them. Wilson despised Wood's constant behind-the-scenes politicking:

In March of that year [1917], despite explicit orders, Wood exasperated Secretary Baker by calling for war against Germany while addressing several large meetings. Although capable of arousing intense enthusiasm and loyalty in those under him, Wood was himself unable to manifest these same qualities toward those over him. He 'had no conception whatever of loyalty to his superiors,' said Secretary Baker; [he] did not know the meaning of the word. He was the most insubordinate general officer in the entire army.[24]

Moreover, Wood was a physical cripple who walked with a limp, caused by a bizarre accident in which he had stood up from his desk and crushed part of his skull against a chandelier. Climbing small hills left him breathless. Much more damaging to his chance of getting Wilson's support as commander of the AEF was his notorious wheeler-dealing. Wood had strong connections with the political elite of Europe, but he was physically unreliable and politically awkward; Pershing was neither.

Few of the top Allied commanders in France had much time for Pershing, but there was nothing exceptional in that; they had little enough time for anyone but themselves. He was, however, subject to some egregious flattery by two of his French aides, who immediately after the war published an appallingly sycophantic account of Pershing and the AEF. Their description of the American commander-in-chief was adulatory:

Clean-cut and expressive of feature, tall and broad-shouldered, with the curt, incisive gesture common to the man of action, impatient with the effort of expression in a foreign tongue [he could not manage a word of comprehensible French, despite having studied it for several years at West Point], and of transforming his thought into activity. General Pershing's energetic profile recalled the line of that bronzed and warlike figure of the Venetian Colleone with clenched fist; typical, also, of those stalwart American men of his, whose sinewy hands would soon be closing upon their fixed bayonets.[25]

Even making allowances for Gallic hyperbole, few of Pershing's fellow generals were quite so dazzled. Two decades after the war Pershing's liaison officer in Lord Milner's office in London recalled an encounter with de Chambrun, one of the authors of this: 'Count de Chambrun, who was a very perfect example of liaison officer, told me that when he was with Marshal Pétain he always told him what a great man General Pershing was and when he was with Pershing he always told him what a great man Pétain was. He said it was astounding that after a number of times of repeating that, they came to believe it.'[26]

Though Pershing was too cold and remote to inspire much genuine affection among his senior officers, none could deny his dedication to duty and the sheer number of hours he put into planning, meetings, inspections. He also had to cope with a prodigious amount of paperwork. None of this voluminous activity was seen by the senior officers who had either been left behind or forced to return to the United States; many of them regarded Pershing with barely disguised contempt. He managed to gather to himself in Paris and at Chaumont a handful of acolytes, pride of place going to Charles Dawes, an extremely wealthy businessman and old friend, whom Pershing plucked from an obscure military position to become head of the AEF's Purchasing Department in France. Old friends were important to Pershing. He also took with him Robert Bacon, former US ambassador to France; at the age of fifty-seven Major Bacon[27] became garrison commander at Chaumont, Pershing's eventual HQ in France, located some 150 miles south-east of Paris.

Dawes was eternally grateful to Pershing for having secured him a commission as a major in the 17th Regiment of Engineers in May 1917. In those early days able men – or at least those with influence, and the two were often one and the same – were rapidly promoted; by July Dawes was a lieutenant-colonel and he ended the war a brigadier-general, a promotion which must have owed a little to his proximity to the centre of power.[28] Dawes, who later gained the nickname 'Hell and Maria',[29] came from old stock; one of his forebears, William Dawes, arrived on the *Mayflower*, while another William Dawes had ridden with Paul Revere. Dawes played a significant backroom role in the First World War, centralizing first the AEF's purchasing in Europe, and then being instrumental in establishing an inter-Allied board of purchasing.[30] Pershing came to rely heavily not only on his social company but also on his advice concerning military strategy. The admiration was mutual; Dawes practically deified Pershing: 'He is very wise. When he starts our offensive it will be kept up. His mind is on essential things [. . .] I have never worked in greater accord with anyone than with Pershing. Reason, and never prejudice, rules with him. He is in the midst of great events – and still greater ones await him.'[31]

Dawes, however, was no diplomat. Lloyd Griscom, Pershing's chief liaison officer with the British War Office in London, was invited to spend a weekend at an English country house where he had the 'stroke of luck' to meet Sir John Cowans, the Quartermaster-General of the British army, a fellow guest. In the night Cowans became very ill. The local doctor was called in and prescribed a purgative. Griscom counselled against that; if Cowans had appendicitis such harsh measures might kill him. Cowans was hospitalized and found to have a burst appendix:

When I saw Sir John Cowans later he said, 'You saved my life; any damn thing you want to know in this War Office, you come to me.' I can say that was very valuable to me [. . .] General Dawes had this very excellent plan to coordinate purchase of supplies for the Army. He had convinced the French and then had to go to London to convince the British, but they are not quick to make any change or take anything new. The important person was my friend, Sir John Cowans. They had this meeting and Cowans said [. . .] 'we'll think about this.' General Dawes got very angry and got up and banged the table and said, 'I won't do any such thing. If you won't attend to this, I will see the Prime Minister. It is time you learned. You have been trying to win this war for four years. Let me tell you an effete monarchy like England will never win this war without our help and we have come here to win it for you.' Sir John Cowans could not believe his ears and rose and passed out of the room and said, 'I have had enough of that man.' That was serious trouble of the highest importance [. . .] I felt something must be done.[32]

Griscom then spent a week with Cowans, trying to undo the damage caused by Dawes's clumsiness. He then went to Paris to see Dawes, who said:

'Do anything you like. I will back you up. My system in business has always been that if a man high-hatted me when I started to talk, I hauled off and hit him in the belly. It is extraordinary how it changes his whole attitude.' I said that it hadn't worked exactly this time and had a meeting with Cowans and they ended as the best of friends.[33]

These kinds of incidents peppered US relations with the British and French. Pershing minimized the opportunity for friction by ensuring that this war would be run as professionally as possible, and not governed by the antics of amateur political colonels, raising their own personal units with a kind of aristocratic amateurism – the kind of flag-waving, feather-in-hat whooping which both Theodore Roosevelt and General Leonard Wood relished. Pershing took the (at the time highly unpopular) decision to refuse Theodore Roosevelt's request that he should be allowed to raise a volunteer division.[34] Given all that Roosevelt had helped him achieve in his career, this was a courageous act. But Pershing was also well aware of the disasters in the Civil War that had been incurred by permitting the like of Roosevelt to intervene; much better to stick with conscription. He would also have been aware that Roosevelt, despite all his promises to the contrary, would have been insufferably insubordinate.

If Pershing valued loyalty, he could be unforgiving to those who seemed to betray or undermine him. He conducted a pointless and time-consuming telegraphic vendetta with General March in Washington, a feud March was equally responsible for perpetuating; both had better things to do. He found it difficult to delegate, and as the AEF grew in size and complexity, his failure to devolve responsibility proved a considerable handicap. Hunter Liggett and Robert Lee Bullard, the only two subordinates to receive the rank of lieutenant-general in the First World War, both received their commands (of the First and Second Armies respectively) far too late in the day, Liggett on 16 October and Bullard on 1 November 1918. Only when it became clear that the administrative burden had become impossible for one man did Pershing split and devolve his power. This inability to relinquish complete control meant Pershing felt himself called upon to pass judgement in areas where he possessed no specialist knowledge or experience, such as aviation. The United States started the war with a Ruritanian apology for an air force, but the Allies relentlessly demanded that US industry design, invent, produce and supply vast quantities of aircraft. These demands largely fell on stony ground but in one respect necessity was the mother of invention. The United States did contribute the design and production of a robust workhorse engine, the Liberty, which the Allies mounted in various aircraft. But while 13,574 Liberty engines were manufactured by the Armistice, only 5,435 actually reached France.[35] Pershing blamed the Allies' onerous demands for the relative failure of the US production of aircraft:

The demands of the Allies for material, for mechanics, for the adoption of this or that type of plane or engine, their efforts to secure preferential treatment from us or from each other, to say nothing of our own interior difficulties as to organization and manufacture, made accomplishments of definite results in preparation very difficult.[36]

General March, however, pinned the blame not on the Allies but on Pershing himself:

While the conditions at home were bad enough in those early days, the confusion existing was largely increased and accentuated by the fact that General Pershing was constantly altering his requests for airplanes. We never knew from day to day where he stood. As soon as we got going on the construction of a type which he had stated was necessary, a cable would come in from him, saying that he did not want that type and asking for something else [. . .] Change after change in the details of planes was cabled to him, until manufacturers simply threw up their hands . . . [37]

But if Pershing was frequently distracted and sometimes countermanded requests directed to the War Department in Washington, he may be to some extent forgiven, if only because unlike his Allied peers Pershing spent much of his war fighting a different struggle on three different fronts – against the Germans, against the Allies, and against his gainsayers back home in Washington.

The Allies subjected Pershing to a guerrilla campaign conducted by some of the toughest bare-knuckle scrappers of the day – Lloyd George, Field Marshal Haig, Marshal Pétain and Georges Clemenceau. They all had one aim, control over the disposition of the doughboys, and, to realize that, they resorted to a tried and trusted diplomatic technique

– backstabbing. In an odd sense the German army posed less of a
threat to Pershing's survival, simply because he could never have
mistaken it for an ally. As Lloyd Griscom argued:

> General Pershing found himself in a situation [. . .] of having great troubles
> with both the British and French, but particularly the British because the
> Prime Minister, Lloyd George, was a very vigorous, opinionated character
> and very obstinate, and the two Allies, France and Britain, had decided the
> best way to use the American forces when they got there [France] was just to
> feed them into the depleted French and British divisions [. . .] In other words,
> to have the Americans fight under another flag. This, of course, was impossible,
> but we had the greatest difficulty in convincing them, and one of General
> Pershing's greatest feats in the war was that he insisted on the policy of having
> an American Army as quickly as it could be gotten together to function. In the
> meantime, for months and months, we went through the most extraordinarily
> unpleasant experiences.[38]

American soldiers did not enter the front line until late January
1918, the 1st Division under General Bullard taking that privilege.
Right up to the last moment much of Pershing's time was occupied in
fighting a rearguard action against pressure to hand over the doughboys
to anyone who asked for them. Dawes observed this struggle at close
hand:

Paris, Monday, January 28, 1918.
The English, notwithstanding their steadfast refusal to mix small units of their
own troops with others – even their colonial troops with their own – and the
French, are endeavouring to persuade the United States to scatter their troops
in small units throughout the French and British line. General Bliss[39] has
acceded to the idea. General Pershing is obdurate in his position against it.
Bliss has not yet gone to the extent, as I understand, of making to Wilson a
recommendation contrary to Pershing [. . .] The President of France, the
British authorities, Lloyd George, General Bliss – all arrayed against John –
mean nothing to him except as they present reason [. . .] I know Wilson will
stand by him in his position, for he is right.
   John wants his troops to go into the line in divisions, thus preserving their
esprit de corps, the pride of their country, the support of the American public,

the honor of our nation. He has no objection to their going into the British or French lines providing they go by divisions.[40]

This struggle was to prove a serious obstacle to achieving victory, and Pershing's post-war reputation has been unfairly blighted because he stood his ground and refused to submit to the demands of the Allies. No American general worth his salt would have done anything less.

7

Ships for Souls

[. . .] the British were bargaining for men to fill their ranks and we were trying to get shipping to carry over our armies.

Pershing[1]

One aspect of the United States' wartime relationship with the Allies, in particular the British, provoked considerable mutual bitterness, though at the time the dispute was largely concealed from public attention in an effort to gloss over the disunity. Friction over how the doughboys were to be ferried across the Atlantic, in what numbers and at what cost, began between the Americans and the British in late 1917 and grew worse as the war dragged on. The issue was never satisfactorily resolved and, had the war not ended when it did, might have seriously affected the US commitment to the struggle in 1919. Underlying the question of how the doughboy army was to be got across to France was the struggle for control of it once it was there.

While initially the Allies tended to dismiss any suggestion that there would be a need for a large doughboy army, that view rapidly changed as the military balance on the Western Front once more seemed to tilt back in favour of the Germans. In the weeks and months following the German spring offensive of March 1918 the Allies began to demand an ever larger US army, while simultaneously angrily complaining about what they saw as the US failure to ship troops with sufficient speed. Yet there was no deliberate procrastination on the part of the Americans; if the doughboys failed to arrived in France at the rate the Allies were beginning to demand, the fault was almost entirely due to the British government's refusal to put enough ships at the disposal of America. Throughout the period of active American involvement, transporting the doughboys to France was largely in the hands of

Britain, then the world's most powerful sea power, which had tightened its control over the country's vast merchant fleet at the start of 1917 by extending its power of requisition.[2]

Underlying this political and logistical mess was a failure on the part of the Allies to agree a coordinated shipping plan. Between April and November 1917 there was no attempt to unite policies on merchant shipping among the Allies and with their Associate, the United States. On 20 November 1917 representatives from the British and American governments met in London, but only to agree to exchange information about what tonnage each had available and what might be the best use of it.[3] This resulted in the Allied Maritime Council being established at a conference in Paris on 29 November 1917 between Britain, France, Italy and the United States, as well as Belgium, Serbia, Greece, Romania and Portugal, with representatives from China, Japan, Cuba, Montenegro, Liberia and Russia. This was a key meeting for the future conduct of the war, as it formulated not only the principle of cooperation between all the participants over the important matter of allocation of shipping; it was also agreed that the United States would provide sufficient transportation for the shipping of an army of 1 million men to France by the end of 1918. This figure was jettisoned in the panic of spring and summer 1918, when the Allies reached such a pitch of despair that they put inordinate pressure on America to ship twice that number of doughboys by late 1918.[4] As Dennis Nolan wrote, 'In a mysterious way British shipping that previously had not been available for the transport of troops was soon forthcoming.'[5]

In the apparent delay in shipping US soldiers to France the Americans were not entirely blameless. The mammoth task of gradually transporting 2 million Americans across the Atlantic, and then keeping them fully supplied with food, clothes, fuel and much else, was inevitably full of mistakes and mishaps, but at least the American authorities wanted to ship troops as quickly as possible. Despite a massive effort there were, however, still only 183,896 doughboys in France nine months after America declared war.[6] One reason for that relatively low figure was the inevitable time lag between the recruitment of raw conscripts and their achieving a state of training adequate to ensure their ability to fight and survive in the trenches. Training of the conscript doughboy army was hardly an overnight job, and the sheer numbers of troops and quantities of gear to be processed imposed enormous strains on US and French ports. While there were never enough ships to transport everything, this shortage was compounded by inefficiency and poor planning in the War Department in Washington. In August 1917 Pershing sent an exasperated cable to the Department, recommending that 'no further shipments be made of following articles [. . .] bath bricks, book cases, bath tubs, cabinets for blanks, chairs except folding chairs, cuspidors, office desks, floor wax, hose except fire hose, step ladders, lawn mowers, refrigerators, safes except iron field safes, settees, sickles, stools, window shades'.[7]

While stuffed to the gunwales with floor wax, the doughboys were desperately short of more essential items. As late as November 1917 Pershing angrily asked Washington to send supplies of winter clothing for the doughboys, only to be told that it was being held back for those in training camps in the States. In that same month his General Staff estimated the AEF would require some 50,000 motor vehicles of all shapes and sizes; not a difficult request, it might be thought, for the world's biggest producers of automobiles and trucks. Pershing was staggered to learn, however, that 'the War Department was waiting for our allowance to be manufactured before sending any to France. This, of course, was quite out of the question, and I suggested that the cantonments at home might use horse-drawn vehicles and that their motor transportation be sent to us.'[8]

The same kind of mismanagement and slackness played the devil at the quayside. The 'improper stowage of cargo – with shifting, damage, and breakage en route' and 'loading heavy objects (locomotives, motor trucks, artillery) above lighter ones (cartons of subsistence stores, etc.) with crushing and destruction of the latter' were rife, while there were frequent incidents of 'men put aboard in winter without adequate warm clothing and blankets [. . .] vessels crowded far beyond troop-carrying capacity (favoring spread of disease) [and] cargo space largely filled with supplies not needed overseas and not asked for by AEF'.[9]

Some hint of the bureaucratic mess that resulted from the sheer scale of the mobilization and the lack of clear-sighted, single-minded control, is given in this episode:

In October 1917 the USS *Nomus* left Newport News with no troops or passengers and but 380 tons of freight (including chewing gum for the Red Cross). Her rated capacity was 6,879 tons. In France she took aboard 500 tons of coal at $25 per ton from the very limited stocks there existing. This fuel cost but $5 per ton at Newport News, and she could readily have loaded 5,000 tons for the use of the AEF, its increased value overseas crediting her with an earning of $100,000 for the eastward trip. Instead, it was estimated that the expenses of the round trip, which consumed 45 days at a daily charter hire of $2,751.60, totalled nearly $189,000.[10]

In another example, in early 1918 the *Oregonian* spent

57 days in one French port, 7 in another, and 51 at sea or in anchorages – a total of 115 days on a single round trip. When she was fortunate enough to find a berth, the average amount of freight unloaded from her daily totalled but 136 tons at one port, 196 at the second. While discharging at one of these, she was compelled to shift berth no less than seven times to permit the adequate handling of different elements of her cargo, whereas presumably not more than one such movement would have been necessary had her loading been scientifically conducted.[11]

Even when the ships had managed to disgorge their cargoes safely, there were snarl-ups in the French docks. In January 1918 there were more than 30,000 damaged and unusable railway carriages laid up in French sidings, with no effort being made to repair them as skilled workers were either at the front or working in munitions factories. That same month some 8,000 tons of supplies destined for the AEF were daily discharged at French ports, but only 3,000 tons a day were shipped out of the ports. This huge backlog of supplies often choked the ports. There were pressing needs for skilled railway and construction workers, for lumber and girders to build railway lines, for stevedores to unload ships, for more men, more supplies, more ships, more everything. The dockside workers in France were running to stand still. It is a wonder that the system did not collapse entirely.

Logistical problems could, however, be overcome with goodwill and thought. They were relatively minor factors in the general paralysis which gripped the first twelve months of transporting the doughboys.

By far the biggest obstacle was Lloyd George's determination to enforce a deal in which British ships would be available at a price – control over the deployment of American soldiers. If the Americans wanted British ships to ferry their troops to Europe, the doughboys would have to serve in British divisions under the command of British generals. Pershing and his General Staff found it incomprehensible that the British were prepared to risk the outcome of the war in this way. Recalling this unseemly episode, Hugh Drum summed up the AEF General Staff's view:

[...] no one in any sane mind can excuse or understand the British attitude on shipping. This attitude nearly lost the war and by delaying the eventual use of their ships for American troops, they are responsible for thousands of lives, etc. Suppose the British, as they could have done as readily as they did in May, June, July and August, 1918, had transported one million American soldiers, or 15 divisions, SOS troops and supplies therefore in November, December, January and February, what a different story![12]

Pershing, Drum and the rest of the General Staff failed both to understand and excuse the British position. If called on to defend it, Whitehall could point to the crippling damage being wrought on British merchant ships by German U-boats in the Atlantic. Throughout 1917 Britain sought to barter ships for souls partly because the Germans then appeared to be winning this sea battle, sinking far more ships than British shipyards could manufacture. These merchant ships were the Allies' lifeline, ferrying supplies essential for both civilians and armed forces alike. The shipping question came to a head following the first successful days of the German spring offensive in 1918; then there began a frantic haste to ship as many US troops as possible – and an even greater desperation in the British and French camps to achieve complete control over their deployment.

In round terms the transportation of one doughboy to France required four gross tons of shipping (mules and horses needed twice that), with a further gross ton perpetually employed in order to supply him. This did not include hospital ships, reinforcements or other vital supplies.[13] In the months following April 1917 the Allies gradually began to look to America to deliver to France a 1-million-strong army by the end of the year. That size of army would have needed, in addition, an estimated 175,000 horses and mules. A simple calculation showed that this was beyond the capacity of the US merchant fleet, which amounted to little more than 3 million gross tons of merchant shipping, 30 per cent of that tonnage being tankers and therefore unsuitable for transporting soldiers. Even if the United States requisitioned all its merchant fleet and sacrificed all its export and import trade – and neglected to take any mules or horses – it would still be unable to ship and supply more than 350,000 soldiers. If the Allies wanted rapid delivery of twice as many more, *they* would have to ship them. To have a million doughboys in France by the end of December 1918, the British estimated at the end of November 1917 that the total tonnage required would be more than 2.3 million gross tons, with a further requirement of more than 1.3 million gross tons to maintain this force in the field. This seemed out of the question, but by a supreme effort that figure of 1 million was achieved as early as August 1918.

In August 1914 Britain indeed ruled the waves, with 4,174 ocean-going merchant ships – almost 50 per cent of the world's total fleet of 8,445 such vessels – with a gross tonnage of more than 18 million tons. Germany ranked a distant number two (743 vessels, 3.8 million gross tons), the United States a poor third (513 vessels, 2.2 million gross tons) and France a long way below that, with 357 ocean-going ships weighing in at 1.6 million tons.[14] Since August 1914 the U-boat war had slowly but surely choked off supplies to Britain. In 1916 the average monthly loss to the British fleet of ocean-going ships totalled twenty-four vessels; in the first six months of 1917 the figure rose to eighty ships. By the end of 1917 the combined merchant fleets of Britain, France and Italy had shrunk from a total of 24.5 million tons to 18 million tons, out of which 5.5 million tons were devoted entirely to supplying the needs of front-line troops.[15] So much hinged upon relatively little. The total value of all the world's ocean-going merchant ships in early 1914 was under £300 million – less than the capital invested in two English railway companies. The total number of the world's merchant seamen during the war was no more than 450,000, a small number compared with the 8 million who were engaged in agriculture in France alone.[16] The actual amount of merchant-fleet steel sunk during the war was about 5 million tons, less than 12 per cent of American steel production in a single year at that time, but little US steel went into shipbuilding. During 1914–16 American shipyards maintained their relatively low output; in 1914 the United States built ninety-four vessels (totalling 201,000 gross tons), against the United Kingdom and Dominions' 714 (totalling more than 1.7 million gross tons).

No one could know this at the time, but by July 1917 the German U-boat campaign against Allied merchant ships had passed its peak of success. The situation at the start of the year seemed ominous to the British; leather had become so scarce that a pair of soldier's boots could not be had for less than £1, much more than the average weekly wage. Sugar had been rationed in Britain since 1914, and luxury foodstuffs completely disappeared. In the two months of April and May 1917, U-boats had sunk 'the stupendous total of one million five hundred thousand tons of shipping. At this rate it was only a question of time until all existing Allied shipping would lie on the bottom of the sea.'[17]

But although butter, flour and other staples became scarcer and many foods had their price fixed by the government, there was never any sign of outright starvation, as became the case in Germany towards the end of the war. In December 1917 the British were, on average, still eating 30 to 40 per cent more food than a typical German family.[18] France was also at the mercy of the U-boat, being entirely dependent on imports for all its oil. Before the war France annually imported about 400,000 tons of oil and petrol. The war increased that consumption to 1 million tons a year. Supplies were likely to be exhausted by 1 March 1918 unless the United States could ship crude oil and petrol to France;[19] in 1917 the monthly demand was for 50,000 tons, yet imports were running at just 30,000 tons. On 15 December 1917 Clemenceau cabled President Wilson, requesting 100,000 tons of oil and distillates to be shipped urgently to France.[20]

By the summer of 1917 British shipping losses were under 350,000 tons a month, thanks to the introduction in May 1917 of the convoy system, backed by both Lloyd George and Woodrow Wilson. By 1918 the shipping loss rate for convoys had fallen to 0.98 per cent, while German submarine losses had risen to 7.4 per cent. But from the British perspective the convoy system was perhaps only a temporary success. It was clear that the more doughboys arrived on the Western Front, more and more scarce shipping would have to be diverted from British needs in order to keep the Americans fed, clothed and armed. A cruel paradox loomed before the Allies: the bigger the American army in France, the slimmer Germany's chance of winning an outright military victory; but the greater was the U-boat's chance of wreaking havoc on the domestic economies of Britain and France through empty soup bowls in Bordeaux or Birmingham.

In April 1917 the Allies hoped that American shipbuilding could be stepped up sufficiently rapidly to obviate the need to take British ships away from the important task of feeding the United Kingdom's civilian population. But it was not until 1918 that US merchant ship production overtook that of the UK[21] and its Dominions, producing that year 929 ships, weighing more than 3 million gross tons, against the UK/Dominions' production of 485 ships weighing 1.6 million gross tons. The bulk of the United States' increased production in 1918 in any case only happened in the last three months of that year.[22] The crisis in merchant shipping was just beginning to peak as America joined the conflict.[23]

In April 1917 America had some 1,500 merchant vessels, about half of which (including tankers) were suitable for ocean-going trade. Of these 3 million gross tons, almost 700,000 tons derived from sixteen German vessels which had been impounded in American ports in 1914, including the largest ship then afloat, the *Vaterland*, which the Americans renamed the *Leviathan*. This sounds like a lot of ships, but was in fact only enough to keep pace with the growing demands of trade. By the end of 1917 the US army had available to it from American sources only 786,000 tons of shipping to transport its divisions across to France.[24]

The Allies were being squeezed from both ends; as the U-boats enforced net reductions to the British merchant fleet, so the combined total import needs of Britain and France had increased by at least 10 million tons since August 1914.[25] By April 1916 the British Shipping Control Committee (established on 27 January 1916 to exercise general supervision over shipping problems) was highly alarmed – the shipping losses caused by German action pointed to a deficit for that year of some 13 million tons of urgent imports of food, munitions and raw materials. Nor were these losses being made good by building new ships; in 1913 British shipyards had launched some 2 million gross tons of ships, and more than 1.5 million in 1914. That dropped to just 630,000 tons in 1916. By the end of June 1916 Britain had 35 per cent less tonnage of shipping than in June 1914, while its imports had shrunk by just 10 per cent. The needs of the war – for greater quantities of heavy materials such as coal, ore, munitions and nitrates, and fewer deliveries of bulkier but lighter materials such as wooden manufactures – exacerbated the problem, as ships built to meet the requirements of peace were put to the service of war. War cargoes were relatively heavier than peacetime cargoes but, for safety reasons (not to exceed the limits of the Plimsoll line), ships would frequently sail the world only half-filled.[26] Lloyd George reasoned that if British merchant ships were to sacrifice grain, munitions, meat, sugar and other scarce commodities in order to carry doughboys, these doughboys must end up under British command.

Besides that, the Allies had never desired an American army in France, only American soldiers under their command:

It should be repeated and emphasized that at the end of November, 1917, the Allied hope lay in American man power, and that British shipping alone could make that man power available in time. But Britain, in effect, bargained her shipping against American soldiers to fill her depleted ranks.[27]

This was an explicit policy of the British, who saw nothing objectionable in assuming that America would simply hand over its own conscripts to a foreign power to use as it pleased. In a letter[28] from General Sir William Robertson to Field Marshal Sir Douglas Haig, dated 10 April 1917, Robertson wrote:

[. . .] we have got America and we shall have great assistance in the way of money and shipping, and I hope we shall get some men. We are going to try to get men as drafts for our own units and have already a recruiting party in Canada waiting for the word to go, but I doubt if the American Senate will stand it. I am also urging them to send some troops to France at once even if only a brigade. It would be a good thing to get some Americans killed and so get the country to take a real interest in the war. Although it will take many months to raise new divisions we hope it may be possible to get over an advance force of say 50,000 men picked from districts as likely to become fairly efficient in a short period of time. We might get these over perhaps by August.[29] Americans can be made into soldiers much quicker than men of most other communities.

In January 1918 Lloyd George informed Colonel House that if 100,000–150,000 US enlisted men could be turned over to the British, then the shipping would be found to bring them across to Europe. The French had no shipping to offer, but were equally determined that doughboys should serve in the ranks of French-officered armies, despite Pershing's objections, based on sensible arguments such as language and cultural barriers. At least the British were direct in their demands and frank in their horse-trading; the French argued that they really only wanted the doughboys in their ranks to ensure that they were properly trained in the arts of trench warfare, whereas in fact, as Pershing believed, 'unofficial information indicates they really want to incorporate our regiments into their divisions for such service in the trenches as they desire'.[30]

Pershing could scarcely believe that the British could be so crude and arrogant in their demands. He later put the problem succinctly:

The question that naturally arose in my mind was that if tonnage was available for this purpose, why had it not been offered to us some time before, or, indeed, why not at that very moment. If the broad view had prevailed that our forces would add just that much to the strength of the Allies, they could have provided additional shipping quite as well before as after the crisis in March. We could then have brought several more divisions to France and had them prepared to go into the line much earlier than was otherwise possible. And it is conceivable that they might have been able to prevent the disasters that came to the British in March and to the French in May. But, of course, the British were not thinking in terms of an American army at all.[31]

Pershing did not blindly oppose the British and French proposals for amalgamation, nor did he dismiss them for crudely selfish motives. He could not afford to; he was fully aware that upon him hinged the possible success or failure of the American contribution. If he opposed amalgamation, and the AEF took longer to build up as a result of

British refusal to divert shipping to US needs, then Pershing would have incurred the blame for any Allied defeat. In a cable to Newton Baker on 17 January 1918 he tussled with this dilemma:

The question of getting our men over as rapidly as possible is being emphasized by both our allies in France. The British have, as you know, made an offer to transport a number of battalions for service with their divisions [. . .] Although in serving with the British we should not have differences in language to contend with, the sticking point of the thing is service under another flag. If human beings were pawns it would be different, but they are our own men and we should therefore study carefully our national sentiment and the attitude of our army and the people toward the proposition. Generally speaking the army would be opposed to it, officers and all, but really the question presented is, can we afford not to send over extra men to help our allies in what may be an emergency when the necessary sea transportation is offered and we have the spare men [. . .] If we agree to this, we must insist upon our men being returned when called for [. . .] We must look forward to bearing a very heavy part in this conflict before it ends, and our forces should not be dissipated except for a temporary emergency. Moreover, it is unnecessary to say, when the war ends, our position will be stronger if our army acting as such shall have played a distinct and definite part.[32]

This is not the argument of a stubborn egoist, determined to cling on to every part of the developing A.E.F in order to promote his own importance. Rather it shows Pershing in a conciliatory light, far more willing to make compromises for the greater good than any other Allied general. On 2 December 1917 the British had proposed a complete amalgamation of US companies into British battalions, an idea that originated from General Robertson. Yet Britain's shipping crisis by this time had passed; instead of weekly losses of some forty ocean-going ships the sinkings were now measured in single digits: 'Out of 149 wheat and sugar ships sailing in convoy from Newport News [in the US] between July 2 and October 10, 1917, only two were sunk, and these were both vessels which had failed to keep in the convoy.'[33]

The convoy system was working so well that by the end of October 1917 of some 100 UK-bound convoys, amounting to 1,500 ships and a total tonnage of 10.5 million capacity, only ten ships (0.66 per cent) had been torpedoed while in contact with the convoy and another fourteen while out of contact with the convoy (making a total of 1.6 per cent).[34] Before the convoy system, an average of 10 per cent of all vessels sailing to the United Kingdom were torpedoed; after it, the loss was below 1 per cent.

No sooner had amalgamation been suggested by the British than a similar idea came from the French: that US troops should amalgamate with *their* armies. Pershing's headquarters staff wrote memos against such notions, and Wilson sent via the War Department a cable in late December 1917, received by Pershing on 25 December, giving Pershing a free hand over the organization and use of the AEF. The negotiations over how many troops the Americans could bring across, and how fast, and to what use they would be put, against the willingness of the British to forgo the use of shipping for their own needs, reached a climax of sorts at a conference at Versailles on 29 January 1918, attended by Generals Bliss, Pershing, Haig, Robertson and Wilson, with Lloyd George and Lord Milner.

At this conference Pershing and his staff reiterated that their priority was the building up of whole US divisions, implying not merely combat troops but all the support services required to feed, supply and care for such troops – in other words, fighting soldiers plus soldiers of the Service of Supply. The British delegates expressed their impatience with such proposals; they did not want scarce space in their transport ships to be taken up by men who would not wield a rifle or machine-gun. All they wanted were combat troops who, after a bit of training in the ways of trench warfare, would plug gaps on *their* parapets. In describing this unseemly rush of the British and French to grab young Americans for battle, Pershing summoned up all the litotes at his command:

The evident rivalry between the British and French for control and use of our forces, even before we had an army in the field, bore out my impression that those two Governments were not working entirely in harmony. It had been apparent from some time that there was a lack of cooperation between their armies. Their efforts were often separate and distinct. First one and then the other would attack, each apparently without reference to the other . . . The absence of entire united effort between the Allied armies on the Western

Front during the earlier years of the war was probably due merely to lack of understanding between the commanders, but its continuance would have undoubtedly led to their defeat.[35]

A compromise of sorts was achieved at Versailles on 29 January 1918, with the so-called Six Division Plan. Under this the British agreed to supply sufficient shipping to bring across six divisions which would be assigned for training to the British sector of the front. The British believed that they had secured an agreement from the Americans to ship six divisions consisting only of infantry and machine-gunners. The Americans, however, understood these divisions to be full divisions, including all the necessary medical, supply, logistical and other non-combatant troops who went to make up a normal division. In Washington, the War Department was bombarded with cables from Pershing's HQ and the British, each trying to ensure the success of their own version of what they understood to have been agreed at Versailles:

The British had kept alive the preferential shipment of infantry and machine-gunners. They had failed to get our consent but the great German attack of March 21st changed the entire situation. This attack [the spring offensive] virtually destroyed the British 5th Army and in a few days drove a salient more than 35 miles deep into the British lines. Priority of infantry and machine-gunners was now recommended by the Military Representatives on the Supreme War Council, and this recommendation was, of course, promptly approved by the Council.[36]

This was not, however, the end of the matter. Newton D. Baker, staunch supporter of Pershing's determination to form an independent American army, was in France during the German spring offensive. He cabled President Wilson that the agreement to give preferential shipping to infantry and machine-gunners should be for a limited time and 'only so long as the situation necessarily demands it', reminding Wilson that the ultimate aim is to 'have its various military forces collected, as speedily as their training and the military situation will permit, into an independent American Army'.[37]

But the British imagined that they had gained an important precedent.

By 3 April 1918 Pershing's staff had received a cable from the War Department saying that Lord Reading, the British ambassador in Washington, had contacted President Wilson

'with the view of obtaining dispatch of 120,000 infantry per month between now and July, infantry and machine gun units only.' Again confusion, mis-understanding and divergent statements of the American program were in full blast. It is impossible to unravel the real cause of all this but it is certain that Lloyd George and Lord Reading thought they were promised 120,000 infantry men per month for the months of April, May, June and July.[38]

It is not clear if Lord Reading did in fact get such a promise. General March, who as chief-of-staff in Washington had huge influence over the War Department, recalled Lord Reading visiting his office on 1 April 1918, where the ambassador allegedly asked for 120,000 US infantry and machine-gunners to be sent each month to augment the British army. Said March:

I told him at once that I would not do it; that our program for shipment of men was a balanced scheme for the organization of our army in France, complete with all its essential parts, including Artillery, Engineers, Medical Detachments, and the Service of Supply, and that I would not change that policy. Furthermore, we had no ships for such a movement, even if agreed upon. If Great Britain would give us more ships, I would fill them to the limit with American troops. Our troop movement abroad was limited only by the ships at our disposal.

He intimated, then, that Great Britain could possibly supply the ships if I would give him the infantry and machine-gun men for whom he was directed to ask.

This was, to me, the sun breaking through the clouds. Every request which we had hitherto made of the British Government for additional ships had been met with statements that all her ships were imperatively needed to bring food and supplies of all kinds not only for her armies in France, including Canadians, Australians, and others, but for the civilian population at home; that they had rationed their people and had given us every available spare ship they had [. . .][39]

March claimed to have told Lord Reading:

'Give me the ships, and I will furnish 120,000 men a month' [. . .] Lord Reading rose, shook hands with me with apparent delight and satisfaction, and told me the ships would be forthcoming.[40]

March felt he had successfully hoodwinked Reading; he had no intention of sending across only infantry and machine-gunners. Naturally, when the British ships started arriving in France the British were angrily surprised to find they carried not just infantry and machine-gun units, but also Service of Supply troops and other non-combatants. They registered strong protests, through Lord Reading, all of which fell on deaf ears. Pershing in London on 22 April – where he had been invited by the British to discuss troop shipments – was handed a copy of a dispatch by Lord Reading to Lloyd George and dated 20 April, in which was quoted at length a memorandum handed to Reading by Baker on 19 April.

This memorandum became known to us as the 'Reading Agreement'. The agreement was long, due to the conditions attached, but the meat of it was that it gave preferential shipment to infantry and machine-gun personnel both in our own and controlled tonnage and in that made available by Great Britain 'throughout the months of April, May, June and July'.[11]

Pershing did his best to dilute the Reading Agreement, extending the priority category to cover not just infantry and machine-gunners but also divisional and brigade HQ staff, signal troops and engineers. He also limited this extended priority to six divisions and for the month of May only. According to Fox Conner this Agreement also 'specified that Divisions and corps should be completed and essential SOS [Service of Supply] troops should be brought over before any further extension of priority'.[42]

On 1 May the Supreme War Council met once more, at Abbeville, where the subject of amalgamation was again top of the agenda. It was a tense summit. According to one witness, Clemenceau opened the meeting with the bald statement that the first business was the allotment of American troops among the Allies. The attitude of both Clemenceau and Lloyd George was that General Pershing had nothing to do with the matter and that the question was purely one of how the Allies would divide up American infantry men and machine-gunners. The discussion was naturally animated. Any American with a single red corpuscle in his veins should glory in the fact that General Pershing pounded the table.[43]

Pershing stood his ground and the US delegation left believing they had secured an agreement for the necessity of the formation of an American army under its own flag. So they may have done. Whatever the truth, Lloyd George was so enraged at what he saw to be Pershing's blind obduracy over amalgamation that he pressed President Wilson, through Lord Reading, to send Colonel House to a conference scheduled to be held at Versailles in June where – according to the British – the major topic would once more be the deployment of American troops. In Fox Conner's view, Lloyd George hoped that by having House attend the meeting he would be able to overrule Pershing.[44]

Over two days of bitter argument this Versailles conference achieved little except a determination by Clemenceau, Lloyd George and Vittorio Orlando, the Italian prime minister, that they would petition President Wilson to raise and send for their use 100 US divisions – a staggering total of more than 5.2 million men, combat and SOS troops.[45] Pershing understandably balked at this demand; if it was currently a struggle to transport and supply 200,000 men a month from the United States, how could America's shipping and the AEF's logistical resources cope with a vastly expanded supply of fresh troops? Even if the numbers of men being shipped could be doubled to about 400,000 a month – in May 1918 233,038 doughboys arrived in France – the implication was that the Allies thought the war would continue well into 1919. Fox Conner, then commander of G-3 AEF headquarters, believed the maximum number of divisions America could ship by 31 May 1919 was sixty-six, about 2.6 million men, based on the amount of tonnage and levels of supply then in existence and likely to become available. This so-called 66 Division Plan was cabled to Washington on 19 June. Undeterred, Clemenceau and Foch motored to Chaumont on 23 June to try to browbeat Pershing into accepting their own 100 Division proposal.

The French backed their insistence by lavish promises of artillery, artillery ammunition, horses and other supplies, and the British had promised tonnage. General Pershing finally consented to join Foch in the 100 Division program for July 1919, and the cable [to that effect] was sent on June 25th [. . .] Whether or not the 100 Division program could have been met is perhaps a matter of opinion. The War Department on July 26th decided on an 80 Division program.[46]

Conner said an 80 Division programme 'called for a total of 4,851,944 officers and men to reach France by the end of July 1919', including 686,825 replacements, making good losses in divisions already serving.

Meanwhile on 26 May the Germans had started their Aisne–Marne offensive, which like others that year proved highly successful in the initial stages. A mood of panic swept through the French, a black despair which clouded the atmosphere at the Versailles summit. Clemenceau announced dramatically in the Chamber of Deputies: 'Je me bats devant Paris; je me bats en Paris; je me bats derrière Paris.' A million Parisians fled Paris, certain that the Germans were about to achieve the final breakthrough.

The clashes between the Allied and US commanders over which flag he would die following were of course far beyond the average doughboy. For many of them the shipping problem meant only one thing – a gruelling voyage and a sharp lesson in military indifference. The most powerful memory most of them had of the war was not the death-or-glory episodes of taking a machine-gun nest by storm, nor even of the delights of French *vin blanc*, but of the crowded, sickening, filthy conditions in which they had travelled across the Atlantic Ocean to arrive at Brest or St Nazaire. The food was often inedible, and on numerous ships chartered from outside the US merchant marine there was a systematic attempt to profiteer at the expense of the trapped doughboys 'by selling foodstuffs (which may have been supplied by the US) at exorbitant prices'.[47] The doughboy expected the best yet often received the worst.

Lieutenant Charles Donnelly sailed from Hoboken on 27 February 1918 aboard the *America*, formerly the *Amerika* of the Hamburg-American line. On board on this sailing were some 5,000 troops, including several hundred officers, a few nurses, and Newton D. Baker, off to see Pershing in France. Baker and the nurses did not move from the top deck – which was out of bounds to ordinary doughboys – throughout the eleven-day voyage. Meanwhile the enlisted men

were quartered in the holds in tiers of bunks, four bunks high. At night all portholes were closed as a protection against detection from submarines, and the ventilation was poor. The smell emanating from these holds was enough to make one sick without any assistance from rough weather. In the staterooms where the officers were quartered, things were much better [. . .] The rough weather lasted several days and tested my ability to withstand seasickness but I never missed or lost a meal. (I didn't do so well coming home.) Things were miserable down in the troop quarters; they were bad enough during smooth sailing but now to the smell of foul air and sweat was added the sickening odor of sour vomit. As far as I know, no-one died from seasickness – although many probably wished they had – but one of my company died from erysipelas. We were fortunate that the influenza epidemic had not struck; later, transports would be returning the bodies of many of the troops who died while en route for France.[48]

Donnelly's was a relatively luxurious trip. In later ones conditions were much worse because the doughboys were increasingly squeezed, sardine-like, into smaller spaces. One of the first steps General March made when he was put in charge of running the War Department in early 1918 was, as he put it, to run the transport service 'as a ferry, and not as a passenger transatlantic service'. March undertook to ship 90,000 men a month. By that he meant cramming as many men as possible into each ship and the cessation of transporting unnecessary items. When America joined the war, the War Department considered it took 50 pounds of supplies of all sorts per man per day to keep the AEF going. March cut that to 40 pounds, then to 30. Still there were never enough ships:

The men were packed in closer and occupied the bunks in reliefs.[49] This was wartime, and any discomfort suffered was slight. This increased the carrying capacity of the ships we had by over 40 per cent . . . The next practical scheme was to shorten the 'turnaround' [. . .] When we first went to France the average turnaround for troopships was 52 days. During November, 1917, this had grown to 67 days; in December it was 64 days – an almost impossible situation. Keen, intensive work brought this down to an average turnaround of 35 days. The *Leviathan*,[50] during the spring and summer of 1918, averaged less than 27 days, and by packing the men in we landed in France each month in this great vessel 12,000 men, the equivalent of a German division [. . .] As these orders became effective, the number of men sailing for France instantly increased. During the month of March, 1918, this number leapt to 84,889. In April we shipped 116,642; in May, 245,945; and in June, 278,664. By June 30th, we had actually landed in France 897,000 men and had on the high seas, steaming toward France, enough more to bring the figure of embarkation up to more than 1,000,000 men [. . .][51]

March attributes the cramming-in of more doughboys to his own logistical genius; General Fox Conner suggested it was in fact thanks to Lloyd George:

On April 2nd, Lloyd George in a cable to Lord Reading complained that ships bringing over Americans were not loaded to capacity. In the same cable, Lloyd George announced that he was sending Graeme Thompson, the British shipping expert, to America. On May 2nd, Admiral Gleaves, in command of our Cruiser and Transport Forces, made two recommendations designed to increase transport capacity. The first was that the number of bunks per standee be increased whenever head space permitted and that certain staterooms be torn out and standees installed. This was immediately done and increased the monthly capacity of American transports by about 15,000 men. Admiral Gleaves' second recommendation was that transports be overloaded to the extent of fifty per cent of berth capacity. This overloading was not put into effect at once. But on May 18th, General Goethals cabled the AEF that as an experiment the *Agamemnon* and the *Mount Vernon* (both of which had sailed on May 16th) were loaded on the basis of three men to two berths. General Pershing was asked for his recommendation and, on June 8th, after the arrival of these ships, he cabled recommending the fifty per cent increase. These measures did not show up in the June arrivals (230,174) but in July, 313,410 officers and men joined the AEF.[52]

In an era when air power was in its infancy, the only way America could get its invaluable reinforcements to France was by sea. Of necessity, that meant the United States was very much in the hands of the British, who then had more than 50 per cent of the world's merchant ships against the less than 10 per cent which belonged to America. Between them, France, Belgium and Italy accounted for even less than the United States. Yet 46.25 per cent of the doughboys were carried in American ships (including those belonging to the enemy and neutrals which had been impounded), only 51.25 per cent in British owned or controlled ships, and 2.5 per cent in others.[53] The failure of the British to provide enough ships at the right time simply because the Americans refused to fight under British command seems, in retrospect, little short of criminal. Rather than accuse Pershing of needlessly delaying the war's end because he stood by his orders, we should consider where the true blame lies.

8

July–December 1917

The British had the dirtiest line of cuss words I ever heard. I liked some of the French soldiers [. . .] The most impressive thing was that each country hated every other country.

Arthur Ellwood Yensen[1]

We are liked for ourselves over here, if we will only be ourselves and not try to imitate anybody.　　　　　　　Charles Dawes[2]

Despite the General Organization Plan Pershing lacked a strategic blueprint for the AEF's deployment until 25 September 1917, when his General Staff produced the document 'A Strategical Study on the Employment of the AEF against the Imperial German Government'. This pessimistically concluded the AEF would be unable to mount a major offensive before 1919, when its objective should be the capture of Metz, some thirty miles beyond the then front line, in Germany. The AEF never took Metz, or even launched an offensive to do so; other more dramatic events got in the way. For now, the priority was to ensure the semi-trained doughboys landing in France were fit to enter the trenches.

By mid-1917 the British and French generals had experienced three years of brutalizing failure. The Western Front, with its mechanized, industrialized nature, had evolved into an apparently unbreakable paralysis. Warfare had become reduced to a primitive level of terrifying yet quixotic crudity, in which chunks of sharpened whirling steel decapitated one soldier while another standing next to him went completely unscathed. Even when not under threat of immediate danger, the front-line soldier had to endure stinking, rat-infested conditions with corpses scattered unburied everywhere, and swarms of black flies alighting on every available surface. Soldiers struggled to prevent themselves from going insane from the ceaseless noise, while the phantom-like insidiousness of poison gas or the ubiquitous mud infiltrated every nook and cranny, rendering every moment a misery. Into these conditions the AEF was inexorably drawn, but before entering this inner circle of hell the typical doughboy went through several unpleasant experiences, all under the rubric of 'training'.

Many months had to be spent by the General Staff in organizing the training of the novice US army, establishing training camps and liaising with the British and French on the best placing of the doughboys into their own training programmes. Ultimately twenty different training schools were set up by the AEF, the most influential being the General Staff College (GSC) established at Langres, commanded by Brigadier-General James W. McAndrew. The GSC was intended to give rapid training courses for new staff officers, instructed by Americans in the American ways of doing things, though British and French officers were attached as advisers. Back in the United States the vast waves of new recruits went through the mills of thirty-two newly-constructed cantonments before being shipped to France. It was to be six months after the declaration of war before the training of the new army really began to pick up speed.[3]

A representative experience was that of Charles Donnelly, who when America declared war had for the previous two years been a Michigan National Guardsman, attached to Battery A of his unit's field artillery. Despite his soldiering background, Donnelly entrained with his formation (as part of the 32nd Division) only on 17 July 1917. The 32nd gathered at Camp MacArthur in Texas, where the Michigan Guard combined with that of Wisconsin. At MacArthur he was given a pile of gear:

[...] uniforms, Stetson hats, leather leggings, oilskin raincoats, web belts, first aid pouches, holsters, extra pistol clips and regulation underwear. That morning the remainder of our equipment was issued: mess kits, saddlebags, shelter halves (two of these were combined to make a pup tent which was shared by two men), tent pegs, little canvas bags with draw strings to hold rations of salt, pepper, sugar and coffee, and Colt .45 cal. automatic pistols.[4]

There then followed months of training and it was not until Wednesday, 20 February 1918 that the 32nd's divisional headquarters arrived in France; the full division only arrived on 9 March. This eight-month process, from the assembly of a new division to its landing in France (by which time Donnelly had been promoted from private to first lieutenant), was not atypical but seemed impossibly slow to the hard-pressed British and French generals. Yet given the conscript doughboys' generally low level of prior training, the scarcity of basic equipment, the lack of trained junior commissioned officers, the shortage of shipping transports, and the bottlenecks at ports both in the United States and France, it was not bad going.[5]

Life in US training camps often appeared unnecessarily harsh to the raw recruit. Arthur Yensen and his brother Walt signed on at the Omaha Army Recruitment Center – the brothers lived in the town of Lowell, Nebraska – in October 1917 and endured all kinds of ill-treatment at the hands of low-calibre NCOs before reaching Fort Leavenworth on 1 November 1917. By then Arthur Yensen was thoroughly sick and tired of the army:

I've been in the Army almost a month now; and I, who was so crazy to join up, could be arrested for saying what I think of it now. I've been bawled out for something every single day. I started in with fresh enthusiasm to do my bit; but instead of finding a history-book army full of noble heroes, all I've found is a pack of imps eternally giving me hell. I like the grub, I can stand the clothes, the drill is all right; but to have someone continually trying to take the joy out of life for no reason at all burns me up and makes me hate to fight for a country that allows such scum to become officers.[6]

He grudgingly acknowledged that 'Physically this life is doing me good; I'm getting heavy and as hard as iron. I couldn't feel better – I feel as if I could whip Germany alone.'

Yensen's sentiments were shared by many doughboys. They hated the army's rules and regulations, yet they loved the outdoor life, the physicality of the work, the heartiness of comradeship. Private First Class Otto Korn, who served in Siberia with the 27th Infantry Regiment, relished each day of his training: 'I loved it. Gained weight. And I fairly bounced out of bed in the morning, oozing with pep!'[7]

Even somewhat sedentary former businessmen discovered an almost schoolboy delight in the novelty of army life. Once he arrived in England in August 1917, 51-year-old Charles Dawes – who had suffered from a troublesome weak ankle, in which a bone would slip out of place 'every year or so' and cause him 'the torments of the damned' until it was reset by a physician – found his new lifestyle gave considerable pleasure:

All the artificial barriers which civil success and wealth have built around one fall away, and leave you but a man among men to make or unmake yourself as in the time of young manhood [. . .] And while in civil life I felt I knew something, at this time and in this life I find I know very little or nothing. But I am learning every day. My hours of work, my time of rising and of going to bed, my food, my habits, my exercise are changed in a revolutionary way from my former life [. . .] The outdoor life – the camp fare – I enjoy everything. I eat beans and cabbage and beets and rice with zest which I never could stand before. Even onions with a small degree of garlic do not stagger me. As for being particular as to whether the service is clean, as I used to be, it never occurs to me to look for dirt, I am so anxious to get something to eat.[8]

Dawes's somewhat Olympian perspective, imbued with the timbre of generations of privilege, no doubt facilitated his schoolboy zest. Matters were rather different for the ordinary doughboy, verbally (and sometimes physically) abused by petty-minded NCOs and junior officers who had frequently only just completed their own training.

Whatever the factors slowing down the flow of doughboys to France, as far as the Allies were concerned all they could see was procrastination when they demanded speed. Relations between the AEF's General Staff and their British and French counterparts became increasingly frosty. It was perhaps inevitable that the euphoria surrounding the first appearance of Pershing and his small band should disperse; less predictable was that it would degenerate so swiftly into outright bickering. General Sir Hubert Gough, commander of the British Fifth Army, received a visit from senior AEF generals in September:

Three of the American Divisional Commanders also came to study the conduct of the battle and stayed about ten days with us. They stayed with me for a night or two living in my mess, and while at Army Headquarters they attended one or two of the Army conferences with the Corps Commanders.

During dinner one evening they told me how disappointed they were at the way they were treated by the French, who were not missing any opportunity of making them pay a good deal extra for everything they had to buy. The price charged for charcoal for use in the trenches for the men's cooking was the item which seemed to have created most soreness! One of them said they had come over 'brimming over with the milk of human kindness for the French, and thinking gratefully of Lafayette' who had fought for them in the days of Washington, but 'the price of charcoal was rapidly drying up the supply'.[9]

In France there was no infrastructure in place to receive, house, feed, arm and inculcate the US army in the ways of the trenches. While the numbers of troops arriving from America were at this stage still relatively low (at the end of August the total strength of the AEF was 1,616 officers and 35,042 enlisted men), a chaotic log-jam inside France was clearly imminent. Pershing tried to forestall this by establishing on 20 August a General Purchasing Board – a committee of ten AEF officers, plus Red Cross and YMCA representatives – under the command of Dawes, who was charged with trying to source as much as possible of the AEF's needs from within Europe to free transatlantic traffic for troops. The notion of centralizing and coordinating the supply process, of organizing a pan-European system for locating and transporting supplies to the army, was completely novel for the British and French. Though for almost three years they had faced a single enemy, they had failed to create a central purchasing board to which Pershing's AEF could attach itself.

The US army was thus forced to build its supply chain from scratch, and was very much left to its own inventiveness to locate horses, fodder, mechanical transport, medical supplies, food, coal and all the other necessities to keep an army in the field. This was no mean task. To transport one American division in France required as many as sixty railway trains.[10] Even the smallest original estimated strength of the AEF, twenty divisions, would thus have required 1,200 trains; yet the French railway system was, by the end of 1917, on its last legs.

The French did not want to hear explanations concerning the delay in sending doughboys. Oscillating between wild euphoria and the blackest of depressions, they focused entirely upon the perpetual threat of the collapse of France. Prime Minister Georges Clemenceau visited the 1st Division (then under the command of General Sibert) in September 1917. He bluntly said he did not wish to hear any more excuses as to why American troops were not arriving in France in large numbers; all he wanted, he said, was soldiers sent as fast as possible, in whatever state, to relieve the exhausted French armies. Said Pershing: 'It was obviously quite out of place for M. Clemenceau to make any such demand, yet there is little doubt that he gave expression to a very general sentiment among the French people at that moment. They simply wanted to see American troops in the trenches.'[11]

The Americans were constantly bemused that the French and British, though fighting a common enemy, rarely consulted one another over plans and usually did not bother to coordinate their offensives. As Pershing noted: 'Each nation had its own aspirations and each sought to gain some advantage over the others. Some of the divergent war aims had to do with territory distant from France, and troops sent there might have been more usefully employed on the Western Front.'[12]

Not until May 1918 did the French and Americans manage to sit round a table and agree on the formation of an inter-Allied committee for centralized purchasing of military supplies (even then the Italians and British did not immediately join). The only reason agreement was reached between Clemenceau and Pershing at this late stage was because of a desperate situation in the supply of horses, the basic means of transport. The French had originally promised to supply to the AEF 100,000 horses (later reduced to 80,000). But even at what Pershing called 'exorbitant prices' the French farmer would not sell his horses to the Americans; the farmers saw no possibility of getting any horses back, and how were they to farm without horses? 'The farmers in general simply would not sell, and one reason given us was that they had the idea that we would thus be compelled to make a large importation of horses, which would give them an opportunity to buy cheaply after the war.'[13]

As the summer of 1917 drifted into autumn the early jauntiness of the first doughboys began to ebb. It gradually became clear that they were in no condition to get into the front line quickly. Gloom descended everywhere, as General Bullard confessed:

I could feel the growing rottenness wherever I was in France. Germany was plainly acquiring friends, spies, and helpers in France these days [. . .] With regard to fighting, a strong feeling of 'Oh, what's the use!' was spreading more and more through France.

To this depression, the slowness of the progress of the American forces in France toward effective entrance into the war contributed [. . .] at the end of September we still had no fighting men upon the front line.[14]

By late October he feared that

we, the United States, came into the war too late. We may perhaps save France from a shameful peace, but we cannot beat Germany. She has beaten Servia, Russia, Belgium and Rumania. She is not beating Italy. France and England are now practically alone in the war and will be until next summer, when we may be able, if England does not starve this winter, to come into the war to a scarcely appreciable extent [. . .] So far as we are concerned, the war is practically lost; we will get nothing out of it, not even barren victory . . . If these things prove true, there is just one man responsible for it, and that is President Wilson. He three years ago prevented any preparation for war by the United States.[15]

Bullard's gloominess was not misplaced. By 1 October, almost six months after declaring war, America had sent France just 65,000 soldiers, scarcely enough men to fling into one day of a medium-sized battle; by Christmas the figure was just 129,000.[16] At the turn of the year, Pershing's enemies in Washington were lobbying hard to have him sacked; newspaper headline-writers were venting their frustration at the inaction. About the biggest news in the AEF so far was the humiliating dismissal of an AEF major-general.

The background to the sacking of the 1st Division's commander, General William Sibert, was symptomatic of the array of problems besetting the fledgling AEF. The 1st Division had spent the last two weeks of July 1917 training with a battalion from an elite French division, the Chasseurs Alpins, known as the Blue Devils. The two sides found the experience a mutual shock. The French could hardly credit that this bunch of rank amateurs, who scarcely knew how to drill, salute or march, were said to be the cream of the US regular army. Of course they were not. As already noted, the majority of the long-standing NCOs and junior officers of the four regular infantry regiments which made up the division had sensibly been left behind in the United States to train the next few divisions. On the other hand the Americans found their French tuition very strange. The doughboys were told to forget the rifle; the most important skill was how to duck into a shell-hole, peep over the top, lob a grenade and then scamper back a few yards to one's own trenches. This sort of fighting the doughboys found distinctly unmanly and possibly even cowardly. It certainly was not the sort of heroic 'up and at 'em' stuff the typical doughboy wanted to hear.

But if the 1st Division was disheartened with their immediate prospects, Pershing was furious at them for failing to meet the high standards he expected of his showcase troops. George Marshall, at that time assistant chief-of-staff in the 1st Division, recalled the type of slackness then prevailing:

As an example of the state of discipline of the First Division, the following incident occurred on our second day ashore. A tall, rangy-looking soldier was on duty as sentinel in front of General Sibert's office. His blouse was unbuttoned and a watch chain extended across the front, between the pockets. A French General, commanding the local region, approached the sentinel and exhibited an interest in his gun. The sentry obligingly handed the General his weapon and retired to the door of the office and sat down on the sill. I personally got him up, got his blouse buttoned and his rifle back. This man was probably one of those remarkably gallant fellows who fought so hard and died so cheerfully not many months later.[17]

On 1 August Pershing inspected the division and was incensed at the sloppiness he encountered:

The prompt assumption of the position of attention marks in the education of the soldier the first complete submission of his will to that of his superior, and is the foundation on which his future efficiency is to be built, and can not therefore be too strongly insisted upon.[18]

In other words, a soldier who salutes and comes to attention smartly is a soldier who will go through hell to beat the enemy. Pershing blamed Sibert for permitting the 1st Division to run to seed, but it was not entirely his fault. For one thing the division arrived in France dressed in the uniforms it had when it left the Mexican border. It was poorly equipped and, in presentational terms (always a source of concern to Pershing), it looked tired and shabby. But Pershing was determined to set an example. On 12 December Sibert was unceremoniously sacked and replaced by General Robert Lee Bullard, who had at the beginning of November already learned through the grapevine what was in store for him and Sibert. Bullard, a tough, no-nonsense Alabaman, did not intend to suffer Sibert's fate:

I took command here on December 14th and General Sibert departed for the United States. Since that day I've been going at a high rate of speed. Everyone and everything is working under heavy pressure. I think I've scared 'em all by telling them that they'd be 'relieved' without any hesitation upon the part of General Pershing if they did not 'deliver the goods'; they must succeed or would lose their commands.[19]

Being busy was one thing, having properly trained soldiers in sufficient numbers to take on and hammer the Germans was something else again. Disaster struck the Allies on 24 October at Caporetto, when a combined Austrian and German offensive masterminded by General Oskar von Hutier broke through the Italian front across a nineteen-mile sector, thrusting sixty miles into Italy and taking more than 300,000 prisoners and 3,000 artillery pieces.[20] Von Hutier's successful tactics (previously equally successfully deployed by him at the battle of Riga in September) eschewed lengthy artillery barrages, instead reinstating surprise as a key element. At Caporetto he staged a brief whirlwind artillery bombardment, followed instantly by extremely heavily armed, highly trained and well-motivated shock troops, who probed to find and then advance through weak spots in the defence. Today such methods sound obvious but were little less than revolutionary at this point in the Great War. The same methods were to be used by the Germans, again with stunning effect, in their offensives of March, April, May and June 1918.

Caporetto was a triumph for the Central Powers but the scale of the collapse at least had the effect of concentrating the minds of the Allies on the urgent need for a greater degree of cooperation. Out of Caporetto on 7 November was born at the Rapallo conference the Supreme War Council, with its permanent seat at Versailles. The SWC was intended to take charge of the overall conduct of the war, but for much of its early existence it was crippled through its lack of executive power. Moreover, it comprised only three permanent military representatives – Marshal Foch for France, General Cadorna for Italy, and General Wilson for Britain. There was no US representative at this stage, though President Wilson gave his approval for the formation of the SWC on 17 November. Pershing was astonished that the establishment of such a body, which could have taken the Allied conduct of the war by the scruff of its neck, caused such disgruntlement:

The commanders of the British and French Armies and many high officials in civil circles were opposed to it. Military commanders were afraid it would result in undue interference with the conduct of operations and it was often referred to in derision as the 'Soviet'.[21]

In fact the SWC was so unpopular in France that its creation was seen as one of the factors in the toppling of the Painlevé government two weeks later; Clemenceau then formed the new administration.

Despite all these obstacles to the smooth running of the Allied and US military strategy, the doughboys were somehow managing to get across to France. The process of shipping them to Europe was often plagued with disruptions. Generals as much as privates were thrown in at the deep end and suffered privations. General Hunter Liggett, one of fourteen commanders of newly-formed US divisions, was sent to France in September at the head of the 41st Division, which comprised National Guard units from eight western states and the District of Columbia. Though the 41st was the fifth division to reach France, Liggett had seen it for only one day in Camp Green, North Carolina, before sailing for Europe. As soon as he disembarked at St Nazaire he was ordered to Ypres, travelling through 'a countryside seemingly populated only by women in mourning and German prisoners at work', before arriving in Ypres to find that he and his staff had parted company from their baggage. 'Mine did not overtake me for a month, and it was in the light marching order of one uniform, an overcoat and a kit of toilet articles that I reported at the headquarters of General Gough's Fifth British Army, not far north of Ypres, in early October.'[22]

On 21 September the first elements of the 26th Division – boasting many sons of New England's wealthy social elite – arrived at St Nazaire. This National Guard contingent was intensely proud of being the first to come to France as a fully formed and equipped division, the 1st and 2nd Divisions having been put together in France. By the end of September the 2nd Division was completed, formed by a brigade of marines, a regular army infantry brigade, three artillery regiments, an engineer regiment and a battalion of field signallers. On 18 October the 42nd Division – composed of National Guard units from almost every state in the Union, and hence called the Rainbow Division sailed for France from Camp Mills, New York.

As the trickle began to turn into a stream, Dawes continued to struggle to persuade the British and French of the wisdom of joining forces in the supply sector, but no one was prepared to cede control over anything. The French began to spread alarmist rumours of running out of fundamental products by the winter. The supply of coal was about to collapse, they argued; this would inevitably bring on civilian riots, and then, given the recent army mutiny, who on earth knew what might happen? Once more panic gripped the French authorities. Where was the fuel supply to come from? Dawes estimated in September 1917 that the AEF alone would require 150,000 tons of coal a month by February 1918:

> Over and above all is the problem of coal and transportation for it for our army [. . .] Winter is coming. France fears a revolution unless her people and army are kept warm, and can give us no coal and little wood. England can give us coal without transportation for it.[23]

Dawes had also discovered soon after arriving in France that French coal mines were being operated at significantly less than full capacity, due to a shortage of skilled manpower. If France was short of coal-miners, perhaps she could use some American coal-miners?[24]

The French government heard that I was about to send an expert to make the examination and requested that I defer doing so. Yesterday [29 September 1917], in answer to my question as to whether this would be agreeable to them, they said that the labor situation and trades-unionism in France were such that the importation of miners would involve them in great domestic embarrassment. We therefore had to give up a plan which I am sure would have greatly relieved the coal situation both for them and us.[25]

The potential shortage of coal was also at that time on the mind of one of Pershing's most able staff officers, Major Nolan. Nolan decided to find out for himself precisely what was the supply and demand situation for French coal. He grabbed one Samuel T. Hubbard, who had travelled out on the *Baltic* as one of three US war correspondents, gave him the rank of major, and put him to work on the coal question:

Hubbard was a graduate of Harvard and a very successful cotton broker in New York City [. . .] as soon as his orders arrived I put him to work at once on a study to determine the truth of the alarming reports that were coming to General Pershing from both French and British official sources that the lack of coal in France during the coming winter was so menacing that it was not unlikely that it might force a peace with Germany. Major Hubbard went about his task at once and in the course of a few days brought me a very complete and detailed report showing that there were ample coal stores in France to supply the French population, to supply our needs, to coal our transports, and even to give Italy certain amounts needed for rail and water transportation. I showed Hubbard's report to General Pershing [. . .] he allowed no one to talk to him about coal after that time. Some time later I asked Hubbard where he had gotten all of his data so quickly on their coal situation. He told me that he had gone at once to the French economic section of their Intelligence staff and had asked them if they had any information on their coal situation. They greeted him with open arms for they were delighted to have someone interested in the subject, because, they informed him, they had an excellent study on it but that they never had been able to get anyone to read it.[26]

While the French teetered on the brink of panic and the British refused to give wholehearted cooperation either in shipping or troops for the Western Front's trenches, at long last the first units of doughboys entered the front line. On the morning of Sunday, 21 October 1917 the 1st Battalions of the four infantry regiments of the 1st Division – the 16th, 18th, 26th and 28th Infantry – had this dubious privilege, some ten kilometres north-east of Nancy, in the Sommerviller sector. Corporal Clarence Mahan's 2nd Battalion, 16th Infantry, occupied a position along the rim of a bald hill that jutted out towards the Rhine–Marne Canal. This was considered a quiet section of the front, or as one doughboy put it, 'the home sweet home sector',[27] where at most a spot of desultory shelling might be expected during their ten-day first taste of the front-line trenches. These tyro doughboys were under the command of French officers of the 18th Division, though their company captains stayed at the head of the troops. Here the opposing trenches were 1,500 to 2,000 feet apart, and the German units were largely second-rate troops. From the French positions could be seen in the distance the long blue line of the Vosges mountains. Villages and farmhouses, mostly intact, dotted the distant landscape. Both sides were well dug in, as there had been no movement here since 1915. There were extensive barbed wire entanglements and well-constructed front- and second-line trenches, with ample dugouts, well-sited gun emplacements and a maze or communication trenches. Though well established, the trenches were hardly comfortable:

At several places along our trench there were narrow tunnels leading down ward into the earth to our sleeping places. To enter, one had to stoop and descend into a dark, damp, smelly hole. When enough depth had been reached the tunnel widened and became level. Short cross tunnels led off of it. There one could sleep if he was tired enough. The whole place was infested with rats, body lice, and bed bugs [...] I chose to stay in the firing trench in preference to that hole in the ground. And I was not sleepy. In fact, it was several days before I could sleep.[28]

Placid though the sector was, it nevertheless gave some enterprising doughboys the opportunity to establish a few records. By 19 October the French instructors felt the American gunners were ready to take a position in support of the front lines, though firing a shot was a very different matter. The 6th Field Artillery, a unit dating back to the Civil War, that night marched twenty miles to Besançon, where they boarded a train to take them closer to the front lines. Even without being under fire, such movements at night were fraught with danger and always likely to degenerate into chaos:

Occasionally a gun or caisson whose drivers had given too much of the road to a passing automobile slid into the ditch and the combined strength of both horses and men was needed to pull it out of the greasy mud. Banks of fog clung to the earth and shut out the big white road at our horses' feet. Riding blindly forward at a brisk trot, barely able to see his own horse's head, a lead driver near the middle of the column rode into a wheel of the carriage in front. Horse and driver went down, tripping the other horses of the team, and in a few seconds several oncoming guns and caissons were piled into a straggling mass of men and animals. Out of the mêlée were dragged one driver with both legs broke and several badly injured horses.[29]

Captain Idus McLendon's C Battery had the honour of firing the AEF's first artillery round into the German lines. But McLendon had to fight very hard – against the French – to get his name into the history books. When McLendon arrived at the front his unit was placed under the command of Commandant Roger Villers, who 'explained to me that this was a very quiet sector [. . .] Tactfully but firmly he impressed on me that excessive activity was to be avoided.'[30] On the night of 22 October C Battery struggled through boggy fields and up slippery clay hillocks, finally managing to haul a Model 1897 French 75mm gun, no. 13579, into position. Captain McLendon then galloped back to try to persuade Commandant Villers into letting him fire the cannon the next morning at first light. McLendon also had to beg for some ammunition for the gun. Earlier that day one of McLendon's lieutenants had visited the French arsenal to collect some shells for the cannon, only to be denied them for failing to have the correct paperwork. Nor did C Battery possess horses or limber by this time, so a dozen of the gun crew carried twenty-four rounds of borrowed 75mm ammunition all the way back to the gun emplacement. After this heroic effort against French obstructionism C Battery deserved its moment of glory, firing the very first shot of the AEF at 6.05 a.m. on 23 October 1917.

It was an emotional moment, as Sergeant Alex L. Arch pulled the lanyard:[31]

All of us stood silent as the shell whistled through the still, frosty air and crashed in the distance. That first shot was directed upon a German battery concealed in a little valley behind the village of Rechicourt, at a range of slightly over five thousand yards from our gun [. . .] The first projectile was shrapnel. We never knew just what damage, if any, the first shot wrought.[32]

A small twist of fate might have seen Arch that day on the receiving end of that very same shell; he had been born in 1895 in Rojtok, in the province of Sopron, in Austria-Hungary, and was brought to the United States when a child aged eight. Captain McLendon later estimated that No. 13579 fired more than 10,000 rounds before being sent back to America, with a preservation order, on 12 May 1918. He certainly felt his tremendous effort had been worthwhile, even though it taught him a lasting lesson in the way the French fought the war:

The French policy of holding us in check was perhaps sensible enough, although at the moment it was extremely exasperating. To permit us to fire at will, meant of course rigorous retaliation by the enemy. Raids would follow, after we had gone perhaps, and the French would have the bag to hold. Hence the cut and dried schedules which were handed us [by the French] on our arrival and to which we had to adhere. Herein lay the answer to the query often put to me since the war: 'Why did not some American captain gallop his battery up to the front, drop trails and let fly a volley into the Boches?' True, this would have been very spectacular play on the traditional American plan – but it would have fared badly with the officer who did that. No. Things did not happen in that fashion. Not a single shot could be fired until the French majors had given their permission.[33]

While the artillery put on a symbolically satisfying first show, the infantry's début was less auspicious. On Friday, 2 November the 16th Infantry Regiment relieved a French regiment in an allegedly quiet sector. Corporal Frank Coffman of F Company, with forty-six men, including four extra automatic riflemen, wrote this account:[34]

Darkness came early, and by five o'clock we were ready to start, each man loaded down with extra ammunition and equipment probably weighing a hundred pounds. It was pitch-dark and raining hard. With French guides to lead us we started in. Over broken duck-boards and shattered trenches half-filled with water we stumbled along through the mud and darkness, finally reaching our positions at ten o'clock [p.m.]. It had taken us just five hours to hike that one mile.

Company F spread itself across a hundred yards of the front trench. Five hundred yards distant, across no-man's-land, were the German trenches. German intelligence had already learned that the Americans finally were in the front line opposite, and the Germans were determined to impose their will upon the novices. From Coffman's squad, Privates Hay and Enright were posted as sentries. Another corporal, Gresham, was in command of a squad further along the trench. Enright and Gresham were old timers, in the regular army several years before America entered the war. Hay had enlisted just before the division left Texas. This was Coffman's lucky night; he was placed on day duty, so together with his five-man squad he went to get some sleep in a dugout to the rear of the front-line trench. Nevertheless he was about to endure one of the nastiest aspects of trench life, a night-time raid under the cover of an intense artillery 'box' barrage.

All was quiet except for an occasional rat-tat-tat from some nervous machine gunner further down the line, or an inquisitive Very light from the enemy trenches across the valley. So, lured on by exhaustion and a sense of safety, we wrapped our blankets around us and prepared for a few hours of restful slumber. False hope.

At three o'clock in the morning the Germans turned loose on our comparatively small position what the French observers afterwards declared to be the most intense bombardment they had ever witnessed. Sixteen batteries of ninety-six guns varying in size from one-pounders to six-inch, threw over in forty-five minutes, according to French estimates, several thousand shells. The only thing that prevented our platoon from being entirely wiped out was the fact that our trenches were deep, and the ground soft and muddy with no loose stones.

After the shelling had lasted three-quarters of an hour the range was suddenly lifted in a half-circle box barrage in our rear to prevent our supports from coming up, and two hundred and forty Bavarians, the widely-advertised cut-throats of the German Army, hopped down on us. The first raid on American troops was in full swing. They had crawled up to our wire under cover of their barrage and the moment it lifted were right on top of us.

Corporal [James B.] Gresham was standing in a dugout entrance when a man in an American uniform came running by and said to him. 'Who are you?' to which Gresham replied, 'An American, don't shoot.' The man replied, 'You are the one I'm looking for,' and immediately shot him through the eye. Private [Merle D.] Hay was also shot through the head by a man in a dark uniform whom he thought was one of his comrades.

The body of Private [Thomas F.] Enright was found next morning on top of the parapet. He had evidently been captured and, refusing to accompany his captors, put up a hard fight before he was killed, as the ground was torn up and trampled down for some distance around his body. His throat had been cut from ear to ear, and his chest ripped open. The medical officer also reported finding twelve bayonet wounds in his body.

The Germans retired after a period of probably fifteen minutes carrying all their dead and wounded, and eleven of our men as prisoners, including platoon sergeant Edgard M. Halyburton and Corporal Mulhall. They cleaned the trench of every piece of equipment they could lay their hands on, and left none of theirs behind as evidence of the unit to which they belonged. Our wire patrol, however, two mornings later found several pieces of their equipment which they dropped on the rush back to their trenches [. . .] we had lost eleven men as prisoners, had seven badly wounded, and three killed. Twenty-one men, or practically fifty per cent of our platoon, were eliminated for further duty by that first raid [. . .] Nine days later, utterly fatigued, grimy, unshaven, and covered with mud, we were relived by the French who once more took their places in the 'quiet' sector.

Corporal Mahan recalled that dreadful night as one of pure fear:

The Germans were shelling all around us. We could not get help as [no] help could get through. I certainly did not want any more of this. We were out ten days which seemed like an eternity. I came through this without a scratch. After this, I never wanted to be a runner. I always thought I was a very good runner, but I must have bettered my best time as I was very scared with all that bombing around me.[35]

Enright, Hay and Gresham were buried with full military honours, but the Germans had struck the first blow against the AEF and throughout the army the mood was sombre.[36] That the 1st Division's General Sibert was a pessimist, who permitted his soldiers to lounge about in a sloppy fashion, was bad enough; that he had also had the misfortune to suffer the first casualties was appalling. The very next night after this raid Bullard was informed he would take over command of the 1st Division.

The year 1917 had been particularly bleak for the Allies; not even the entry of America into the war had wrought the yearned-for change. On the evening of Friday, 30 November Charles Dawes, ever the businessman, drew up a balance sheet. On the debit side he found:

1st. We fear invasion of France by the Germans through Switzerland. Eighty per cent of the Swiss army is said to be pro-German. If Germany starts through, it is doubtful if Switzerland will fight them. She may fight for Germany. The situation there seems bad.

2nd. If the Germans come through Switzerland the frontier defense calls for troops which it will be difficult to furnish.

3rd. France is 'fed up' with war. Only the entrance of the United States into war prevented her from going to pieces before this. In the case of invasion through Switzerland the effect on the morale of France may be disastrous.

4th. In getting troops and supplies from America we are not as yet handling the shipping problem right. We are not loading ships to fifty per cent of their carrying capacity – lacking coordination on the other side between the source of supply and the docks, and proper handling of the docks. We are not unloading ships expeditiously on this side. In America the control of ships is still considering commerce with South America, for example – when we are in a death struggle.

5th. Military coordination between the Allies is sadly needed.

6th. Revolution is feared in Spain which will much lessen France's current supplies if it occurs.

7th. Our line of communication is delayed by lack of equipment (engineering, etc.) from the United States. In this our danger lies in our being blocked with freight when its real movement commences, say three months from now.

8th. The release of the German divisions from the Russian line, the capture of over 2,000 Italian guns [at Caporetto], means increased pressure on our French lines eventually.

9th. Peace seems in the atmosphere.

Against that, the credit position included:

1st. France will probably hold for another season. If she does, especially on the western part of the western front, a general retirement of the Germans can be forced. This should greatly impair German morale and perhaps cause internal and political collapse in Germany.

2d. English morale is in no danger. The United States is new in the struggle, and if she gets in in time will greatly improve the general morale.

3d. Germany probably cannot organize any considerable system in her conquered territory which will prove of *immediate* military importance to her. She is wearing down in man power. The Allies are still increasing.

4th. We probably underestimate the extent to which the German army and morale has been affected, and also the strength of the internal desire for peace which, with a proper basis such as an important military reverse, should crystallize into revolution.

5th. We have the best of the food and supply situation.

6th. Coordination is improving, though far from what it should be along all lines.

7th. Only about 40 of say 160 German divisions released from the Russian lines will probably be effective military forces.

8th. Italy is holding.

9th. That *status quo* is against Germany.[37]

Six months had elapsed since Pershing arrived in France and there was, according to the British and French, little evidence of the AEF proving to be the longed-for saviour. As for the Americans, they were still trying to come to terms with what seemed to be the form for fighting the war – an almost complete lack of cooperation, and frequent irreconcilable discord, between the British, French, Belgian and Italian

military and political authorities. It was incomprehensible to many of
the senior officers on Pershing's General Staff, newly arrived in France
in mid-1917, that the British and French had so utterly failed to wage
war in a joint capacity. No wonder they had been brought to the brink
of disaster; they faced an enemy who had the benefit of fighting
singlemindedly. As late as 3 December 1917 Dawes confided to his
journal his irritation at one example of this failure to forsake national
feelings for the common interest:

Sunday [. . .] I arranged with Van de Vyvere [the Belgian minister of finance
and a close personal friend of Dawes], who is here representing Belgium at
the Inter-Allied Conference, an effort to get Belgium to turn over to the AEF
600 locomotives which are now rusting on the tracks idle, and which Belgium
declines to give to England or France, having already given them 1,100 and
wishing to retain these so as to be sure to have them to start business within
that poor country when the war closes . . . England and France (that is, their
War offices) are very angry with Belgium for not turning over these last 600
or 700 engines.[38]

Dawes got his locomotives, on the same terms as the British and
French got theirs from the Belgians. He immediately turned them over
to the French, who were in charge of running the railways in France.
Dawes regarded this as a significant victory; but given that the Allies
had been fiercely criticizing the Americans for failing to get their troops
and supplies into the front lines fast enough, it appears ridiculous that
he was spending his time on solving an emergency that could, with
goodwill, have been resolved months before America declared war.

In early September 1917 Pershing had, with some prescience, forecast
to Dawes that thanks to US intervention the Allies would secure victory
by Christmas 1918, despite the desperate situation in Russia. But he
was also alarmed at the ham-fisted way in which his British and French
colleagues conducted operations:

He said that one trouble which he saw was the difficulty the French, English
and Italians experienced in securing between themselves the best methods of
cooperation; that this condition was improving, but that the recent offensives
of the French and English, though arranged to be simultaneous practically

throughout, failed to be so, and as a result after one offensive was through the Germans could move and did move their troops over to combat the other.[39]

Following the initial débâcle of the 1st Division, Pershing spent a few days considering how best to send a signal to the AEF that he would not tolerate being embarrassed by it, ever again. He decided that the doughboys, particularly those from the soft, preening outfits formed from the National Guard, needed toughening up. Thus on 11 December the 42nd Division was ordered to begin a series of marches which the doughboys of the Rainbow Division would never forget. On that bitterly cold winter's day they started a 35-mile march south, taking two and a half days to get to the La Fauche area. On Christmas Day, in a ferocious snowstorm, the division was ordered to start an immediate 47-mile march to the area south of Langres. Over the next three days the Rainbow – many of whose men lacked coats and few had gloves – slogged through blizzards on roads where every step felt as though it were on glass.

As 1917 ended it was evident that although America was now in the war it would only influence the outcome if it could quickly send over masses of troops. Private Winters Fehr, attached to Base Hospital no. 32, arrived at Brest on Christmas Eve, 1917. His first impressions of France were that there were 'too damn many foreigners'. He quickly realized there were so few doughboys around that he himself was the foreigner. By the end of the year the United States had four combat divisions in France: the 1st (Regular); 2nd (Regular and Marine); 26th (New England National Guard); and 42nd (Rainbow). Together with the 41st Division these were designated the First American Army Corps, to be placed under the command of Major-General Hunter Liggett in the middle of January 1918, with its headquarters at Neuf-château. Four divisions with one on the way hardly impressed the British and French, who were making increasingly loud noises about American foot-dragging; why, nine months after the United States declared war, had only 183,896 Americans – and not all of them combat troops – arrived in France?[40]

The answer partly, as we have seen, is that the US army was ill-prepared and undersized for the kind of conflict it was to engage in.

There was not much anyone could do to hustle any faster the enlisted thousands into a fit shape. Nor were the Americans much slower than their Allies when it came to training men for the front. James Norman Hall, an American citizen who found himself engaged in 'three weeks of solitary tramping in the mountains of North Wales', decided on 18 August 1914 to join up with 'Kitchener's Mob', the title of his exceptionally good account of fighting on the Western Front in 1915–16. He then underwent another eight months of training in Britain, being transported to France in May 1915, where it was another month before he actually went into the front line. But that was in 1915; in 1917 there was much less patience.

At the same time the Americans were utterly bemused by some of the practices that had grown up since the start of the war in 1914, which seemed to them to hinder the active prosecution of the war – and surely that was why all of them were there? As well as developing the habit of letting certain sectors of the line become sleepy rest-homes, the Allies had some peculiar attitudes when it came to interrogating prisoners, as was discovered by the Major Hubbard, attached to G-2 (Intelligence), who had helped Nolan discover the truth about coal supplies. Hubbard visited his opposite numbers at British GHQ for briefings on 18–23 December 1917. He was astonished to discover that German prisoners-of-war normally had about their person a document called the 'Soldbuck' (actually *Soldbuch*), their pay book:

This book contains practically all the information regarding the soldier [. . .] In reference to the Soldbuck the English are rather handicapped as they have an agreement with the Germans not to take away the pay books by either side. Great care should be taken that no such arrangements are made by us with the Germans as this book is of the greatest value. On account of this arrangement it is necessary for the British to have every prisoner interviewed and his answers written down on a classification sheet which must be gone over in great detail afterwards and entails a great deal of extra work.[41]

The French did not have the same problem with *Soldbuchen*. By February 1918 they had collected more than 300,000 of them.

On 27 December one of the more unusual doughboy regiments arrived in France – the 369th, the last National Guard regiment organized in the United States. The 2,000 men and fifty-six officers of what had formerly been New York's 15th Regiment were almost all black. The most training these intelligent, educated and willing men had received was three weeks' close and extended order drill between 15 July and 3 August, and various night school and correspondence classes. When they arrived at St Nazaire, this supposedly combat outfit was immediately put to work on something no white combat regiment ever had to face – manual labour,

and every imaginable duty except preparation for combat. It is not an exaggeration to say that the men of this regiment never saw their rifles except by candle light, or in the case of that part of the regiment excused from manual labour on the Sabbath Day, from December 27 to March 12th when it was turned over to the French Army as an American combat unit.[42]

The 369th's caring and dedicated commander, Colonel William Hayward, did his professional military career no good by submitting such pointed testimony in 1919. The tide of the time favoured instead people like Bullard, a southern racist of the old breed. On 28 December Bullard was told by Pershing to get ready to take the 1st Division back into the front line, attached to the French army under the command of General Eugène Debeney, former chief-of-staff to General Pétain. 'Pershing,' said Bullard, 'is looking for results. He intends to have them. He will sacrifice any man who does not bring them.'[43]

9

Killing Time

Think of standing up to your knees in water all night in a trench,
looking and listening for Bosche, or, worse, going out on patrol
into No Man's Land in the driving rain, peering into the darkness,
seeing spooks every minute, trying to get a sight at the Hun before
he pots you with a rifle or rips a dozen machine gun bullets through
your anatomy.   Major Hugh Ogden[1]

We were greener than grass on St Patrick's Day.
                            Private Malcolm D. Aitken, 5th Marines[2]

If the French army's weakness was 'that its leaders were committed to
an aggressive strategy which was beyond their tactical powers',[3] then
the AEF's, at least in its early days, was that its tactical aggression far
outstripped its strategic experience. Its pugilistic ambition was huge;
its punch puny. Despite this Pershing was confident that he, and he
alone, knew how to break the stalemate in trench warfare. It would be
done, he frequently declared, by reinstating the rifle as the pre-eminent
infantry combat weapon, and by getting the ordinary soldier to adopt
a much more aggressive attitude. Pershing believed and said that the
Allied armies had lost sight of the importance of open warfare. There
was too much emphasis on trench combat tactics; the rifle was the
thing.

As well as marking him as incorrigibly naive in the eyes of the Allied
commanders this attitude failed to take note of several realities, not
the least of which was a severe shortage of rifles back in the States. It
was all very well placing renewed emphasis on the rifle, but not much
good would come of this if the raw recruit could not learn how to
shoot one. When in September 1917 Forest Mead joined the 356th

Infantry Regiment, 89th Division, he found something missing: 'We had no rifles in Base training [. . .] For a few weeks, we trained with wooden ones. Then I was transferred [overseas], I believe they got rifles in early Nov. '17.'[4]

Matters had scarcely improved by the time Pablo Garcia enlisted in the same regiment in April 1918:

We barely were taught how to use our rifles and gas masks. We did not even have rifles at first, and had to make dummy rifles out of wood [. . .] The helmet was ridiculous. It looked like a saucepan, and it looked like it was made of some inferior metal which would hardly stop a rock, let alone a bullet.[5]

Private Robert Glover was drafted into the 89th the same month as Garcia. His feet hardly touched the ground at Camp Funston in the United States, spending just enough time to 'get inoculations and equipment' before being shipped to France. Glover was in the 342nd Machine Gun Battalion but the first time he got to handle or fire a machine-gun was in France.

By the end of the war many doughboys were flung into battle inadequately prepared:

The necessity to speed troops to the front likewise affected individual training. Many untrained replacements, for example, reported to combat divisions in the latter stages of the war. In late September 1918 the 77th Division received 2,100 replacements. Over half lacked rudimentary infantry skills. Many had not been issued weapons prior to reporting to the division and did not know how to care for or use a rifle. The day after receiving these replacements the division jumped off at daylight as part of the Meuse–Argonne attack.[6]

Poorly trained and armed, the average doughboy nevertheless had bags of innate courage and stamina by way of compensation. These qualities were vital since he was led by officers who had as little knowledge of trench warfare as he did. Officers trained at West Point immediately before April 1917 still studied the wars of the past, not the present:

As far as the Academy was concerned, the first three years of the war in Europe need never have taken place. No attempt was made to learn from it or to apply its lessons to the curriculum. In the department of military art, the cadets continued to concentrate on and visit Civil War battlefields; while the French army bled to death in front of Verdun, the cadets at West Point inspected Gettysburg [. . .] The instructors continued to emphasize cavalry tactics and made no attempt to teach the cadets anything about trench warfare. The first mention of the war came in 1916, when the head of the department of modern languages reported, 'On account of the war abroad, no request was made to send officers to Europe to study French and Spanish.'[7]

Despite this ignorance, graduates of West Point dominated the top leadership of the AEF. Of the eventual thirty-eight corps and division commanders in France, thirty-four were West Point graduates; out of the 474 generals who were in the US army during 1917 to 1919, 27.8 per cent were from West Point.[8] Yet if the teaching of tactics and strategy at West Point was backward-looking and largely irrelevant to the realities of the Western Front, the Academy's harsh and often cruel discipline, combined with its self-proclaimed high moral code, nevertheless schooled its young men in one crucial requirement for battle on the Western Front – a willingness to suffer:

Losses per thousand among first lieutenants who were Emergency Officers [non-regular army] serving in the theatre of operations were 30.3; among West Pointers in the combat zones the figure was 195. For all junior officers, regardless of their assignment, the losses per thousand among Emergency Officers were 21.5; among West Pointers they were 41.9.[9]

When the first contingents of the AEF arrived in France its senior officers, Pershing included, were contemptuous of the trench-bound stalemate that prevailed. They correctly grasped that true victory would only derive from doing things differently. But while they understood the problem they had little idea of a solution. All too often they appeared to believe that because the British and French had taken such a battering over the past three years then they had lost the necessary willpower that the Americans possessed. Sometimes, such as at Belleau

Wood in June 1918, the kind of reckless courage based upon such profound ignorance as the AEF's commanders initially displayed did indeed prevail. But the longer the AEF fought the more its senior officers came to realize that an indomitable will was insufficient without tanks, aircraft, plentiful artillery and, most important of all, intelligent coordination of all elements. General Bullard perfectly embodied this contradiction between contempt for the shrunken spirits of the British and French and a recognition that the AEF had a lot to learn:

Among the officers of the 1st Division there largely prevailed our old idea that experience in war was the only proper teacher of war-making, and that war having come, schools should cease: we should take the field and learn war there [. . .] These ideas remained among Americans until they had seen real war at the front. Then every commander wanted officers and men who had been through the schools. The demand for [training] school instruction became so great that it could not be met.[10]

Along with the rest of the senior commanders of the AEF he was deeply shocked by the type of training organized by the French for the doughboys soon after they arrived in France:

The first thing that impressed itself in our practical training beside our Allies was the immense emphasis placed by both French and British upon purely trench warfare [. . .] It was commonly said that if you took at this time a French or English soldier out of the trenches and into the open he felt like a man stripped of everything. From what I personally saw, I can believe this. In the training of the 1st Division with the 47th Chasseurs [the French regiment conducting the training at Gondrecourt] and with the 18th French Division a little later, an enormous system of trenches, covering miles and miles, was dug, at the expense of very great labor and patience, for the purpose of making the training realistic [. . .] In the construction of these works the French soldiers spared no labor. They did it with as good will, apparently, as if they were constructing trenches for their own protection upon the actual line of battle; which is saying a good deal, for, as we all later learned, the French soldier was a wonderful trench digger. Wherever he stopped within reach of an enemy's shells he never rested until he was in a hole, and it may be said that he never rested elsewhere than in a hole.[11]

Bullard's characteristically robust view was widespread among the AEF. Some other senior officers were prepared to recognize that they had much to learn from the more experienced, if not more imaginative, and much more bruised French and British. Lieutenant-Colonel Johnson Hagood of the 7th Field Artillery was a professional artilleryman. Soon after arriving in France he and colleagues spent time translating into English the French Drill Regulations. They were

all astonished to find the extent to which the French excelled in their artillery methods. In our Coast Artillery methods at home we had never taken into consideration the fact that the earth was a sphere and that all trajectories lay in the plane of a great circle. Therefore every projectile fired in the northern hemisphere will drift to the south. Nor had we ever considered the fact that the rotation of the earth had any great effect upon trajectories. There are two such effects. One is caused by the fact that a projectile going away from the center of the earth cannot maintain its terrestrial angular velocity. The other is that at the moment of discharge the terrestrial component or velocity is tangent to the trajectory but is not tangent at the point of impact. It has a lifting effect upon projectiles fired towards the east and a depressing effect upon those fired towards the west.[12]

By April 1917 the Germans had already made considerable territorial gains and the onus was on the Allies to try to winkle them out. When in August 1916 Erich Ludendorff and Paul von Hindenburg replaced Falkenhayn as joint heads of the German High Command they set about preparing a series of theoretically impregnable defensive lines along the Western Front, to which the German divisions withdrew once they were completed. The Hindenburg line (also called the Siegfried line) consisted of a front zone about 8,000 yards deep; 600 yards behind that was the main line of defence, with three interconnected trench systems, consisting of large, well-protected and deep dugouts in which the troops lived most of the time; concrete emplacements dotted these trenches, with machine-guns inside them. The whole line was also defended by carefully sited artillery batteries, with highly developed map grids for pre-arranged firing. From this massive structure, which took months to prepare, the Germans believed they could fend off any Allied attacks while they prepared for their own, and they hoped final, offensive. The Germans had withdrawn some thirty kilometres to occupy this new defensive network, consisting of a battle zone of three parallel trench lines of 1,500–3,000 metres in depth, sited wherever possible on reverse slopes beyond the view of Allied observers and also beyond the reach of artillery. This kind of defence in depth was to cause enormous trouble to all the Allied armies – including the AEF – in 1917 and 1918. Bullard made the contemptuous accusation that if French troops dug trenches whenever they stopped, there was a good reason – they were always subject to the possibility of harassing artillery fire from well-positioned German defences. The French historian Marc Ferro suggests that, if anything, the French probably dug too few trenches:

Germany had set an example, with systems of trenches, equipped with parallels, saps, communication-trenches, dugouts and listening-posts. The British followed the example; the French and Russians less so, since they never imagined they would be buried there for three years.[13]

During the war units of the AEF participated in thirteen battles:

Operation	Numbers engaged
1917	
Cambrai, 20 November – 4 December	(detachments)
1918	
Somme, 21 March – 6 April	2,200
Lys, 9 – 27 April	500
Aisne, 27 May – 5 June	27,500
Noyon–Montdidier, 9–15 June	27,000
Champagne–Marne, 15–18 July	85,000

1918
(the following Allied offensives)

Aisne–Marne, 18 July – 6 August	270,000
Somme, 8 August – 11 November	54,000
Oise–Aisne, 18 August – 11 November	85,000
Ypres–Lys, 19 August – 11 November	108,000
St-Mihiel, 12–16 September	550,000
Meuse–Argonne, 20 September – 11 November	1,200,000

(*on the Italian front, 1918*)

Vittorio–Veneto, 24 October – 4 November	1,200

It can be seen from this that the AEF did not become centrally involved in fighting on the Western Front until the middle of 1918; in other words there were but six months for the doughboys to establish their combat reputation, to demonstrate their fighting abilities and valour, and for Pershing to show that his powers of generalship were as good if not better than those of his rivals among the French and British armies. What did this fine aspiration to do things differently actually boil down to? Ultimately, often little more than a re-assertion of the importance of the rifle. General Bullard spoke for all the senior officers in the AEF, Pershing included, when he said it was absurd the British and French had apparently lost all confidence in this weapon:

In the American Army the rifle has always been the essential weapon. The infantry of the 1st Division, in its training area at Gondrecourt, concerned itself at once with rifle ranges for practice in individual shooting. The fine 47th French Chasseurs beside us began to talk to us about the use of the hand grenade and the digging of trenches and accustoming ourselves to the use of the gas mask, asserting in substance that there was little use in warfare for the individual rifle or pistol; that the artillery would do all the shooting for the infantry; the infantryman would advance with his gun slung over his shoulder and use grenades against machine-gun nests. Without gainsaying our very agreeable and tactful instructors, we adhered to our individual rifle shooting and learned all their grenade-throwing and gas work also. This had to be done very tactfully.[14]

1. The Draft: Newton Baker (blindfolded) draws the first number for the 2nd round of conscription, 27 June 1918.

2. General John Pershing (centre), commander-in-chief of the American Expeditionary Force.

3. A British captain shows rookie doughboys how it's done. Training by British officers in US bases was one of the more successful collaborative efforts.

4. The enemy: a German front-line soldier in 1918, equipped with extra cartridges and grenades.

5. Doughboys entertain French soldiers in the front line, 16 April 1918.

6. Doughboys frequently complained about monotonous rations, but these two from the 18th Infantry, 1st Division, seem content.

7. Cigarettes and chocolate were important perks for front-line troops. These two US inspectors are exercising some quality control.

8. Fraternization with French women was officially discouraged, but widely practised. This picture shows 2nd Lieutenant E. E. Clark of the 35th Division receiving some French tuition in June 1918.

9. The AEF's racial segregation extended only to black Americans. Apart
from that prejudice it was ethnically very diverse. This photographic portrait
is of Private F. F. Berchardt of the 35th Division. Berchardt was from Wacoma,
Minnesota, and was of German–Swedish descent.

10. Private John Elk, a full-blooded Sioux of the 35th Division. Native Americans were often used for important communications tasks, their languages defeating German attempts at 'code-breaking'.

11. Corporal Samuel G. Morse of the 808th Pioneer Infantry Regiment, 12 October 1918, on the Meuse-Argonne front. Most black American dough-boys were restricted to menial tasks, such as labouring and grave-digging.

12. Members of the 369th Infantry Regiment, 93rd Division, on the Atlantic crossing. The 93rd was one of just two combat divisions of black Americans permitted to serve in France.

13. An AEF trench mortar squad pulling a 6-inch Newton mortar into position. The AEF suffered throughout the conflict from inadequate supplies of heavy ordnance.

14. October 1918. A German machine-gun emplacement prepares for action against AEF divisions in the thickly wooded Argonne forest.

15. This photograph shows a Salvation Army volunteer rolling pastry for doughboy dinners. The Salvation Army's unstinting generosity won the lasting affection of many doughboys.

16. One of the greatest irritants for the doughboys was the ubiquitous louse. Most soldiers in the front line became infested at some point in their service. Here men of the 2nd Field Signal Battalion have their garments treated by an (ineffectual) delousing machine.

17. Belleau Wood, June 1918 Troops of the 2nd Division man a 37mm gun
in an effort to dislodge the astonishingly stiff German resistance.

18. 26 June 1918: soldiers from the 32nd Division setting up a French-made 37mm (1 pounder) gun on the Alsace front. The AEF was almost entirely dependent on the French and British for any weapons heavier than pistol or rifle.

19. Stretcher-bearers of the 32nd Division bringing in a wounded doughboy on 1 August 1918 at Courmont. Note the wounded soldier's tightly clenched fists: pain relief was primitive and scarce.

20. The first tank of the AEF's 27th Division to go into action was destroyed by a German direct hit near Ronssoy, on the Somme. The AEF had no US-manufactured tanks, but depended entirely on what it could wring from the British and French High Commands.

21. A French 340mm gun manned by troops of the US Coastal Artillery unit, on 29 September 1918, behind the Meuse–Argonne front. The 340mm gun could send shells almost twenty miles into German defences.

22. French-made light Renault tanks – manned by doughboys – go into action on the Meuse–Argonne front on 26 September 1918. Most were quickly out of action, through German gunfire or mechanical breakdown.

23. Doughboys head out to conduct a trench raid. Round their shoulders are canvas bags, loaded with hand-grenades. They do not carry rifles, which were usually useless in such close combat.

24. 16 July 1918. Dead German troops, left behind in the wake of a successful advance by the 1st Division at Missy au Bois.

Pershing was a strong exponent of a return to mobile, open-order tactics, in which expert marksmanship with the rifle instead of a strong grenade-throwing arm was the most useful skill to possess. Yet in early 1918, by the time the AEF was actually ready to fight, this seemed to many rather like a Christian in a Roman arena believing that if only he could run fast enough the lion would eventually get tired.

It is easy to see why Pershing placed so much emphasis upon skill with the rifle; this was what the US army was good at. America had designed and built the finest rifle of the time, the Springfield 1903, which was accurate up to 1,000 yards and beyond and, in trained hands, capable of extremely rapid fire. American marksmanship was internationally established:

There was no questioning the superiority of the Springfield in point of accuracy. Time after time we pitted our army shooting teams against those of other nations and won the international competitions with the Springfield. We won the Olympic shoot of 1908 over England, Canada, France, Sweden, Norway, Greece and Denmark. Again, in 1912, we won the Olympic shoot against England, Russia, and Austria-Hungary [. . .] in all these matches the Mauser rifle was fired by various teams; but the Springfields never failed to defeat this German weapon, which it was to meet later in the fighting of the world war.[15]

In many parts of rural America AEF recruits had grown up regarding a rifle as part of the family. Private Malcolm D. Aitken enlisted in December 1917 and by June 1918 he was boasting that he and his pals in the 5th Marines were easily capable of accurate shooting at 500 yards or more: 'the closer they got the more accurate [. . .] Pick out one man for [a] target was always our forte, whatever the range or fire routine.'[16]

Right from the start Pershing criticized the British and French methods of training, even though he admired the British training for trench warfare which

taught their men to be aggressive and undertook to perfect them in hand-to-hand fighting with bayonet, grenade and dagger. A certain amount of this training was necessary to prepare the troops for trench warfare. Moreover it served to stimulate their morale by giving them confidence in their own personal prowess.[17]

But he thought the French had given up on aggression and that French teaching would have 'seriously handicapped' his embryonic army. In particular he wanted to reinstate the rifle as the central weapon of the infantryman:

The armies on the Western Front in the recent battles that I had witnessed had all but given up the use of the rifle. Machine guns, grenades, Stokes mortars, and one-pounders had become the main reliance of the average Allied soldier. These were all valuable weapons for specific purposes but they could not replace the combination of an efficient soldier and his rifle.[18]

The trouble was that good rifle-shooting was no longer enough to win battles. The criticism to be levelled at Pershing is not that he desired a return to a form of combat that dispensed with fixed defensive positions but that he had insufficient imagination to see how best to achieve this. In his memoirs he was able to bask in the gritty glories of some doughboy units who, through sheer willpower derived from inexperience, were able to launch and push home a few attacks against heavily defended German positions; but the truth of it is that these successes were few and far between, and did not result in a qualitative change in the nature of the combat. By the time the doughboys were fighting in their biggest battle, the Meuse–Argonne in late October 1918, they were taking as much if not more punishment from well-defended German emplacements as any of their British and French comrades elsewhere on the line.

Pershing used his memoirs to construct a *post hoc* theory based on the pragmatic day-by-day decisions that had to be made in the strenuous days of 1917 and 1918. He disputed that trench warfare was either a totally new phenomenon or that it was here to stay and had displaced older, more fluid forms of combat:

Many Allied writers had proclaimed that trench warfare was a development of the World War which had made open combat a thing of the past. But trenches were not new to Americans, as both the Union and Confederate armies in the Civil War had used them extensively [. . .]

To bring about a decision, that army must be driven from the trenches and the fighting carried into the open. It is here that the infantryman with his rifle, supported by the machine guns, the tanks, the artillery, the airplanes and all the auxiliary arms, determines the issues. Through adherence to this principle, the American soldier, taught how to shoot, how to take advantage of the terrain, and how to rely upon hasty entrenchment, shall retain the ability to drive the enemy from his trenches and, by the same tactics, defeat him in the open.[19]

This is deeply misleading. Riflemen shooting from entrenched positions was the exception, not the rule in the Civil War, which had also been a war of enormous fluidity and movement. The riflemen of the AEF did not, as Pershing implied, turn the balance against entrenched German troops. In a couple of small engagements heroic American infantrymen armed with little more than rifles assaulted, and sometimes even took, erstwhile impregnable positions. But there were many more occasions when the doughboys found themselves engaged in fruitless slogging bouts – whistles blowing, up out of a trench, following a rolling barrage and with luck taking the first-line trenches of the enemy – of the kind witnessed throughout the war before the AEF arrived. Pershing was right; skilled riflemanship was relatively rare on the Western Front in 1918. But he failed to grasp, or preferred not to understand, why that was the case. Most other generals and armies had by then adjusted to the short-term, rapid encounter, short-distance attack, in which there was little chance to exercise accurate marksmanship over 500 yards; better by far a strong right arm to lob grenades a few yards further than the next man. In France, other talents had to be honed. Although Pershing emphasized the importance of rifle skills and marksmanship, what the AEF's tactics came down to in the end were, at least initially, nothing new:

Both the Germans and the Allies watched the American military intervention with amazement. The Americans perished in the same way that all the parties involved had perished during the first years of the war: side by side and wave after wave. Even the British officers, who served in the most conservative army in the whole war, found the American mode of action astonishing. At the risk of exaggeration, it can thus be said that the army of the United States set off to battle in 1918 as if the Great War had just begun, and had to discover the hard reality of trench warfare all over again.[20]

Pershing's methods (or at least those of his senior commanders), of winkling the Germans out from their defence emplacements and into an open field of battle, was little different from the tried and failed techniques of British, French and German commanders, much earlier in the war – frontal assaults by serried ranks of heavily equipped soldiers.

The Americans [in 1918] were following closely the precedent of the BEF [British Expeditionary Force] of the early years; after their great fight at Belleau Wood it was remarked how their dead, especially the dead of the Marine Corps, lay in beautifully ordered lines where the traversing machine-guns had caught them.[21]

The ordinary doughboy's experience of the war and the preliminaries to combat were no different from those of the British and French footslogger. One marine recalled his unit's journey up to the front lines and thence into the conflagration at Belleau Wood:

Camion travel at first, rain, mud, bombings, and transport of every shape and kind, including men, going in or coming out; the center of the road was open for Command, Ambulance, and such, first one way, then the other. Dark as black as you want to call it. No lights except on vehicles, no smoking in ranks, no food, no rest. Just slosh along keeping in touch with [the] man ahead, with your outstretched fingers. After falling in the slippery, slidy water-filled side road area (a large ditch yet). After much time as this we lined out across an area among some small trees, shrubs and grassy stuff. After a very short breath word was passed: 'Walking barrage due in five minutes, take care. Listen for whistle for advance; good hunting; first objective, line of trees yonder. Regroup, assess, and continue when organized, as soon as possible, so not to lose barrage effect to second objective, another small hill with trees. Consolidate line and stand by for counter attack, or further orders.'[22]

There were generals on the Allied side who were capable of great creativity and who began to crack the German defences, but ironically Pershing quarrelled bitterly with the best example, John Monash, commander of the Australian Imperial Force (AIF) in 1918. In his memoirs Pershing makes no reference to Monash who, at the battle of Hamel, which started in the early hours of 4 July 1918 and was over in ninety minutes, put into practice what Pershing only ever theorized about – a combined tank, infantry, artillery and aircraft attack which forced the enemy into the open and defeated him in a battle of movement and carefully planned manoeuvre, the like of which had rarely been seen since 1914. Only hours before the battle Pershing had discovered that ten doughboy companies were being lent to Monash for the attack. Pershing saw this as yet another example of an attempt to undermine his command of the AEF's troops and refused to let Monash have the men. In the end Monash demanded and secured the participation of four doughboy companies from the 33rd Division; they performed courageously and suffered about 140 wounded.[23] Monash's clear and decisive victory was bought at relatively little cost (about 1,400 casualties, mostly lightly wounded, while 1,600 prisoners were taken). Monash's methods had in any case been tested earlier, by the Germans. By early 1917 the German High Command was steadily coming to grips with the principles of success for Western Front combat:

In the early summer of 1916, the Germans had captured a French document entitled 'The Attack in Trench Warfare'. Unlike the British, they translated it; unlike the French, they adopted it. Its author, Captain Andre Laffargue, called for new infiltration tactics by *groupes des tirailleurs* for an in-depth attack designed to disrupt the enemy, to destroy only his main centres of resistance, and to infiltrate his defensive zone as deeply as possible. Special assault troops would lead the charge. Artillery bombardment would be sudden and cover the full depth of the field . . . the Germans first practised principles similar to these at Riga in the east in September 1917, at Caporetto in October 1917, and at Cambrai in November 1917. Their greatest application, however, would come in France in March 1918.[24]

The theory of such tactics was practically advanced by Ludendorff, who in October 1916 ordered the development of battalion-strength units of storm troops (*Stosstrupps*), highly trained, well-equipped, well-fed and housed, and strongly motivated specialist assault troops, whose task in attack was to infiltrate the enemy's positions, bypassing resistance and ploughing on, as deeply as possible, in order to sow destruction and demoralization far behind the front line. They had orders not to lay siege to any well-defended position but to push ahead, leaving it for later comrades to isolate and absorb.

Thus by mid-1918 – the moment when the doughboys finally consti-tuted a key element in the Allied military force – there was a looser form of trench warfare than previously seen, but it had become more flexible for a number of reasons, few of which owed much to Pershing's generalship.

Pershing's aspirations for his doughboys to be seen as contributing a vital part in the downfall of the Germans were laudable, but all too often the raw material of his armies had plenty of enthusiasm and not much else. Even in late 1918, when the Allies had begun to break through the solid defence networks of the Germans and force a greater fluidity onto the battlefields, the typical doughboy was scarcely able to cope with the demands made by flexible and fast-changing conditions of combat. An AEF field artillery major, himself a trained regular army officer, pinpointed this problem. On the morning of 18 July Major Raymond Austin's battalion was in support of the 16th Infantry Regi-ment, part of the 1st Division assaulting German positions in the Aisne–Marne offensive which was controlled by the French. The 16th rapidly reached its third objective of the day, and would soon be beyond the support range of Major Austin's guns. He began to consider where he should move his batteries so that they could continue to give that urgently needed support:

We had changed from the stereotyped trench warfare to a warfare of manoeuvre, a warfare which requires a great deal more military knowledge and ability to carry on properly than it does to 'sit tight' 'holding a sector' [. . .] Many an officer of a few months' experience in a sector like the Toul sector, who was an expert in figuring firing data in a dugout and pointing guns in an emplacement, soon realized that there was much in field soldiering that he hadn't yet learned [. . .] In my battalion I have only two officers with as much as 20 months in the army – most of the lieutenants have been in one year or less. They are fine, bright fellows who learn quickly, but who have had almost no work in the open warfare training which the Regular Army has always received, and the result was that I had to perform as anything from Battalion Commander to 1st Sergeant of a battery.[25]

Indeed, on 20 July 1918, the third full day of the offensive undertaken by several AEF and French divisions to recapture Soissons, anyone who had observed the attacks launched on the Somme the same month two years earlier would have felt they were witnessing a re-run of recent history:

At 10 a.m. our Infantry advanced to the attack of Berzy-le-Sec [. . .] and we shifted our fire out of our own sector to help them with a rolling barrage. The capture of Berzy-le-Sec was a wonderful example of steadiness and determination in troops already tired from two days and nights of fighting. They advanced steadily behind the barrage, walking along with apparently all the calmness and unconsciousness of danger of a drill ground. Shells striking among them, men falling dead and wounded, seemed not to affect in the slightest the ones who were left. Not a man ran forward, not one lagged behind – it was just a normal steady walk forward, hesitating for a few moments at enemy trenches while their bayonets struck downward, and then the march continued up and over a ridge [. . .][26]

In September 1918 the training section of AEF GHQ, G-5, made a report on the doughboys' combat performance. It dourly noted that despite the exhortations to adopt an offensive spirit,

'The principles enunciated [. . .] are not yet receiving due application.' Assault formations had been too dense and lacked flexibility; scouts were seldom used; supporting arms were improperly employed; and junior officers displayed little initiative [. . .] By the time of the armistice, American units were becoming more tactically proficient. 'Rapid progress in the art of war was everywhere to be seen. Divisions were more mobile, formations less dense; suitable maneuvers in the attack were more often seen; and vastly better advantage was taken of cover. Commanders and staffs were generally more confident, and worked with greater sureness and dispatch.' Clearly the AEF learned to fight by fighting, as much as by Pershing's insistence on open warfare.[27]

Even when, as the initially successful Aisne–Marne offensive which opened on 18 July showed, it became possible to break the apparently impenetrable German front lines, the logistical problem of supplying the advancing forces across no-man's-land inevitably and swiftly restored the *status quo*. Most pursuits into German-held positions found the AEF's supporting artillery, field kitchens, ambulances, ammunition trains and assorted other vital paraphernalia having to cross mile after mile of ground which, according to one combatant at the St-Mihiel attack on 12 September, was impossible to traverse except with great care and very slowly: 'One cannot say the ground is pock-marked with shell craters – it is nothing but holes. One steps from one into another. For miles stretch battered trenches, and the territory is thickly strewn with "duds", unexploded grenades [. . .]'[28] And this in a sector where there had been relatively insignificant amounts of fighting since late 1914.[29]

In fairness to Pershing there were a number of aspects to his generalship which should be recognized and praised. He never wavered in his conviction that a breakthrough to victory would be achieved, while many Allied generals, particularly the French, oscillated wildly between euphoria and despair. Major-General Bullard, commanding the AEF 1st Division, discovered in September 1917 just how deep was the French misery when he attended a French officers' training school in Alsace-Lorraine. It was attended by senior French officers – colonels and generals – only. Bullard recalled:

I was impressed by the difference between the French officers' public show of confidence about winning the war and their private and confidential feeling that there was almost no chance of winning as the conditions then stood. The French newspapers and French official utterances were very optimistic [. . .] Not so this session of high military officers. They frankly faced and acknowledged that there was almost no chance of victory.[30]

And Pershing certainly worked well with the raw materials he was given. The lack of experienced junior officers gave Pershing and his senior commanders little choice but to take short cuts, not least by forming the divisions of the AEF into units much larger than most contemporary generals thought suitable for manoeuvrability, ease of supply, firmness of command control and other key battle factors. It was early on decided that an AEF division would have some 27,000 combat troops[31] – more than twice the nominal size of a British, French or German division and, by the latter stages of the war, when the European combatants' reserves had become severely depleted, more than five times as big – largely because there were insufficient numbers of officers of adequate calibre and experience to spread across the greater number of divisions had they been any smaller.[32] One entirely predictable consequence of opting for such large divisions was that Pershing's wish for warfare that combined speed of manoeuvre, flexibility, and taking advantage of opportunities as they presented themselves was made much more difficult. The lack of sufficient numbers of good junior officers and NCOs across all the divisions rendered even more remote the possibility of realizing Pershing's ambition of forcing the war back onto an open plane.[33] A number of the National Guard divisions were seriously undermined by their lack of strong and experienced officers, as Colonel Hugh Drum acknowledged in his diary at the end of January 1918:

Our 1st div went into the line for permanent use on Jan 16 [...] The 26th div goes in for training with the French near Soissons soon [...] This is a militia div. It has all the defects of the system. The men are good but the officers are poor. We are going through a process of weeding them out. It will take time to do this [...][34]

A hint of the serious problem caused by the absence of a sufficiently large and experienced officer cadre comes through in one of the reports Major Paul Clark submitted to Pershing. On 8 March 1918 Clark recorded a conversation with Commandant Rozet of the French GHQ 3rd Bureau (Operations). Rozet was Clark's opposite number, in charge of liaison with the AEF. Rozet had just returned from a visit to the 42nd (Rainbow) Division of the AEF. It was a delicate conversation; Rozet thought the National Guardsmen 'had the making of first-class soldiers' but they had some serious failings:

[...] the non-commissioned and company officers betrayed a great lack of confidence in themselves, a lack of comprehension in their duties, as a result of which there was a corresponding lack of confidence on the part of the men in their non-commissioned and company officers [. . .] the men individually were splendid material, displayed every readiness and needed only that their non-commissioned officers and officers should have the understanding and comprehension that will enable them properly to direct their men [. . .] the trenches occupied by the 42nd Division were dirty and unkempt and they did not seem to realize that it requires constant work to maintain trenches in condition [. . .] the 42nd Division were too confident during the daytime – that is they too often showed themselves and looked over the top of the trenches – showing a disdain for concealment, and in contradistinction at night, were too fearful and too easily frightened and appeared ready to fire upon slight provocation, a condition fraught with danger to themselves.[35]

Rozet also thought that there were 'lots of officers in the 42nd Division of all grades who should be eliminated'; they simply were not up to the job. One of Rozet's criticisms betrays the rather bureaucratic[36] and atrophied nature of the French conception of staff officers' duties:

He said that the officers of the Staff whose offices were at Luneville spent too much time walking about the trenches and mingling with the troops and too little time in their offices and in contact with the officers of the French staff; that though it is important that Staff officers should have a full comprehension of the life and problems of the troops, at the same time their principal work is at the headquarters [. . .]

Even though the French officers encountered by Clark were always working to a scarcely concealed agenda – exercising all possible leverage upon Pershing to have the doughboys trained by and amalgamated with French units – their criticisms of the AEF's officer cadre were not always wide of the mark.

Yet against all the handicaps the quality of the AEF was impressive, largely because the individual soldiers were physically strong, enthusiastic, fresh and possessed of a tremendous spirit. Some of the AEF's divisions gained the reputation of being hard-bitten, tough outfits; others were dispirited. By comparison with the British and French armies, both shattered by years of bitter and largely fruitless fighting, the AEF was a race of youthful, vigorous giants. The doughboys impressed a young Vera Brittain, whose fiancé had died in the war.

Serving as a nurse in France she saw one day a large contingent of unknown, unrecognized soldiers marching towards Camiers. In *Testament of Youth*, she said they were so sprightly and upright that she thought them 'Tommies in heaven': 'I pressed forward with the others to watch the United States physically entering the War, so god-like, so magnificent, so splendidly unimpaired in comparison with the tired, nerve-racked men of the British Army. So these were our deliverers at last.'[37]

The doughboys who were first in the field may have provided little by way of immediate results in terms of territory recaptured or prisoners taken; but the intangible benefits brought by their presence must have been enormous. After the British Fifth Army was broken by the spring offensive of March 1918, the ranks of the British battalions were manned largely by troops who would have been rejected earlier in the war:

Britain was indeed nearing the bottom of her well of manpower. Conscription had been effective for nearly two years and the age for service had been raised to 50 and even, in some cases, to 55. The new men filling the ranks were those returning after their second or third wound, men who had been upgraded in their medical categories to a flattering extent, grandfathers, and boys with the down still on their cheeks [. . .] The British divisions from April, 1918, onwards were largely composed of soldiers who might well have still been at school [. . .] The British divisions, though they had halted the German onrush, had so exhausted themselves in the process that a major counter-offensive in 1918 would have been beyond their strength. The same thing applied even more forcibly to the armies of France.[38]

Assessments by German military sources tell a sometimes contradictory tale about the AEF. The Germans were clearly surprised not only by America's ability to raise, train (no matter how poorly), and then equip and ship to France a massive army in a relatively short space of time and from a totally unpropitious starting point. European professional soldiers were, however, generally inclined to be contemptuous of the US armed forces both before and during the First World War, at least up until the AEF's first major action on the Western Front. Any army which depended on a part-time militia, organized on quasi-democratic grounds, was suspect to a European professional officer:

Germany military opinion, however, tended to regard such a militia system, backed up by a small, standing, 'mercenary' army, as obsolete and possessing a very low level of military efficiency [. . .] German observers fully appreciated America possessed a 'huge reservoir' for a wartime voluntary army (14,767,011 on 1 January 1908), but in the short term the US could not despatch an expeditionary force of more than 200,000. In these circumstances, America's military potential had to be considered irrelevant for the European balance. Moreover, despite attempts by American military reformers to copy German military regulations (as the British did too), the American standard still seemed to fall well below the European norm. In 1912 the American Secretary for War, Henry S. Stimson, himself described the combat worth of the army, divided up in 49 garrisons over 24 states and territories, as zero.[39]

But there is good cause to suspect that German intelligence reports belittling the combat efficiency of the doughboys during the war did so partly to boost German morale. It is rare that staff reports can be magnanimous enough to concede that defeat occurred simply because the enemy was intrinsically better; better equipped, better led, better prepared perhaps – but not innately superior fighting material, which was in many respects the case in 1918. If it were possible to match the typical AEF soldier with his German counterpart in 1918 the balance sheet would probably have put experience, wiliness, weariness, hunger, anxiety, illness, and personal initiative on the side of the German; while fearlessness, fitness, inexperience, naivety, poor basic military skills, determination, and above all a sense of justice would be the basic composition for the doughboy. German analysts immediately after defeat attempted to explain their humiliation by resorting to the 'stab-in-the-back' theory, the *Dolchstoss*, in which the doughboys arrived on the scene not to scale an impregnable castle but to assist in pushing over an already rotten termite heap that had been eaten away from within. Yet both arguments are obviously true: while the AEF was slow to get into the front line, its growing presence was, by mid-1918, a guarantee that the war could not now be lost; this in turn discouraged German politicians, generals and civilians from hoping that they might hang on and secure a negotiated peace. The mere presence of growing numbers of Americans was an enormous factor in the minds of front-line German troops considering whether to fight or flee; it was equally influential in the rear, among the generals and politicians. Ludendorff in 1927 had no doubt about what swung the balance of the war, when he discussed the Second Battle of the Marne:

> With more than a million fresh, young, ardent Americans pressing forward into the battle, the result was inevitable [. . .] The tremendous superabundance of pent-up, untapped nervous energy which America's troops brought into the fray more than balanced the weakness of their allies, who were utterly exhausted.
>
> It was assuredly the Americans who bore the heaviest brunt of the fighting on the whole battlefront during the last few months of the war. The German field army found them much more aggressive in attack than either the English [sic] or the French. [. . .]
>
> Regarding the actual fighting of the Americans, their attacks were undoubtedly brave and often reckless. They lacked sufficient dexterity or experience in availing themselves of topographical cover or protection. They came right on in open field and attacked in units much too closely formed. Their lack of actual field experience accounts for some extraordinarily heavy losses.[40]

Ludendorff's 1927 opinion was supported by a report dated 28 October 1918 written by someone who was extremely well placed to understand the strengths and weaknesses of the doughboys, General von Gallwitz, who was then busily engaged in trying to fend them off in the Meuse–Argonne offensive. Von Gallwitz summarizes perfectly the strengths (youth, freshness, vigour, numbers) and weaknesses (recklessness, naivety, impetuosity) of the AEF:

> The Americans are particularly fresh and numerically strong. They have also put excellent material into the first combat divisions. Men in their twenties. But these good divisions have suffered absolutely colossal casualties. The Americans are affected by this. Their morale is therefore not elated. Their political awareness is shockingly low, but they are men of fresh, rude strength and in their prime. But it may be assumed that the reinforcement transports

will now bring the older classes. The Americans are to be highly rated as enemies, but due to heavy losses their offensive power has now greatly declined. But after reinforcements they will undoubtedly proceed to new attacks.[41]

It must also be said that the German army faced by the AEF in 1918 was not the same impressive force which swept all before it in 1914. After March 1918 most divisions were 50 per cent below strength, and elite I Class Divisions (the German army categorized its divisions into four classes) were few and far between. The Alpenkorps, 1st Guard, 1 Bavarian, 10th Reserve, 12th, 17th, 26th, 33rd, and 50th Divisions were regarded as I Class. The most common type of division was the II Class, deemed to be average, meaning it was reliable but that was about all. III Class divisions were considered adequate for most defensive duties, but poor in attack. IV Class units, mostly Landwehr, were regarded as suitable only for defence in normally quiet sectors. In late 1917 when the German High Command reorganized its divisions for the series of offensives in spring and summer 1918, it developed three other categories: the highly trained and splendidly equipped *Stoss* divisions, geared up entirely for relentless assault; the average divisions and the position-holding *Stellungs-Divisionen*. Out of a total of some 250 divisions, only seventy were regarded as being of *Stoss* quality.

The reality is that the inexperience and poor leadership of its junior officers, together with the relatively untrained nature of most of the soldiers, negated the impact of the AEF's freshness and high morale; its quality was crucial in morale terms but only its quantity swung the balance. The unquenchably high morale of the doughboys (a result partly of not having spent long in the trenches) enabled them to press home the kind of attacks that, had they been launched even a few months earlier in the war when the German divisions were less disillusioned and more determined to resist, would have caused considerably greater slaughter among their ranks.

10

Filth, Food and
Fornication

War is [. . .] 75 per cent an engineering and sanitary problem
and a little less than 25 per cent a military one [. . .] some of the
reckless courage of the American troops in the late war was
stimulated by the knowledge that in front of them were only
the Germans, but behind them were the assembled surgeons of
America, with sleeves rolled up.   Hans Zinsser[1]

The conventional view of life on the Western Front in 1917–18 is that
of an unending, continuous version of hell, with a permanent threat
of being mashed, mangled, torn asunder and ripped apart. Yet while
the conditions under which most soldiers existed for most of the time
were upsetting and offensive, life-threatening events resulting from
military action were comparatively unusual in the daily existence of
the typical doughboy. The suffering he most commonly endured
derived from more banal things, such as being perpetually at the mercy
of the elements, a poor diet, the filthy grime, and the ubiquitous 'cootie'
or louse. The stench of living and dead bodies, the appalling noise and
excruciating boredom, added to the awful purgatory. After a few weeks
on the Western Front in the early part of 1918 Private Yensen conducted
an audit of his enemies, ranked in order of dread:

Our officers head the list, because they never do us any good; they're cranky,
arrogant and unreasonable. They have so much power that they can have us
shot for nothing if they want to; and since we have no protection against
them, I call them our arch-enemies.

The weather ranks second because in these leaky clothes, the cold rain and
mud are slowly sapping the life out of us [. . .]

The mules come third because they are mostly white-eyed outlaws – so dangerous that the civilians sold them to the army to get rid of 'em. We have to take care of them before ourselves, which is all the way from disagreeable to impossible.

Our leaky clothes come fourth because only our steel helmets turn water – and they sit way up on our heads like pie-pans instead of coming down around our ears where they could do some good. Our wool clothes would be fine if they fit and were of a comfortable design and were protected by rain-coats that were rain-coats. Our feet are wet *all* the time [. . .]

The cooties come fifth [. . .]

The canned potato-meat hash comes sixth because it gives us heartburn. Our rations are half meat and the other half is made up of potatoes, bread, coffee, rice, dried carrots and too little fruit. We crave sweets, milk and fruit.

Homesickness comes seventh. Most of us have never been away from home before, and we're so hungry for a little womanly affection that it's awful.

The Germans come last, because if it wasn't for them we could go home![2]

When he and his brother Walt were demobilized at Fort Wayne, Indiana, in August 1919, they quickly found themselves some girls, one of whom said it must have been dreadful to have been shelled: 'Why, no!' Walt said, 'It was the only thing that made the war interesting.'[3]

It was impossible to keep clean in the trenches. Dirt bred disease, and with only the most primitive drugs, many diseases which are today innocuous could be life-threatening. They also sapped the AEF's fighting power. Official figures show 71 per cent of duty-time lost in the AEF in France was through disease, against just 22 per cent from battle injuries. In 1918, influenza, pneumonia and other respiratory diseases caused 17.33 per cent of all AEF hospital admissions for disease and 82 per cent of illness-related deaths. The same year the total number of AEF soldiers admitted to hospital for disease was 2,422,362; for ordinary injuries 182,789; just 27,855 were hospitalized as a result of battle injuries.[4]

Officers were as prone to succumb to bullet or bug as their charges, but their daily grind was rather less onerous thanks to their entitlement to a servant. In his time 2nd Lieutenant John D. Clark had several:

Every officer had his own orderly (popularly referred to as a 'striker' or 'dog robber') who took care of his horse and performed other personal duties. It was always a voluntary assignment which carried some extra income provided by the officer. At the time we went into the Champagne [the Allied attack started in that region on 3 October 1918], I had a fine young lad named Martin Roy, who hailed from the Pennsylvania coal fields. One day he spoke to me and said that in as much as the echelon [a position in the rear] was so far behind the gun positions it might seem that he was shirking danger; therefore, he requested assignment with the guns. Although I explained that the echelon assignment was only temporary, he persisted in his request and I had him transferred. The next day he was killed.[5]

The average doughboy who saw any action at all – and many did not – spent around seven days under fire all told. This statistical flattening-out of their experience inevitably disguises the individual intensity of many soldiers' experience, but one thing united them all – the louse, 'cootie' or 'seam squirrel'. These parasites were not merely a nuisance. They were also the cause of many of the trench fevers that would afflict soldiers for several days, laying them low with fierce temperatures and bodily weakness.

The vermin were about the size and color of small grains of uncooked rice until they would gorge themselves on the blood of their victims. Apparently their digestive system was in the shape of a cross, since when they were well-fed a black cross could readily be seen. The troops considered this a black German Iron Cross. It was a standing joke that there was no point in scratching because the little buggers had legs on both sides. The Army had a 'delousing' program which consisted of, thank God infrequent, visits of a large tank-truck-like device and a steam generator. We were required to completely disrobe and toss our clothes into a bundle which was then thrown into the tank and live steam cooked the bugs. During this time we froze, of course, since the contraption never came on a nice warm day, but usually made its appearance during the winter months. After submitting to this we were louse-free until we crawled back into the hay beds, when we again became infested.⁶

There was not much to be done about the cootie, except to grin and bear it. In a June 1918 issue of *Stars and Stripes*, 'W.D.B.' offered this 'remedy' for the cootie:

First, get a rope or wire, rope preferred, that is about 30 feet long and has two ends. Be sure you get both ends. Then place one end on the ground and the other in the air, climb up and place some cheese or butter – butter preferred – on the top, then come down and hide. You will not have to wait long before a Mr Cootie will be along. He, of course, hears the butter or cheese up on the rope or wire, and goes up to get a bite. Now, climb up yourself and cut the wire or rope about two feet below Mr Cootie and place on that end an ice cream cone. Then come down and hide. Mr Cootie will get all the butter or cheese he wants and start down, not knowing the wire or rope is cut, and fall in the ice cream cone and freeze to death.

The same cheese or butter will work for a day or more, if you remove the dead immediately.

The cootie was but one element in a generally filthy existence, a lifestyle which shocked and distressed most doughboys, who could never accustom themselves to the coarseness of the French billets – usually farmyard buildings – they were expected to occupy when in the rear areas. US armies traditionally built their own encampments but the exigencies of trench warfare made this expensively pointless and French billets were generally used. Many doughboys decided that a leading feature of the French character was a distinct lack of interest in basic hygiene:

[To] one of the conditions of this life of billeting the American soldiers never did fully adapt themselves. It was to the *fumier* – the heap of manure piled at the front door of every villager – the sign of his thrift and even of his wealth, but a disagreeable thing, irritating and dangerous in the dark, and a kind of front yard ornamentation to which our soldiers could never grow accustomed [. . .] this one little thing was the cause of more impatience and irritation of American soldiers toward the French population than anything that I can now remember. The French villagers' habit of having farm animals and people living close together under the same roof was repulsive to our sensibilities.[7]

Food – or rather the poor quality of it – was another item constantly on the mind of the doughboy, a source of jokes, grousing and ever-receding promise. Sometimes they struck lucky, as did 1st Lieutenant Donnelly, who had a delightfully authentic introduction to French cuisine, being served for his first breakfast in a comfortable house

croissants, Bar-le-Duc redcurrant jelly and hot chocolate [. . .] The previous night I had been too tired to take a good look at my quarters; now, in the light of a cloudless day, I saw that I had not only a bedroom but also a large living room, both with tiled floors and beamed ceilings. There was a big window facing the river, from which there was a panoramic view of the Cher valley; never again during the war would I have such pleasant living arrangements.[8]

But for the vast majority there never seemed to be enough to eat. All too often they were dished up a variant on what they feelingly called 'slum' or 'goldfish' – respectively a basic stew of infinite variety but little appeal, and canned salmon. Another staple was 'monkey meat' (variously described as 'Argentine horse meat' or 'corned beef'). When they were permitted to light fires – a rarity in the front lines – the soldiers would invariably add whatever ingredients they could lay their hands on to the 'monkey meat' to produce 'slum'. Soon after arriving in France Private Benjamin Dexter 'Heard a ruckus; a whole contingent came along. They had a stretcher with an imitation of a monkey. They had a sign, saying, "Be it resolved. When we get home again we will petition Congress to enact laws to the effect that in future wars troops won't have to eat his ancestors."'[9]

The average doughboy was generally much fitter, healthier, younger, better fed and paid rather more than either his Allied comrades-in-arms or his German enemy. In fact a doughboy's rations were – in theory – the best enjoyed by any soldier in the conflict.[10] The American garrison ration of the time, if issued in its entirety, had a total fuel value of 4,100–4,200 calories; the British was 3,000–3,600; the French 3,400.[11]

In 1917–18 the average US soldier ate nearly three-quarters of a ton of food each year at a cost (not counting transport and handling costs, and because of food shortages in Britain and France the overwhelming bulk of US rations were shipped from America) of about $165. The daily cost of feeding the US army in 1918 was estimated at $2,500,000. A billion cans of food were sent from the United States to the AEF in France in 1918.[12]

AEF soldiers individually were on a notional ration of 456 pounds of beef a year, or 1.25 pounds a day, though few regularly received this. This meat was no prime rib steak but usually canned Argentine beef which had been frozen and packed in Chicago, and had often seen better days. Army regulations permitted the substitution of pork, in the form of bacon, for 30 per cent of the beef ration. In any case the practice, especially under battle conditions, was very different from the theory. Private Malcolm D. Aitken, of the 5th Marines, recalled later the kind of stuff his comrades received when engaged in the fight at Belleau Wood in June 1918:

We had been living on cold canned tomatoes, cold canned beef and Argentine Bully Beef (French Ration, in red or blue #1 size can. The red one always had a slice of carrot on the top and was in demand, for it was thought better chewing. Once a day while we were still in [the] fox-hole [. . .] a member of the ration gang would stroll along the line with a #10 size can of the sweet, rough, juicy French Quince jam, ladling a spoonful on our messpan lid as he went along. This, one day, resulted in a whizbang centering on the flashing movement of the can; one hit fore, next one hit after him, and he really started going, throwing the jam in the direction he thought we should be. We picked up what we could after the can and he and the whizbang had proceeded down the line. What if dirt was with it?[13]

But despite the inevitable complaints from the rank-and-file, that the doughboys got as much as they did was a further testament to the almost superhuman logistical effort involved in transporting vast quantities of food across the Atlantic. After the war one senior officer calculated the total food consumption of the US army at its peak, of almost four million men, during 1917–18, using the graphic image of regarding the whole as if it were one single meal consumed by

one gigantic figure in khaki [. . .] Let us start off with the main course; the
roast of beef placed before this giant weighs 800,000,000 pounds; and this is
flanked by a rasher of bacon weighing 150,000,000 pounds more. The loaf
from which his bread is cut required over 1,000,000,000 pounds of flour in
its making, and to spread it required a lump of butter weighing 17,500,000
pounds, and another lump of 11,000,000 pounds of oleomargarine, As a side
dish there is provided 150,000,000 pounds of beans, baked [. . .] The potatoes
for this meal weighed 487,000,000 pounds, and to add gusto to his appetite
there were served 40,000,000 pounds of onions. Scattered over the table are
such items as 150,000,000 cans of peas, corn and string beans. His salad
contains 50,000,000 cans of salmon and 750,000 tins of sardines. The large
bowl of tomatoes received 190,000,000 tins of solid pack, and for dessert he
had 67,000,000 pounds of prunes and 40,000,000 pounds of evaporated
peaches and apples. The sugar for sweetening the various dishes on the table
weighed 350,000,000 pounds, and he washed it down with a draught made
from 75,000,000 pounds of coffee diluted with 200,000,000 cans of evaporated milk, and for this meal the American people paid $727,092,430.44. It is
estimated that each soldier weighed 12 pounds more at his discharge than
when his enlistment or the Selective Service Act brought him into the Army,
hence this giant arose from that meal with 45,000,000 pounds of added brawn
and energy which will be felt for generations to come.[14]

Statistics cut little ice with the typical doughboy, whose experience
of rations could be very poor indeed:

To read the official reports of the Army Quartermaster after the war, one
would think that we had lived high on the hog. This was relatively true in the
rear areas but not in the combat zone. We had two meals a day, most of the
time. The ration was supposed to be canned meat, hard bread, beans, potatoes,
dried fruit or jam, coffee, sugar, salt and pepper. Substitute items were canned
tomatoes, canned salmon, powdered eggs and corn syrup [. . .] For weeks
we had only substitute items instead of the regular ration; even bread was
scarce and the coffee was lukewarm slop by the time it came to us. Most of
the time we had canned salmon and canned tomatoes with coffee. I became
so sick of salmon [. . .] that it was years after the war before I could eat any.
As for the eggs, out of respect for the innocent and patriotic hens who did
their best for the war effort, I refrain from commenting on the terrible

transformation to which their eggs were subjected before they came to us.[15]

Throughout history, for soldiers the best-tasting food has been that which is either scrounged or stolen. In the First World War the appalling conditions made any meal even slightly out of the ordinary seem fabulous. Private Yensen and his buddies decided to acquire some food to celebrate the Fourth of July, 1918:

Today was the Fourth of July; so eight of us either bought, or stole, the following: half a gallon of jelly, a pound of butter, a cake of cheese, a long loaf of French rye-bread, four packages of hardtack, a can of tomatoes, a can of corn bill, a sack of peanuts, a sack of almonds and oodles of doughnuts. All this we carried back into the woods, built a fire and gorged ourselves. On the way home we all said it was the best Fourth of July we'd ever had, meaning, of course, that it was the best meal we'd had in a long time.[16]

While the doughboys were accustoming themselves to the privations of trench life, their families in America were increasingly subject to strictures from the federal government, interfering in all aspects of daily life, not least what was on the dinner table. The 'Clean Plate' campaign, started in the States by Herbert Hoover, who had been appointed America's national food tsar following his remarkable success at organizing charity relief for occupied Belgium, swung into action soon after America entered the war. Hoover's propaganda drive was aimed at persuading Americans to think that they too could do their bit for the war effort by eating everything and leaving no waste.[17] As in other quarters of US civil existence this basically sound idea soon developed into a nationwide frenzy, and spilled over into the AEF. On 29 April 1918 Bulletin No. 21 emanated from GHQ AEF at Chaumont, signed by General James Harbord and stamped 'By Command of General Pershing'. This piece of bureaucratic nonsense dealt with the baking of loaves in a new style; item 4 gave instructions as to how the loaf must be sliced:

This new loaf, being about 12 inches wide and about 24 inches long, should be cut in half, through the long dimension, so as to leave the halves about 24 inches long and about 6 inches wide, and of the same thickness which the loaf had when baked. After the loaf is thus divided it should be turned up on edge, with the edge made by the first cutting operation flat on the table. Then slice by using the sawing motion, cutting the slices from the top edge, through the loaf, to the table.[18]

As the war dragged on into late 1918 the Allies' demands for increasing reinforcements meant that many elements of a healthy diet were left behind on the quaysides of US ports. Fruit and vegetables were squeezed out in favour of more soldiers. Many doughboys found themselves consuming an unbearably dull diet, consisting, bizarrely enough, of a lot of tomato juice:

During the spring of 1918, when the necessity of transporting troops reduced transportation of supplies to everything but essentials, it became necessary to eliminate to a great extent from AEF shipments canned vegetables and fruits such as peas, corn, sweet potatoes, asparagus, pineapple, pears, and apples. As a result, tomato purchases exceeded those of all other vegetables combined, the Army taking 45 per cent of the total American pack. Because of its food value and slight acidity, a quart of tomato juice was equal to several quarts of water for thirsty field parties, and it also was of great value in feeding soldiers in the trenches.[19]

Nutritious and thirst-quenching it may have been, but doughboys often longed for something rather more potent. US soldiers were officially permitted to buy 'light wines' and beer but other fortifying drinks, such as champagne, whisky and brandy, were banned, and any establishment where such spirits were sold was off-limits. Of course this semi-Prohibition was vigorously challenged whenever possible and despite Pershing's pretence that there was 'comparatively little drinking in our armies and what there was decreased noticeably after the prohibition of strong drink',[20] the doughboys did their fair share of boozing. Indeed, many of them abandoned their old teetotal ways for the pleasures of the bottle – any bottle. Charles Donnelly, then twenty-one, had been teetotal all his life before landing in France but within his first week he 'soon got acquainted with a local drink called *vermouth et cassis* which was rather sweet and gave no hint that it was alcoholic until a few had been drowned; then it had a sneaky way of letting you know that you should have stopped before you took the last one or two.'

A couple of weeks later he was sampling champagne and 'learned that night that champagne will give one the worst hangover of any alcoholic drink, except perhaps absinthe'.

Yet despite the ban on the consumption of strong liquor, and the ease of access to alcohol in France, the officially recorded degree of alcoholism in the US army dropped to a remarkably low level during the two war years, at just 2.5 cases per thousand in 1917 and 1.1 in 1918, against an average 18.44 cases in the previous decade.[21]

There was a degree of hypocrisy in the way the AEF's top officers handled the alcohol question, just as there was over the issue of sexual relations with French and, later, during the Occupation, German women. The AEF's senior officers paid lip service to concern over the morals of the ordinary soldier, but the provision of YMCA and other voluntary organization entertainments, clubs and shows, along with the establishment of some educational outlets, was made partly with a view to the public image back home, and partly from the belief that the devil finds work for idle hands. In any case, the AEF's General Staff undermined the dignity and practical efforts of the army chaplains, who had as their main concern the troops' moral welfare. In the summer of 1917 Samuel Arthur Devan, a Baptist minister at Bryn Mawr, Pennsylvania, applied for a commission as a chaplain in the army. He was assigned to the 58th Regiment of the Coast Artillery Corps. It is quite evident from many accounts, including Devan's, that officers felt that while alcohol was perfectly acceptable for themselves, it should certainly be denied to the enlisted men – and especially black Americans:

July 11th. Last night we had some little excitement among the higher officers here. The colonel who is sometimes very unmanageable went off on a rampage on the subject of drinking. Possibly I had given the key-note to the day by having (soon after breakfast) asked for clemency for a man, McKnoll, who has been in the pen longer than is good either for him or the service. My right to prefer the request was cordially admitted, but the request itself was most vigorously refused. By evening the colonel was in a very wrought up state, and, as it chanced, several circumstances came to light which rendered him even more so. He was for issuing orders of a drastic kind that we all felt would be harmful. The question of liquor here is an extremely delicate and difficult one. No one is a more whole-hearted adversary of alcohol than I am, but I know that drastic rules that have no possibility of being enforced, in a country like this, are far from being a satisfactory solution.[22]

Devan's pragmatic attitude concerning alcohol should also have been implemented concerning fornication. The doughboys were subjected to a somewhat more stringent regime in this respect than any other troops on the Western Front. It was not even clear if simple fraternization with local women was permitted. One of the more gifted memoirists from the AEF's ranks was Captain (later Major) Arthur W. Little, of the 369th Infantry Regiment. Little served happily with the 369th for two years but found the AEF a generally exasperating organization:

The American Expeditionary Forces had the American law-making habit to an exaggerated degree: orders were ground out more rapidly than they could possibly be read and digested by anyone who had anything else to do. As for remembering them – such a thing was out of the question [. . .] Some of these law-making orders were comical. There was one that was presented to us just before going ashore at Brest that always impressed me as being a perfect example of the product of a small man in a big place. And I don't know who wrote the order either. In effect this is what it said:

'Officers are not permitted to be seen in public with women of bad reputation; and a woman of bad reputation, for the purposes of this order, will be considered to be, any woman who may be seen in public with an officer.'[23]

As for the type of women who might conceivably have been deemed at the time to be of 'bad reputation' – prostitutes – the AEF tried to impose on the rank-and-file soldier impossible standards. The French embraced the inevitable and established a system of licensed brothels behind the front lines: establishments with a blue light over the front door were for officers, those with a red light were for other ranks. The typical charge was 15 francs for thirty minutes, or about $2.85 at the contemporary exchange rate. British troops were perfectly free to visit these establishments until in May 1918 the British War Office ruled them out of bounds. Even then the British authorities preferred to turn a blind eye. For the first four months after arriving in France the doughboys were not under any formal ban from visiting brothels. This changed once Pershing realized how serious a problem VD was for the British and French, who both lost millions of troops' days each year as a result of sexually communicable diseases. Doughboys were then formally banned, on pain of severe punishment, from visiting brothels:

Venereal diseases were from the first the subject of grave concern to General Pershing, and he took a great and useful interest in their prevention. The problem was aggravated by the fundamental differences of opinion between the French and the Americans as to the best means of prevention and control. The French believed that the legalization and control of prostitution were important and highly desirable, and they acted on that belief. The Americans believed that such measures were pernicious and most undesirable, and they acted on their belief. These contradictory opinions were never brought into accord.[24]

Being barred from bordellos is one thing, abstinence is another. There is no way of quantifying how many doughboys had sexual relations with prostitutes or those who did not charge for the service, but it is evident from the archives that the typical AEF soldier had a normal inclination to indulge this need whenever possible. Various inter-Allied conferences were held throughout the war on what Pershing euphemistically referred to as 'this age-long evil', all failing to persuade the French to close down the licensed brothels. Some AEF chaplains tried to persuade men of the dangers of VD, rather than preach the virtues of prophylaxis: 'We had [a] saying "15 minutes with Venus and 3 years with Mercury." This was prior to the invention of penicillin.'[25]

Enlightened officers and voluntary workers from the many organizations in France tried to encourage the American soldiers to take disease-preventive measures. This often fell on deaf ears. Arthur Yensen confessed to his diary while in England *en route* to France that he was glad the war was being fought there rather than in England because the English girls he saw were singularly unattractive. But French sexual mores were puzzling for many doughboys, who had been raised in a more conservative and prudish environment. They failed to understand that French frankness about sex was just that, an open-minded recognition that the impulse towards procreation was not possible to repress and indeed should not be stifled but recognized and accepted. As Yensen wrote in July 1918:

Most of the Americans mistake the frank attitude of the French people on matters of sex for vulgarity, which, of course, is causing a great deal of misunderstanding. Some of the boys say there isn't a decent woman in France, while the rest of us argue that there are as many good women in France in proportion to the population as in America. Here if you ask a decent French woman to go to bed with you, she'll politely say no, and instead of being insulted, will tell you where to go to get what you want – always keeping herself above reproach.

Ordinarily we get acquainted with only the lowest class here just as we did around Ft. Leavenworth or Kansas City; so it's my contention that we can't judge the women of France by the scum we meet here any more than we can judge the women of America by the chippies that congregate around the army camps back home. If I had a daughter I wouldn't trust her very far with the average man in this outfit, and I suppose the respectable French people feel the same way.[26]

Sex, and the effort to get it, was a common preoccupation of dough boys, no matter where they found themselves. Thus Douglas Osborn, a 2nd Lieutenant of the 31st Regiment of Infantry on his way through Japan to Vladivostok, recorded on 21 March 1919 how he and a couple of comrades visited a bar in Nagasaki:

Red and Frank picked up a couple of girls in there. As for me, I can't see anything in em at all. There is one girl in there tho, that is really pretty. Then we bummed around some more & went for a ride way out to the end of town to some baths that are very much patronized by men and women in summer. After dinner a whole party of us went up to a bath house and I had a bath where a Jap girl comes in washed me all over. Gee! It was some time![27]

Captain Joseph Loughran, a Roman Catholic army chaplain, volunteered in December 1919 to act as chaplain to those units of the 27th Infantry stationed at Lake Baikal in Siberia. When in January 1920 the Americans received orders hurriedly to pull out of Siberia, it was Loughran's job to marry all the doughboys who were keen to wed their Siberian sweethearts. He was then placed in command of a special train – dubbed the 'Bridal Special' by Colonel C. H. Morrow, commander of the 27th Infantry – to transport the seventy-eight brides from Lake Baikal to Vladivostok, a distance of 2,400 miles, which took three weeks, thanks to the antiquated state of the locomotives and the collapsing box-car carriages. During the journey the Bridal Special arrived at Chita, a junction where the Trans-Siberian railway intersected with the Chinese Eastern Railway, to Peking.

It was a bitter, cold night when the Colonel's [Morrow's] train drew alongside ours. A guard came from his train and told me that the Colonel would like to see me. I complied and met the Colonel in his very de luxe and lavish Wagon-Lit coach, which was in striking contrast to our barren, box-car quarters [. . .] Then he asked me a rather ridiculous question, (in view of the freezing weather). He wanted to know whether my brides had had a recent bath. I naturally replied, 'Certainly not.'

Now the Colonel knew, as we all did, that every Russian city of the size of Chita would have a public bath, so he turned to me and said, 'Chaplain, I wish these women to have a bath, and you will personally supervise it.' I said, 'Very well sir,' of course.

When I returned to my car, I sent for the sergeant and gave him the order to take the women to the public bath in groups of ten, and to personally supervise the operation. He gave an audible groan. However, he promptly gathered the complaining women together, and I saw him take the first group of ten to the public bath. Since he was a fine soldier, I am sure that he carried out the command to the letter, as he subsequently reported back to me.[28]

Yet perhaps the anti-VD propaganda worked, after all. In 1917 more than 12 per cent of the US army reported sick with various types of venereal disease, a figure large enough to cause real concern but still below the 16 per cent of 1902.

Venereal disease was not, however, the biggest cause of non-combat debilitation. While there were 57,195 cases of VD admitted for medical treatment in the AEF (causing 1.7 million days lost from duty in 1918), there were more than 40 million days lost from duty from all types of disease that same year. Compared with just 12.5 million days lost as a result of injuries sustained in battle, it is clear that dirt, lice, cold, damp and poor diet posed threats to health three times greater than a German machine-gunner.[29] But death was ultimately relatively even-handed; if you were a doughboy you had about as much chance of dying from influenza as from a whizz-bang. In 1917–18 the AEF suffered 50,714 deaths from disease and 52,423 as a result of injuries associated with combat, including those lost at sea.[30]

Disease, boredom, lassitude, exhaustion – all excellent breeding grounds for moral decay and collapse into sin. Surely Pershing would have realized this and exercised great care to nurture his army chaplains? Not a bit of it. By 2 August 1918 Samuel Devan was confessing to his journal in a bitterly despondent fashion:

Am quite disgusted tonight. After fighting for two days to get a Summary instead of a General court martial for a boy who, exasperated beyond endurance, beat up a bullying sergeant, I returned to my room and found some unflattering communications from the Chaplain's Office of General Head quarters of the American Expeditionary Force, communications which showed just how contemptuous the Army heads are of their Chaplains. I was told that 'the question of transportation at the front is a problem which has to be solved by each one (i.e. Chaplain) according to circumstances. The elements of transportation are lacking and are not provided by the Quartermaster except in exceptional circumstances. So that a Chaplain at present has to avail himself of such occasional opportunities which fall in his way when motor vehicles are passing thru, or by horse and even bicycle.

Moreover, Devan was also informed that night by official communication that chaplains would no longer be permitted to wear the insignia of the regiment or division to which they were attached – and this was on top of an army rule that no chaplain would be promoted to any rank higher than 1st Lieutenant before he had completed seven years' service.

No transportation, no training, no office, no corps, no rank, no funds. 'Here is no straw and no clay – now, go and make bricks!' they command. This gives them a reasonable excuse for complaining that Chaplains are inefficient, that good men will not go into the Army and all the other ways they have of finding fault [. . .] In the medical corps a man may be made a colonel right out of civil life [. . .] But a Chaplain must begin as a 1st Lieut. and remain that for seven years. Were he as efficient as St Paul or the Archangel Gabriel he could not be promoted short of that time, though to say the truth, it is probably [*sic*] that either of those worthies would be more likely to receive a dismissal 'for the good of the service' [. . .] So much for the rank awarded to a chaplain. Not even that is to be taken away – no insignia of rank of any kind may be worn henceforth, nor may he show to what arm of the service, or what regiment he belongs, tho the wearing of that has always served as a tie that helped bind a chaplain affectionately to the officers and men of his regiment. The idea is to make it plain to all the world that the chaplain is neither a soldier nor an officer – only a chaplain.

The chaplains looked to the voluntary services to help them keep the doughboys from falling into immorality. But these agencies were not on the whole popular with the majority of doughboys. In Siberia the YMCA was nicknamed 'You Must Come Across' because it seemed to make the soldiers pay for everything, including cigarettes, which were notionally free to all serving American soldiers overseas. Only one agency gained the undying and unforced affection of the doughboys – the Salvation Army. When he was eighty-seven years old, former Corporal Charles Bishop, intensely proud of his membership of the 26th (Yankee, National Guard) Division, still remembered the generosity and courage of the Salvation Army officers he met:

Greatest & best non combat outfit, SALVATION ARMY, right at the line along with us. Wearing gas masks and helmets like us Doughboys, and made D.Nuts right when the shells were flying. Also huts back or the lines. AND NO money was needed if you had none which we had very little but the SA everything free. The only & only outfit that ever gave us free coffee D.Nuts cigs clean socks [. . .] They were our real Buddies of our men and [. . .] they never forgot us and we will never forget them.[31]

Yet despite all these hardships and the threat of suffering any number of excruciating ways of dying, the war brought out a degree of dedication and loyalty from the American soldier scarcely seen before or since. The total number of instances of soldiers going absent without leave was 4,316 (in the United States and abroad) between 6 April 1917 and 30 November 1918, while between 6 April 1917 and 31 December 1918, 5,584 were charged with desertion, and 2,657 were convicted. The death sentence was passed on only twenty-four of those deserters, and inflicted on none of them. The 1917 rate of desertion was lower than in any year since 1909; and in 1918, the desertion rate was the lowest in percentage terms since 1830. Running away in France of course made rather less sense than running away in the United States; deserters found it less easy to go undetected. But although the AEF had its fair share of stragglers, when the shells started flying and conditions grew rough, by and large it was an army of cohesive power, fuelled by a united sense of purpose.

11

January–June 1918

War [is like] being carried in a two-handed basket, by two of His
Satanic Majesty's Imps, grinning and yowling; the rougher the
going the bigger the grin and the fiercer the yowling as they carried
me through the thirteen different kinds of hell.

Private Malcolm D. Aitken[1]

As 1918 opened, Colonel Hugh Drum feared the worst for the coming
year:

From a military view point Germany is stronger in the West today than she
has been since 1914. She [has] 170 divisions at least against British 54 and
French 93. Germany can in the next three months bring to the Western Front
230 Divs including 25 Austrian [. . .] I am fearfull [*sic*] that we are falling
into a French and British trap [. . .] they are persistent in their endeavors to
have us let them absorb our Army in theirs [. . .] They want to fill them up
with our inf. If I did not feel that Germany could be held by the B & F I would
not oppose it. If this is the only way to hold him next spring it is all right, but
I believe that Germany's defeat is to come in 1919 & by us. The longer we
put off forming Armies corps etc the longer Germany will be able to stand up
– then what about peace terms, we have no Army etc, how about the effect
on our people [. . .]

We have 180,000 men (Jan 27 1918) in France. Only 85,000 of them are
with the fighting troops.[2]

In the scales against Drum's gloomy foreboding was set the gathering
flood of doughboys sailing across the Atlantic. On 6 February Donnelly
– now part of the 1st Battalion of the newly-formed 119th Field
Artillery Regiment – was on his way to Hoboken via New Orleans,

headed for France. The send-off for his 32nd Division from Camp Robinson had scarcely been the heroic farewell he had hoped for. As they marched to the train,

> some townspeople stood on the curbs and watched with varying degrees of interest. A few older men yelled some good-natured jeers: 'You going to lick the Kaiser?' and 'Why don't you get some real jobs instead of playing soldier?' There was no apparent hostility but I was a bit shocked to realize that some citizens looked upon the National Guard as less than heroic.[3]

On 27 February Donnelly and his buddies were handed their full kit at Hoboken, the main embarkation point in the States for the doughboys:

> Each man was issued a pistol belt, first aid kit, extra blouse and breeches, extra pair of shoes, haversack, blanket, rifle, bayonet and scabbard; they already had mess kits and canteens. For my part [he had been promoted to 1st lieutenant] I had to supply myself with two uniforms, boots, puttees, shoes, shirts, underwear, socks, six white stocks, six white shirts, bedding roll with two blankets, musette bag, gas mask, folding wash basin, folding bucket, hatchet, pup tent with pegs, overseas cap, garrison cap, Sam Browne belt, mess kit, pistol, pistol belt, extra clips for pistol, first aid kit, folding shovel for digging foxholes, toilet articles, binoculars, flashlight, raincoat, overcoat and two footlockers to hold the stuff [. . .] tons and tons of unnecessary equipment were shipped to France, stored in warehouses for the duration and finally shipped home again without ever being used.[4]

Donnelly's transport, the *America*, arrived in Brest on Sunday, 10 March. The port was, as usual, completely jammed with ships, stevedores, supplies and soldiers. The general chaos was a sight to behold. Next morning Donnelly, still on board the *America*, watched a couple of lighters come alongside and begin to unload. In one of the huge nets coming up from the holds he spotted one of his footlockers. He could tell it was his because he saw inscribed on it a large red circle of his own creation. The net was so heavy it looked as though the crane might topple over. Out it swung, over the ocean and snap! – all the gear crashed into the water. When he left France in 1919 Donnelly was given his missing footlocker; its contents were ruined after having spent a year in salty waterlogged storage.

But at least Donnelly landed safely on shore; a few did not. Thanks to the convoy system almost all the doughboys were ferried safely across the Atlantic, but to claim (as some historians have) that no doughboys died as a result of U-boat attacks is not correct.

At the Armistice the American Expeditionary Force, with a ration strength of 1,876,000, was actually larger than the BEF [British Expeditionary Force]. For both Britain and America, this huge concentration of military strength constituted the main effort of the nation in the war. And the U-boats proved powerless to prevent it, or even diminish it; the great hosts crossed the oceans of the world and the Narrow Seas without losing a man, a horse, or a gun.[5]

Not the U-boat, as it proved, but an unsuspected enemy was most fatal to our expeditionary soldiers on the ocean. *The submarine was not able to sink one troopship on the way to France*: the influenza epidemic of the autumn of 1918 cost the lives of over seven hundred American soldiers at sea.[6]

The truth is rather different; doughboys *were* torpedoed and some died in the freezing waters of the Atlantic, though relatively few, and the first such casualties did not occur until late in the war.[7] On 5 February 1918 the *Tuscania*, then a Cunard-owner liner (and thus a sister ship to the equally unfortunate but much better remembered *Lusitania*), was the first troopship carrying doughboys from the United States to France to be torpedoed in the First World War. She was attacked without warning in that killing ground favoured by U-boats, off the coast of Ireland. Contemporary accounts show this was no isolated catastrophe. The sinking of the *Tuscania* was followed by that of the *Moldovia*, another British auxiliary cruiser, in the English Channel in the early morning of 23 May 1918; she carried men of Companies A and B of the 58th Infantry Regiment, on their way to join the 4th Division in France. Fifty-five of them died, fifty-three from Company B, most of them trapped in the fore part of the ship, where the torpedo struck; another of Company B died of his injuries later, and one member of Company A was killed.[8]

But the *Tuscania* was the biggest disaster in the ferrying of American soldiers to Europe. Launched in September 1914, the *Tuscania* made her maiden voyage to New York in February 1915. When first floated she was considered the finest – and, at more than 550 feet and 14,348 tons gross, she was the biggest – of the Anchor line's fleet of five ships. In 1917 the Anchor Line leased the *Tuscania* to Cunard as a transatlantic troopship. On her last voyage she left the port of Hoboken, New Jersey, on Thursday, 24 January 1918. Besides her crew of 384 she carried more than 2,000 doughboys from the 6th Battalion, 20th Engineers, destined for the Service of Supply as well as medical units, three air squadrons, and four small units of the 32nd Division. The *Tuscania* was captained by a veteran of Atlantic crossing, Captain Peter McLean, a 51-year-old Glaswegian. Camouflaged with black-and-white zebra stripes and armed with a rapid-fire 4-inch gun, its destination was Le Havre. The *Tuscania* sailed as part of a thirteen-ship convoy, number HX-20. Among their number was the *Baltic*, which on this trip was carrying Canadian troops.

In the gathering darkness of the early evening of 5 February, with a ferocious squall blowing up, it was a miracle that the attacking U-boat could see clearly enough to hit anything. At about 5.40 p.m., when 'several hundred lumberjacks from the woods of Wisconsin and Michigan, forestry engineers, and aero-squadron men were at supper', the *Tuscania* was hit by a single torpedo.[9] The ship listed quickly onto her starboard side, where the torpedo had struck.

General Pershing asserted that while the *Tuscania* was sinking 'the fine discipline of the men and the efficient handling of a difficult situation by those in command, together with the splendid work of the British Navy, contributed to account for relatively light casualties'.[10] Accounts differ; others have argued that aboard the *Tuscania* there was some panic as in their anxious haste the crew and soldiers bitterly discovered that much of the lifeboat tackle had rusted. All knew that in the icy cold, pitch-black Atlantic there was precious little chance of survival. More than an hour after she was hit the *Tuscania* was still afloat, and some lifeboats had been launched. Two of the convoy's escorting British destroyers scoured the area, looking for survivors and depth-charging the U-boat. Some

800 of the *Tuscania*'s passengers and crew were rescued by the destroyer *Pigeon*. About five hours after being hit, the *Tuscania* finally slid below the waves, seven miles north of the Rathlin Island lighthouse.[11]

As so often, it was not the torpedo itself which caused the large loss of life, but the appalling weather conditions, the sub-zero temperature of the sea, and the swift onset of pitch-black night making searches impossible. The destroyers brought into the northern Irish port of Londonderry about 1,350 men, and to Larne another 550. Hundreds of others were thrown onto the coast in their lifeboats. Some sank beneath the waves very quickly. Certainly,

all the *Tuscania*'s company were not so fortunate as to land in Ireland. There were hundreds of men in the ship's boats which rowed away as she sank. These had the wind and the swift set of the North Channel current to contend with and these drove them eastward upon the jagged rocks of Islay. And it was here that so many were killed or drowned when their boats crashed upon the rocks. The people of the island did all that was humanly possible to rescue them when the lifeboats and rafts came plunging in during the early morning at several points along the rough coast. While they did save hundreds who might otherwise have been lost, 182 of the *Tuscania*'s soldiers were flung ashore lifeless. Of these, only 170 could be identified. As the victims had come in at rather widely separated places, they were buried as near as possible to these places in four cemeteries overlooking the sea.[12]

The sinking of the *Tuscania*

created a sensation in England as well as in the United States and the newspapers in both countries rang with it. This was the first time that a vessel filled with American troops on their way to the theater of war had gone to the bottom. Had it not been for the intrepidity of the convoying British destroyers and a measurable factor of pure Chance, most of the 2,500 men aboard her must have perished.[13]

One American probably never forgot the *Tuscania* until his dying day. On 20 March 1918 Elmer White was dragged by a war-frenzied mob from his home in Yerington, Nevada, lashed to a stake and then whipped, tarred and feathered before being kicked out of his home town. His crime? A fellow citizen thought they saw him celebrating the sinking of the *Tuscania*. In the anti-German hysteria which had swept America following the declaration of war it was all too easy to fall foul of such mobs.

Although the doughboys had begun to take casualties and were at long last getting a taste of combat, they still had not taken the initiative to any large degree, much to the irritation of Colonel Drum:

I am trying to have our people pull off a raid. We must do something to insure their morale. This theory of letting the Boche do it all is getting on the nerves – somehow the French seem to avoid letting our men do anything. The [1st] div is now commanded by General Bullard but he is under a French corps commander who holds a tight rein. Hope that something will be done soon. We are different from the French and need different methods, aggressiveness in us is the result of success. We must capture a few Germans – even if we pay for these in losses.[14]

The uneasy stalemate ended on 21 March when the Germans opened an offensive along a fifty-mile front against the British Fifth Army, virtually destroying it and penetrating the British rear areas to a depth of almost forty miles. The British army's losses between 21 March and 2 May were 280,000 dead and wounded, while those of the French were almost 60,000–70,000. There was a desperate need for reinforcements to stave off complete collapse along the British lines, and some units of the AEF were ordered into the fray. The Allies should have been better prepared for this offensive than they were. After all, they had good intelligence as to what the Germans were planning; even Pershing had been informed. On 15 February Major Paul Clark, Pershing's personal representative at the French GHQ, reported to Pershing a conversation with Major Rozet, one of his main contacts:

I asked what were their anticipations in regard to the [widely expected] German attack and Major Rozet said that it was believed that toward the end of this month the Germans would make a serious effort to break the line. At what places I asked. He believed that the principal German effort would be made between St Quentin and Cambrai, and also probably in the vicinity of Rheims. I asked why. The three principal reasons he gave were: (1) The first area named was the junction point of the French and British Armies – always a delicate point; (2) The line between the two cities named offers the Germans 30 kilometers of front best suited to an offensive on their part; (3) That this was the terrain which the Germans had abandoned, and that the French, anticipating that the Germans would not seek to return over it, had not expended the amount of effort to rehabilitate it – to fortify it – that they had spent on other parts of the line, and that this fact was known to the Germans, that is to say there was a lack of shelter – villages and forests were destroyed – and that it offered the most favorable place for the employment of gas, which no doubt would be an important factor in the attack.[15]

The only aspect of this analysis which proved incorrect was the date. Rather than towards the end of February it was almost the end of March when fifty-two elite attack divisions and eleven ordinary divisions broke the British Fifth Army.

There were by this time 251,889 doughboys in France. Those units of the AEF training with the British were allocated by regiment to British skeleton divisions, to be tutored in such specialisms as the handling of machine-guns. After that, the regiment would be attached to a British division in line, under the command of AEF officers. The theory was that this trained doughboy regiment would then gradually combine with other elements of the division, until the full division was ready for front-line duties. In fact, all the divisions sent to train with the British were urgently needed to help halt Ludendorff's spring offensive; only the 27th and 30th had time enough to complete their period of training. Various of the earliest divisions to arrive had now entered the front line, mostly under French supervision. On 16 February the first elements of the 42nd (assigned to the French Seventh Army Corps) went into the line of the Baccarat sector of the Vosges mountains, near Luneville, where they carried out further training programmes. The Baccarat sector was some eight miles long amid beautiful wooded hills and, because of the high terrain, almost guaranteed to be safe from any serious offensive. The 2nd Division (regulars and marines) went into line, again under French command for training purposes, on the west side of the St-Mihiel salient, near Verdun. By 15 March the AEF had suffered 136 killed in action – only two more than those who had died accidentally. Far more – 641 – had already died of various diseases.[16]

These were uneasy days, with both British and French commanders just one step away from panic as the long-expected German explosion, which smashed into the junction of the British and French armies between Cambrai and St Quentin, seemed to be unstoppable. Field Marshal Sir Douglas Haig said the British were now with 'their backs to the wall', fighting for survival along a battle front of 150 miles. On 28 March Marshal Foch had been made Supreme Commander of the Allied forces in France; that same day Pershing pledged that all his doughboys would be at the service of Foch – thus at one level suspending the interminable debate about who should control them – in the desperate effort simply to hold back the flood-tide of German storm troops. Between this point and the AEF's assault on the St-Mihiel salient in September Pershing exercised no tactical command over the AEF. Yet another German offensive was launched on 27 May, this specifically against the French; by 31 May Soissons had been captured and German troops had reached the Marne and Château-Thierry, thirty miles from their starting line, practically annihilating the French Sixth Army. Only where the AEF's 2nd and 3rd Divisions barred the German advance did the line hold. All this German activity in the spring of 1918 once more brought to the fore the Allied demand to be able to control, through amalgamation, the deployment of the doughboys. The issue came to a head at the Abbeville conference on Thursday, 2 May. At this session of the Supreme War Council (SWC) Pershing spelt out the fundamental reason why he was opposed to amalgamation. It was a compelling argument:

We all desire the same thing, but our means of attaining it are different from yours. America declared war independently of the Allies and she must face it as soon as possible with a powerful army. There is one important point upon which I wish to lay stress, and that is that the morale of our soldiers depends upon their fighting under our own flag.

America is already anxious to know where her army is. The Germans are once more circulating propaganda in the United States to the effect that the

Allies have so little confidence in the American troops that they parcel them out among Allied divisions.

The American soldier has his own pride, and the time will soon come when our troops, as well as our Government, will demand an autonomous army under the American High Command.[17]

He concluded that he was prepared to re-examine the question in June, but no more than that. The session broke up acrimoniously.

As if to rub salt in the wounds Pershing received a letter from Haig soon afterwards, dated 5 May:

Dear General Pershing,

I beg to enclose a note showing how I stand in the matter of Artillery Personnel. You will see that there is considerable shortage, and consequently if you could arrange to let me have 10,000 American Artillerymen, it would be of very great assistance to us.

With kind regards,

Believe me yours very truly,

D.Haig.[18]

Pershing may have stood his ground when it came to control of the white doughboys under his command, but he showed less concern for the black regiments entrusted to him. He offered the black American 92nd Division to Haig:

As you know, all of our infantry and machine gun units to be embarked in the near future are destined for service, for the time being, with your forces. I accordingly replied to the cable [. . .] to the effect that the 92nd (colored) Division could be included in the troops to be assigned to the forces under your command. It now appears, however, that the British Military Attaché in Washington has made a protest against including any colored battalions among the troops destined for service with your forces and that he has stated that this protest was made in behalf of your War Office.

You will, of course, appreciate my position in this matter, which, in brief, is that these negroes are American citizens [. . .] Naturally I cannot and will not discriminate against these soldiers.

I am informed that the 92nd Division is in a good state of training [in the United States] and I have no reason to believe that its employment under your command would be accompanied by any unusual difficulties.

[. . .] May I not hope that the inclusion of the 92nd Division among the American troops to be placed under your command is acceptable to you and that you will be able to overcome the objections raised by your War Office?[19]

On Monday, 13 May Lord Milner replied to Pershing's offer. Years of diplomacy had rendered him unable to frame the word 'no' and he merely replied that 'a good deal of administrative trouble would, I think, necessarily arise if the British Army had to undertake the training of a coloured Division'.

The British and French hunger for American soldiers to replenish their shattered, shrunken divisions at this stage of the war is entirely comprehensible. Equally so is Pershing's determination not to give way. For him it was an important political as well as military point that he and he alone should decide the fate of the army under his charge. One of the AEF's better generals, Hunter Liggett, summed up the US relationship within the Allied camp:

From the day of our declaration of war until less than a month prior to the Armistice, our Allies endeavoured – by argument, cajolery, flattery; by counsels of panic and prophecies of disaster; by social, political and military pressure; ingratiating, plausible, necessitous; diminishing as our troops began to show their wares, but not abandoned until victory was certain – to sway the United States from its insistence on an independent American Army working in concert with the Allies under the strategic direction of an Allied generalissimo.[20]

Liggett saw 'nothing sinister in these efforts [. . .] With no understanding of our national psychology, it was reasonable, even obvious, as they saw it, to use the AEF as a replacement depot from which to fill their depleted ranks.'

In their efforts to get hold of American troops, British and French military and political leaders did their utmost to ignore, belittle and undermine Pershing. They even sometimes simply behaved as though he was not there, as in one episode concerning the French promise –

broken almost as soon as made – that France would supply the AEF with 80,000 mules and horses, from a total of 160,000 to be requisitioned within France during June–July 1918. French farmers did their utmost to avoid sending their precious beasts off to be slaughtered and Paris was unable to secure anything like the promised quantity of horses and mules. André Tardieu – director of the General Commission for Franco-American War Affairs and former ambassador to the United States – then cabled his successor in Washington and instructed him to ask the US War Department to begin shipping horses and mules from America at the rate of 35,000 animals per month, rising to 60,000 a month; and this was at a time when the British and French were exercising every possible pressure upon Pershing to ship nothing but combat infantrymen and machine-gunners. Not only did Tardieu not bother to inform Pershing of his cable to Washington, he completely confused the War Department, which had previously received an order from Pershing that the rate of shipping for horses and mules should be 8,000 per month, so that the extra quantities of combat troops could be accommodated.[21]

At the same time as fighting for the right to lead his own army, Pershing was also trying to tackle the Germans. He had asked for the AEF to be allowed to take up its section of the front in what he regarded as the enemy's solar plexus, along the river Meuse and the Argonne forest. This whole region was elaborately and ingeniously fortified; the Argonne forest concealed all kinds of artillery, machine-gun and other emplacements, while the German-occupied heights of Montfaucon, some 500 feet above the plains, gave a perfect wide-ranging observation area and a strong defensive position. The area was covered in dense woods and thickets and criss-crossed by steep and rocky ridges and ravines. It was by far the strongest natural defensive length of the Western Front, and the Germans had made the best use of what Nature offered them.

The start to the AEF's contribution to smashing their formidable set of defences was somewhat inauspicious, with General Bullard, in command of the 1st Division, losing half his command as it vainly attempted to enter the front line for its initiation into trench warfare. The other half fortunately was not lost, as it was (deliberately) left behind in the training area at Gondrecourt. The 1st Division had spent the first week of January engaged in trench manoeuvres, preparatory to going into the front line, in one of the coldest winters for many years. By the time they were deemed ready to take over the defence of one small part of the front protecting France – no more than six kilometres – persistent snow and rain had created first a muddy swamp, followed by another freeze, turning every bit of flat ground into a skating rink. They were destined to take over from the French a low-lying, mud-filled series of trenches and dugouts with the ground steeply rising before them, occupied by the much better placed German lines. As the division moved up to the front its commanding general had a first taste of just how difficult it would be to return to open, fluid, flexible manoeuvres; the cramped French roads had been so heavily shelled that all progress was at a snail's pace:

Vehicles, animals, and men were in a struggling mass in blockade and delay along the road: for the first day of the march half of them were continually in the ditch. [By nightfall] The men of perhaps one third of the column might as well have slept in the houses from which they had started in the morning, so little distance had they gained [. . .] Darkness found the division widely scattered. I do not know how it slept or how it passed the night. I attempted ineffectually in an automobile to follow during a portion of the course. It was impossible. After a mile and a half or two miles I gave it up and returned to the place whence I had started in the morning. The trip had taken me in an automobile nearly half a day [. . .][22]

Bullard established the 1st Division's headquarters at Mesnil-la-Tour, equidistant between St-Mihiel and Pont-à-Mousson. Captain (later Major) Raymond Austin of the 6th Field Artillery was one of the 1st Division's few regular army officers. He got an early glimpse of the German positions from this sector, having gone on reconnaissance there a few days before the rest of his comrades struggled up the road. Austin's first port of call was a French command post just to the rear of the front line where he was, of course, entertained to lunch before getting down to business:

After lunch the French major took me out to the edge of town and up into an observation post cleverly camouflaged in a shell-wrecked house, from where I got my first view of the French lines below me, no-man's-land, and the German trenches beyond, the communication trenches, ruined villages on or near the lines, etc. etc. The country across there is desolate – not a blade of grass or a living being in sight. Occasionally a lone German can be seen back of the lines, but in general everyone keeps out of sight and all you see is shells bursting over apparently deserted country – yet you know that down in the ground there are thousands. Roads are camouflaged by artificial hedges, painted canvas, etc; gun position, observatories, etc., are likewise concealed, even wagons and trucks themselves are daubed up to make them less visible. Most of the dug-outs are rather comfortable, depending on their location with respect to drainage, etc. Some are thirty feet underground – the deeper the better when the Boches start work on them.[23]

Austin was occupying a command post close to the ruined town of Beaumont at this time, from where he had a panoramic view across the St-Mihiel salient:

Beaumont is on a high but not extremely steep ridge which runs for miles from Pont-à-Mousson to Flirey, Beaumont, Rambeaucourt, etc. Seicheprey is at the foot of the slope just beneath Beaumont. From Seicheprey north there is a broad, rolling valley, dotted with towns formerly held by the Germans – St Baussant, Lahayville, Richecourt, Nonsard, Pannes, etc. From almost any point along the Beaumont ridge a great Panorama is visible. The country is spread out before you like a map, beginning far to the left where the valley narrows noticeably toward Saint Mihiel, and opening wider and wider as the gaze passes to the right. Looming up high and commanding all the country for miles and miles in all directions is the great fort of Mont Sec which the French once took and held for seven hours with the loss of nearly one thousand men per hour. On the far side of the broad valley is a long ridge similar to the Beaumont ridge. Vigneulles is just at the base of this ridge, and Hattonville, near where our line now rests, is just at the top of the ridge. From the heights the valley appears quite even and smooth, but it is really broken by many smaller valleys and hills, streams, woods, etc.[24]

Austin's assistant in this reconnaissance, a lieutenant, wryly commented: 'I believe that at this particular moment you and I form the point of the spear that Uncle Sam, with all his effort, is trying to stick into Kaiser Bill.' In fact the first spear-sticking came not from the 1st Division but the Germans.

Despite Austin's being entertained to a good lunch by French officers, at the higher levels of interaction there was often, even at this precarious stage of the war, a failure of cooperative spirit on the part of the French. Soon after being attached to the French GHQ as Pershing's personal liaison officer in February 1918, Major Clark received a request from Colonel Leroy Eltinge at Chaumont, Pershing's HQ. The air was full of (largely correct) rumours of a major German offensive; Eltinge had been assured by Major Serot of the French GHQ that the AEF could have a copy of the plans for the deployment of the French First Army in the event of such an offensive:

I saw Major Serot several times in regard to this matter. In condensed form his reply is to the effect that at first he expressed great surprise that the maps and papers had not been delivered to Colonel Eltinge; second, that he would take steps to bring about delivery; third, that it would be impracticable to permit the papers in question to leave I Army Headquarters. These statements were made, respectively, at the three different interviews I had with him.[25]

As late as May 1918 the mutual discord often reached a level of frank and cordial dislike. Major Lloyd Griscom[26] was invited to take tea with Lloyd George soon after he arrived in London as Pershing's personal liaison officer with the British War Office. Lloyd George was in an irascible mood:

Lloyd George, while I was having tea with him, astonished me by starting in to tell me what a foul commander they had in the field, Sir Douglas Haig. 'It is unbelievable,' he said, 'but he lost 700,000 men last summer unnecessarily. I want to remove him, but cannot find anybody to replace him.' [...] He then started in to say how badly General Pershing was behaving [...] He repeated the old story about sending our troops to fill their depleted divisions, etc. I said, 'General Pershing has discussed that with you, Mr Lloyd George, and considers it settled.' He said, 'Yes, but I don't.' So that was the nature of my opening talk with the Prime Minister.[27]

Nor were the British and French simply hostile towards the American leadership; they had plenty of contempt for each other, too. Before he left France to take up his job in London, Griscom sensibly did the rounds of the British and French GHQs in France to inform himself more fully. He was astonished at the level of mutual distrust:

General Pershing also credited me to the French Government and the French War Office, so I went there and had an interview with the Chief of Staff of the French Army in Paris. He astonished me by pulling out a great typewritten document and handed it to me and said, 'Will you please deliver this to the British and put in a good word for us?' He said, 'The truth is that the British are not putting their manpower in the fighting line; they're putting them in the Navy, which isn't fighting, and in the coal mines and sending them on nice ships all over the world, but they aren't getting killed.' I looked over this thing and saw an amazing indictment, which had taken some months to prepare, to show how their Ally was playing a mean game [. . .] What an opening that we have made for me in London![28]

Amidst all this fruitless squabbling the AEF was rapidly growing; between April and July 1918 about 1 million American soldiers stepped off the boat in France. Private Arthur Yensen's transport, the *Orduna*, arrived safely in Liverpool on 27 March 1918. His unit travelled across the Atlantic 'as third-class passengers – way down in the hold, where the air is so sickening that it would turn a dog pale'. By 7 April, having spent a few days in camp in Winchester, England, Yensen's outfit arrived in France where they got their first view of German prisoners, about 600 of them:

The Germans were a dizzy-looking bunch; none of them dressed alike. Covered with mud, they reminded me of tired horses. They were larger than the British and looked as if they might be better soldiers. Compared to us, they looked stronger and heavier, but more clumsy and stupid. An average comment from us was, 'Aw hell, they don't look very bad to me!'[29]

In the United States the War Department, meanwhile, was functioning with scarcely any greater sense of urgency than one year before.

On his first day in the office, 4 March 1918, March was staggered at what he found in the War Department:

I talked over with General Biddle [whom March was replacing] the methods of conducting business which were in force at that time, and when he had concluded what he had to say, asked him one question: 'What are your office hours?' He replied that he generally left the office at about five o'clock and that he did not come back at night unless there was some special cable from Headquarters in France which required his personal attention.

I came down to the War Department that night and found the General Staff offices dark, nobody was there; I wandered along the deserted corridors of the War Department, nobody was in the Acting Secretary of War's office. In front of the Adjutant General's office I found the corridor piled high with unopened mail sacks, and nobody was there to open them. I finally found one officer on duty, Major W. K. Wilson of the General Staff, in charge of the code room, and he was the only officer I did find.

The next night the entire General Staff were on duty, and they stayed on duty at night until the end of the War. All the other offices and bureaus of the War Department took up the work without regard to hours, and in a very short time the piles of unopened mail sacks vanished.[30]

And in France, although the German offensives were initially very successful, in quantity of munitions, tanks, aircraft and artillery, the Allies entered 1918 with considerable superiority. At the start of 1918 they could count upon some 18,500 artillery pieces (against Germany's 14,000), 4,500 airplanes (against 3,670) and about 800 tanks, of which Germany possessed only a handful.[31] In qualitative terms, however, there was still plenty of room for improvement; General Bullard of the 1st Division was still unhappy about the quality of the officer material he was receiving: 'I have much difficulty in getting officers who know anything. All are untrained, and many of even our regular officers can never be worth anything in this war, unadaptable and immovable.'[32]

At this stage of the war, relatively early for the doughboys, the promise of combat still had a kind of Boy's Own Paper quality to it, a sense of imminent adventure long since lost among the doughboys' allies. Although a relatively senior officer in command of several batteries of artillery, Captain Austin nevertheless found plenty of time and scope for mounting his own occasional one-man trench raids. At the end of March he wrote to his mother that he had met in the front line the Paris correspondent of *Leslie's Weekly*:

I took him down to the front lines and we went the length of the American sector [the Toul sector at that time] through the front line trenches. At one point we crawled out to a listening post less than 20 yards from the Boche front line trench where we could hear them talking. We were right at the edge of their wire. We heard a Boche sniper fire his rifle about 25 or 30 yards to our right, so we slipped back to our front line where I got a hand grenade. Then I slipped back only part way, so as not to expose the position of the listening post, and waited until the sniper fired again, and then heaved the grenade over to where the sound came from and skipped back to our lines. When the grenade went off it sounded like a mine exploding.[33]

A year after America joined the Allies some of the AEF's commanders were finding their feet and there was a growing confidence among the US soldiers and their officers about their grasp of techniques in this new and strange type of warfare, a confidence which was more solidly based than the early bravado of months before. 'Our patrolling and raiding were steadily improving and were now regularly successful,' recalled General Bullard, adding, 'with experience came skill and comparative safety.'[34]

On 4 April the 1st Division, which had been holding nine miles of muddy front line on the south side of the St-Mihiel salient, was relieved by the 26th Division, the New England National Guardsmen under the command of Major-General Clarence Edwards. The hand-over was extremely acrimonious and Bullard later said that it was 'altogether the most irritating experience of my life. It was a vicious blow from behind.' He accused Edwards of being 'so fault-finding and officially critical of our shortcomings, and made such bad reports of us to our common military superiors, that for long afterward we were kept explaining, fighting our own people behind while we fought the enemy in front.'[35]

The switch of divisions was appallingly handled and revealed serious flaws in the AEF's logistical abilities. Some 28,000 men, 1,700 animals and 1,000 vehicles were pulled out, and the same number put into the line. The ensuing chaos jangled the nerves of the 26th's officers, and they were not helped by constant small-scale patrolling by the Germans, determined to probe and uncover the weaknesses of this new unit. The soldiers of the 26th Division were a rather haughty bunch, considering their social backgrounds raised them above the hoi polloi, the bulk of the AEF:

Many of the companies represented the center of social life of a New England town, these cadres dating back in history to pre-Revolutionary times [...] These Yankees had an independence, a dignity about them. When replacements began to be drafted, and a Vermonter received the White House greetings, the local weekly might say that 'Mr Obadiah Littlejohn has accepted the position of Private in the United States Army.' [They] did not care a damn about the Regular Army; they held themselves better men than the catch-all Regulars of the peacetime Army. Officers knew all their men; knew where they lived, had talked with their mothers. They had a fierce loyalty, and when they were elected to an officer's rank, even the many who had stooped to the chicanery of militia politics to gain a commission, set about, conscience-stricken, to make officers of themselves [...] When they came ashore in France in September, 1917, their infantry were the best-coached riflemen the American Army sent over. They were commanded by a West Pointer, Major General Clarence Edwards, himself frowned upon by many of his fellow Leavenworth graduates for his effusive magnetism and charm.[36]

The sector which the 26th had taken over, like all in the St-Mihiel salient, was completely dominated by the sugarloaf-shaped Montsec, a 457-feet-high protuberance 2,000 yards behind the German lines. The Germans had converted Montsec into a perfect platform from which to observe the Allied lines. It allowed observation of the entire country for miles. Riddled with concrete tunnels, emplacements and carefully concealed observation posts, Montsec was thought to be the most impregnable position anywhere in France. From 4 April almost every night saw tussles in no-man's-land. On the night of Saturday, 20 April a fearsome barrage opened up on the 26th Division's trenches on a two-mile front, encompassing the village of Seicheprey. It was a perfect night for causing maximum confusion, with a heavy fog, and at 5 a.m. a large German raiding party of between 1,000 and 3,000 men plunged out of the darkness. In an hour of savage fighting they wrenched Seicheprey from the New Englanders and pushed more than a mile into the US lines. The 26th counter-attacked but failed to recapture the town; the next day the Germans withdrew and the doughboys had the humiliating experience of being allowed to re-occupy what they were expected never to lose in the first place.

The Germans made the most of this early success against the Americans, going so far as to deliver lengthy reports with pictures of the affair to neutral countries. Berlin radio even broadcast a boastful account of how the Americans had been resoundingly thumped. The 26th had taken the AEF's worst battle casualties of the war so far: 1 officer and 80 men killed; 11 officers and 176 men wounded; 3 officers and 211 men gassed; 5 officers and 182 men missing and prisoners. Major-General Edwards lost something for ever too – the confidence of the AEF's commander-in-chief.[37] Something would have to be done to recover what was for Pershing a dreadful loss of face. He could not immediately sack Edwards, who had powerful political supporters in Congress, but he would eventually obtain retribution.

In May 1918 the mood in the Allied camp was extremely gloomy, if not outright defeatist. In Britain, Private Benjamin Dexter, of the AEF's 82nd Division, found utter hopelessness when travelling through it to France. Things were 'not what we expected. The English people were critical, said we were too late, one person said "the Hun was artillery 3 lines deep, from the Channel to the Swiss line. When they attack, their planes darken the sky." '[38]

More than ever before the doughboys needed to prove themselves. But where? And how?

12

Cantigny and Belleau Wood

The Marines fighting in Belleau Wood are magnificent, but theirs is a useless sacrifice.   Major-General Joseph Dickman[1]

We kill or get killed.   Anonymous doughboy at Belleau Wood

The place selected to demonstrate that the AEF could take the initiative in battle was a small, once pretty village lacking any strategic or tactical importance. Now reduced to skeletal ruins, Cantigny was in other words the perfect spot for a gesture. If the doughboys managed to wrest it from German control, they would prove to both Germans and Allies that they were a force to be reckoned with. If they failed, the humiliation would not damage much more than their pride. Cantigny was close to the point of the furthest advance of the German storm-troops in the March 1918 spring offensive. If relatively meaningless in strategic terms, a victory here would nevertheless bolster the jittery morale of the doughboys, many of whom were by now almost unbearably keyed up, desperate to get into action but also fearful of failure.

Pershing had high hopes of success in this engagement. He believed the AEF was by now beginning to amount to a respectable army, at least in sheer size. By the end of May 1918 the AEF had eleven combat divisions, 290,765 troops out of a total force of 488,224 in France and Britain.[2] The total strength of the army, including those in training in the States, was now about 1,900,000, including more than 790,000 volunteers. The combat troops in France were defending a 35-mile front, twice that held by the Belgian army. The 1st Division was with the French near Amiens, the 2nd, 26th and 42nd were occupying usually quiet sectors, while the 32nd was preparing to go into the line.

The 77th Division – along with four regiments of railway engineers, one regiment of pioneer engineers, a telegraph battalion, six base hospital teams and almost 10,000 men of the American air service – was in support with the British. Three more divisions were ready to sail from the United States, and, more remote still from the fighting, another 263,852 US-based infantrymen were deemed good enough to be ready to receive training in France.[3]

By 20 May the 1st Division had spent a month in the lines opposite the small village of Cantigny, three miles west of Montdidier. It was at that time part of a French corps under the command of General Eugène Debeney. The village of Cantigny sat at the tip of a small German-held salient projecting some three miles into the Allied lines. The AEF and French trenches were some 700 yards from the village. Every angle of approach to Cantigny was covered by German flanking machine-gun fire, and the Germans often drenched the entire Allied lines with shrapnel and gas. On 15 May Debeney had suggested to General Bullard that his 1st Division might like to wrest Cantigny from its German occupiers. This was something of a poisoned chalice; the French had twice previously taken and lost the very same obscure hamlet. To lead the assault Bullard chose the 28th Regiment, commanded by Colonel Hanson Ely, a 6 feet 2 inch, 220-pound, beefy regular army soldier, one possessed of a fearsome reputation: 'If Ely asked his mess attendant for a cup of coffee, the request had the tone of a battalion fire chief ordering a hoseman back into a burning building. When he was silent, which was not too often, he continually worked the leathery muscle at the corner of his jaw, as if banking the fires that smoldered in his rasping vocal chords.'[4]

The timing of the attack, which started on 28 May, was unlucky for the AEF. On the previous day the Germans had themselves launched another offensive on a fifty-mile front across the Chemin des Dames, a fifteen-mile-long ridge east of Soissons. This was supposedly a quiet sector, chosen by Ludendorff primarily as a means of diverting Allied reserves from the British sector of the front, to the north, preparatory to delivering a further offensive against the British in June or July. At 1 a.m. on Monday, 27 May the Germans pounded the French lines using high explosive and gas to terrorize and deracinate the rear areas to a depth of twelve kilometres. After a three-hour artillery blizzard, seventeen German divisions burst across the French lines, held by six divisions. By 11 a.m. the Germans had reached the French second lines, at the river Aisne; by nightfall they were easing their tired feet in the river Vesle, a total incursion twelve miles deep and thirty miles wide, and one of the most successful attacks of the war up to that time. Next day the Germans marched into Soissons; by the end of the third day of the attack they had penetrated the Allied defences to a depth of more than thirty miles, captured 650 artillery pieces, 2,000 machine-guns and 60,000 (mostly French) prisoners. Day four of the attack saw them on the Marne, with minor bridgeheads across it. The French reserves thrown into the offensive were routed, the French General Staff in despair, and the politicians in Paris prepared to scurry away to Bordeaux. On the weekend of 1–2 June, more than 1 million civilians are estimated to have fled Paris, convinced that the Germans, now less than forty miles from the French capital, would be marching down the Champs-Élysées within a week.

The battle of Cantigny was thus overshadowed by a much larger and strategically more vital engagement. That did not matter in itself; of much more serious consequence was that the defence of Paris sucked away from the doughboys at Cantigny the weapons essential for securing swift success. Observation aircraft and heavy artillery, both supplied by the French, were quickly withdrawn, to be thrown desperately into the breach opening up before Paris. The doughboys can and did swiftly take Cantigny (the German divisions holding Cantigny were not crack units; the 82nd Reserve was categorized as a third-class division, while the other division, the 25th Reserve, was in such bad shape that it was defined by the Germans as little better than a labour unit), but lack of these vital arms made holding on to the village much more difficult than it need have been.

Cantigny was situated on the slope of a long, rather steep, high ridge; the Germans occupying the upper ground had an excellent observation platform for studying and shelling the 1st Division. At the start of the attack the doughboys were to be supported by French aircraft, French flamethrower units, twelve French heavy tanks and almost 400 artillery pieces of various sizes. In addition, the 1st

Western front line 1918 ground held by British and American armies

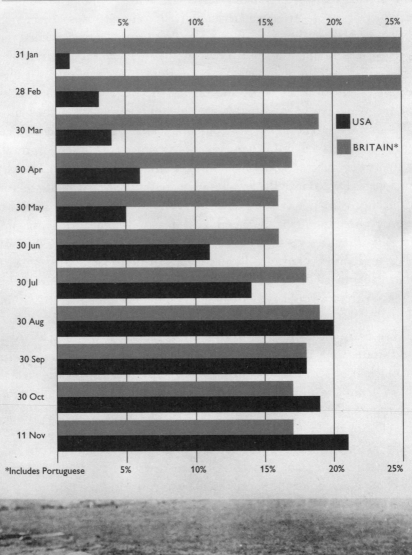

| | 5% | 10% | 15% | 20% | 25% |

31 Jan
28 Feb
30 Mar
30 Apr
30 May
30 Jun
30 Jul
30 Aug
30 Sep
30 Oct
11 Nov

■ USA

■ BRITAIN*

*Includes Portuguese

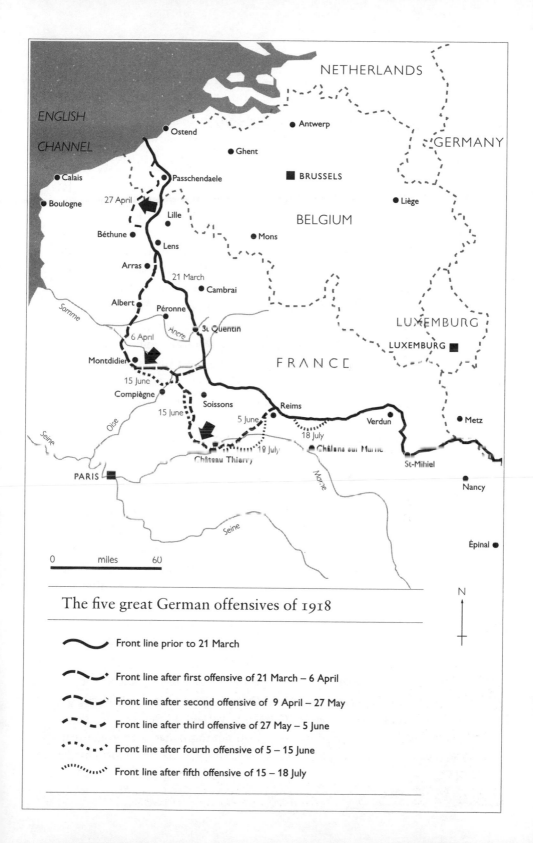

The five great German offensives of 1918

Front line prior to 21 March

Front line after first offensive of 21 March – 6 April

Front line after second offensive of 9 April – 27 May

Front line after third offensive of 27 May – 5 June

Front line after fourth offensive of 5 – 15 June

Front line after fifth offensive of 15 – 18 July

Division's 6th Field Artillery Regiment and machine-gun battalions, an engineer company and two extra rifle companies from the 18th Infantry Regiment (also of the 1st Division) were in support.

It may have been a sideshow in the context of the much larger German offensive threatening Paris, but for those who took part it was a shattering experience.[5] From Colonel Ely down to the lowest private, Cantigny was a searing crash-course (it only lasted from 28 to 31 May) in bitter and degrading Western Front combat.

On Monday, 27 May, 1st Lieutenant Daniel Sargent, of the 5th Field Artillery Regiment (1st Division), woke early in the Bois de Plainville, some two miles south-west of Cantigny, a village which he thought was 'shaped like a ship with its bow pointed toward us'. Sargent was a reserve officer in the regular army and had been attached to 'F' Battery, armed with French-made 155mm howitzers, for nine months. That morning Sargent was ordered to report to brigade head-quarters at Tartigny, two miles to the south-west of his position. At Tartigny he was met by Colonel Charles de Chambrun, a liaison officer attached to Pershing – itself an indication of how closely interested both the French staff and Pershing were in this relatively minor fracas. De Chambrun told Sargent that his ability to speak a little French meant he was being appointed artillery liaison officer between the 1st Division and the French artillery. Sargent's job would be to occupy an observation post (code-named 'Pennsylvania') in front of Cantigny, and from there report (via field telephone) on the progress of the infantry assault artillery 'if they called me up to inquire about it'.[6] 'Pennsylvania' was at the point of a wood jutting out towards Cantigny, on the right of the one-mile-wide front of the attack. After conferring with de Chambrun, Sargent trudged the battle front to familiarize himself with its layout, so that next day he would have a clear idea of the lie of the land. He was a little shocked when he reached 'Pennsylvania' to discover it

was not a well-equipped observation post [. . .] only a fox hole in it three feet deep [. . .] From it one could well observe. Lying on my belly beside the 'fox hole' I took a good look at Cantigny. It stood on the top of a slope, beyond a hollow in front of me. It seemed not more than a good golf-ball drive away from me [. . .] It had been fought through back and forth by the

Germans and French in April, but appeared to be still intact. It looked peaceful enough, but completely unoccupied.

At 'Pennsylvania' on the morning of 28 May, Sargent was joined by two French officers, an American infantry lieutenant (whom Sargent refers to in his memoir as 'L.C.') and a doughboy sergeant. Preliminary range-finding shelling of the German positions in Cantigny started at 4.45 a.m., the men gradually making their adjustments with single shots here and there. The full-scale bombardment started at 5.45 a.m. Captain Raymond Austin was that morning in command of a battery of field artillery:

The ground was pounded to dust by our shells – all that was visible was the heavy smoke hanging over Cantigny and the ridge [. . .] the preparation stopped at 6.40, giving 5 minutes for the formation of the attack proper. One, by one the batteries dropped their fire onto the line, one here and another there, then others would drop in between and link up until along the whole front of the attack there was a perfect, even line of bursting shells a mile long. Then at 6.45 as though by the command of a single officer, although in reality each battery worked independently by pre-arranged schedule and synchronised watches, the barrage moved forward at a rate just fast enough for the infantry to keep up with it at a walk. At the same time as the barrage left the line of departure (our front line trenches) the infantry suddenly appeared on the slope of the ridge close behind our barrage – a long brown line with bayonets glistening in the sun. They seemed to have sprung from the earth, as in reality they had when they went over the top. They walked steadily along behind our barrage accompanied by the tanks which buzzed along with smoke coming out from their exhausts and their guns. As the line reached the crest and was silhouetted in the morning sun [. . .] it looked like a long picket fence. Occasionally a shell would strike among them and a gap would appear among the pickets, then quickly close.[7]

The waves of doughboys attacking on the comparatively tiny front went over the top in just the same fashion as their British and French allies had been doing for almost four years. They were probably unable to do much more than walk, as each was plodding towards death loaded with '220 rounds of ammunition, three sandbags, two hand grenades, one rifle grenade, two water canteens, two iron rations, one shelter half, two cakes of chocolate as emergency rations, plus one lemon and wads of chewing gum as thirst quenchers'.[8]

For once, the preliminary bombardment – just one hour, comparatively short by Western Front standards – had succeeded in its main task of softening up resistance to the point where it crumbled and posed little or no obstacle to the first attack wave. Captain Austin reported that 'our losses in the attack proper were comparatively small', and added that 247 prisoners were taken (other sources put the tally at about 100 prisoners and some fifty AEF casualties), but the attack quickly degenerated into a messy to-and-fro. The Americans suffered their biggest losses only after taking the village. German defenders had sheltered in the deep, well-protected basements of houses during the preliminary bombardment. The US advance was swift and rather casual; many of the German defenders who came up from their shelters found themselves *behind* the doughboys who had pushed a considerable distance east beyond Cantigny. A little after 7 a.m. it appeared to Lieutenant Sargent that Cantigny was taken; there had been no signs of resistance and the only soldiers he had so far seen breaking into a run that morning were some Germans who had come

running out of Cantigny toward the tanks with their arms raised in surrender [. . .] Then at about 7.10 a.m. everything changed. Our artillery fire had pretty much ceased, but a German artillery fire took its place. Huge German shells began to fall on Cantigny and they raised a cloud of yellow smoke, similar to that which we had seen raised by a bombardment a few minutes ago.

German shells were beginning to fall around 'Pennsylvania' too; one of the French officers, a young cadet, hysterically ran into the woods behind them. This was as nothing to the reaction of Sargent's fellow AEF officer, who together with Sargent was

squirming now and then to the right or left as if thereby to evade a shell that we heard screaming towards us. While engaged in this futility, Lieutenant L.C. began what seemed to me an inappropriate social conversation. 'Lieutenant Sargent,' he began. 'Do you remember the date of your commission as first lieutenant?' I answered, 'September, 1917.' 'But,' he said, 'my commission was dated August, 1917, which makes me your senior, in which case I suppose this "fox-hole" falls to me.' At this he ensconced himself in the three-foot hole, protruding from it like a jack-in-the-box with a broken spring.

The Germans launched a series of counter-attacks, beginning at about 4.30 p.m. with a huge artillery bombardment, followed by a wave of German infantry attacking the village at 5.10. At one point Major Theodore Roosevelt – son of the former president – led the 1st Battalion of the 26th Infantry across the fields in front of Cantigny, to plug a gap. A second and then a third wave of assaulting Germans were courageously repulsed.

In the early morning of the second day of the battle (29 May) matters were becoming so confused that Lieutenant Sargent was ordered to enter Cantigny to act as an on-the-spot liaison officer between the infantry and artillery. Guided to a chalk cliff on the edge of the village he found himself taken to a cave which, it turned out, was the headquarters of Colonel Ely. In the twenty-four hours since the start of the attack approximately 30 per cent of the 28th Infantry had become casualties, most as a result of the intense German air and artillery bombardments. Those not dead or wounded were utterly exhausted, as were the artillerymen who vainly did their best to support them:

Some of our companies were practically annihilated and others held on without budging an inch, with their officers dead. In the last two counter-attacks the Boches brought up tanks as a sort of final resort and we caught the tanks in our barrage and they never even reached our front lines. In 72 hours I had six hours' sleep, which was getting off easy. Cantigny is in sight. All that's left of it is the place where it was and dead scattered around, mostly Germans, as we lost few in the attack.[9]

For Sargent the experience was chilling. Inside the cave were several lanterns

which revealed Colonel Ely seated on what seemed to me to be a horse saddle. His staff were ranged along the wall about him, in front of him on the floor was the depressing sight of the artillery officer that I was relieving. He was staring up at the ceiling glassy-eyed.

Colonel Ely, whom I, of course, had never seen before wore a sleepless look, but he had a most calming presence and calming look, and he addressed me by name, which was a calming thing to do. 'Lieutenant Sargent,' he said. 'You are succeeding the artillery officer that you are looking at. You are to go to the command post of the 2nd battalion of the 28th Infantry in Cantigny, which is not far from here. The battalion commander is Major Roussel, who may not be expecting you for the telephone wire between him and me has been momentarily cut, so that I can't announce your arrival. A runner will guide you to Major Roussel's command post and you can tell him that I have sent you. Once in the dug-out, you will have the task of relaying requests for barrages from the infantry to the artillery. You will do this by telephone which will begin to function again shortly.' He nodded, to send me on.

Sargent made his way unscathed to the dugout – 'a black hole that stared out of the ashes' in a 'featureless field' – which was a former wine cellar, no more than seven feet high. He discovered Major Roussel, who was sitting on a shelf 'rasping' out orders, plus an assortment of French and US officers; Sargent's arrival made seven in total. A fellow 1st Lieutenant turned a spigot on a nearby hogshead and passed him a mug of 'Normandy cider': 'I much enjoyed this cider. It was a Godsend.' The infantry major initially did not think much of Sargent, referring to him as 'Mr Artilleryman'; but after Sargent had managed to direct some fire on to a troublesome battery of nearby German howitzers and put them out of action, his prestige grew. Late in the afternoon of 29 May Sargent was relieved by another artillery lieutenant, when the German guns had fallen silent. The Germans had finally relinquished hope of recapturing and holding this meaningless speck of rubble.

For General Bullard, Cantigny was

the first serious fight made by American troops in France, and it was greeted enthusiastically as a wonderful success. I know that it was so carefully prepared that it could not have failed, but it is a fact also that the execution by the troops was very good [...] The total losses and evacuations of the [1st] division, on account of this fight, amounted to some thirteen hundred men

[. . .] Cantigny, in itself, was a small fight. Hundreds greater had preceded and would follow it in the mighty war. But Cantigny was, nevertheless, one of the important engagements of the war in its import to our war-wearied and sorely tried Allies. To both friend and foe it said, 'Americans will both fight and stick.'[10]

And die, he might have added. A few days after the battle Captain Austin wrote to his mother: 'when the wind is right you can smell Cantigny two miles away'.[11]

After Cantigny Pershing's tail was up. It proved to him that his doughboys were not only as courageous as any other soldier on the Western Front, but that they were capable of delivering on his promises. It marked a psychological turning-point for Pershing; the poor relation perched on a rickety chair at the edge of the family party now felt his rightful place was at the top table: 'I remember particularly Pershing's banging his fist down on the table and shouting out, "I am certainly going to jump down the throat of the next person who asks me, 'Will the Americans really fight?' " '[12]

'The Boches certainly were whipped for once,' said Captain Austin, but he was forced to admit in his same letter home that it was a close thing. Fear of both the Germans and Pershing goaded the doughboys and their field officers into making tremendous efforts. Pershing had ordered that not an inch of Cantigny was to be relinquished; Bullard, Ely and every subordinate officer below them realized that their future careers depended on that order being obeyed.

Meanwhile the Second Battle of the Marne, which lasted from 27 May to 6 August, was underway. The French began to panic; what had started out as a moderate push began to seem much more successful, and the Germans were always ready to reinforce success. The city of Reims had been their initial target but suddenly it seemed that Château-Thierry, even Paris, might be open to them. A desperate Pétain appealed to Pershing to lend whatever help he could to try to stem the tide of field-grey uniforms. The most vulnerable spot, the tip of the German thrust, was the town of Château-Thierry, lying on the Marne. The only relatively close doughboy divisions which were also in a condition of combat-readiness were the 3rd Division, another US regular army formation under Major-General Joseph T. Dickman, then in training near Chaumont, along with the 2nd Division, under Major-General Omar Bundy, in reserve near Chaumont-en-Vixen. Both were some 100 miles away from Château-Thierry. Dickman was ordered to transport the 3rd as quickly as possible to Château-Thierry. On the afternoon of 30 May the 7th (motorized) Machine Gun Battalion of the 3rd Division set forth, followed by the infantry and engineers that evening. The 2nd Division was also ordered to the fray. It moved by truck on the night of 30 May towards Meaux, twenty miles east of Paris, whence the troops marched towards Château-Thierry.

The 7th Machine Gun Battalion was the first to reach Château-Thierry on the afternoon of Friday, 31 May, and a handful of doughboys – armed with two Hotchkiss machine-guns and led by Lieutenant Bissell, a recent graduate of West Point – rushed immediately across a bridge and to the outskirts of the town, despite their long, tiring journey. That night they marched into Château-Thierry, where some elements of a battalion of French colonial infantry were desperately hanging on, fending off the German vanguard. Still other French troops were already fleeing, clogging the roads. The Americans were too late, said the *poilus*; but the Americans still kept coming, spoiling for a fight.

By 2 June the whole of the 3rd Division's infantry had caught up and the French commanding officer, General Mondesir, now had 17,000 US troops to hold back the Germans. Château-Thierry was held. By 6 June the doughboys were themselves on the offensive, together with French units; the 3rd Division recaptured Hill 204, just outside Château-Thierry, and thus secured for the Allies domination of the town, while the fight for Belleau Wood and the village of Bouresches was that same day commenced by the 2nd Division. From this moment on the lines were stabilized and the German offensive here went no further.

On 1 June the 2nd Division deployed near the village of Lucy-le-Bocage, strung across the Paris–Soissons highway in support of two French divisions that had orders to fall back through American lines. With his troops providing such support for the nearly broken French divisions, Pershing was in an obdurate mood when André Tardieu called on him in Paris and started to criticize the AEF's staff and organization. Pershing immediately shut him up, as these were subjects that he could not possible know about [. . .] I intimated that we had had quite enough of this sort of thing from the French, either military or civilian, and suggested that if his people would cease troubling themselves so much about our affairs and attend more strictly to their own we should all get along much better [. . .] the constant inclination on the part of a certain element among the French to assume a superiority that did not exist, then or at any later period, added to the attempts of some of them to dictate, had reached the limit of patience.[13]

Pershing's decision to tolerate no more unfair criticism of his staff or troops was immediate severely tested at another meeting of the Supreme War Council, its sixth session, which started on Saturday, 1 June. The SWC again returned to the vexed question of the nature and numbers of American troops to be shipped to France. Pershing refused to accept that this was a topic within the remit of the Council and suggested a meeting outside the Council's orbit to discuss it, which was agreed. On the afternoon of 1 June, while the threat to Paris was mounting, Lord Milner, Pershing, Generals Foch and Weygand, with Colonels Conner and Boyd of the AEF, met in Clemenceau's office. Foch was in a high state of anxiety: 'He was very positive and insistent and in fact became quite excited, waving his hands and repeating, "The battle, the battle, nothing else counts." '[14]

Pershing was not being merely bloody-minded; there was a serious risk that if Foch got his way and no other troops but infantry and machine-gunners were shipped across at the rate of 250,000 a month in June and July, then the ports and railway lines might collapse under the pressure of too many combat troops and not enough SOS labourers to prevent the whole transportation infrastructure from breaking down. The meeting was heated; Lloyd George played his usual underhand role and announced that he thought President Wilson would be 'deeply interested' in Foch's views. The meeting adjourned until the following day, when battle was joined again – a reprise of the inconclusive debate seen a month before at Abbeville. On the afternoon of 2 June Foch, Clemenceau and Lloyd George resumed their bombardment of Pershing, demanding shipments only of infantry and machine-gunners in June and July. Pershing was adamant. Lloyd George then tried a different method of attack: '[He] said the Allies were in a sense in the hands of the United States. He spoke of the generous and chivalrous attitude of President Wilson and said all they could do was to acquaint him with their needs and call upon him to come to their aid.'[15]

In others words, if Pershing would not give him what he wanted, then perhaps Wilson would. Clemenceau backed up the British prime minister and Foch then asked for an astonishing 300,000 US soldiers a month to be sent, and a total of 100 divisions. Without these numbers of doughboys, said Foch, it was 'impossible to foresee ultimate victory in the war'. The wrangling went round and round the same themes – how many US soldiers would be shipped, when would they arrive, did Pershing fully understand the crisis besetting the Allies? 'The whole discussion was very erratic, as one of the Allies would take exception to nearly every statement made by the other,' commented Pershing. Those sitting round the table could not even agree how many divisions they already had; Lord Milner said it was 169, Foch 150. Lloyd George, foolishly enough, interjected that 'he could not understand why all the losses fell to the Allies and none to the Germans'. Foch then threw in a sidelong jibe at Britain, commenting that the Germans handled their replacements better than Britain; what other explanation could there be for Germany, with a population of 68 million, managing to maintain 204 divisions, while Britain, with a population of 46 million, could manage just 43 divisions?

Patience wore thin on all sides. Eventually Pershing proposed that he, Foch and Lord Milner should draft a cable to Washington on the subject of priorities in the shipping of troops in June and July. Signed by those three and sent 2 June, it made the following recommendations:

A. For the month of June: 1st, absolute priority shall be given to the transportation of 170,000 combatant troops (viz., six divisions without artillery, ammunition trains or supply trains, amounting to 126,000 men and 44,000 replacements for combat troops); 2d, 25,400 men for the service of railways, of which 13,400 have been asked for by the French Minister of Transportation; 3d, the remainder to be troops of categories to be determined by the Commander-in-Chief, American Expeditionary Forces.

B. For the month of July; 1st, absolute priority for the shipment of 140,000 combatant troops of the nature defined above (4 divisions minus artillery, etc.

etc., amounting to 84,000 men plus 56,000 replacements); 2d, the balance of the 250,000 to consist of troops to be designated by the Commander-in-Chief, American Expeditionary Forces.

C. It is agreed that if available tonnage in either month allows of the transportation of a larger number of men than 250,000 the excess tonnage will be employed in the transportation of combat troops as defined above.

D. We recognize that the combatant troops to be dispatched in July may have to include troops with insufficient training, but we consider the present emergency is such as to justify a temporary and exceptional departure by the United States from sound principles of training especially as a similar course is being followed by France and Great Britain.[16]

Thus Clemenceau and Lloyd George may be said to have got their way to some extent, but only under great pressure. As Pershing commented,

What a difference it would have made if the Allies had seen this [the necessity of having a strong US army in France] a year or even six months earlier and had then given us assistance in shipping! Certainly, the situation had been clearly understood since the preceding August [. . .] The Governments [. . .] understood in August that the constitution of our army in France depended upon sea transportation, but they took no steps then to provide it. On the contrary their minds were centered on using America as a reservoir from which men could be drawn to serve under an alien flag. They failed to understand the psychology of the American people. They failed to foresee the results. They failed to do the only thing that good judgment dictated, and that was to assist by all possible means the organization of a powerful American army and to transport it to France at the earliest possible moment.[17]

This SWC conference took place in a highly-charged atmosphere. It seemed to many present that the game might soon be up, and that the Germans, pushing towards Château-Thierry, which was just forty miles north-east of Paris, would soon be in possession of the French capital. The AEF's 2nd Division – comprising the 9th and 23rd Infantry Regiments, and the 5th and 6th Marine Regiments – had been designated to relieve the 1st at Cantigny, but such was the sense of apocalypse in the Château-Thierry region that it was ordered into the line to the left of Château-Thierry itself, near the village of Vaux and a small forest nearby, Belleau Wood. The names of these villages were to be burned for ever into the memories of those who fought there, as indeed would the chaos of orders, countermanded and yet again countermanded, with the French commanders continually contradicting themselves in the flux of battle, horrified that they might go down in history as the ones who lost Paris:

So great was French confusion in constantly changing combat orders for the 2nd Division that Germans who later interrogated their first US Marine prisoners were astonished to discover that wounded sergeants with three hash marks did not know how the Leathernecks and Doughboys reached the wooded patches due south of Belleau Wood. 'They are kept in complete ignorance,' Lieutenant von Buy of Intelligence reported to his commander [. . .] 'They cannot name the towns they have passed through.'[18]

It rained incessantly throughout the days of the to-and-fro struggle over Belleau Wood, an insignificant piece of woodland in the middle of France, where the doughboys were under constant artillery fire and periodic strafing by German aircraft, who appeared to have complete supremacy.

Among those who fought at Belleau Wood was William A. Francis, a twenty-year-old ruddy-cheeked Texan and former clerk, now a private in the 5th Marines, 2nd Division. On the night of 31 May he was ferried by train, with the rest of the 2nd Division, to the town of Meaux, twenty miles east of Paris on the Marne: 'We were met at the station by a great number of French peasants who were trying to get a train for Paris; they were very excited, saying the Germans were only a few kilometres away, that we were going to sure death.'[19]

From Meaux they hiked for two hours uphill. They could feel the ground vibrate with the sound of heavy artillery gunfire. They then waited for several hours before being collected by American-made trucks, which took several more hours to ship them to the third line, along roads choked with traffic, refugees and some fleeing French troops. John Thomason, a lieutenant with the 5th Marines, recorded his impressions:

No man who saw that road in the first days of June ever forgot it. A stream of old men and children and old and young women turned out of their homes between two sunrises, with what they could carry in their hands. You saw an ancient in a linen smock and sabots, trundling a wheelbarrow, whereon rode a woman as old as himself, with a feather-bed and a selection of copper pots and a string of garlic [. . .] Women carrying babies. Children – solemn little boys in black pinafores, and curly-headed, high-nosed little girls, trudging hand-in-hand. People of elegance and refinement on inadequate shoes. Broad-faced peasants. Inhabitants of a thousand peaceful little villages and farms, untouched by the war since 1914. Now the Boche was out again [. . .] There were French soldiers in the rout, too. Nearly all were wounded, or in the last stages of exhaustion. They did not appear to be first-line troops; they were old, bearded fellows of forty and fifty-five, territorials, or mean, unpleasant-looking Algerians, such troops as are put in to hold a quiet sector.[20]

The marines had a professional *esprit de corps*, even though there were few veterans in their ranks. Private Malcolm Aitken had arrived at Brest on 6 May; a month later he was in the thick of the fighting at Belleau Wood where 'there was none of this "gallant charge, with officer, drawn sword leading, and the Colors the center of things".'

Aitken, Francis and the rest of them ditched their packs, keeping only their blankets and emergency rations. In the last month they had neither shaved nor bathed; they had taken a drenching from the skies every single day. They marched on towards their unknown destination until, after several more miles, they were handed two more bandoliers of ammunition. Eventually they reached Lucy-le-Bocage, where Briga-dier-General James Harbord, whom Pershing had placed in command of the marine brigade for this operation, had established his HQ. Francis found that 'Lucy' was a hot spot:

The Germans are shelling us pretty hard and the town is practically destroyed [. . .] A building on our right is burning, and as the flames light up the ground around us I can see dead Marines lying in the narrow road [. . .] At three o'clock [a.m.] we started again for the front trenches; we must reach the front line before daylight. The woods we are going through is [sic] very dense, it seems impossible to make our way through, the limbs from the trees are hitting us in the face and the men are cursing like the devil. The line has been broken several times, it is very hard to keep closed up for men are falling into shell holes and old trenches and it is very dark. If the man in front of you were to get three feet away you would surely be lost [. . .] The lines are so complicated that you are likely to run into the German trenches at any time. After a miserable night of hiking we reached the front-line trenches and were told to dig in immediately, and believe me we surely did [. . .] The Germans are shelling us very hard; a shell hit close by caving in our dug-out. A friend by the name of Burke was just killed, a piece of shrapnel taking his head off.[21]

Francis found himself a dugout, no more than three feet deep, and settled down in six inches of water to try to get some rest. The 2nd Division were now in support of the French, who were making a stand along the line of the villages of Bouresches, Belleau, Torcy and Bussiares. Between 2 and 4 June the Germans launched sporadic night raids on the French and Americans. Francis and his comrades fought for their survival:

The second night we were here the Germans attacked us. It is almost impossible to describe what we went thru. The Germans came down the hill firing everything at us, machine guns, rifle and hand grenades. We opened up immediately with our rifles and threw hand grenades as if they had been baseballs. We could not see them, but we knew that they were only a few yards away and that they were set upon taking our trench. They would hold up for a few minutes and start all over again. But we never let up with our fire for a minute; kept throwing hand grenades. This lasted all thru the night, and they finally decided that there was too many of us for them so they fell back to their old positions. A boy next to me threw a hand grenade and hit a tree in front of our trench, it bounded back on our parapet and exploded, we saw it just in time to hit the bottom of our trench and keep from getting killed. I could hardly keep from laughing for the boy on the other side of me started cursing because he came near getting killed by one of our own men.[22]

By the night of 5 June the line being held south of the Marne from Château-Thierry for almost ten miles east comprised the 3rd Division (AEF) in Château-Thierry; the 39th French Division; the 2nd Division

AEF, and finally, on the far east of the line, the 167th French Division. The 2nd Division was now part of the 21st French Army Corps, under Major-General Jean Degoutte.

On 5 June senior US and French officers on the ground debated what to do. Harbord and his senior staff had no maps and little or no knowledge of the local situation; they had simply been thrown in to plug a gap. One French colonel suggested to the commander of the 5th Marines, Colonel Wendell C. Neville, who wore his Medal of Honor with some pride, that the best thing to do was to retreat. This was an unfamiliar word to Neville, who replied: 'Retreat, hell. We just got here.'[23]

If there was to be no retreat then, said Degoutte, there must be a counter-attack. The 2nd Division was ordered to cross the wheatfields separating their higgledy piggledy trenches and shallow dugouts at 5 a.m. on the morning of Thursday, 6 June. They were to seize the crest upon which sat the town of Bouresches and Belleau Wood. There were no tanks or flamethrowers available for the attack, and only a relatively thin rolling artillery barrage; the infantry would have to press it home. There were to be three attacks altogether – on 6, 9 and 12 June – before the marines were relieved on 17 June. They were then dragged back into the attack to try to finish the job on 25 June. Rarely had a square mile of forest seen so much bloodshed.

On 6 June Bouresches was taken after bitter fighting by the 6th Marines, who through sheer grit also managed to get a toe-hold in Belleau Wood. But this wooded area was devilishly well defended; machine-gunners had inserted themselves in perfect, naturally created defensive holes in small nooks and crannies of rocky boulders, or were completely masked by dense undergrowth which had been untouched in centuries. The 6th Marines

attacked across the open, losing hideously. Platoons were shot down entire [. . .] Lieutenant Robinson got into Bouresches, with twenty men out of some hundred who had started, threw the Boche out, and held it. They gained a footing in the rocky ledges at the edge of the Bois de Belleau, suffering much from what was believed to be a machine-gun nest at this point. They tried to leave it and go on, with a containing force to watch it; they found that the whole wood was a machine-gun nest.[24]

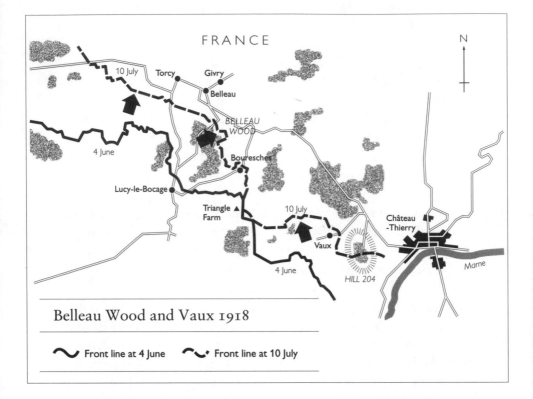

FRANCE   N

Belleau Wood and Vaux 1918

Front line at 4 June   Front line at 10 July

On the left of the assault the 5th Marines struggled to advance a kilometre towards the village of Torcy, taking Hill 142 by midday. Many legends were forged at Belleau Wood on 6 June, and none quite so long-lived as that surrounding a 49-year-old gunnery sergeant with the 73rd Machine Gun Company of the 6th Marines. Daniel Joseph Daly was a small man, just 5 feet 4 inches. But he was clearly tough, thanks to nineteen years with the marines; he had twice been awarded the Navy Medal of Honor, at Peking in 1900 and in 1915 for service in Haiti. Daly's legend was forged by a journalist, the ubiquitous Floyd Gibbons who was to lose his left eye later that day while getting too close to the action at Belleau Wood. Gibbons was with Daly's unit when it attacked the Germans on the morning of 6 June. Almost instantly the marines were pinned down in the open wheatfields that lay between their lines and the wood. Gibbons then captured the story of 'Devil Dog Dan', as Daly was christened on that day:

A runner came scrambling through the brush, and handed the old Gunnery Sergeant a sheet of paper. He read it quickly, then glanced along the line of the dug-in platoon. He stood up and made a forward motion to his men. There was slight hesitation. Who in the hell could blame them? Machine gun and rifle bullets were kicking up the dirt, closer and closer. The sergeant [Daly] ran out to the center of his platoon – he swung his bayoneted rifle over his head with a forward sweep. He yelled at his men: 'Come on, you sons-of-bitches! Do you want to live forever?'

Where Daly led, the marines followed.[25]

But by 10 June the Germans were still stubbornly clinging on to Belleau Wood, and the marines were almost exhausted. Brigadier-General Harbord called for relief; his brigade had been in constant action for thirteen days, with little water and no hot food. At AEF headquarters at Chaumont, Fox Conner, head of Operations (G-3), instructed Major Richardson, Chaumont's liaison officer with Degoutte: 'On that question of relief, leave that matter entirely to the French. Do not insist on any relief. The reports that we have show that conditions are not very bad.'

Degoutte thus informed Harbord that there could be no question of relief until 25 June. Harbord exploded and, thanks to his longstanding friendship with Pershing, got his way and managed to have Conner's decision overruled. The 7th Infantry of the 3rd Division was then lent to General Omar Bundy, the 2nd Division's commander, for six days. On the night of 15 June this regiment started moving into Belleau Wood, which although reported clear of the enemy on 12 June was not wholly and finally captured until fourteen days later, thanks to the participation of the 9th and 23rd Infantry Regiments of the 2nd Division. Lieutenant-Colonel John P. Adams, commanding the 7th's 1st Battalion, informed Harbord that the battalion's attack would commence at 3.15 a.m. on 21 June, but first he had some big demands to make. He asked for 1,000 hand grenades and other munitions, for food to be sent to the attacking company as it had not eaten in more than twenty-four hours, and for a heavy artillery barrage to be mounted against the wood: 'The wood is almost a thicket and the throwing of troops into the woods is filtering away men with nothing gained [. . .] I can assure you that the orders to attack will stand as given, but it cannot succeed.'[26]

Adams was right; the attack failed, as did that of the 7th's 3rd Battalion on 22 June, in which Sergeant Alison Page, the nineteen-year-old son of Walter Hines Page, the US ambassador in London, was killed. During its time at Belleau Wood the 7th, already hammered from its defence of Château-Thierry, lost what little ground the marines had first gained. On 21–22 June the 5th and 6th Regiments of marines went back into the wood, relieving the 7th Infantry. The marines found the Germans still grimly clinging on, as if aware that to concede ground now might mean having to do so all the way back to Berlin:

Good German troops, with every device of engineering skill, and all their cunning gained in war, poured into the wood. Battalions of Marines threw themselves against it. Day and night for nearly a month men fought in its corpse-choked thickets, killing with bayonet and bomb and machine-gun. It was gassed and shelled and shot into the semblance of nothing earthly. The great trees all went down; the leaves were blasted off, or hung sere and blackened. It was pock-marked with shell craters and shallow dugouts and hasty trenches. It was strewn with all the debris of war, Mauser rifles and Springfields, helmets, German and American, unexploded grenades, letters, knapsacks, packs, blankets, boots. A year later, it is said, they were still finding unburied dead in the depths of it.[27]

The already bitter fighting now became extremely callous. The doughboys were (unofficially) ordered to take no prisoners. This was one of the rare occasions when hand-to-hand combat with bayonets, knuckledusters and something the doughboys called a 'toad sticker' – a 6–8 inch triangular steel blade set on a knuckle handle – came into use. Private Aitken became 'quite adept' with the toad sticker:[28]

We lost several men and had a lovely bayonet scrap in a counter attack. This time they [the Germans] failed to break. How they could stand up under our fire I don't know because it was murderous. They didn't have a chance as we rushed them down hill. The roar we gave as we came out was spontaneous and we went at it hammer and tongs. We used But-strike (*sic*) and slash no sticking because of pressure. It must have lasted a good fifteen minutes before they finally broke. We followed them for fifty yards and they put up a splendid defense, but to no avail. We drove them off easily according to the report turned in. There were no trees or brush to hamper our charge and we sure charged. The afterglow was interesting: most of us just sat down and cried. Jim Lannon was gone and so many of our best friends. We saw them fall. However we got our revenge. At last I know Grandad's feeling of willing to fight with your bare hands. You sure had to be fast and furious.[29]

On Sunday, 25 June Belleau Wood finally and lastingly fell into the hands of the AEF. Colonel Paul Malone, commander of the 23rd, reported his regiment on that day alone suffered 855 casualties, 334 of them from gas. He estimated 4,000 gas shells had been fired on his positions in the wood. The marines had certainly been savaged. Their two regiments, half the divisional strength (or roughly 13,500 men), had suffered 113 officers and 5,598 men killed, wounded and missing; the 9th and 23rd together lost 65 officers and 3,496 men.[30]

Was it worth it? General Bullard thought so. 'The marines didn't "win the war" here. *But they saved the Allies from defeat.* Had they arrived a few hours later I think that would have been the beginning of the end: France could not have stood the loss of Paris.'[31]

Private Aitken[32] was one of just twenty survivors from the 250 original members of Company D. At the start of the battle he was a mere novice; by its end he was a hardened veteran:

We are in little foxholes in reserve after the Belleau woods and Boureoches fracas. Alas only a few are left of the gang. We buried skads of them this morning, some very badly decomposed as they had been in the hot sun for two days. They were bluish-black in color and the odor beggars description. It was a job and a half to get their dogtags and personal effects. Took quite a time. After laying them side by side forty or so to a 6ft trench we stood with uncovered heads while the service, short and to the point was recited. There were some twenty of us on this detail and we recognized several of our former friends. We had to go out with stretchers and pick them up very carefully and roll them into the trench in a very careful manner after having been searched for personal effects etc. The one tag was left on the body, the other attached to a rude cross at the head. The Chaplain kept score in his little book, listing the effects under the name and address of the body when possible. Just as the final prayer was being recited the first of a bracket of three shells lit a little in front and to the right scattering the first dirt on the bodies and on us. It was 20 feet or more away so we didn't duck much. The next shell arrived within the minute and went over us about the same distance, we ducked and tried for cover, by throwing ourselves on the ground, for no time was to be lost. The third of the group made a direct hit on our beautiful trench. Two of the detail were killed and three wounded. We buried the pieces and said some more hurried prayers, took our wounded to the PC reported the casualties and here we are. C'est le Guerre.[33]

After the battle, the honours to those who survived:

We were called to an area, a few at a time and there was some Brass (a Major and Colonel from our GHQ and a couple of French Field Brass, with the sweeping moustache, and wine breath). Each of us received a Croix de Guerre from one of the brilliant bodies, and was he dressed; colored uniform, medals, the works; a kiss on both cheeks accompanied the presentation, no written citation. We had saved Paris; Belleau Wood was now formally known as the Bois de la Brigade, de la Marine; hurray for our side.[34]

Though the 2nd and 3rd Divisions were valiantly holding back the Germans, the panic among the Allies obviously began to wear down Pershing's resistance to their demands for more and more combat troops. By the end of the month the AEF had 40,487 officers and 833,204 enlisted men in France, a significant force.[35] Yet by now the French were convinced that nothing less than 4 million doughboys would suffice to beat the Germans, and even then only by the spring of 1919. Pershing pointed out that this would necessitate an extra million men in France simply to service and supply this massive army, which in any case would be the equal of 200 British and French divisions, when at this date the combined British and French strength was no more than 162 divisions. Pershing thought the maximum number of troops that could be shipped by early 1919, given logistical considerations, would be 3 million, or 66 to 70 divisions. In a cable sent to the War Department on 21 June Pershing asked that sufficient men be conscripted to achieve an 80-division-strong AEF by April 1919, with 100 divisions by July of that year:

The morale of the French Government and of the High Command is believed to be good but it is certain that the morale of the lower grades of the French Army is distinctly poor. Both the French and British people are extremely tired of the war and their troops are reflecting this attitude in their frequent inability to meet successfully the German attacks. It is the American soldiers now in France upon whom they rely. It is the moral as well as material aid given by the American soldier that is making the continuation of the war possible [. . .] The war can be brought to a successful conclusion next year if we only go at it now.[36]

Despite the pervasive gloom within the Allied camp, Cantigny and Belleau Wood had proved to Pershing that his soldiers could fight as well as anyone, and he was determined no longer to be bullied by the French and British. Talking to General Bullard about relations with the Allies after Cantigny and Belleau Wood, he asked Bullard:

'Do they patronize you? [. . .] Do they assume superior airs with you?'

'No sir,' I answered, 'they do not. I have been with them too long and know them too well.'

'By—! they have been trying it with me, and I don't intend to stand a bit of it,' he said, vehemently. He meant it.[37]

13

July–August 1918

If those in front of us are fair specimens of the average American troops, and there are as many as they say there are, then good-by for us.   Gefreiter Earl Recklinghausen[1]

Since the spring, the trickle of doughboy divisions landing in France had begun to turn into a flood. On 13 April the 77th (the Metropolitan, recruited from New York City) – the first division of the National Army, as the designation for the conscripted divisions had it – landed in France; after preliminary training it went to relieve the 42nd Division in the quiet Baccarat sector of the Vosges, where it had been in line for 140 days. The 5th (Red Diamond) docked in France on 1 May; the 35th on 11 May; the 4th (the Ivy) on 17 May; the 82nd (called the 'All American' because it took its draft from right across the nation) on 13 May; the 28th (Pennsylvania National Guard) on 18 May; the 33rd (the Illinois National Guard, known as the 'Prairie') on 24 May; while on 30 May the first units of the 80th (or Blue Ridge) Division and on 31 May those of the 27th (New York) began landing. Nine more divisions, including the two comprising black Americans, the 92nd (known as the Buffalo) and 93rd, as well as the 89th, arrived in June and July. The start of the summer saw twenty combat divisions in France; seven were in the Marne area, around Château-Thierry; four were with the British; and the other nine were either training or headed for it in the Vosges mountains.

By now both the 1st and 2nd Divisions had proved they could halt the most aggressive German attacks and capture fiercely held German defensive positions. In mid-July 2nd Lieutenant John D. Clark felt a new confidence in his own and his unit's abilities, able to tough out anything:

'Shock troops' we are, I guess. For on the evening of the 14th [July] we received orders to pack and move out. We traveled for two days and nights with practically no sleep or food – drivers went to sleep in the saddle, falling forward on their horses' necks. Last night we finally pulled in, finding ourselves in the Villers-Cotterets sector [. . .] the roads are choked with troops, ammunition and supplies. During the night and this morning I saw a large number of tanks going forward [. . .] The troops which have been massed here [for the assault on Soissons] are the best of the French army. That we are joining them is a sign that we have gained some prestige.[2]

His 1st Division had by now endured three nights of continuous marching. Exhaustion overcame many of the doughboys, including Major Raymond Austin, who was so washed-out that he began to hallucinate:

After the first day and night I didn't feel sleepy at all (it was really the third night without sleep as I had had one night of seven hours out of four days previous) but got dull in thought and action, and the last night I began to 'see things'. Distant objects like stars, lights, lone trees, etc., would move back and forth, and the road would seem to creep like the track when you look at it from the end of a train.[3]

The 1st Division marched to within ten miles of the French capital, and Austin became quite sick. His regimental surgeon, Major Bealo (who was himself to die a few days later), ordered him to stay in bed. Austin was fortunate; his bedridden state meant he avoided being immediately ordered with the rest of his regiment to march another twenty kilometres towards the supposed front line, 'only to receive orders when they arrived at their destination at 2 a.m. to return to the place they had just come from. They got back about noon, and at 3 p.m. the guns and gun squads and the necessary officers were loaded on trucks and taken to the front.'

Austin, by now in command of three batteries of the 1st Battalion, 6th Field Artillery, had been hauled from his bed to assist in the halt of the last great German offensive of 1918, the crossing of the Marne, which commenced with a tremendous artillery barrage (from an estimated 336 guns) at midnight on 14 July. This was the fifth German offensive in as many months. The German Seventh Army, under General von Boehn, crossed the Marne west of Epernay in the early hours of 15 July. He faced a weakened French Fifth Army, which included two Italian divisions and some elements of the AEF's 28th Division, which had arrived in France less than two months before. At the far western extreme of the German attack was the AEF's 3rd Division under the redoubtable Major-General Joseph Dickman. Within Dickman's division was the 38th Infantry Regiment, soon to become the stuff of yet another battlefield legend.

The 38th Regiment was commanded by the superbly named Colonel Ulysses Grant McAlexander, who for weeks had been preparing his defensive positions on the south bank of the Marne. McAlexander, another West Pointer, was almost fifty-four. He was a fine soldier and had been with the 1st Division since it landed in France in June 1917, but he did not see eye-to-eye with General Bullard and had left the 1st Division for the 38th Regiment in May 1918. Since then he had spent his time carefully organizing three battalions of the regiment in a defensive position of four lines of resistance: along the bank of the Marne river; the Paris–Metz railway (some 350 yards back from the river); in a line along an aqueduct; and in another along some woods. To the left of the 38th, the neighbouring 30th Infantry Regiment had made scant defensive preparations, while on McAlexander's right flank the French 131st Regiment was even less concerned to prepare for any assault, claiming instead to be making ready a form of what it called 'elastic defence' – which for McAlexander hinted very strongly of a readiness to run. McAlexander stationed several companies in depth down his right flank, just in case the French collapsed and exposed his flank. His lack of confidence in the French was criticized at the time but proved to be remarkably prescient.

As the German bombardment started in the early hours of 15 July, one of the 38th's forward companies, G, under the command of Captain Jesse Wooldridge, was dug in along a 600-yard length of the river bank. Wooldridge watched as, under cover of the artillery, German soldiers of the 10th and 36th Divisions crossed the sluggish Marne in pontoon boats and over a light floating bridge. To Wooldridge's right were Companies E and H. They opened fire and quickly sank all the German pontoons, while on the left flank the 30th Regiment was, predictably, beaten back from its poorly prepared defences. On McAlexander's right flank the French 131st Regiment quickly fled without putting up much resistance. General Dickman had ordered the 38th not to surrender or retreat; to have done so would have given the Germans two valuable roads upon which they could have more easily transported their attacking armies, having captured the towns of Varennes and Mézy. For a distance of up to five kilometres on either flank the 38th was thus surrounded by German attackers. Yet for three magnificent days the 38th, well dug in on its flanks and determined not to cede an inch of ground, grimly held on and denied the field to the Germans, whose two attacking divisions were gradually reduced to shreds by the 38th. Wooldridge, who personally led several counter-attacks and whose company ended up taking more than 400 prisoners, found by the end of the battle he had 'fourteen bullet holes in my blouse'. Three of his company went 'raving mad'.[4] Altogether 2,917 officers and men of the 38th were to die in the course of the war; this action alone cost it 20 per cent in casualties, normally enough to break any unit's will to continue fighting. McAlexander was immediately dubbed 'The Rock of the Marne'.

The exemplary behaviour of the 38th Regiment was a salutary lesson for the Allies in what was to be the Germans' last great offensive of the war. Three days after it started the French army, under General Gouraud, had managed to repel the attack all along the Champagne front. The Germans found themselves over-extended in the Marne salient, a long, narrow salient which ran from Soissons to Reims. They had in the past month tried on two occasions to burst through it, but had only succeeded in deepening it and thus exacerbating their supply problems. Now Marshal Foch was determined to recapture Soissons, by striking at the hinge of the Marne salient. At his disposal he could eventually count on 1,200 pieces of artillery, 500 tanks and 1,100 aircraft, as well as the French Tenth and Sixth Armies, twenty-four divisions in all. Lieutenant-General Bullard was instructed to take command of the 1st (under the immediate command of Major-General Summerall) and 2nd (led by Major-General James Harbord), form them into the American Third Corps, and assemble in the forest of Villers-Cottêrets to attack the western side of the Marne salient as part of the French Tenth Army.

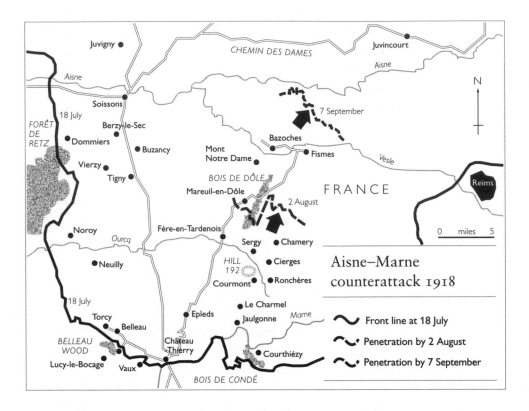

Juvigny

CHEMIN DES DAMES

Juvincourt

Aisne

Aisne

Soissons

18 July

7 September

FORÊT
DE
RETZ

Berzy-le-Sec

Bazoches

Dommiers

Buzancy

Mont
Notre Dame

Fismes

Vierzy

Vesle

Tigny

BOIS DE DÔLE

FRANCE

Reims

Mareuil-en-Dôle

2 August

Noroy

Fère-en-Tardenois

Ourcq

Sergy

Chamery

Aisne–Marne
counterattack 1918

Neuilly

HILL
192

Cierges

Courmont

Ronchères

0   miles   5

18 July

Le Charmel

Torcy

Epleds

Jaulgonne

Marne

Belleau

BELLEAU
WOOD

Château
Thierry

Courthiézy

Front line at 18 July

Lucy-le-Bocage

Vaux

BOIS DE CONDÉ

Penetration by 2 August

Penetration by 7 September

In this counter-offensive the French constituted 80 per cent of the
Allied forces, spread across a 27-mile front. In order to gain the
advantage of surprise, there was no preliminary bombardment. The
key objective was the Fère-en-Tardenois railway, the only line of
communication of the German army inside the Marne pocket. The
German front was held by the Seventh Army, with twelve divisions in
the front line and eight in reserve. Opposing was the French Tenth
Army (under General Mangin) from the Aisne to the Ourcq (the French
1st, 20th, 39th and 11th Corps); the 1st and 2nd Divisions of the AEF,
and the 15th Scottish Division. The French Sixth Army (under General
Degoutte, with the French 2nd and 7th Corps) plus the 14th and 26th
Divisions of the AEF, from the Ourcq to Château-Thierry.

Now rallied from his fever, Major Austin began to grasp the scale
of the imminent offensive:

Truck trains in endless numbers moved along every road, batteries or light artillery, immense tractor-drawn 6, 8 and 12 inch guns, staff cars hastening in all directions, blue snake-like columns of French infantry, regiments of Senegalese troops (big negroes whose blackness makes the blackest negroes I have ever seen pale in comparison), brown-skinned Moroccans in olive drab uniforms similar to ours, groups of Indo-Chinese laborers, strangely camouflaged tanks, military police at all turns and cross roads directing traffic, like policemen in a big city [. . .] I saw ten trainloads of tanks, averaging about 25 tanks per train. They were of all sizes – a large part of them were enormous things – real land battleships carrying a three inch gun and several machine guns, others were smaller like the ones we had at Cantigny. Also trainloads of airplanes, solid box car trains of bread, gasoline tanks, ammunition dumps, everything in the world seemingly – and very nearly true literally. And all this was for just one small part of the line.[5]

As usual, there was considerable logistical chaos within the AEF before the battle for Soissons, which started on 18 July. Huge traffic jams clogged the roads. Orders were immediately countermanded and fresh orders given. In the darkness, officers lost their units and units mislaid their officers. The fact that all the preparation was in haste and carried out at night meant the whole attack was in jeopardy before it even started. On the night of 17 July, along three roads leading to the sector of the front where the Americans were to form up for the attack, some 67,000 men, 5,000 animals and 3,000 vehicles struggled to move forward in a drenching downpour. Not that the AEF's commanders were solely to blame; most of the time their French comrades, nominally responsible for the overall conduct of this attack, rarely informed them as to what was going on. The roads surrounding the jump-off points were

one solid mass of tanks, ammunition trains, trucks, infantry, and artillery. The Boches evidently suspected nothing and so did not shell the roads much. If they had had any idea that the attack was coming at that particular time they would have shelled heavily, of course, and the results in that compact mass would have been terrible.[6]

Major Austin 'despaired' of being able to struggle through this mess to get his ammunition caissons to his guns in time for the opening of the attack, particularly as the guide who was to take him to his command post managed to lose him in the town of Coeuvres in the early hours of the morning ('I could have shot that man with great satisfaction, only he was nearly as much distressed as I') just before the attack was due to begin, at 4.45 a.m. on Thursday, 18 July. Lieutenant Clark was scarcely on time at his post, either:

It was after 11 o'clock [p.m.] before the barrage data [for next morning's attack] became available and I started the trip to deliver them. It had rained to add to the normal darkness. The road was now clogged with artillery, tanks, ambulances and every conceivable vehicle. For long periods nothing moved. I rode a large rangy horse who seemed to possess a sixth sense when it came to finding an opening in the traffic [. . .] It seemed miraculous but we got to regimental headquarters just before midnight with the barrage orders. As I was riding back to brigade, there seemed to be an open stretch of road just ahead and I started to trot. Then there appeared to be a darker shadow approaching and I reined in the horse just in time to avoid running into a column of infantrymen who were dog-trotting in the mud with each man holding onto the shoulder of the man in front of him. They were to reach the front just in time to shed their packs and go over the top. These were some of the men General Harbord [in command of the 2nd Division] was relying on to make the attack but of whose whereabouts he had not the slightest idea.[7]

Major Austin located his command post just before the start of the rolling barrage, which began immediately in front of the French and American lines and was timed to move forward at the rate of 100 yards every three minutes. Every fourth shell was of smoke, intended to confuse the enemy's machine-gunners. Austin's command post was in a trench on a high ridge on the far side of Coeuvres, an ideal spot from which to watch the battle as it unfolded across a forty-kilometre front that morning.

When the artillery 'cut loose' it made the ground tremble and every hill and valley was just a mass of flashes in the dim light of early morning. I never realized that there was that much artillery in the world. The guns of my three American batteries (I also had three French, but saw little of them as they did only barrage work) were set almost hub to hub and there were many batteries above and below them on the same hillside [. . .] The Infantry went forward in a long line extending as far as could be seen to either side, the successive waves following each other at even intervals.[8]

Private Francis in the 2nd Division had never seen anything quite like it:

I will never forget the sight when our artillery opened up. It was worse than any electrical storm I have ever seen. The whole sky seemed to open up for it became as light as day. This put new life into us and we went over as if we had just hopped off the trucks. It was impossible to hear anyone talk, and the artillery kept a continual roar day and night. It seemed like thunder and it didn't even let up for five minutes.[9]

According to Lieutenant John Clark the attack 'came as a surprise to the enemy', and the German trenches were soon overrun by the 1st Division's 16th Infantry. Major Austin quickly limbered up his batteries and pursued the retreating Germans, giving much-needed field artillery support. A 'few hundred yards' brought his gunners to the first German trenches 'where lay a few gray-coated Germans and an occasional American', and on across the second line of trenches across fields 'dotted with dead. The farther in we went the more dead we found as the Germans use the "coil spring defense" which consists in holding the front line lightly, the next a little more strongly, and so on [. . .] This "disposition of troops in depth" is now used by both sides.'

Lieutenant John Clark's twenty-second birthday fell on 19 July. He thought it might be his last and he wrote a farewell letter to his parents. Had he been able to read Clark's diary entry for 19 July (where he notes that he has just learned the Soissons–Château-Thierry road has been crossed), Pershing would have been delighted at the vindication he implicitly receives there:

It is now open warfare, movement being carried on irrespective of whether it is day or night. Our batteries are lines up in the open, firing with practically no concealment, the enemy planes are thick overhead [. . .] It is all like a great cinema, constantly changing, constantly moving. Cars, trucks, men, horses, aeroplanes – all in a jumble.

This jubilation was premature, even though at this stage the German rout seemed complete. Major Austin quickly established a new firing post at an old German emplacement and commenced firing at Germans who were 'fleeing along the roads and fields in droves pursued by tanks which fired at them with machine guns and "75" cannon. Evidently the attack surprised the Boches and our losses the first day were comparatively light. By the next day they had reorganized, sown the ground with machine guns, and we lost heavily from then on.'

Outside his command post were two wounded Germans, 'one a lieutenant fatally wounded. It would have been a mercy to have shot him but no one had the heart to do it, and he lay there raving all day, and died about 7 p.m. The other was a boy of 19, shot through the legs and hands. His hands were mere shreds but he had lots of nerve and we did what we could for him, and about 10 p.m., after the American wounded had been removed, we had him carried in by some Boche prisoners who happened to pass there.'

By 5.35 a.m. on the first day of this attack the French and Americans had reached their first objectives; the Germans had failed to dig in, perhaps in the belief that they would soon be moving on Paris. But this offensive threatened to go the way of many others – a stunning first-day success accompanied by tremendous euphoria, to be swiftly replaced by a growing realization that the initial impact could not be sustained. The tanks that had proved so effective on Day 1 were 'practically out of the fight after the first day. They were not used at all after the second day', according to Major Austin. As ever, the old-fashioned generals still in command could not rid themselves of their blind adherence to superseded ideas; thus in this offensive regiments of cavalry were waiting in the wings, as usual:

There were several thousand French Cavalrymen (lancers) near us awaiting a chance to break through the lines. They had large bodies out on reconnais-sance and the Boche went after them pretty hard. The Germans had ranged on the crest to our front where the national road runs and as these troops of cavalry came galloping over the crest they fired upon them heavily and horses and men would fall rolling and kicking as the shells fell among them. It was very spectacular and occurred often during the day, but we hated to see them coming as it meant a shelling for us as we were just back of the crest.[10]

And once again it seemed to the doughboys on the ground that the Germans had complete control of the skies above. During the night of the first day of the battle the American and French positions were strafed by low-flying German heavy bombing aircraft, called Gothas:

[. . .] they dropped wonderfully brilliant illuminating shells that hung in the air for many minutes lighting up the ground below almost as brightly as the sun, and the planes, being on the far side of the light, were invisible to our machine gunners, who could direct their fire only by the sound of the motors [. . .] Then, with their targets brilliantly illuminated, they dropped heavy bombs that burst with terrific concussions, tore big holes in the ground, and covered everyone with showers of dirt and stones. I have never felt so helpless in my life and how we got through without losing a lot of men and most of the guns is almost inexplicable. The ground all around was pitted with big holes and the whole place covered with loose dirt and rocks, but we had almost no casualties, as luckily no bombs struck directly in the trenches which were dug near the guns.[11]

On Friday, 19 July the doughboys began to learn just how difficult it was to turn the initial advantage gained by a surprise assault into a full-blown breakthrough. That day the 2nd Division

lost half its men. Part of the division will be relieved tonight, but the battle is not nearly over. We have gained from ten to fifteen kilometers in depth, but the Boche have now had time to recover to some extent and will undoubtedly counter-attack within a few days. Their artillery has been active today – too close for comfort when everyone is in the open. The Boche are supreme in the air and have amused themselves today by flying over and popping at us with their machine-guns from a low altitude.[12]

On this same day Major Austin also began to observe how stubborn German machine-gunners, well hidden and entrenched and thus able to avoid the barrage, could inflict heavy damage on the attackers. One machine-gun casualty was the 16th Infantry's Major Theodore Roosevelt Jnr, shot in the leg, placed on a battery limber by Austin and sent to the rear. Once again well-dug-in machine-guns, supported by carefully ranged artillery, demonstrated that the most vigorously pursued open warfare would grind to a halt. While he was attending to the needs of Major Roosevelt, Austin was also trying to bring his A Battery forward, to direct fire onto a machine-gun nest which was holding up the advance of his particular sector of the front line. The machine-gun was rapidly knocked out and the

gunner of that machine gun, strange to say, was captured unharmed and brought in to my PC with some other prisoners. He said he was a Saxon and belonged to the famous Kaiser Wilhelm Regiment. He wore the Iron Cross Ribbon. The Boche machine gunners seem to be the best and nerviest men they have. There have been cases where German machine gunners have been found chained to their guns but these cases are extremely exceptional and men so placed were certainly put there for punishment for some misdeed. I have never known of such a case personally. The gunner I speak of was a surly sort of brute but he held up a part of our line practically single-handed. With him was a boy of 19, who said that the day before he had come to the front for the first time.[13]

On all sides, the toll was acute. Lieutenant Clark recalled that a senior 1st Lieutenant, Ed Blanchard, 'an efficient and popular officer', was by this time suffering from complete exhaustion, and little wonder – that day the batteries of the 15th Field Artillery fired a thousand rounds per gun, and the barrels became red-hot:

By noontime [on 20 July], Eddie was going around with his mouth hanging open – an obvious victim of 'shell shock' [. . .] We told him that he ought to go back for a rest but he maintained that he was all right. Early in the afternoon we summoned an ambulance and sent him back to the hospital. Later, we heard that he had died, so we divided up his usable belongings. I think I got his bedding roll.[14]

Late on Saturday, 20 July, the now almost exhausted 2nd Division, which had found its advance for the first few miles 'nothing but a hike', was relieved from the front line of the assault by French troops. Their hike by evening slowed to a crawl, bogged down outside the well-defended town of Vierzy. But because of the desperate nature of the situation its artillery remained in line, to continue trying to help press the attack home; the 15th Field Artillery was not relieved until 25 July. The resulting confusion of having US-commanded artillery working in support of French infantry was noted by Lieutenant Clark. The battalions of the 12th and 15th Field Artillery were limbered-up, ready to follow the advancing French infantry, who failed to make any impact on the by now prepared German positions. One battalion from the 15th and another from the 12th failed to hear the order not to trot behind the French and galloped straight into German artillery and machine-gun fire, with heavy losses before withdrawing. And there were penalties, as well as benefits, to be gained from a return to open warfare. On 20 July, Clark noted: 'Our position was wholly exposed to observation as the Boche had supremacy of the air, and, as we expected, on the afternoon of the 21st the Boche started to shell us out. All they had to do was to direct fire from a balloon on a beautiful target [. . .]'[15]

No sleep, little food or water, constant harassing counter fire, the trauma of spending what little spare time there was burying dead comrades, the smell of death and the cries of the wounded – after three days of this any unit's will to press on would begin to suffer.

The attack began to flag and on Sunday, 21 July it came to a standstill for three days. The Germans still held the higher ground on the Chandun plateau, and were fighting for every inch of ground. The 2nd Division had advanced some seven miles but at terrible cost, with almost 50 per cent casualties in some units.[16] Austin proudly walked off the battlefield with the only souvenir he craved – an Iron Cross, which he obtained from an officer named Roesch. His battalion marched all night on the 22 July to Mortefontaine and in a few days was removed by train to a rest area, with 24-hour passes for visits to the nearest city, Nancy.

Meanwhile the 1st Division had been pulled into the conflict on 20 July to accomplish something which had proved beyond the French 1st Moroccan Division: the taking by storm of the heavily defended village of Berzy-le-Sec, occupied by the 1st Prussian Guards Division.

The 26th and 28th Infantry Regiments were ordered to attack the village at 2 p.m. Wave after wave of doughboys marched down the wooded slopes towards Berzy-le-Sec that afternoon, to be mown down by machine-gun fire. Major-General Summerall visited the lines after this failure and ordered the now depleted ranks of the two regiments to be filled with all the available cooks, orderlies, clerks, engineers and military police – and for the attack to be resumed the next morning. At their head was Brigadier Beaumont Buck, who drove his men to take the town while it was saturated with artillery fire.

On the night of 19–20 July the Germans evacuated the south bank of the Marne. The infantry of the 1st Division was now devastated, with 8,365 casualties, 1,252 of them dead; 75 per cent of all officers above the rank of captain, 60 per cent of all infantry officers, and 50 per cent of the enlisted men were casualties in this action. As the 'Big Red One' was relieved by the 15th Scottish Division on the night of 22–23 July, the 5th and 6th Artillery Regiments of the 1st Division put up a terrific barrage to speed them into the attack.

For some of those who took part in the early days of the battle for Soissons it felt like a watershed. According to Lieutenant Clark,

Soissons marked the turning point of the war. The 1st and 2nd American Divisions with the French 1st Moroccan Division (including a regiment of the famed Foreign Legion) turned the tide of war definitely in favor of the Allies. Although the Germans fought stubbornly to the end, they were henceforth always on the defensive.[17]

This was true, though the cost of forcing them onto the defensive was high; but such high casualty rates could be sustained by the Americans, anticipating the imminent arrival in France of hundreds of thousands of eager new young conscripts.

By the end of July the AEF had 54,224 officers and 1,114,838 enlisted men in France; of the latter, 175,000 were employed by the Services of Supply (SOS). Together with General Harbord, Pershing set off to inspect the SOS on 5 August, and discovered that despite the shortage of shipping transport, the Tours headquarters of the SOS, whose chief quartermaster was Brigadier-General Rogers, had enough rations to last for forty days (amounting to some 90,000 tons), but the truck and automobile situation was desperate, with just 50 per cent of what the SOS required. At the Tours base hospital he visited some of the casualties from the recent action on the Marne:

Passing through one of the wards of this hospital, I spoke to a fine-looking young soldier who was sitting up in bed and asked him where he was wounded, meaning to inquire as to the nature of his wound. In reply, he said, 'Do you remember, Sir, just where the road skirts a small grove and turns to the left across a wheatfield, and then leads up over the brow of the hill? Well! right there, Sir.'[18]

Elsewhere on the front, as the 3rd Division crossed the Marne on the morning of 21 July into Château-Thierry, it found the town virtually empty. The same morning the 26th Division, who had taken over the Belleau Wood sector, were also to attack; but they too found the Germans had gone. The two divisions pursued the Germans, who were carrying out a carefully prepared rearguard action to shrink the Marne pocket and straighten their front line between Soissons and Reims. The 32nd Division followed up the 3rd and 26th, and 1st Lieutenant Charles Donnelly led his gunners through the grisly battlefields:

Our recent companions-in-arms, the Yankee Division, had captured the area we had just entered only a few days before; there had not been time enough in which to clean up the battlefield. Dead men and horses littered the fields and putrefaction, aided by the warm weather, was well along. Of all the odors I have experienced, none is as repulsive as the sweetish, nauseating smell of rotting flesh, especially in hot weather. Up to that time I had never smoked but I needed something to help me cope with the stench. A field agent of the Knights of Columbus [one of the many US voluntary organizations in France] came by at about that time, giving away tobacco, writing paper and other things soldiers needed. I told him my problem and he gave me some cigars, Prince Albert, and a corncob pipe; I have been a cigar smoker from that day on.[19]

By the night of 26–27 July, the German-held Fère-en-Tardenois was under threat, and the Germans retreated again; Fère-en-Tardenois was taken on 28 July by the French 62nd and the AEF's 42nd Divisions.

By 4 August, harried by the 1st, 2nd, 3rd, 4th, 26th, 28th, 32nd and 42nd Divisions of the AEF in relatively small engagements, the German line had moved back along the river Vesle, which stretched from Reims to the Aisne river, which ran through Soissons. In eight days of fighting during this skilful German retreat the 42nd Division lost 184 officers and 5,469 men, but gained seven miles, while the 32nd had gained twelve miles and sustained 3,547 casualties. On 6 August, Foch was made Marshal of France; the French and Americans reached the Vesle and the advance was halted, as the Germans concentrated the majority of their reserves behind this line. Pétain received the Médaille Militaire (the second highest French military honour) and the Grand Croix de la Légion d'Honneur was awarded to Pershing. In three weeks the Germans had lost all the gains they had made between 27 May and 15 July, the salient was sliced off, and more than 18,000 German prisoners and 700 guns were captured.

The Second Battle of the Marne was a significant turning-point; from that time until the end of the war the Germans were outmanoeuvred and facing defeat. A breathing-space was again available (though of course intense shellfire and raids continued)[20] in which Pershing returned to his ultimate ambition – the creation of the independent and autonomously commanded American army. On 10 August he issued the formal order bringing the American First Army into being; its first task would be to rid the Western Front of that persistent carbuncle, the St-Mihiel salient, which had been jutting into the French lines since the start of the war. This was to be a showcase attack, a combined American and French effort, the first by the newly-formed First Army, and the means by which Pershing would demonstrate to all that the doughboys fought differently, better, and achieved greater things than anyone else.

It was certain that the psychological effect on the enemy of success in this first operation by the American Army, as well as on our Allies, our own troops, and our people at home, would be of signal importance. The attack must, therefore, not only carry through, but a serious hostile reaction must be made impossible.[21]

While Pershing planned his assault at St-Mihiel, on 8 August the British army surprised everyone by breaking through the German lines around Amiens. Ludendorff called this 'the Black Day in the history of the German Army in the war', as the Germans lost 700 officers and 27,000 men killed, wounded or taken prisoner, on the first day alone. By 12 August the Second Battle of the Marne had come to an end, Soissons was again in French hands, and on 13 August 1918 Pershing, Bliss and several members of the 33rd Division were decorated by King George V at the division's headquarters. Pershing received the Grand Cross of the Order of the Bath, Bliss the Order of St Michael and St George. But still the Allies tried to persuade Pershing to throw his troops into Allied custody; the King even raised the subject during the ceremony. Two days later Pershing was shown by Clemenceau a note sent to him by Lloyd George, in which he explained why he was so keen on having doughboys sent to train with the British and augment the British reserves:

I did not consider my demand excessive for it must not be forgotten that the greater part of the American troops were brought to France by British shipping and that because of the sacrifices made to furnish the shipping our people have the right to expect that more than five divisions of the twenty-eight now in France should be put in training behind our lines.[22]

In the phrase 'our people have the right' is the essence of the way in which Lloyd George and most of the other senior figures in the Anglo-French alliance regarded the AEF: as an entity over which they should have been accorded complete authority. Towards the end of August Lloyd George cabled Clemenceau that he had reason to believe that the United States was now planning to put eighty, not 100, divisions on the Western Front by July 1919, adding that this reduced programme could depend upon assistance from British shipping:

I regret to declare that we shall not be able to continue our help as far as cargoes of merchandise are concerned and that we shall probably have to cut down tonnage assigned for troop transportation. In the last few months we have lost several troop transports of large tonnage.[23]

Lloyd George cited 40,000 cotton workers idle in Lancashire and a lack of coal holding up ships in British ports as reasons why he might not be able to furnish the number of ships needed for the transportation of more doughboys. Yet by this time it was apparent to most that the U-boat threat had receded beyond serious concern. The truth is that he was irritated by his failure to get his own way with the doughboys.

By 31 August Lieutenant Clark's guns were in the usually quiet sector near St-Mihiel, an area he found 'most tranquil', the repose disturbed only by 'being bothered with the usual endless series of formations, drills, inspections and classes'.[24] There would soon be much greater bother.

14

Siberia

In the first place there was no war; in the second, there was no enemy, and in the third, there was nothing to fight about. And yet!! We engaged the Russians on six battle-scarred fronts [...]

Brigadier Johnson Hagood[1]

We came out from Vladivostok to catch the Bolshevik
We chased them o'er the mountains and we chased them through the creek
We chased them every Sunday and we chased them through the week
But we couldn't catch a gosh darned one.

Sung to the tune of *The Battle Hymn of the Republic*

While hundreds of thousands of Americans were fighting for the liberation of Belgium and France, machinations were going on in Washington to send some of them even further afield – to Russia, which by the middle of 1918 was partly under the control of the Bolsheviks. On 6 July 1918 the citizens of Vladivostok, one of the world's least accessible spots, woke to find themselves under yet another new administration. On this morning they found themselves being governed by the oddest bunch yet, the 'Allied Powers'. Copies of a proclamation were pasted up around the city, informing its inhabitants that, as the activities of 'Austro-German agents' were threatening calm and peaceful business, they were now 'under the provisional protection of the Allied Powers'. The proclamation was signed by Captain Badiura of the Czechoslovak army; Colonel Pons, chief of the French military mission attached to the Czechs; Captain Paine of the British Royal Navy; Vice-Admiral Kato of the Japanese Imperial Fleet; and Admiral

Knight of the United States Navy. Thus began one of the more bizarre episodes of the First World War, the opening round of Allied intervention in the internal affairs of Russia.[2] None of the Allied powers who took this high-handed action emerged from it with any glory. Some, including the United States, thrashed about with little or no idea as to what they were even trying to achieve. The best that can be said about the doughboy contingent sent to various parts of Siberia – 'a witch's cauldron of blood, politics, pillaging and intrigue' – as part of this Allied intervention is that it abused its power rather less than any of the other participants.[3]

As many as 15,000 American soldiers were at different times during 1918–22 part of this *de facto* army of occupation, spread out across some 4,000 miles of north and east Russia at the height of the early days of the Russian Revolution. President Wilson's decision to join this expedition was one of his most ill-judged moves, and cast a pall over US–Russian relations for many years to come. As always, it was much easier to send troops in than it was to get them out. This particular policing adventure left an extremely bitter taste in the mouths of many Americans back home.

Following the March 1917 revolution, which established the Provisional Government, and the revolution of October, which brought the Bolsheviks to power, Russia was no longer a dependable ally for the British and French. On 12 February 1918 the Bolsheviks declared that Russia would no longer continue the war against the Central Powers. Russia's collapse signified a huge disaster for the Allies, who almost overnight lost some 12 million Russian soldiers fighting in their cause. More than seventy German divisions, or almost 2 million soldiers, were freed to join the fight in France. Moreover, Germany gained the vital wheat, coal and iron reserves of the Ukraine.

The origins of Allied intervention in Russia arose in a note sent on 20 February 1918 by the military representatives at Versailles to the Supreme War Council, recommending the occupation by the Allies, the United States and the Japanese of the stretch of the Siberian railway which ran from Vladivostok to Harbin and its terminal, a distance of 780 miles.[4] The eventual agreement placed a ceiling of no more than 10,000 troops from each of the participants, a figure adhered to by everyone except the Japanese, who rapidly sent as many as 80,000 soldiers to Siberia. General Tasker Bliss confidentially wrote to General March that

the whole question is one fraught with grave possibilities. The intervention, over a large part of Siberia, of a large Japanese army, raises the question of when and how they can be made to get out. I have often thought that this war, instead of being the last one, may be only the breeder of still more [. . .] The British and French are convinced that the proposed intervention is the only way of consolidating a strong sentiment in Russia favorable to the Allies.[5]

Brigadier-General Johnson Hagood, one of the AEF's senior officers, ridiculed the Siberian adventure of the AEF as 'a superduper example of what is called "civilian control of the army"'. Other US generals were equally scathing, believing it would do nothing but damage army morale and national interests. General March believed the sending of US soldiers to Russia was a monumental folly; it diluted the army's manpower, stretched the already seriously depleted shipping fleets to snapping point, and involved America in a theatre of war where, even at the time, it was patently evident that mutual treachery was lying in wait for the unwary. Pershing, however, always the loyal, obedient servant to his political master, supported Wilson's decision to send a token force.

Most of the doughboys who went to Russia survived, but many were traumatized by the climate, the living conditions, and the almost complete inability to tell who was the enemy, who the friend. Although the Allies ended bitter enemies of the Bolsheviks, confusingly enough they also occasionally fought alongside some elements of the Bolshevik forces. On 6 July 1918 a treaty was signed between the Murmansk Soviet and representatives of Britain, France and the United States in which the two sides agreed to take coordinated action against the Germans and Finland (Finland had thrown in its lot with Germany in opposition to Russian domination). This treaty remained in force throughout the Allied occupation of Murmansk. British troops fought alongside Russian communist troops against a Finnish White Army which, under German command, had made deep incursions into

Russian territory; the Finns were finally routed at Ukhtinskaya on 1 September.[6]

The joint Allied expeditions to north Russia – to Murmansk and Archangel, two ports on the White Sea just south of the Arctic Ocean, and to Vladivostok – were nominally intended to recover vast quantities of Allied-owned arms and supplies sent to assist the Russian war effort. A second and equally important task was to supervise the extrication from Russia of as many as 120,000 Czechoslovak troops[7] who wished to continue fighting the Germans on the Western Front. These soldiers had become trapped inside Russia after Leon Trotsky signed the peace treaty of Brest-Litovsk on 3 March 1918. The Czechs were veterans of the south-western campaign in the Ukraine and remained bitterly opposed to the Central Powers: 'These Czechs, in Siberia, were remarkable soldiers and always looked the part. There seemed to be no triflers in their ranks, and when they were assigned to a military duty they brooked no interference with their proper performance of that duty.'[8]

Siberia covers more than 5 million square miles, about 75 per cent of the land mass of Russia. Through this region ran the Trans-Siberian railway, connecting the main industrial centres from Moscow through to Harbin and thence on to Vladivostok. For such a vast country as Russia there were in 1917 just 42,000 miles of railway track, 76 per cent of it single-line. There is little question that the collapsed condition of Russia's railways played a major part in the country's inability to fend off the German attacks on the eastern front; it became impossible to supply the front-line troops adequately. In Siberia the primitive single-track, narrow-gauge rail link was the only significant line of communication and supply. It controlled access to massive dumps of munitions, food, fuel, coal, and other war supplies that the Allies had stockpiled in the ports of Archangel and Vladivostok.

In Murmansk and Archangel alone more than 600,000 tons of Allied munitions and military equipment had been landed. The Bolshevik government repudiated the debt for this and the stores at Vladivostok. By the time of the Russian Revolution the US War Department estimated there were, rusting in Vladivostok's quayside warehouses, 400,000 tons of steel, copper, brass and lead, barbed wire, rails, automobiles and trucks, machine tools, and munitions. When 43-year-old Colonel Fred Bugbee arrived at Vladivostok on 6 September 1919 to take over command of the 31st Infantry Regiment he was astonished to find 'immense piles of war material scattered all around both in and outside of town. One pile of boxes containing rubber must have about three-quarters of a million dollars' worth in it. This is just a sample. It was all shipped here to the Russian government and the Siberian railway wasn't able to haul it away before the country broke down.'[9]

Bugbee was relatively late on the scene; as even then there were still vast amounts of materials still to be shifted it does not require a conspiratorially-minded analysis to suspect that the Allies were as interested in staying put in Russia as in expediting the removal of supposedly essential war supplies.

The Soviets had instructed the Czech Legion, which was strung out along almost the whole length of the Trans-Siberian railway line, to leave the country via Vladivostok, to be ferried to France by Allied ships; but as the Czech troops began moving towards Vladivostok, the Soviet leaders in Moscow intervened to have them declared prisoners-of-war, disarmed, and kept in camps until the end of the war. The Czechs resisted this and fighting broke out between Czech armoured trains and local Soviets along the line.[10] From then on there was open warfare between the Soviets and the Czechs, who constituted such a powerful factor in the Siberian wastelands that they frequently stayed put for months at a time and set up their own local government. More than 12,000 Czechs reached Vladivostok by 21 April 1918, where their political, ethnic and military cohesion immediately gave them control over the city, which was in chaos.

The remaining well-armed and combat-hardened Czech legionaries commandeered some 190 trains, which served them both as homes and rolling fortresses; they printed their own newspaper and even their own paper currency. Trotsky, the Russian secretary of war, ordered all Red Army commanders along the Trans-Siberian railway to halt the Czech Legion's advance eastwards; in retaliation the Czechs began to shoot up everyone who stood in their way. By the middle of 1918 the Czechoslovak troops controlled the entire Trans-Siberian railway between Kazan, on the Volga, to Vladivostok, with the exception of the sector between Chita and Habarovsk. For almost six months the Czech soldiers fought the Red Army to a standstill at the Volga, the only defensive line against the Bolsheviks' march eastward, withdrawing from that front only after the signing of the Armistice on 11 November 1918.

This challenge to Soviet rule opened up a space for local peasant cooperatives and town councils to re-establish themselves and loosely group around anti-Bolshevik counter-revolutionary forces, the Siberian version of which was led by Admiral Alexander Kolchak, who on 18 November 1918 proclaimed himself 'Supreme Ruler' of Russia and established his headquarters at Omsk, 3,700 miles west of Vladivostok.

Into this snake-pit President Wilson blithely ordered an initial 5,000 doughboys, most of them without winter clothing and with almost no idea of what their mission was to be once they had arrived. As with the AEF, quite a few of them arrived in Russia without having gone through even basic training. Private Joseph Ahearn, in the 31st Infantry, recalled:

The first time I was handed a rifle was when our troop train stopped going from Vladivostock to join 'F' Co, of the 31st Infantry. Found the rifle was loaded, but wasn't even shown how to fire it. Just told to 'Walk Post' until relieved. Received recruit training after joining 'F' Co. in old Russian barracks at Razdolnoe.[11]

When 2nd Lieutenant Alf Thompson of the 31st Infantry arrived in Vladivostok on Wednesday, 21 August 1918 he still had no proper uniform, such had been the hurried departure of the expedition:

We were all shipped as sergeants. Our commissions had not come through from Washington when we left, but when we arrived in Siberia our commissions did come through and we were second 'looies'. They didn't have any way of equipping us with officers' uniforms as none of that material came with us to Siberia, so I had no insignia, no officers' bars nor regimental insignia or officers' puttees or any of this. We just had our enlisted man's uniform.

It was a struggle to equip myself as a second lieutenant. Other officers in the regiment got me bars – some of theirs – and regimental insignia, but I couldn't get a pair of leather puttees to save me, so I used regular enlisted man's rolled leggings.

On our first leave we went to town and in a store window was a beautiful pair of riding boots. They looked wonderful – shiny and bright. I went in and paid a ghastly price for them [. . .] Then I was really equipped as a second lieutenant, right down to my boots. The first march we made was in the rain. Those boots spread apart just like paper – in fact, they were paper.[12]

Private Francis Sterling, in the 27th Infantry, was a farm labourer who enlisted to escape the tedium of toiling on the land. He had no training at all before he arrived in Siberia:

A German prisoner of war taught me the American manual of arms in Berouka, Siberia [. . .] What training you got was your GI issues and got on Transport Logan for a 30 day crossing of the Pacific Ocean, ending in Vladivostock Harbor, Siberia, 7 days in quarantine, then 8 days crossing China to Berouka.[13]

This was a soldier who was to find himself very shortly confronting some of the most barbarous bandits of the day. As for the 4,487 doughboys who comprised the 339th Regiment (the majority of them from Michigan) which was sent to Archangel, they were equipped in Newcastle, England, with Russian rifles before leaving for Siberia. The bayonet was immovably fixed to these rifles, which were so inaccurate they were said to be able to shoot round corners. Each man had fired just ten rounds from his rifle before the regiment left Newcastle on 26 August 1918.[14] When they got to Archangel one of them found there were '269,831 inhabitants, of which 61,329 are human beings and 208,502 are dogs'.

The intervention by the United States in Siberia aroused the wrath of many Americans, not least because President Wilson in taking this momentous step seemed to by-pass all civil and military authority. Pressure had been put on him by the Allies. Hagood in his memoirs poked fun at Wilson:

Woodrow Wilson, Constitutional Commander-in-Chief of the army and navy and of the militia of the several States when called into the service of the Union, had been provided by Congress with a Ministry of War, a General Staff, and everything needful for such a purpose, but instead of making use of these facilities, he resorted to an *Aide Mémoire*. Now as a military man I do not know what that is. I do not find it in the dictionary and from my slight knowledge of French, I should judge that an *Aide Mémoire* was a string that you tied around your finger or a piece of paper upon which your wife had written a list of things that you were to bring back from the store.

But no! It was a declaration of war! or something akin to that, though not aimed at any particular person or thing. Congress, charged under the Constitution with declaring war, raising and supporting armies, making rules for the regulation and government of the same, was not consulted.[15]

The officer charged by the US War Department with the thankless task of helping unravel this unholy mess was a straightforward but intelligent Texan, Major-General William S. Graves, who in July 1918 was stationed at Camp Fremont in California, training a group of recruits he hoped to lead into France as the fully-fledged 8th Division.[16] Instead he received on 2 August 'the most remarkable telegram that has ever emanated from the War Department. It read: "Take the first and fastest train out of San Francisco and proceed to Kansas City." '[17]

Two days before, on 31 July, an Allied squadron of ships had headed from Murmansk (where Brigadier-General C. S. S. Maynard was in command of the British forces) to Archangel with 1,400 soldiers of eleven different nationalities, including a small American contingent from the USS *Olympia*. The day after, 3 August, saw the first landing (of British soldiers, the 25th Battalion of the Middlesex Regiment) in Vladivostok, followed by the French on 9 August and the Japanese on the 12th. The US troops destined for Murmansk – the 339th Infantry Regiment, together with the 310th Engineers, the 337th Field Hospital and the 337th Ambulance Company, all diverted from the 85th Division which arrived in France 3–11th August 1918 – arrived there on 4 September and were immediately distributed across a wide front of about 450 miles, under British command.

In the waiting-room of Kansas City's railway station on 4 August 1918 was Newton D. Baker. The Secretary of War was himself hurriedly preparing to take a train to Washington DC. The meeting between these two old friends was brief; Baker merely said that Graves was to make ready to go to Siberia, that Baker was sorry it was not to be

France, and that even General March in the War Department (another old friend of Graves) was unable to persuade the President against this expedition. 'The Secretary then handed Graves a sealed envelope and departed, saying "This contains the policy of the United States in Russia which you are to follow. Watch your step!! You will be walking on eggs loaded with dynamite. God bless you!! Goodbye!" '[18]

Inside the envelope was a copy of the *Aide Mémoire*, addressed to no one, signed by no one. This had been typed by President Wilson in person. Hagood was disgusted with the verbal miasma of the *Aide Mémoire* which, he said,

was couched in diplomatic language. That is, language that could not be readily understood by persons of average intelligence; but could easily be made the subject of controversial interpretations at international gatherings. It read as if it might be intended for the Supreme War Council in Paris; for our French, British and Japanese allies; for the Russian people; or for mankind [...]

There were seven pages of typewritten matter and on the sixth page thereof was a 182-word sentence, the latter part of which read:

'and it (the government of the United States) proposes to ask (our allies) to unite in assuring the people of Russia in the most public and solemn manner that none of the governments uniting in this action in Siberia, or in Northern Russia, contemplates any interference of any kind with the political sovereignty of Russia, any intervention in her internal affairs, or any impairment of her territorial integrity now or hereafter'.

It does not appear whether Mr Wilson ever did actually put this proposition up to the allies. But if so, they paid no attention to it. Graves took it to mean 'Keep out of foreign entanglements,' and with the unflagging support of Secretary Baker and General March, he stood by that to the end. But others including our State Department and the Intelligence Section of our General Staff, took it to mean 'Make the world safe for Democracy by destroying Bolshevism.'[19]

The British, French, Japanese and the rest of the seven nations who made up the original expeditionary force, including the United States, had neither the intention nor any interest in staying neutral; from the start they openly opposed and whenever possible attacked the

Bolsheviks. The numbers very quickly built up until by October there were about 9,000 US soldiers in Siberia, along with 72,000 Japanese, 1,000 French, 1,600 British, 2,000 Italians, 4,000 Romanians, 4,000 Serbians, 12,000 Poles and almost 4,200 Canadians. All threw in their lot with Admiral Kolchak, whose repressive autocracy and whose ferocious opposition to the Bolsheviks – whom he defined as anyone who did not support him – perfectly suited the Allied cause. Kolchak was no fool; he had been on three scientific expeditions to the Arctic, and had served with distinction during the First World War. He had even visited America in the summer of 1917, sent on a mission by the Provisional Government. One of his closest aides described him as

a big, sick child, a pure idealist, a convinced slave of duty and of service to an idea and to Russia; certainly a neurasthenic, quick to flare up, very wild and uncontrolled in the expression of his dissatisfaction and anger, lacking in selfish interest and amour propre, he hates all violence and arbitrariness, but because of his rash temper he often goes beyond the limits of the law; always he is under another's influence.[20]

The fact that Kolchak's generals and soldiers waged their war against Bolshevism with particular brutality, slaughtering *en masse* those they suspected or simply disliked, did not trouble any of the Allied officers present – except for General Graves. Two of Kolchak's leading generals waged a form of Mongolian genocide across Siberia, ravaging the land and murdering any Russian who stood in their way. Grigori Mikhailovich Semenoff and Ivan Pavlovich Kalmykoff practised such extreme cruelty on the local population in east Siberia that the Bolsheviks were frequently welcomed with open arms by the peasantry; Semenoff – an illiterate but quick-witted Cossack – relished telling nervous audiences that he could not rest easily at night unless he had killed at least one person during the day. They both felt themselves to be entirely above local and international law; Kalmykoff hanged two members of the Swedish Red Cross.[21]

Some years after the war one of the US soldiers stationed in Vladivostok, Colonel Homer Slaughter, alleged that the British invited the Americans to share in the payment of $50,000 a month to Semenoff, claiming that Semenoff with from three to five thousand men could easily push on to Irkutsk and thus stop the movement of both prisoners of war and supplies from Vladivostock west to Germany. Later the British more formally repeated their request to America to join them in hiring Semenoff and finally Japan joined with the British in openly paying and supplying him.[22]

While Japan used the chance to land its troops legitimately in a part of the world it had long lusted after, General Graves tried to conduct a strictly neutral policy, for which he was as loathed by the Allies as Pershing had been in France.

The very first US troops to arrive in Siberia, on 16 August 1918, had been sent from base at Manila in the Philippines. These fifty-three officers and 1,537 enlisted men of the 27th Infantry were followed a few days later by the forty-six officers and 1,375 men of the 31st Infantry, who arrived on 21 August; Brigadier-General Graves arrived on 1 September and took command of what was officially called the American Expeditionary Force, Siberia.[23]

Half the 27th were sent to the Trans-Baikal area, while the other half were ordered to take up positions at Habarovsk, on the Amur river. The poor condition of the railway meant that it took the regiment almost a month to arrive at their designated positions. Half of the 31st, meanwhile, had a slightly easier existence, being ordered to remain in Vladivostok to act as port guard, while the other battalion was parcelled out in small detachments along the railway line from Vladivostok to the Suchan Valley, the area's big coal-mining district. These troops were also charged with guarding the Red Cross trains in the region. The American North Russia Expeditionary Force – under British command – saw its first troops land at Archangel on 4 September 1918.

The American public learned officially of these manoeuvres on 17 August 1918, when the US State Department issued a press statement which said, among other things,

the only present object for which American troops will be employed will be to guard military stores which may subsequently be needed by Russian forces and to render such aid as may be acceptable to Russians in the organization of their own self-defense. With such objects in view the Government of the

United States is now cooperating with the Government of France and Great Britain in the neighbourhood of Murmansk and Archangel. The Government of the United States wishes to announce to the people of Russia in the most public and solemn manner that it contemplates no interference with the political sovereignty of Russia and no intervention in her internal affairs, *not even the local affairs of the limited areas which her military force may be obliged to occupy* [my italics] and no impairment of her territorial integrity either now or hereafter, but that what we are about to do has as its single and only object the rendering of such aid as should be acceptable to the Russian people themselves in their endeavour to regain control of their own affairs, their own territory and their own destiny.

This was entirely specious; the US government was well aware, as were the other participants, that it was engaged in blatant interference in the internal affairs of another country, though at least their commanding officer, unlike others, did his best to ensure that there was no systematic policy of intervention:

The Japanese at once commenced a pacification campaign which amounted to an extermination of Bolsheviki, through the action of punitive and searching columns sent out into the villages away from the railway. The Americans on the other hand merely guarded the railway sectors and sent out no columns unless attacked, when they attempted to inflict punishment by direct pursuit of the attackers. Otherwise the American soldier lived on terms of friendship with the local inhabitants whether Bolsheviki or 'White', or partisan. The simple fact that the American soldier found no enemies and made only friends later became the basis of the charge that they also were Bolsheviki. The Russians not in contact with the American soldier believed it. The British fostered the idea. The Japanese contributed confirmatory lies of American deserters captured fighting with the Bolsheviki. The French, always realists and keen, smiled; it was not their quarrel, and they had an axe to grind with both the Russians and the British.[24]

Yet while their commanding officer wished to remain neutral, the ordinary doughboy was forced by the situation to take sides and make judgements, and they generally tended to be anti-Bolshevik. Throughout the winter of 1918–19 the Murmansk front was a more or less constant flashpoint, with Allied troops continually clashing with Bolshevik forces. The first US casualties there were sustained on 16 September, with four deaths and four wounded in two separate gunfights.

Graves arrived in Vladivostok having received, as he put it, 'no information as to the military, political, social, economic, or financial situation in Russia'.[25] Ironically, by the time he arrived one of his tasks – the opening of the Trans-Siberian line in the rear of the Czech Legion to assist their passage to Vladivostok – had already been accomplished by the ferociously hard-fighting Czechs themselves.

To have sent a senior officer of the US army into any foreign territory lacking such vital basic intelligence would have been extremely dangerous; to have sent one into the poisonous cauldron of the Russian Revolution, when the British, French and Japanese were each working to their own fixed agenda and against those of their 'allies', bordered on the criminal. It is testimony to the hard work and steely determination of Graves that his Expeditionary Force largely escaped serious tragedy. Kolchak's brutality and those of his two senior commanders, Semenoff and Kalmykoff, disgusted the Americans. The Kolchak soldiers,

under the protection of Japanese troops, were roaming the country like wild animals, killing and robbing the people, and these murders could have been stopped any day Japan wished. If questions were asked about these brutal murders, the reply was that the people murdered were Bolsheviks and this explanation, apparently, satisfied the world [. . .]

There were horrible murders committed, but they were not committed by the Bolsheviks as the world believes. I am well on the side of safety when I say that the anti-Bolsheviks killed one hundred people in Eastern Siberia, to every one killed by the Bolsheviks. It was my judgement when in Siberia, and is now, that Japan always hoped, by fostering these murderers, that the United States would become disgusted with conditions, withdraw her troops and request Japan to go in and clean up the situation.[26]

Semenoff controlled the area around Chita by operating a fleet of heavily armoured trains, each of which had a suitably unpleasant name. His flagship was called 'The Merciless'; others were 'The Destroyer' (which had a crew of fifty-seven and was protected by half an inch of armour plate over eighteen inches of concrete), and 'The Terrible'. In June 1920 an American railway executive recalled his encounters with Semenoff:

His train lay alongside of mine for more than ninety days, so that I knew the gentleman quite well, and when you hear stories about the 'nationalization' of the Russian women [. . .] I want to tell you this – and I do not think you are going to see it reported in the newspapers – General Semenoff had thirty of the most beautiful women that I ever saw held in his train. He ran back and forth over the Trans-Siberian railroad, robbing and pillaging. He robbed the Chinese banks and custom-houses. In three days' time in Chita he took sixty million rubles and stripped every man, woman and child, taking every bit of valuables that they had about them. I was there at the time.[27]

American troops were fired on by 'The Destroyer', which they captured, after the death of two of their number and the wounding of others. But diplomatic pressure brought to bear via Kolchak's Washington supporters forced General Graves to return the train.

Kalmykoff, a Cossack, was equally brutal; his men had the habit of whipping any Russian women they discovered frequenting the company of US soldiers, and of throwing dead horses into American camps from their passing trains. Both enjoyed the backing, financial and with weapons, of the Japanese: 'Semenof [sic] and Kalmykoff could not have existed but for Japan. Unprincipled bandits, robbers, murderers and paid Japanese agents, their primary duties were to bait and to harass the Americans.'[28]

Not only were Japan, Britain and France ranged against General Graves over the issue of supporting Admiral Kolchak (though all of them had pledged their neutrality before arriving in Siberia) but so too was the US Consul-General in Vladivostok and many elements in the War Department in Washington, particularly in the person of Brigadier-General Marlborough Churchill, head of the military intelligence service, the Military Information Division. General Graves's own chief of intelligence, Major David P. Barrows (who went on to become president of the University of California), received reports from around the country, some of which were highly tendentious, including this from Captain Montgomery Schuyler, who had just returned from a visit to Omsk, where Kolchak had established his headquarters:

[. . .] the coup of Admiral Kolchak's friends whereby he assumed the role of Supreme Governor was absolutely necessary if the whole of Siberia was not to fall ripe into the hands of the Bolsheviks [. . .]

It is probably unwise to say this too loudly in the United States but the Bolshevik movement is and has been since its beginning guided and controlled by Russian Jews of the greasiest type, who have been in the United States and there absorbed every one of the worst phases of our civilization without having the least understanding of what we really mean by liberty [. . .]

Unfortunately, a few of our people in the United States, especially those with good lungs, seem to think that the Bolsheviks are as deserving of a hearing as any real political party with us. This is what the Russian cannot understand and I must say that without being thought one-sided, I should not hesitate to shoot without trial if I had the power any persons who admitted for one moment that they were Bolsheviks. I would just as soon see a mad dog running about a lot of children.[29]

Captain Schuyler was in Omsk from 8 December 1918 until 26 April 1919 and was heartily sick of the murder and mayhem he saw there, but he clearly overstepped the bounds of duty in this report; what is more interesting, perhaps, is that he felt no inhibitions about so doing. Intervention by American troops into the internal affairs of Russia was an everyday occurrence, and those who did it saw nothing untoward in it.

Boredom and loneliness were the two big problems facing American soldiers stationed in Siberia. 'Drinking and chasing women seemed to be the most prevalent' off-duty recreations, according to Private Joseph Ahearn. Along with that of most of his comrades, Ahearn's lasting impression was a constant sense of 'What in hell are we doing here? After a while, we figured we had come over there to keep the Japs from taking over, the English came over to keep an eye on us, the French to check on the English, and so on. The only real friends I could see were the Czechs.'

15

September 1918

Wars are won by the side that accomplishes the impossible.
George Marshall[1]

The load placed upon the doughboys was, inevitably, very unevenly distributed. As we have seen, the first doughboys off the boat gained the most battle experience and that in turn ensured that they were in the greatest demand. As the Germans pushed and probed, testing for weak spots everywhere, the AEF's first-comers were thrown into breaches up and down the French sectors. The 2nd Division's Major Austin – who by September 1918 was one of 61,061 officers and 1,354,067 enlisted men in the AEF – had since his arrival eight months before been in almost continuous action. Austin managed to wangle himself some leave in the latter part of August and early September and spent it sightseeing in Biarritz, Marseilles and Paris. He rejoined his regiment in the first week of September near Pont-à-Mousson, where his command post was just outside Beaumont: 'less than 500 yards from the P. of C. which I had last winter,' he coldly observed in a letter to his uncle.[2] He was soon hard at work in the one battle of the AEF which was an unalloyed success – the snapping-off of the St-Mihiel salient.

Pershing was immensely enthusiastic about the assault on this salient, which had butted into French territory almost since the start of the war, an offence to French dignity and pride. To slice it off and hand it back to the French would, Pershing correctly believed, deliver tremendous kudos for the AEF which, despite the bloody achievements at Cantigny, Belleau Wood and Château-Thierry, had yet to be involved in a large-scale offensive. But two weeks before St-Mihiel was due to be attacked Foch and Pershing were engaged in yet another bout of vitriolic wrangling, yet again over the issue of who had the authority to dictate the movements and efforts of the twenty-seven divisions of the AEF.

First captured by Bavarian troops in 1914, the town of St-Mihiel – some twenty miles south-east of Verdun – had remained in German hands ever since. By crossing the river Meuse at this point the Germans had cut all major Allied railway communications with Verdun. The total length around the perimeter of the salient, which enclosed some 150 square miles of French territory, was approximately forty miles. Thirty-two miles directly beyond St-Mihiel itself was the prize Pershing craved most of all, the great German fortress of Metz. Foch had formally given Pershing the job of reducing this salient as far back as 24 July, and after he had formed the American First Army (with himself in command and Colonel Hugh Drum as his chief-of-staff), Pershing was raring to go.

By 16 August he had issued preliminary instructions for an early-September offensive. More than 550,000 doughboys were assembled and 3.3 million artillery rounds were to be lobbed into the German positions. In the original plans the British promised to supply the AEF with some heavy tanks, but, as so often, when the time came they were not available to the Americans. The British said they could not spare any, 'not at all to my surprise,' noted Pershing rather sourly.[3] Foch, however, agreed to supply five battalions of light tanks, three to be crewed by French, the other two by Americans, the latter under the command of Brigadier-General Rockenbach. Air support was also in French hands. As originally conceived, the assault plan dictated that the western face of the salient was to be attacked by three or four AEF divisions with five or six French divisions on their left, while the major assault would be an entirely AEF operation against the southern face.

There was the usual flurry of intense planning and training, but it all threatened to be for nothing when on Friday, 30 August – just a week before Pershing hoped the attack would commence – Foch visited Pershing and told him that the St-Mihiel attack would have to be scaled down as a result of the successful British offensive at Amiens. On 8 August the British had scored a major victory against the Germans, who by now were so weakened that (unknown to the Allies) Ludendorff had recommended to the Kaiser that he start immediate peace negotiations. Foch understandably wanted to reinforce that British success, which had been followed up by similarly effective British attacks all along the Western Front's left sector. Foch proposed, therefore, that rather than pinching out the St-Mihiel salient, the Americans should attack it on the southern face only, while several of the AEF's divisions would be diverted to carry out an assault in the Argonne–Meuse region, once again of course under the command of the French. Even worse, as far as Pershing's dream of an independent AEF effort was concerned, Foch suggested that the AEF divisions removed from St-Mihiel be sent to the operation in the Aisne under the command of General Degoutte, a French general who had gained a notorious reputation in the AEF for the careless sacrifice of doughboy lives. Foch's new plan originated in the offices of Field Marshal Haig, who had abrogated the agreement to provide heavy tanks for the St-Mihiel attack.

Pershing angrily repudiated Foch's proposal and all the old ill-will between the two quickly rose to the surface. Foch accused Pershing of failing to pull his weight, while Pershing forcefully reminded Foch of his agreement to support the formation of an independent American army with its own sector of the front. Pershing declared: 'Marshal Foch, you have no authority as Allied Commander-in-Chief to call upon me to yield up my command of the American Army and have it scattered among the Allied forces where it will not be an American army at all [. . .] While our army will fight wherever you may decide, it will not fight except as an independent American army.'[4]

On Monday, 2 September they met again to try to thrash out a compromise. Following their shouting match of 30 August, both had cooled considerably. Pershing told Foch he believed 'we should unite in carrying out vigorous offensives to the fullest possible extent [and] I explained that if it should be deemed necessary to abandon the St-Mihiel project in order to begin the larger offensive, which he had decided should be west of the Meuse, I would abide by his decision.'[5]

This was against Pershing's better judgement. He felt that not only would reduction of the salient be a tremendous boost to morale, it would also offer the real possibility of posing a threat to the important railway supply network of Mézières–Sedan–Metz, as well as the strategically vital Briey iron-ore region.

A highly unsatisfactory compromise was reached, one it should have been obvious was bound to cause enormous problems for the AEF. It stipulated that, once the American First Army had taken the salient, it would immediately swing north and begin a second offensive, in the Meuse–Argonne region, no later than Wednesday, 25 September. In his anxiety not to abandon the St-Mihiel plan Pershing overlooked the logistical problems this agreement entailed. After the war, Pershing recognized the daunting mission he had set for his precious soldiers:

Our commitments now represented a gigantic task, a task involving the execution of the major operation against the St-Mihiel salient and the transfer of certain troops employed in that battle, together with many others, to a new front, and the initiative of the second battle, all in the brief space of two weeks. Plans for this second concentration involved the movement of some 600,000 men and 2,700 guns, more than half of which would have to be transferred from the battlefield of St Mihiel by only three roads, almost entirely during the hours of darkness. In other words, we had undertaken to launch with practically the same army, within the next twenty-four days, two great attacks on battlefields sixty miles apart [. . .] It was only my absolute faith in the energy and resourcefulness of our offices of both staff and line that permitted me to accept such a prodigious undertaking.[6]

It might also look, in retrospect, that Pershing was prepared to risk the AEF collapsing into utter chaos, endangering the lives of many thousands of doughboys, simply to satisfy personal vanity. What prevented the assault on the St-Mihiel salient and the abrupt lurch by the AEF to fight in the Meuse–Argonne from turning into a disaster was that the doughboys caught the Germans slightly off-guard, in the middle of a planned withdrawal. Had Pershing insisted on sticking to the original plan, of taking the salient and pushing on to Metz, the AEF's First Army might have turned this planned German retreat into a complete rout. It is equally possible, of course, that the logistical poverty of the AEF might have meant that any offensive against Metz might have rapidly petered out.

Thus, late in the day all the carefully prepared plans for taking the salient had to be scrapped. Captain George Marshall, who had gained a considerable reputation for his operational planning skills with the

1st Division staff, was given the tough assignment of preparing a new plan, one which would enable the AEF to move swiftly from St-Mihiel to a distant, new offensive. The battle to regain St-Mihiel was scheduled to start on 12 September; on 8 September General Drum sent for Marshall and told him the ghastly news that the AEF's First Army now had to move rapidly on after St-Mihiel some sixty miles north, in good order and without revealing to the enemy its intentions, so that it could start a fresh offensive on 25 September.

About ten minutes' consideration made it apparent that to reach the new front in time to deploy for a battle on September 25th, would require many of these troops to get under way on the evening of the first day of the St-Mihiel battle, notwithstanding the fact that the advance in that fight was expected to continue for at least two days. This appalling proposition rather disturbed my equilibrium and I went out on the canal to have a walk while thinking it over [. . .]

I remember thinking during this walk that I could not recall an incident in history where the fighting of one battle had been preceded by the plans for a later battle to be fought by the same army on a different front, and involving the issuing of orders for the movement of troops already destined to participate in the first battle, directing their transfer to the new field of action.[7]

Marshall – who was later to orchestrate so finely the US military effort in the Second World War – could not recall a precedent because there was none. Pershing was asking the impossible and in so doing revealed himself to be neither a great man nor a great general. While the essence of the former might be said to be a willingness to sacrifice personal ambition for the greater good, that of the second is an ability to know when to give ground and when not to. On this occasion Pershing was guilty of the error of accepting half-measures. He should either have recognized, along with Foch, the importance of reinforcing the success of the British and French breakthroughs to the north, or continued to insist upon implementing his own agenda. Instead he accepted an almost fatal compromise.

Marshall was acutely aware of how fragile were the prospects of a middle-ranking officer who failed Black Jack. One slip could trash one's entire career:

The development of the American Expeditionary Forces was marked by a series of personal tragedies suffered by officers assigned important tasks and who, with the limited means or facilities at their disposal, and the short time usually available, were unable to produce the desired result.[8]

Fear of failure before this big occasion, the first test of whether the AEF could successfully mount a large-scale offensive, gripped officers everywhere and often for a very good reason – many outfits were already exhausted. Samuel Devan, chaplain of the 58th Regiment, Coastal Artillery Corps, captured his unit's mood in his journal entry for 25 September:

Little to mark the day. The regiment is not in condition, I am beginning to fear. Too frequent shake-ups among the officers, and the uncertain tenure which almost everyone has on his position have weakened the whole of the outfit to an alarming degree. This perhaps would not be perceptible except to one who was well 'on the inside'. There is a very serious lack of coordination among the several units of the regiment, and a good deal of organization selfishness which works to the detriment of the whole. It is very unfortunate for things to be in this condition just before we go to the front.[9]

Private Arthur Yensen was convinced that the sharp 'us-and-them' divide prevalent in many parts of the AEF was responsible for the relatively poor shape of his unit: 'I've noticed a big difference between the officers and the enlisted men. The officers, who have better chow, clothes, and quarters, and are allowed to think once in a while, still look like men; but the rest of us look more and more like tired, dumb, demagnetized, colorless, half-dead war horses.'[10]

It is almost entirely to Marshall's credit – and the sheer slogging guts of several thousands of doughboys – that the swerve north from St-Mihiel was accomplished at all. The large manoeuvre developed into an ugly fractious mess, but at least Marshall created a theoretical infrastructure in which it could be attempted. By the end of 12 September Marshall's plan was on Drum's desk. The next morning Drum sent for Marshall; Pershing wished to see him. As they went into Pershing's office Drum casually remarked, 'That order for the

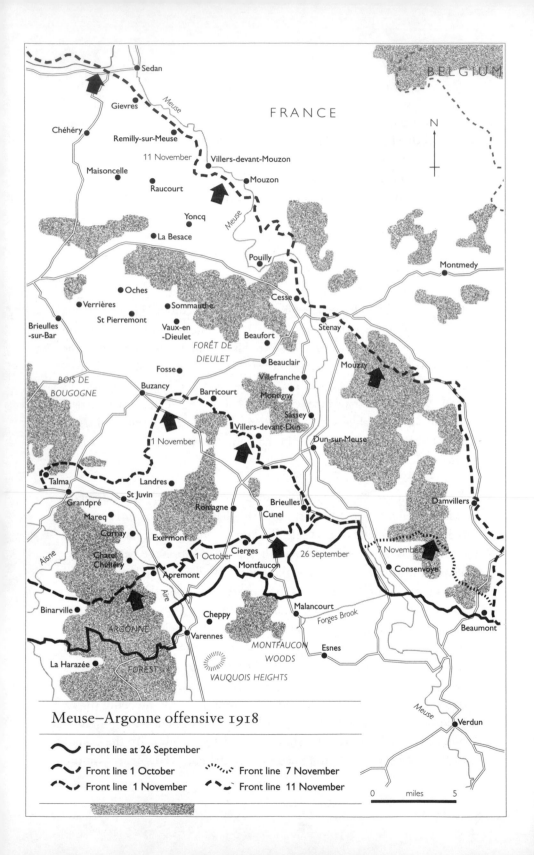

BELGIUM

FRANCE

Sedan

Gievres

Meuse

Chéhéry

Remilly-sur-Meuse

Maisoncelle

11 November

Villers-devant-Mouzon

Raucourt

Mouzon

Yoncq

Montmedy

La Besace

Meuse

Pouilly

Oches

Cesse

Verrières

Sommauthe

St Pierremont

Stenay

Brieulles
-sur-Bar

Vaux-en
-Dieulet

Beaufort

FORÊT DE
DIEULET

Mouzay

Fosse

Beauclair

BOIS DE
BOUGOGNE

Buzancy

Barricourt

Villefranche

Montigny

Sassey

Villers-devant-Dun

Dun-sur-Meuse

1 November

Talma

Landres

Grandpré

St Juvin

Damvillers

Mareq

Romagne

Brieulles

Cornay

Cunel

Aisne

Exermont

Cierges

Chatel
Chéhéry

1 October

Montfaucon

26 September

7 November

Consenvoye

Apremont

Aire

Binarville

Malancourt

Beaumont

ARGONNE

Cheppy

Forges Brook

Varennes

Esnes

La Harazée

FOREST

MONTFAUCON
WOODS

VAUQUOIS HEIGHTS

Meuse

Verdun

Meuse–Argonne offensive 1918

〰 Front line at 26 September

〰 Front line 1 October ⋯〰 Front line 7 November

〰 Front line 1 November 〰 Front line 11 November

0   miles   5

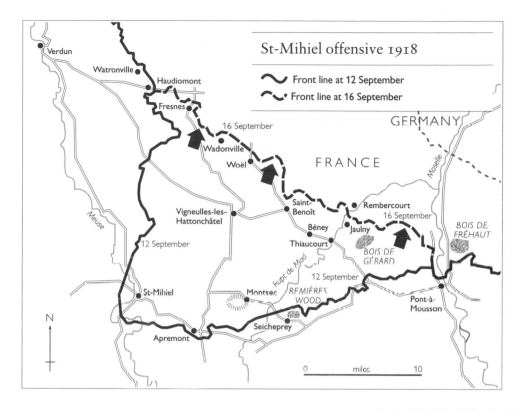

St-Mihiel offensive 1918

∿ Front line at 12 September
∿• Front line at 16 September

Verdun
Watronville
Haudiomont
Fresnes
16 September
Wadonville
Woël
GERMANY
FRANCE
Moselle
Saint-Benoît
Vigneulles-les-Hattonchâtel
Rembercourt
16 September
Béney Jaulny
BOIS DE FRÉHAUT
12 September
Thiaucourt
BOIS DE GÉRARD
Meuse
Rupt de Mad
12 September
St-Mihiel
Montsec
REMIÈRES WOOD
Pont-à-Mousson
N
Apremont
Seicheprey
0   miles   10

Meuse–Argonne concentration you sent last night is a dandy. The General thought it was a fine piece of work.'[11]

In the build-up to the assault many AEF divisions were crammed into the line around the St-Mihiel salient. The order of battle for the main attack was the 1st Corps, under Lieutenant-General Liggett, comprising the 82nd, 90th, 5th and 2nd Divisions from east to west, on the right, from Clemercy to Limey. The 4th Corps, under Lieutenant-General Dickman, had the 89th, 42nd and 1st Divisions, and took the next place in line. The 5th Corps, under Lieutenant-General Cameron, with the 26th and part of the 4th Divisions, assisted by the French 15th Colonial Division, was to take the secondary attack against the western face of the salient. The tip of the salient – the town of St-Mihiel itself – would be attacked by the French 2nd Colonial Corps, under General Blondat. Facing this force of more than 400,000 Americans and 48,000 French were eleven German divisions, about 75,000 troops, occupying some of the finest defensive positions on the Western Front. For some AEF divisions – the 5th, 82nd, 89th and 90th – this was their first taste of combat. Some divisions were squeezed into very small spaces; the 2nd, for example, commanded by Major-General John Lejeune, occupied a front of just half a mile, close under the dominating Montsec which, at more than 450 feet above the plain upon which most of the battle would be fought, looked like being the toughest objective in the assault. General Bullard said of this formidable obstacle that

from it nothing was hidden [. . .] you felt as if you were under the eye of God, threatening and inescapable. Miles back, even as you emerge from the ancient Forêt de la Reine, lifting up your eyes to it, you involuntarily shrink, stoop, and double up, thinking to avoid its eye. Useless! Montsec, with its careful German soldier-observer, saw all. He traced our trenches and marked our roads [. . .] he easily spotted our artillery positions and knew our dumps of materials and ammunition. Of camouflage there were miles for the roads and acres for the gun positions, but they hid nothing from the eye of Montsec.[12]

To have a hope of concealing from German observers on Montsec the assembly of half a million men, their equipment, rations, ammunition and all other necessities meant doing everything by night. By day the troops were under strict orders to keep under cover and not to move, so that enemy spotter aircraft would be deceived. The AEF General Staff did their best to keep an element of surprise, and even fed the Germans a ruse suggesting there would be an attack in the direction of Mulhouse, in the south-east, with the objective of an assault up to the Rhine. Pershing's chief of intelligence, Brigadier-General Nolan, issued 'confidential' orders to Major-General Bundy – who was kept in the dark to make the bluff even more credible – to establish a headquarters at Belfort and to plan for an eventual strength of seven divisions to be used in an attack. This deception was capped by Colonel Arthur Conger, who typed out a spurious letter to General Pershing reporting that all was ready for the big attack through the Belfort Gap. Conger then deliberately left the carbon paper screwed up in his waste-paper bin in his rented room in the Hôtel Tonneau d'Or in Belfort. Conger left the room for a few minutes and, when he returned, discovered the carbon sheet had mysteriously disappeared.[13]

Even this elaborate bluff failed to prevent the Germans from guessing what was afoot. On 8 September Lieutenant John Clark – already feeling very exposed beneath Montsec – commented:

That the Boche knew we are here is very evident, for yesterday a balloon message came over, which read – 'To the 9th Infantry – we know you are here and we are — ready for you.' I really feel sorry for them, because if they are ready for the ninth, or any others of our division, as they say, they must have made their wills and resigned themselves either to death or a prison camp. For our motto is 'Let's go!' and no Boche obstacles have stopped us yet.[14]

And for weeks before the event Paris had been buzzing with talk about the Americans taking St-Mihiel:

Every supply officer up and down the long line of communications who had received an order to send an abnormal amount of his special stock in trade up to the St-Mihiel salient by September 10 predicted to a few friends that the American Army would attack. The Paris papers openly hinted at the time and the place, and the Swiss papers in their guess only missed the date by one day.[15]

So much for carefully constructed intelligence hoaxes.

The assault on the St-Mihiel salient started in heavy rain at 5 a.m., preceded by a four-hour preliminary bombardment, on the chilly morning of Thursday, 12 September. Ground conditions were appalling; it had been raining continuously for four days. For the offensive the Americans and French mustered 3,010 artillery pieces, 1,681 manned by AEF gunners, 1,329 by French, to cover a total front of 62.1 kilometres with an average of 194.7 guns per kilometre.[16] Some 40,000 tons of artillery shells had been placed in ammunition dumps close to the front line, and were then brought further forward to nineteen railheads before finally being transported by animals. Air superiority was ensured by a force of almost 1,400 Allied aircraft, including British bombing squadrons and 600 French planes. One weakness was the lack of heavy tanks; just 267 French light tanks took part in the assault, 154 of them manned by American crews, including one Lieutenant-Colonel George Patton. To bring up the requisite amount of ammunition and other supplies the SOS had reconstructed more than fifteen miles of road, using in excess of 100,000 tons of rock. There were 20,900 hospital beds and sixty-five evacuation trains prepared for casualties. This was an attack in the traditional mode of the Western Front, with masses of infantry tackling equally large masses of infantry, like two ponderous giants struggling to push each other over.[17]

The night before the attack Sergeant Rudolph Forderhase was sitting in a muddy, slippery trench at the bottom of a steep slope. It was a tense time, waiting sleeplessly for the jump-off:

Each man was issued two extra bandoleers of ammunition. We hated these for the way they tortured us. The cloth they were made of was very thin [. . .] they held fifty cartridges in clips of five rounds per clip. A bandoleer was slung over each shoulder and this made the flimsy cloth of the bandoleers [. . .] bring so much pressure on both sides of the neck, that it was torture. We were checked and re-checked not only for ammunition, but grenades, intrenching tools, first aid kit, and rations.[18]

All this preparation resulted in something of an anti-climax for, to the astonishment of many doughboys, when in the early hours they went over the top they found almost no resistance. In fact many of the German positions had already been vacated, leaving behind only a token rearguard force. Practically the only serious opposition came from the final trench in the Quart de Réserve, which was a small wood, about a mile square, midway between Seicheprey and Nonsard. The 1st Division found itself facing intense fire here from machine-gunners and sustained about 600 casualties before the wood was subdued. Elsewhere it was pretty much of a walkover, so that by 7 a.m. on the second day of the attack the first patrols of the 1st Division linked hands with those of the 26th Division in Hattonchâtel, thus sealing off the salient. This great expanse of French territory was once more in Allied hands.

Sergeant Forderhase's experience was a common one that first day:

We were not supposed to reach our objective until late afternoon the next day. We could easily have reached it at 10 a.m. The enemy had not expected us to attack until at least a day later. He had, therefore, chosen to move his artillery the day we attacked. This saved many lives for us. Also, the new tactic of dispersing our troops in wide interval and depth, saved many lives. Also, we made no effort to take Mont Sec by frontal assault.[19]

Montsec was simply by-passed and mopped up later. Writing to his uncle, Major Austin caught the scale of the defeat:

Their resistance was feeble so far as artillery was concerned, and their Infantry, so much of it as was within the zone of our artillery preparation, was badly shaken. Not a shell landed anywhere near my batteries and during the whole fight not more than four shells fell near enough to me to be dangerous [...] the Boche evidently left in great haste as our advance was extremely rapid. In one place an excellent dinner, ready to be cooked, was left – steaks, potatoes, cheese, etc. One of my batteries got two cows and several had pigs, chickens and a great number of rabbits. The main idea of the Germans seems to have been to get out of the salient and about all we had to do was to follow them up [...] The whole thing was a walk-over for us [...]

Raymond.

PS. I forgot to say that Mont Sec was not taken by storm. In fact, it was not attacked at all. There was simply a lot of artillery put against it to neutralize its fire and the attack went around it. The Boche had to leave Mont Sec or be left stranded there. So they withdrew from the position.[20]

The first German prisoners started arriving in the rear of the AEF lines within a few hours of the attack's opening shots. Despite their withdrawal plans and their four strongly built defensive lines (including the Hindenburg as the fourth), the Germans – mainly poor-quality troops sent there to rest – were winkled out in a trice. Major Austin was still full of the easy victory when he wrote home on 29 September, happily repeating the words of Pershing, spoken when visiting the 1st Division just before the St-Mihiel attack:

'Nothing that I could say, could add lustre to the glorious deeds of this glorious division.' After the attack he visited us again and said, 'This is known as the shock division. It is the *First* Division, the model after which other divisions pattern': so you see why I talk so much about the *1st* Division.

This was his last letter: Major Austin was killed in action soon after. His grave is number 35, row 33, block F, in the Meuse–Argonne Cemetery at Romagne-sous-Montfaucon.[21]

The AEF's First Army was lucky that the Germans were already vacating the St-Mihiel salient, one of the most systematically entrenched German defensive positions on the Western Front, with barbed wire so thickly strewn that in places it was possible to put planks on top of it and walk across. Had there been fierce resistance, that wire would have been the end of many a doughboy; it had been scarcely touched by the artillery. George Marshall calculated (rather optimistically) that it took 'five hundred shots from a 75 [. . .] to cut a gap five meters wide and ten meters long. At least a whole day [of bombardment] would be required to cut the minimum number of gaps considered necessary [at St-Mihiel].'[22]

To defeat the barbed wire some doughboys carried rolls of chicken wire eighteen feet long, which they unravelled across the worst thickets. The French were so impressed with the swift decisiveness with which the salient was captured that they sent a team of senior officers to examine how it was done: 'One of these officers, after his reconnaissance, remarked in all seriousness that the Americans had the advantage over Frenchmen because of their long legs and large feet.'[23]

But there was no secret that the French could discover, except that the doughboys either cut themselves passages or, as Pershing put it, 'they have walked over these wire entanglements with much skill, rapidity and decision. It is interesting that our infantry soldiers should see for themselves the nature of the difficulties thus overcome and that they should persuade themselves that they also are capable of doing as much on occasion.'[24]

Fortunate they may have been in catching the Germans in retreat, but this relatively bloodless victory was a remarkably useful morale boost for the Allies. It was also a serious psychological blow to the Germans; even though they were conducting an orderly withdrawal, the ceding of any ground in the coveted territory of Alsace-Lorraine was a bitter blow. Moreover, no soldier finds it heartening to retreat, whether that retreat is planned or unplanned. On the other hand it might be said that Pershing was very unfortunate; had he not been forced to compromise on his original plan but been permitted to head full-speed for Metz, he might have become famous as the general who ended the war. Certainly George Marshall, who in the post-war period acted for a time as Pershing's amanuensis and was thus a slightly partisan observer, thought that a possibility:

Had not the operation been definitely limited in order to permit troops participating in it to be withdrawn immediately and marched to the Meuse–Argonne in time for that battle, there is no doubt in my mind but that we could have reached the outskirts of Metz by the late afternoon of the 13th, and quite probably could have captured the city on the 14th, as the enemy was incapable of bringing up reserves in sufficient numbers and formation to offer an adequate resistance.[25]

The Germans counter-attacked the salient several times after 13 September, but in a desultory, half-hearted fashion; the new line became established along Haudiomont/Tresnes-en-Woevre/Doncourt/Jaulny/Vandières. The prisoner bag was satisfactory without being enormous; just 16,000 Germans fell into the hands of the AEF, along with 450 guns, at the cost to the AEF of a few hundred deaths among the 7,000 killed, wounded and missing. Pershing believed it a clear and laudable victory, which 'probably did more than any single operation of the war to encourage the tired allies'.[26]

As a real American victory and on a large scale, unlike Cantigny or Belleau Wood, it certainly filled many doughboys with jubilation and delighted the French, who thought it 'magnificent, superb, inspiring'.[27] But the AEF struck lucky at St-Mihiel, and never again had such a cake-walk. Those divisions who were quickly diverted from St-Mihiel to the Meuse–Argonne would look back on St-Mihiel with relative fondness.

Even at this late stage of the war the clash of politicians' egos in the Allied camp offered the Germans some hope that internal disarray might play into their hands. For one thing, neither the British nor the French gave up the struggle for control over the doughboys, despite the good show they had put on at St-Mihiel. Soon after the battle Newton Baker visited France and then travelled to London, where among others he met Lloyd George, accompanied by Lloyd Griscom. In London they discovered a plot to unseat Pershing:

Lloyd George delivered a harangue about how our army was not cooperating with the French and British, but going our own bull-headed way and it was a peril to the Allied cause, and the British were giving their whole shipping, sacrificing their food and their own supplies to bring our troops over, but they were no good when they got here. Mr Baker interrupted him, jumped to his feet, banged on the table, and said that under the circumstances, he was sure the President would agree that we send no more troops to France. Lloyd George said, 'I don't quite mean that.' [Baker then] informed the Prime Minister that when the American Government and the President wished advice from any foreign country as to who should command our armies, they would ask it but until they did, they didn't want any advice. He sat down and Lloyd George simply saluted and the meeting adjourned.[28]

Even the Italians wanted to nab doughboys for the ranks of their divisions. Pershing recalled an incident of Friday, 6 September 1918, when he was in the middle of trying to organize the St-Mihiel attack. General Diaz, the Italian commander-in-chief, insisted that Pershing see him:

[. . .] in the course of our conversation it developed that the real purpose of his visit was to ask that American troops be sent for service with the Italian armies. In framing his request, he at first mentioned twenty divisions, and as I showed no evidence of surprise, having become quite accustomed to that sort of thing, he possibly thought that was a favorable sign, so while the interpreter was translating what he had said he interrupted and raised the number to twenty-five divisions. With all the auxiliary services that would have been required to constitute an army of that many divisions, it would have reached the modest total of 1,000,000 men.

This request, coming from one in his position, was so astonishing that it was difficult to regard it seriously [. . .] I merely let him know very politely that we were in need of troops ourselves and could not send any more to Italy [. . .] I suggested to General Diaz that it would be of immense help to the Allies if the Italian armies could assume the offensive also and take advantage of the situation in which the Germans found themselves with all their forces in France engaged on the defensive. He said his staff were studying the matter, but that if his troops should attack now he would have no reserves left for operations the following spring, a course of reasoning which was not easy to follow.[29]

As soon as it was evident that the St-Mihiel salient was secured Pershing started ordering units out of the attack and to re-form before marching north to the Meuse–Argonne area, where the enemy was to be assaulted across a 24-mile front. The Meuse–Argonne campaign was originally conceived of as a two-army attack, with the American First Army on the right and the French Fourth on the left, both aiming to cut the Lille–Metz railway line in the region of Mézières–Sedan. The hope was that by doing this the Germans would no longer be able to ship troops and supplies east and west behind their lines, thus bringing their defence to a halt.

But the problems it presented to Pershing and his General Staff were enormous. For one thing, their front line would be served by just three railway lines and only three narrow, badly shelled roads. Traffic chaos was inevitable, as more than 600,000 men and their equipment attempted to squeeze into a tight area. Despite his good staff work, Marshall's well-laid plans to shift masses of troops from St-Mihiel sixty miles north began to fall apart immediately, as the ceaseless rain and collapsed infrastructure brought everything to a grinding, boggy halt. Thousands of horses died on the roads, adding to the chaos.

Ten doughboy divisions, more than 250,000 men, were designated to take part in the first assault wave of the Meuse–Argonne offensive, while those divisions in reserve (the 1st, 2nd, 3rd, 5th, 29th, 32nd, 82nd and 92nd) accounted for at least another 200,000. These divisions collectively faced eighteen German divisions, about 125,000 troops. The Americans on this occasion had 189 light tanks, all French, and no heavy tanks. Some 821 aircraft joined in on the American side, more than 600 of them flown by American pilots.

The natural defensive strengths of the Meuse–Argonne region were some of the most formidable anywhere on the Western Front. Between the heights of the river Meuse and those of the Argonne forests lay a river valley, crossed by several lines of natural strongpoints, including the heights of Montfaucon, then those of Romagne, and finally those of the Bois de Barricourt and the Bois de Bourgogne, which were some twelve miles from Pershing's start-line. Each of these positions, which completely dominated the French and American lines, was heavily defended. To these natural slopes and forests the Germans had added dugouts, trenches, concrete emplacements, jungles of barbed wire, well-concealed machine-gun pits with perfectly interlocking fields of fire, and heavily camouflaged artillery positions. In four years the French had shied away from even thinking about attacking such an efficiently defended area. The Germans gave every appearance of intending to stay for ever in their four successive lines: the first, or Hindenburg; the second, the Giselher Stellung; the third, the Kriemhilde Stellung; and the fourth, the Freya Stellung – the three last named after Wagnerian witches. These four networks of defensive positions extended north-west from Metz in the south. They were widely separated near Paris but closely converged in the Meuse–Argonne region.

The Argonne woods were not tree-lined beauty spots but thick, dense undergrowth, giving a splendid natural defensive position encompassing not just the forests but also ten square miles of rivulets, streams, ravines, cliffs and rocky promontories, some of which stood above 300 feet. In the middle of the Giselher Stellung was Montfaucon, a dominating hill some 1,250 feet high in a region which itself is 1,000 feet above sea-level. Montfaucon provided admirable observation for the German defenders, giving them commanding views of some 80 per cent of the surrounding battlefield. The German first line of defence was largely a lightly defended observation line; the second (which ran through Apremont, Montfaucon and Sivry) was the main bulwark, roughly 6,000 metres from the front line; the third, prepared but unmanned, ran through Grandpré, Romagne and Brieulles; and the fourth, which was laid out but neither prepared nor manned, ran through the Bois de Barricourt. Apart from the front line all the others ran along high ridges.

At the start of the Meuse–Argonne offensive the left wing of the American flank was formed by General Liggett's 1st Corps, positioned in the Argonne forest. On the far left was the 77th Division, the so-called 'Times Square' Division; next to it was the 28th, from Pennsylvania, half in and half out of the forest; the right hand of the 1st Corps was taken by a fresh division, the 35th, formed from the National Guard of Kansas and Missouri. Next in line came the 5th Corps, the far left of which was formed by the 91st, the 37th (National Guard) in the middle, and the 79th on the far right. Their target for the first day was Montfaucon – which Pétain did not expect to be captured before Christmas. On the extreme right of the American line was the 3rd Corps, with the 4th (regular) Division on the far left, next to which came the 80th 'Blue Ridge' Division, and on the furthest right came the 33rd Division, primarily Illinois National Guardsmen.

On Thursday, 26 September 1918 the Meuse–Argonne offensive opened. The initial artillery bombardment was conducted by 3,980 guns of different calibres, a staggering 96.8 guns per kilometre.[30] The strategic target for the First Army of the AEF was the citadel of Grandpré, an ancient town sitting on the crest of a hill with the Bois de Bourgogne as a backcloth, east of the junction of the rivers Aire and Aisne. The First Army was intended to form a link with the French Fourth Army under General Gouraud, forty five miles east of Reims. The prize of Reims was to prove elusive in more than a month of savage slogging, though the 77th Division reached the outskirts of Grandpré on 9–10 October.

Ultimately this offensive was to push the German defenders back thirty-two miles to the north and fourteen miles to the north-east. When the Armistice was declared the Meuse–Argonne campaign was still in progress and the battlefront here had been extended to cover ninety miles. At the time the guns stopped firing on 11 November 1918 it was touch-and-go whether the AEF could have pushed the Germans back much further or whether they would have had to dig in for the winter, strategically defeated and crushed in spirit. Eventually more than 1,200,000 doughboys, in both combat and SOS units, took part in this vast battle, in which Pershing's aspiration of returning the conflict to an open, flexible style of warfare was tested to the limit.

On other fronts, the end of September 1918 saw a series of auspiciously successful Allied actions which taken together seemed to portend a general collapse for the Central Powers, though few among the Allies were prepared to consider this possibility just yet. On 21 September General Franchet d'Espérey launched an attack on the Macedonian front, and broke through the lines of the Bulgarian armies; on 23 September General Allenby successfully led the British against the Turks in Palestine; on 27 September the British First and Third Armies renewed the offensive begun at Amiens. The AEF's 2nd Corps, consisting of the 27th and 30th Divisions (both National Guard), was performing well with the British Fourth Army in the assault on the 6,500-yard Bellicourt Tunnel on the Cambrai–St Quentin Canal, used to shelter German troops, 125 miles north-west of the Meuse–Argonne battle. Both divisions had spent all their time since landing in France training with the British; the 30th Division was to gain more Medals of Honor than any other. By this time most were in British uniforms, their own having been worn to shreds. On 29 September the 2nd Corps assaulted the defences at 6 a.m. and overran three interlocking trench systems to take the ridge line of the tunnel, part of the Hindenburg line. The tunnel itself was an underground city, with its own power-generating system and telephone network; it was heavily defended and extended for about three miles, just behind the Hindenburg line. In a bloody and ferocious struggle the 27th incurred more than 8,000 casualties and the 30th more than 7,400 before the tunnel fell to them and the accompanying British divisions.

But in the Meuse–Argonne offensive the doughboys quickly became bogged down in the nightmarish landscape of impressively constructed and well-defended German defences. Pershing's view after the war was, as ever, rather too rose-tinted: 'The vast network of undestroyed barbed wire, the deep ravines, the dense woods, and the heavy fog made it difficult to coordinate the movements of the assaulting infantry, especially of some divisions in battle for the first time, yet the advance throughout was extremely vigorous.'[31]

Many of the AEF's divisions, such as the 79th, found themselves marooned in their own barbed wire early in the assault. What was so menacingly different about the barbed wire at the Meuse–Argonne against that of St-Mihiel? Nothing, of course; just that here there was no intention on the part of the Germans to sacrifice a single inch of ground.

Nevertheless, there were some initial successes. The 3rd Corps under General Bullard, to the extreme right of the AEF's line, adjacent to the river Meuse, stormed across the Germans' second position, the Giselher Stellung, by darkness on the first day, while the 4th Division advanced four miles. But the central thrust by the 5th Corps, under General Cameron, to capture Montfaucon, failed; by late on 27 September the 5th Corps had made progress but the following day German resistance everywhere stiffened. The 79th Division – little more than raw recruits, in France only since 3 August and insufficiently trained – was twice thrown out of the Bois des Ogons, and again the next day. The 4th, 28th, 33rd, 35th, 37th, 80th and 91st Divisions were either bogged down by murderous machine-gun and artillery fire, thrust back by counter-attacks, or made only minor advances. In the Argonne forest the 77th Division encountered especially ferocious resistance. In the first four days of fighting the First Army west of the Meuse made a maximum advance of about eight kilometres; good by the standards of the time, but by no means the unalloyed success Pershing craved. He wrote later:

The enemy has been struck a blow so powerful that the extreme gravity of his situation in France was obvious to him. From the North Sea to the Meuse his tired divisions had been battered, and nowhere with more dogged resolution than in front of the American First Army, his most sensitive point.[32]

This was wishful thinking. In fact the German divisions facing Pershing's army were heavily outnumbered – there were in line just eleven undermanned divisions – and of poor quality, yet they nevertheless prevented his troops from breaking through. The terrain, the stretched lines of communication, the lack of horses and mules to haul cannon and supplies, the overcrowded roads crossing no-man's-land – all these greatly handicapped the progress of the First Army, but there is no avoiding the fact that the green AEF divisions thrown into this battle were revealed as grievously inexperienced and sometimes poorly led. Casualties were unexpectedly heavy. Pershing used the 32nd and 3rd Divisions to relieve the 37th and 79th respectively, while the ubiquitous 1st Division under General Summerall took over from the badly bruised 35th. The 91st was placed well in reserve, while the 92nd was handed over to the French 38th Corps.

By 27 September the momentum of the whole offensive had been slowed to a virtual halt by the failure of the 79th Division, men largely from Pennsylvania and Maryland, to take the town and hill of Montfaucon. The division's commander, Major-General Kuhn, unceremoniously sacked Brigadier-General Robert Noble, whom he held responsible for a failure to press home the attack. Yet for Captain Charles Donnelly, in the neighbouring 32nd Division, it was quite clear where the blame should be laid. On 29 September he was standing outside his command post when

Major-General Joseph E. Kuhn appeared. Kuhn, who had once commanded the Army War College, was acknowledged by the army to be erudite as to the art of warfare at higher levels but was lacking in experience of commanding troops above the regimental level, as, indeed, were most of the American division commanders. The General and his aide were afoot, dressed in well-pressed spotless uniforms, shining boots and wearing stocks. Stocks were made of stiff white linen and were worn inside the stand-up collars of blouses on social or formal occasions, but on a battlefield during combat? This was the commanding general of the 79th Division! He stopped about fifty feet away from us and sent his aide to ask what the situation was like with the 199th. I had an immediate dislike of the general. Why send his aide to get information which we could have given him directly? It seemed as though he did not want to get too close to us for fear of getting contaminated in some way. The aide, a young lieutenant, was burdened with his own trench coat and the general's, a pair of field glasses, map case, his own and the general's gas masks and attached to his Sam Browne belt were a pistol, ammunition clips, first aid kit, canteen and a compass. I thought to myself: 'You old bastard. You treat your aide as though he were a servant. And the way your troops are behaving reflects the kind of leadership they have been getting.'[33]

Every available Allied artillery piece deluged Montfaucon with gas

25. Doughboys were packed like sardines on the transports which ferried them across the Atlantic to Europe. Many found conditions on board, such as this photograph shows, more intolerable than those in the trenches.

26. In the morgue at Antwerp, coffins of dead US soldiers await the journey home. Most of those who died remain interred in France.

27. The French-made 75mm light artillery piece was the commonest cannon used by the AEF. This photograph shows Captain I. R. McLendon commanding Battery C, 6th Field Artillery, at Beaumont on 12 September 1918. Battery C fired the 1st shot by the AEF.

28. On the Meuse–Argonne front in September–November 1918. The lack of usable roads and the sheer volume of traffic constantly threatened to choke the advance and paralyse the prospect of victory. This shows conditions at Esne, 29 September 1918.

29. Exermont, in the Ardennes, 7 October 1918. Doughboys of the 18th Infantry, 1st Division, scurry for shelter as the Germans begin shelling the village, just captured by the Americans.

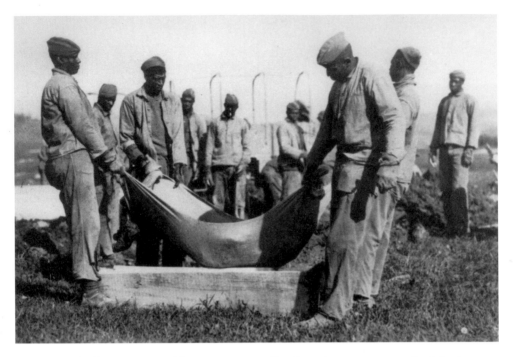

30. Black American soldiers were generally given the most unpopular jobs in France. Here, members of the Quartermaster's Corps Graves Registration Service place a body in a coffin, prior to burial.

31. Left: Major Charles Whittlesey, commander of the so-called 'Lost Battalion' of the 77th Division, shortly after his hapless unit was rescued by (right) Major Kenny's 307th Infantry Regiment, Argonne Forest, October 1918.

32. A pause for celebration. Doughboys liberate some German refreshments on the Meuse–Argonne front, October 1918.

33. Lucky escape. Private Mere Lipsky of the 326th Infantry Regiment inspects the bullet hole in his helmet, sustained during combat in the Argonne Forest on 11 October 1918.

34. The face of war. A casualty from the 110th Infantry Regiment gets first aid on the battlefield during the Meuse–Argonne offensive in September 1918.

35. 'Calamity Jane' – the French-made 155mm field artillery piece which fired the last shot by the AEF: official time, 10:59:59, actual time 11:05 a.m., 11 November 1918. 1st Lieutenant H. F. Phillips is preparing to pull the lanyard of #2 gun, Battery E, 11th Field Artillery.

18352

36. As the offensives by the AEF began to meet with success, there was little or no concern to bury enemy dead: most doughboys gradually acclimatized themselves to the presence of corpses everywhere. This photograph shows dead German machine-gunners.

37. An unusual picture, showing dead doughboys in a trench at Beaulicourt. The US War Department discouraged such photos in order to preserve morale. Someone has (vainly) tried to scratch out the visible face on this picture's negative.

30640

38. New Yorkers of the 27th Division, in a photo taken on 4 November 1918, demonstrate their indomitable sense of fun by making a fashion parade of captured German body-armour.

39. At Remoiville, on the Meuse–Argonne front, 12 November 1918. News of the Armistice filters through to these men of the 6th Infantry Regiment.

40. German soldiers cross the Rhine back into Germany after the Armistice. Many doughboys could not understand why their own battlefield success was not pressed home to bring about a complete rout.

41. This is no defeated rabble but a well-ordered withdrawal: German officers lead their men across the Rhine after the Armistice.

42. Ladies of the night – and day. Doughboys who were posted to Siberia in 1918 and the following years found a cornucopia of fleshly pleasures awaiting them, including these women of a Vladivostok brothel.

43. This rare picture shows two alleged Bolshevik 'spies', with hands tied behind their backs, in the foreground. In the background are some American and Russian soldiers. Despite official orders to avoid intervening in internal Russian affairs, US soldiers gleefully participated in drives to hunt down, capture and kill Bolsheviks.

44. Bakharitza, Russia, 6 September 1918. In the foreground are American sailors from the USS *Olympia*, just back from an anti-Bolshevik armed expedition. In the background are US soldiers of the 339th Infantry Regiment.

45. 'Die Wacht am Rhein' –
an entertainment by
doughboys of the 1st
Division's engineers,
performed on 7 February
1919: members of the cast.

46. After the Armistice,
doughboys who formed
part of the Allied Army of
Occupation in Germany
found plenty of time for
horseplay and relaxation:
two officers get acquainted
with a pantomime horse on
27 February 1919.

47. Cochem, Germany, 23 January 1919. Many doughboys found Germany to be more pleasant than they expected – and Germans to be far more welcoming than the French.

48. Hats off! President Woodrow Wilson finds cause for joy in Paris on 14 December 1918, while President Poincaré of France looks into the future with less ebullience.

and high explosive. In the early morning of 27 September patrols from the 37th and 79th Divisions had battered their way into the outskirts of Montfaucon. One doughboy – Lieutenant-Colonel George Patton, whose French light tanks had participated in the frontal assault on Montfaucon – was not present to watch the final capture of the town on the second day of the battle. His squadron had advanced far ahead of the 35th Division (which they were meant to be supporting) and had reached the village of Cheppy. Deadly machine-gun and light-artillery fire had prevented the 35th from making much headway, and many of the soldiers had simply become lost in the thick early-morning fog. As the fog lifted, Patton's tanks and about 100 infantry-men he had collected came under intense fire; at about 10.30 a.m. Patton was hit in the leg by a machine-gun bullet. By midday the 79th Division had managed to take Montfaucon, but by this time the Germans had managed to bring up reserves and stiffen their other defensive lines.

The left wing of the assault, the 1st Corps, came under particularly heavy and well-sited artillery fire. The 35th Division, whose targets were first the Vauquois Heights and then the town of Varennes on the river Aire, were especially savaged. Varennes was taken at considerable cost by late on 26 September; in four days' fighting this single division suffered 6,000 casualties and advanced six miles, before being relieved on 1 October by the 1st Division. Next in line, to the left of the 35th, was the 28th, the 'Iron Division'; it managed to smash its way through the barbed-wire emplacements in the valley between the Argonne forest to its left and Varennes to its right, on a one-mile front, but then came under intense fire from a rocky outcrop extending from the forest. There its men were pinned down for twelve days, suffering 6,149 casualties in the process before they were relieved by the 82nd Division. To the far left the already under-strength and exhausted 77th Division, which had marched continuously for the past nine days to get into position for this offensive, was in perhaps even worse circumstances, having begun on the first day to make good progress – about one mile on a five-mile front. Some of its recently arrived replacement troops did not know how to load a rifle or throw a grenade; hardly the sort of calibre required to storm the fortresses and underground camps of the Argonne forest.

By 1 October the whole attacking force had in total advanced but four miles, over some of the worst terrain and most densely defended positions to be found in the First World War. The Meuse–Argonne offensive was threatening to turn into a costly and humiliating débâcle, and the doughboys' victory at St-Mihiel began to look as though it might have been a fluke.

16

October 1918

Now the Germans were killing lots of the boys.

William Francis, 5th Marines

Bulk cancels out experience.   Liddell Hart[1]

In the four brutal days of 25–29 September the AEF's First Army had sustained 45,000 casualties, a rate of destruction as bleak as at almost any other period in the war. In another ominous reminder of the previous ghastly campaigns of 1916 and 1917, its advance had slowed almost to a halt. The Meuse–Argonne campaign was threatening to fall apart, with serious consequences for the reputation of every senior figure in the AEF, from Pershing down. What could be done to salvage the wreckage?

The first two weeks of October were undoubtedly the most difficult in the brief history of the AEF. While its broad front offensive was stuck in a quagmire, the news from a wider perspective was already beginning to overshadow the doughboys' efforts. International newspaper headlines in the first week of October were dominated by an armistice proposal from Germany; and influenza was scything through the ranks of the AEF. General Hagood, now chief-of-staff of the Services of Supply, wrote on 7 October that the arrival camp at Brest had so far reported 1,540 cases of influenza, 1,062 incidences of pneumonia and seventy-seven deaths. He was receiving reports of soldiers dying 'at the rate of about one every ten minutes [. . .] We got information that another convoy had arrived in England with about 250 deaths and that a convoy of 2,400 men had arrived at St Nazaire with 400 sick. All of this trouble really originated in the United States, as sick people are put on board these ships.'[2]

In France the weather was becoming increasingly miserable, with incessant rain and bitter cold day after day, adding to the already crippling transportation difficulties. On the Meuse–Argonne front the doughboys had no choice but to use roads destroyed by years of artillery bombardment. In such circumstances, pushing home an advance against increasingly impregnable defences was well-nigh impossible. Pershing would not let up: 'the thing to do was to drive forward with all possible force'.[3] Easier said than done, for this part of the Hindenburg line, part of which was on the top of the Romagne Heights, enjoyed a panoramic view of the plain across which the doughboys would have to advance. Matters were not helped by Clemenceau trying to take a Sunday saunter on 29 September, to observe how the AEF was faring in the Meuse–Argonne battle. His chauffeur set off for Montfaucon, but

The road he took was crowded with trucks that morning, due especially to the trains of the 1st Division, which was going to the front to relieve the 35th. He failed to reach Montfaucon and left rather disappointed, thinking no doubt, that our transportation was hopelessly swamped, as we soon began to hear criticisms to that effect not only by the French but even by some Americans.[4]

Stallings describes the visit with more brutal honesty:

On the road to Montfaucon he saw field guns fall into shakily bridged craters, and fifty pairs of arms lift them to level road again; exhausted horses dropping dead, replaced by men manning tug ropes; broken-down trucks lifted by cordons of Doughboys to any level spot off the road and instantly swarmed upon by mechanics; forage trains intermingled with life-or-death ammunition trucks, water cart loads of corned beef, and ambulances with ambulatory wounded perched on rooks. Clemenceau had never seen the Doughboys in action, believing many were still interspersed by battalions into the trained fabric of the French Army, and he never recovered from his shock at this seemingly endless pandemonium [. . .][5]

Indeed the roads were swamped, but it was only partly the fault of poor staff and logistical work; the French had compounded the confusion by failing to keep their promise to provide the AEF with sufficient numbers of horses and mules, while the lack of motor transport was a direct result of the Americans giving in to Allied demands to prioritize the shipping of combat troops from the United States. In any case the appalling conditions of the three available roads would have defeated the efforts of a whole regiment of traffic police. A single AEF artillery brigade on the march stretched for almost twenty kilometres; it took two hours for the column's tail to reach the point from where its head had set off. More than fifty-five such artillery brigades were deployed in the Meuse–Argonne; little wonder that Clemenceau's most vivid memory of his failed visit was of one vast logjam.

The poor results of the AEF in the first few days of the Meuse–Argonne offensive were immediately and carefully analysed by the Inspector General of the First Army. The problems he found ranged from a failure to make full use of carrier pigeons, through a complete communication failure between and within regiments, brigades and divisions, to a shortage of rifles, helmets, gas masks and gun oil. On top of that there was a growing problem with demoralized stragglers, clogging up the rear areas. This huge offensive had been allocated only 189 tanks, all of them light and easily put out of action; ten days later only eighteen were still functioning. Far from being the well-ordered demonstration of open warfare which Pershing had longed for, the first Meuse–Argonne offensive was an under-resourced, poorly planned and hastily executed effort, highly reminiscent of many such episodes previously conducted by the British and the French. The root cause, of course, lay in the decision to move rapidly from the St-Mihiel offensive to this new attack.

The failure of the First Meuse–Argonne (as it became known) was all the more disturbing because at the start of the campaign the odds were heavily in favour of the Americans and French. Even when the attack caused the Germans to draw off another 16 divisions from the French sector of the front, the AEF was still far superior in numbers and arms. Admittedly the attack was against very carefully planned defences, and the divisions thrown into the fighting were often quite inexperienced, but the lack of careful advance planning humbled the doughboys on this occasion:

The trouble was not merely that the troops were fresh – perhaps it was mostly that the arrangements were fresh. The Americans had scarcely a week of real preparation – an astonishing contrast with the months which preceded the French and British offensives of 1915, 1916, and even 1917.[6]

In the hope of averting a looming disaster, the 1st, 3rd and 32nd Divisions – held back in reserve behind the original jump-off line – were rushed to the front line. But on 29 September Pershing suspended all offensive operations while he and his staff tried to work out how best to get themselves out of this hole. On 1 October the AEF's guns fell silent; only in the Argonne forest was there any movement between that day and 4 October. The first phase of the Meuse–Argonne officially came to an end on 3 October. The nine fresh divisions which took part – the 28th, 33rd, 35th, 37th (all National Guard), and the 77th, 79th, 80th and 91st (all National Army, i.e. conscripted), and the 4th (regular) – had in the first two days swept much before them (apart from at Montfaucon) but their energy and enthusiasm had run into a brick wall.

News that the AEF had suspended the offensive deeply angered the French and British. Everywhere else on the Western Front the onward drive was continuing; why should the AEF hold back? Within a week of his frustrating outing, Clemenceau instructed Foch to suggest to Pershing that the French Second Army should take over command of those divisions on the left of the AEF First Army that were in and near the Argonne forest. This implied that Pershing had lost control of the massive First Army, and that it should be reduced to a more manageable size by giving control of some of it to the French. Pershing was enraged. He told General Weygand, Foch's emissary, that his men 'seriously objected to service in the French Army'. In the middle of October Foch and Pershing met at Bombon, the GHQ of the Allied armies, for one of their most fraught discussions. Foch criticized the American effort by saying that on all other parts of the front 'the advances are very marked. The Americans are not progressing as rapidly.'[7] Pershing correctly replied that the Americans were facing some of the worst terrain and most toughly defended positions on the whole front, and that the doughboys were pinning down many German divisions and drawing others away from other sectors of the front. This was not good enough for Foch, who said: 'I would like to see the Americans advance more rapidly,' adding, 'I only consider results.' Pershing reiterated that the AEF's advance was as good as any army could achieve in the circumstances: 'The Germans could hold up any troops Marshal Foch has at his command [. . .] Nothing any French general could say will put more goodwill, energy, or coordination into our operations. I have done all in my power, as have the officers under me.' The failures of the AEF were not in will and determination and courage, but in transport, planning and training, and none of these were solely the responsibility of the Americans. Pershing presented his plan to form two American armies but Foch did not even glance at them. Wearily, he merely gave his assent to their formation, and the acrimonious meeting ended without clear resolution. Foch reported what had passed to Clemenceau, who decided to try to have Pershing dismissed.

Pershing formed the Second Army of the AEF, placing Bullard in charge of it, on 12 October, in response to the obvious broadening of the offensive on German positions. Liggett took command of the First Army. Both were recommended by Pershing for promotion to lieutenant-general. In these shuffles Pershing became Commander of the Armies of the United States. The formation of two American armies was in part an acknowledgement that the scale of the First Army, as the current difficult circumstances of the First Meuse–Argonne had revealed, was too unwieldy, particularly given the many other demands on Pershing's time and energy. By taking the over-arching title of Army Group Commander, above the commanders of the First and Second Armies, Pershing was also now equal in status to Haig and Pétain, and in France responsible only to Foch. Dickman was placed in charge of the 1st Corps, taking over from Liggett; Summerall took over from Cameron as commander of the 5th Corps, while Cameron returned to lead the 4th Division. The 4th's previous commander, General Hines, moved to lead the 3rd Corps. With these new designations it was time to plan how best to resume the Meuse–Argonne campaign.

While the AEF's generals were considering their options in what was to become the Second Meuse–Argonne battle, many doughboys of the 77th Division were stuck in the thick of the Argonne forest.

Unaware that it had been called to a halt they were still engaged in fighting the First Meuse–Argonne. This confusion helped to give rise to yet another tale of valiant doughboy heroism, that of the so-called 'Lost Battalion', the myth once more helping to disguise the reality of serious incompetence. In continuing the struggle, the 77th Division had by Tuesday, 1 October captured the so-called Bagatelle Pavilion, a relatively luxurious underground German camp, and were in sight of another, the Palette Pavilion, deep in the densely wooded and ravine-riddled forest. All the 77th Division knew or cared about was that the forest was a serious threat to Pershing's left flank, and its mission was to clear it. The 1st Battalion of the 308th Infantry Regiment, part of the 77th Division, was commanded by Major Charles W. Whittlesey; the 2nd Battalion by Captain George G. McMurtry. Both battalions had already taken heavy punishment and were down to about 50 per cent strength, altogether around 800 men. Whittlesey's unit had already once during the campaign found itself isolated in an advanced pocket and had had to be rescued. On the morning of 1 October the two battalions were ordered to attack across a ravine inside the forest, but were severely mauled by superbly well-positioned German defenders. In the early afternoon of the next day Whittlesey's battalion broke through, followed by the 2nd Battalion, taking thirty prisoners as the Germans retreated to stronger defence works. The 1st Battalion (Companies A, B and C), and the 2nd Battalion (Companies E, G and H) now found themselves trapped on a road running along one side of a steep ravine. They decided to dig in for the night.

Overnight they were reinforced by the ninety-seven survivors of Company K of the 307th Brigade; Whittlesey sent out a runner to attempt to contact the two separated companies, D and F, but the runner never made it. Whittlesey's position was dire:

Whittlesey now knew he was bagged with elements of three infantry battalions and his machine gunners – 650 American soldiers trapped in a slender oval, with fourteen elements of a fresh German division, including riflemen, machine gunners, shock companies, flame throwers and mortar-men, skillfully positioned in a full circle around them at a radius of about two hundred yards. At this point, Whittlesey sent two of his eight carrier pigeons to Alexander, asking for ammunition, rations and support, giving his approximate whereabouts, an obscure road he occupied in a depth of 70 yards on a 350-yard line.[8]

The possibility of surrender never occurred to the trapped dough-boys. Major Whittlesey, a bespectacled, academic-looking graduate of Williams College in Massachusetts, began to send out by carrier pigeon a stream of increasingly dire situation reports. Surrounded, his men had to sit tight and await rescue. The stalled Meuse–Argonne offensive was by now gearing up again, with the replacement of the smashed 35th Division by the 1st Division. The remaining elements of the 77th Division meanwhile were ordered to strike left and try to reach Whittlesey's men. By 4 October Whittlesey's situation was becoming desperate, as shown by this message he sent at 10.35 a.m. that day:

Germans are still around us, but in smaller numbers. We have been heavily shelled by mortar this morning. Present effectives A.B.C.E.G & H companies 175; E Co 307th 45; M.G. Detachment 17 – total here about 235.

Officers wounded Lt. Harrington, A; Capt. Strohnel, C; Lt. Buckler, G; Lts. Peabody and Revnes of M.G.; Lt. Wilhelm Co. E miss.

Cover bad if we advance up the hill. Very difficult to move the wounded if we re-change our position. Situation is cutting into our strength rapidly. Men are suffering from hunger and exposure, and the wounded are in very bad condition. Cannot support be sent at once.

(signed) Whittlesey.[9]

That morning, 4 October, the Second Meuse–Argonne (also known as the Champagne offensive) began with a rolling barrage at 5 a.m. The initial aim was to capture the Romagne and Cunel Heights to the right of the line, and the wooded heights of the Argonne forest to its left. The First Army – comprising the 3rd Corps (from right to left including the 33rd, 4th, and 80th Divisions), the 5th Corps (from right to left, the 3rd and 32nd Divisions), and the 1st Corps (comprising the 1st, 28th and 77th) – were engaged, with the French Fourth Army to its left. Once again, the doughboys encountered ferocious and dogged resistance; in three days the 4th Division, attempting to scale the Cunel Heights on the far right of the attack, gained scarcely a mile, and were still overlooked by the Germans on the Heights above. Right across the line the same story was told: unparalleled resistance, very heavy casualties, little or no advance.

So much for open warfare. The AEF could take small comfort from the fact that the French were doing little better on their section of the same offensive. The French Fourth Army, commanded by General Gouraud, was equally bogged down in its struggle to break through to the left of the Argonne forest. Foch asked for AEF reinforcements for the Fourth Army and Pershing sent the valiant 2nd Division, by now one of his – or indeed anyone's – finest fighting units. The French Fourth Army faced yet another series of formidable obstacles, the most intimidating being the range of hills comprising the Mont Blanc ridge and Hill 210, overlooking the village of Somme-Py, itself some twenty miles north-east of Reims. The 2nd Division had arrived on the battle-field in haste on the night of 1 October, under the command of Major-General Lejeune, a tough and experienced marine. A brief but violent French and US artillery bombardment at 5.50 a.m. on Friday, 4 October was followed by the 2nd Division attacking just before Somme-Py, heading north-north-west to assault Mont Blanc, which so far had completely pinned down the French. The marines hoped to take Mont Blanc's left flank, while the doughboy brigade of the division swept up its right; the two would then roll up the middle, taking what protection they could from the hill's wooded, rocky slopes. In that first day alone they advanced six kilometres, and the marines crested Mont Blanc within three hours of the jump-off, their aggressive spirit across the open ground being bolstered by supporting tanks. Private Francis of the 5th Marines was again in action:

It was cold and we were wearing overcoats. I usually went over the top with a loaf of bread inside my blouse if it was possible to get one, and I was always eating on it, not especially as I wanted it but because it took my mind off the fighting sometimes [. . .] We broke the German lines and gained our objective [Mont Blanc] the first day.[10]

On the right, the doughboy brigade under the command of General Ely raced 3,000 yards up the Souain road, heading north, and stormed the right-hand flank of the ridge. By the evening of 4 October the marines and doughboys shook hands on Mont Blanc's summit, having killed those German defenders who would not accept ejection. Lejeune was by this time thoroughly contemptuous of his French allies who, he said, had utterly failed to protect the flanks of his 2nd Division, as had been agreed before the assault was launched. He cabled Pershing at AEF headquarters that he would resign his commission rather than fight with French liaison officers alongside him again.[11]

On the second day the failure of the French to keep pace began to threaten this initial success of the 2nd Division. As Private Francis wrote,

we advanced too far, the French did not keep up with us, so that we were being fired upon from the front, each side and nearly from the rear. We were afraid that the Germans were going to close in together in the rear and cut us off from our lines. We fought desperately to keep the Germans from carrying out their plans. We were on a prairie with machine gun bullets hitting all round. They were hitting only inches from me on each side, and knocking dirt into my face [. . .] Late in the afternoon we took a German trench. A German intelligence officer started running, but was shot by a boy with a rifle grenade. His clothing caught fire a little further on and he fell. A man ran up and shot him, and still he was not dead. A fellow took his glasses from him as a souvenir and then an officer shot him three times. We were always called souvenir hunters, but this was the limit. I could hardly keep from laughing at the time.[12]

The American soldiers on Mont Blanc had fought for twenty-four hours without water or food; in a lull in the fighting they now began scavenging among the water bottles of the dead lying at their feet.

Meanwhile in the Argonne forest, on the left wing, Whittlesey's 'Lost Battalion' was still surrounded. The poorly trained 77th was being crucified. Aircraft from the US 50th Aero Squadron tried to drop medical supplies, food and ammunition to the beleaguered unit on the afternoon of 5 October. Whittlesey's men then suffered the indignity of being shelled by French artillery, working from the wrong map references. By 6 October these doughboys were in a sorry state, taking dressings from dead men to use on the wounded, among many of whom gangrene had already set in.

Between 7 and 11 October the AEF was involved in four separate actions, including one in which the 30th Division (under Major-General Lewis) went in to bat on the British sector. On 7 October the 1st Corps (the 1st, 28th and 82nd Divisions) attacked the eastern edge of the Argonne forest; on 8 October the French 17th Corps, supported by the AEF's 29th and 33rd Divisions, attacked east of the Meuse; on 9 October the 5th Corps attacked the Romagne Heights again. By the end of Tuesday, 8 October the hamlet of St Etienne-à-Arnes was in the hands of the 2nd Division. Thanks to their courage and stamina the French advance had been given a dramatic impetus but 'it was the most costly of our battles', Lieutenant John Clark recalled. The 2nd Division's losses from 2 to 10 October (when the 2nd Division was relieved) were 41 officers and 685 men killed, 162 officers and 3,500 men wounded, 6 officers and 579 men missing: a total of 209 officers and 4,764 men.[13] Despite the promise of French support much of the burden of prising the Germans out of this strategically vital position fell on the shoulders of American soldiers, though the French official reports of the action held otherwise, much to the chagrin of the Americans, then and later:

Back at Pétain's Group of Armies Headquarters, a résumé of the Mont Blanc operation mentioned that, 'In the course of the first day's advance, the 5th Regiment of Marines sent a detachment to the [French] XI Corps to help it clean out the German trenches.' Inasmuch as the French were two kilometers from those German trenches at the time, wits of the 3rd Battalion, 5th Marines, devised a new series of verses for the immortal 'Mademoiselle from Armentieres', one of which ran like this:

> Oh, the general got the Croix de Guerre,
> Parley-voo.
> Oh, the general got the Croix de Guerre,
> Parley-voo.
> Yes, the general got the Croix de Guerre,
> But the sonofabitch wasn't even there;
> Hinkey-dinky, parley-voo.[14]

The costs to the AEF were mounting fast. Between 26 September and the middle of October it had sustained 75,000 casualties. Influenza had become a serious problem, with 70,000 AEF cases hospitalized in France; at its peak the death rate from influenza and associated illnesses such as pneumonia reached 32 per cent.[15] These pressures began to bite and Pershing was forced to reduce the size of a company from 250 to 175 men.

The 'Lost Battalion' meanwhile had nearly been overrun. Medical supplies had been used up; 50 per cent of the original troops were wounded or killed; food and water were almost exhausted. McMurtry was hit by shrapnel in the knee. Grenades continually rained down from the steep slopes above them. An attempt at an air-dropped supply by DH-4s came to grief, the aircraft being shot down while the supplies landed outside the doughboys' defensive perimeter. Lieutenants Harold Goettler and Erwin Blackley, pilot and observer, were shot down in the afternoon of 5 October on their second run over the battalion; their deaths gained them posthumous Medals of Honor. On Sunday, 6 October a lieutenant and two privates from the 'Lost Battalion' managed to steal through the German lines, bringing with them valuable information concerning its precise location. Next day nine starving doughboys from McMurtry's H Company slipped away to try to retrieve some of the air-dropped rations; five were killed and the other four taken prisoner in an ambush. One of their German captors was an English-speaking officer, Lieutenant Fritz Printz, who had worked in the United States as a representative for a German company. On his initiative one of the doughboy prisoners, Private Lowell R. Hollingshead, was – under considerable protest by Hollingshead, who felt it was a dishonourable thing – nominated to return to the battalion with a request for surrender. The note came into Whittlesey's hands late that afternoon. It read:

To the Commanding Officer – Infantry, 77th American Division.

Sir: The bearer of this present, Private —, has been taken prisoner by us. He refused to give the German Intelligence Officer any answer to his questions, and is quite an honourable fellow, doing honour to his Fatherland in the strictest sense of the world.

He has been charged against his will, believing that he is doing wrong to his country to carry forward this present letter to the officer in charge of the battalion of the 77th Division, with the purpose to recommend this commander to surrender with his forces, as it would be quite useless to resist anymore, in view of present conditions.

The suffering of your wounded men can be heard over here in the German lines, and we are appealing to your humane sentiments to stop. A white flag shown by one of your men will tell us that you agree with these conditions. Please treat Private — as an honourable man. He is quite a soldier. We envy you.

The German Commanding Officer.[16]

But it was late in the war, and far too late in this particular life-and-death struggle for chivalrous gestures. The reaction of the trapped doughboys was a round of yelled abuse, to which the Germans responded by sending in a flamethrower crew, which was soon picked off by the battalion's only machine-gun still in working order. When it seemed as though all their efforts would finally be for nothing, late that same day Lieutenant-Colonel Eugene H. Houghton (who like many Americans had in 1915 joined the Canadian army and later transferred to the AEF) led an attack by the 307th Infantry and finally broke through to the 'Lost Battalion'. They found just 195 men unwounded. After five days of isolation and more or less continual attack many of those were too weak from hunger and thirst to walk.

Despite losing touch with the rest of his division, Whittlesey and his fellow survivors were converted into overnight heroes. Whittlesey was immediately promoted to lieutenant-colonel, McMurtry to major, and both were awarded the Medal of Honor. Once started, the legend quickly spread – helped on its way by a junior reporter attached to the AEF in France, Damon Runyon – that Whittlesey's response to the surrender offer was 'Go to hell!', though his actual reply was rather more mundane. Whittlesey survived the war, but perhaps something ate into his heart and mind. After the war he disappeared one night from a ship sailing to Havana; it was assumed he committed suicide.

As the legend of the 'Lost Battalion' was being born, another was in the making. To the right of the Argonne forest was the 82nd Division, commanded by the splenetic Major-General George B. Duncan who had earlier been removed from command of the 77th Division when questions were raised over his physical fitness. The 82nd had arrived in France on 21 May 1918. Raised late in the war, it had no special recruiting-ground and settled for calling itself the 'All-American Division'. It was composed largely of backwoodsmen from Tennessee along with a sprinkling of city types, and had acquitted itself well at St-Mihiel. On the morning of 5 October the division moved into the line beyond Apremont, on the Aire river and west of the village of Exermont, replacing the exhausted 28th Division and consolidating the Americans' grip on Hill 223. The 82nd's orders were to cut through the Decauville railway connection, which ran north–south and helped to supply the German units in the Argonne forest. The Germans had drenched the whole area in mustard gas when, on the morning of Friday, 8 October, the leading assault battalion of the 328th Infantry attacked without the support of the promised preliminary barrage. Its mission was to take the railway line which lay two miles ahead of them.

In their midst was Acting Corporal Alvin York, a farmer from the mountains of Tennessee who had a huntsman's skill with a rifle, being able to hit the mid-point of a half-inch cross drawn on a piece of paper nailed to a tree 100 feet away. He kept a diary, which was strictly against army regulations. York had been with Company G, 328th Infantry, since the 82nd Division assembled and trained at Camp Gordon, Georgia, in February 1918; he recalled later that his company captain, E. C. B. Danforth, would line up the men and ask if any of them were keeping a diary. York, a sincere Christian convert who had initially considered refusing to serve on the grounds that the Bible said murder was wrong, found it impossible to lie directly to Danforth:

I told him I was not admitting whether I did or didn't, and he told me it would betray a lot of valuable information to the Germans if I was captured. And I told him that I didn't come to the war to be captured, and I wasn't going to be captured, and that if the Germans ever got any information out of me they would have to get it out of my dead body.[17]

In the early hours of 8 October the Tennesseans ascended Hill 223, their jumping-off point. At 6.10 a.m. the battalion, with York's platoon in the second wave, began its charge across a triangular-shaped valley several hundred yards wide. This was almost like a death funnel, as German machine-guns lined the valley's flanks and topped its apex.

Inevitably, the rush was stopped dead in its tracks; 'our boys just went down like the long grass before the mowing machine at home,' said York, who calculated they were facing about thirty machine-guns hidden on the ridges 300 yards in front and to their left. Together with Harry Parsons, his platoon sergeant, York's squad and some others – seventeen in all – tried to work their way round the left flank. This was the reality of Pershing's open warfare, as York and the others debated among themselves, on the crest of the ridge, whether to take the machine-gunners in the flank or continue to move further back, to come from behind. They chose the second course:

We opened up in skirmishing order and flitting from brush to brush, quickly crossed over the hill and down into the gully behind. Then we suddenly swung around behind them. The first Germans we saw were two men with Red Cross bands on their arms. They jumped out of the brush in front of us and bolted like two scared rabbits. We called to them to surrender, and one of our boys fired and missed. And they kept on going. We wanted to capture them before they gave the alarm. We were now well behind the German trench and in the rear of the machine guns that were holding up our big advance.[18]

The three doughboy squads, now behind the German machine-gunners, alighted upon the HQ of the German unit, where they captured several orderlies, runners, stretcher-bearers and a major without firing a shot. By now some of the German machine-gunners had turned round and were firing on the infiltrators, killing six and wounding three, leaving just eight doughboys to press home their advantages. Their position became much uglier when yet more gunners switched their aim and, from a distance which York estimated was about thirty yards, began killing or scaring into retreat all the non-commissioned officers, leaving York in command:

And those machine guns were spitting fire and cutting down the undergrowth all around me something awful. And the Germans were yelling orders. You never heard such a racket in all of your life. I didn't have time to dodge behind a tree or dive into the brush, I didn't even have time to kneel or lie down [...] As soon as the machine guns opened fire on me, I began to exchange shots with them. There were over thirty of them in continuous action, and all

I could do was touch the Germans off just as fast as I could. I was sharpshooting. I don't think I missed a shot. It was no time to miss. In order to sight me or to swing their machine guns on me, the Germans had to show their heads above the trench, and every time I saw a head I just touched it off. All the time I kept yelling at them to come down. I didn't want to kill any more than I had to. But it was they or I. And I was giving them the best I had. Suddenly a German officer and five men jumped out of the trench and charged me with fixed bayonets. I changed to the old automatic and just touched them off too. I touched off the sixth man first, then the fifth, then the fourth, then the third, and so on. I wanted them to keep coming. I didn't want the rear ones to see me touching off the front ones, I was afraid they would drop down and pump a volley into me.[19]

York kept cool and, concealed in high brush behind a tree trunk, picked off Germans whenever they popped their heads up. Too close to them to risk a grenade – and the machine-gunners themselves were unsure where their captured rear-line comrades might be – the Germans tried to rush the demon rifleman. When that failed, a German major – who later turned out to have lived for several years in Chicago – surrendered to York. York had by this stage killed more than twenty machine-gunners. Those of his squad who were still alive rose up and helped him disarm about ninety Germans who were then marched back through the German front line, York using his Colt .45 against the temple of the German major to persuade him to get others to surrender *en route*. By the time York and his handful of doughboys reached their own lines he had taken 132 prisoners.

York was ordered to report to his brigade commander, Brigadier-General Lindsay, who said:

'Well, York, I hear you have captured the whole damned German army.'

'Only 132 of them,' replied York, who almost single-handedly put out of action thirty-five German machine-guns and ensured that the 82nd's assault on the railway went through as originally planned. Awarded the DSC and immediately promoted sergeant, York then personally received his Medal of Honor from Pershing. York was indeed exceptionally courageous but he remained a modest man, later telling Brigadier-General Lindsay: 'Sir, it is not man power. A higher power than man power guided and watched over me and told me what to do.'

On 10 October the 82nd took the town of Cornay, slightly to the north of where York's company had been pinned down.

On the far right flank of this extending front the 33rd, 26th and 29th Divisions were all engaged in a bitter and ultimately unsuccessful fight to gain the peak of the Consenvoye Heights, upon which dominating position the Germans had a host of cannon which was splintering the doughboys' right flank. On 8 October these three AEF divisions, plus two French, were ordered to advance frontally to the Meuse, take Consenvoye village, put pontoon bridges across the Meuse and scale the Heights. The assault was an unmitigated disaster. The French collapsed, the 29th was parcelled out among them to bolster their efforts, and on 9 October for some inexplicable reason the 33rd Division attempted to cross the two narrow pontoon bridges not at night but in broad daylight. That day there was plenty of heroism; many of the 33rd's doughboys managed to cross the Meuse only to find themselves pinned down in a maelstrom of machine-gun fire. The stalemated struggle over the next three days saw the 33rd take considerable casualties until on 12 October it was accepted that the attack had, once again, petered out.

The supposed failure of the 26th Division to press home the attack with sufficient ardour gave Pershing the opportunity he needed to take revenge for what he perceived to be the earlier irresponsibility and disloyalty of General Clarence Edwards, who was abruptly sacked from command of the 26th Division and replaced by Brigadier-General Frank E. Bamford from the 1st Division. Bamford in turn pillaged the 26th's senior ranks, kicking back to the United States Colonel Logan of the 101st Infantry, Colonel Hume of the 103rd (on 6 November) and (on 9 November) dismissing Brigadier Cole of the 52nd Brigade and seven majors. All these officers were National Guardsmen. There was bitter and enduring resentment among the 26th's rank-and-file that their hand-picked officers should be so summarily jettisoned by the regular army. The story of Edwards's dismissal is covered in barnacles; there have long been accusations against Pershing that he let personal jealousy get in the way of his professional judgement. If true, it would not have been the first time. Certainly Pershing could never abide non-professional soldiers, though Edwards was as professional a soldier as they come – another West Point graduate.[20] But it was equally true that under Edwards's leadership the division had stalled in front of the Consenvoye Heights; under Bamford they were revitalized.

By mid-October many among the Allies and the AEF began to sense that the Germans might be on the run. And yet the conflict remained astonishingly close, right up to the final hurdle. For one thing the vast quantities of artillery shells consumed in the final days threatened to halt the Allied offensive. In the first ten months of 1918 French shell production for the sturdy 75mm light field gun[21] was enormous, but at the end of October demand began dangerously to exceed supply. Between 11 and 20 September production averaged 210,000 shells per day, but those in charge of French supplies expected this rate of production to fall as low as 180,000 shells per day because of the army call-up of skilled munitions workers. On 21 March, French 75mm shell reserves stood at 3,663 'lots' (one lot = 6,000 rounds), i.e. 21,978,000 rounds. By 12 October the reserve was down to 399 'lots', i.e. 2,394,000 rounds – a reduction of nearly 90 per cent. On days of heavy fighting in the final days of the war the daily consumption was as follows:

26 September	1,842,000 rounds
30 September	853,000
1 October	300,000
2 October	288,000
3 October	330,000
4 October	491,000
5 October	353,000
6 October	275,000
7 October	223,000
8 October	446,000
9 October	320,000
10 October	244,000

Given the lowest projection for output of 75mm shells, the available reserve, and a low daily average of expenditure of 250,000 shells, the

French were on course to run out of 75mm ammunition by the end of November. No doubt there would have been a desperate campaign to withdraw munitions workers from the front and send them back to making shells before a total collapse occurred. But the situation was not clear-cut, and the AEF certainly experienced some very hard going in the attacks of 7–12 October:

[. . .] the enemy contested every inch of ground and the severe fighting that occurred before positions could be captured was scarcely realized outside of our own army. Our troops were engaged in some of the most bitter fighting of the war, forcing their way through dense woods, over hills and across deep ravines, against German defense conducted with a skill only equalled by that of the French in front of Verdun in 1916. Yet all our corps advanced their lines, the V capturing elements of the Hindenburg Line, which our troops were now facing.[22]

On 14 October the AEF commenced its third effort to take the Romagne and Cunel Heights, and finally to extricate itself from the Argonne forest. On the right of the line was the French 17th Corps, to the east of the Meuse, and containing the 29th and 33rd Divisions of the AEF; next came the AEF 3rd Corps, commanded by General Hines (the 4th Division under General Cameron, the 3rd under General Buck, the 5th under General McMahon); then the 5th Corps, led by General Summerall (with the 32nd Division commanded by General Haan, and the 42nd under General Menoher); then the 1st Corps under General Dickman (comprising the 82nd Division under General Duncan and the 77th under General Alexander). Between 14 and 16 October the dogged, slow-paced slogging matches resumed all along the line; stalemate prevailed.

On 13 October a section of the 77th, including Captain Julius Ochs Adler – whose family owned the *New York Times* – led an assault on one of Grandpré's more difficult emplacements, St Juvin, managing to capture it after some intense fighting. That same night the 78th Division, who called themselves 'The White Lightnings' (after the whisky-distilling skills of the rural areas of their home states of New York and New Jersey), relieved the 77th. Meanwhile, units of the French Fourth Army had taken the village of Talma, north-west of Grandpré, only to be driven out by the Germans on 14 October. On 15 October the 78th Division re-took a farm outside Talma, and there then followed nine days of ferocious combat before Talma was once more in Allied hands.

Every objective was taking far too long to be picked off; far from being ready to pack up and leave, the Germans seemed to be increasingly determined. Grandpré only fell on Sunday, 27 October, by which time the 78th Division had sustained 5,000 casualties and its German defenders were all either dead or taken prisoner. Grandpré symbolizes the kind of resistance put up by the Germans on the US front; it was fighting to the bitter end, with little or no quarter given on either side. Everywhere German heavy machine-guns continued slaughtering doughboys; the 4th Division made no headway at all, while the rest of the 3rd Corps struggled to advance. The 5th Corps fared slightly better, the 32nd Division showing great valour and determination; on Monday, 14 October its 64th Brigade captured one of the Hindenburg line's most important strongpoints, the Côte Dame Marie. The town of Romagne and the eastern half of the Bois de Romagne were taken by the same division on the same day. On 11 October the 42nd Division relieved the 1st Division, which had suffered enormous casualties in taking two high ridges from the Germans on the outskirts of the small village of Exermont. The 42nd then proceeded to force its way from Exermont through the western half of the Bois de Romagne, the 84th Brigade under Douglas MacArthur scaling the heights of the Côte de Châtillon; but it was another four days, with 3,000 casualties sustained by his brigade alone, before the 42nd grabbed Châtillon's defensive system, part of the Kriemhilde Stellung. In those four days the Rainbow Division's centre covered less than a mile of ground.

The fighting was just as bad here as at any previous time or place on the Western Front. On 12 October Private Albert Ettinger, a Rainbow Division doughboy, was in a foxhole, taking cover from German artillery:

I wanted to smoke and had plenty of tobacco and paper for making cigarettes, but damn it, I didn't have a match [. . .] Consequently, I went over to the next fox hole to get some matches.

In this fox hole was our Color Sergeant, Bill Sheahan, who didn't have to be there in the first place, and another doughboy I didn't know. I got some dry matches from them and squeezed back into our fox hole. No sooner had I rolled and lit a cigarette than there was a terrible explosion! Both Sherwood and I were stunned and buried in mud. We managed to dig ourselves out of our hole, heard shouts, and discovered that the shell had landed in the adjacent hole where those two fellows had been. There was no sign of Bill Sheahan, and the other fellow had both legs blown off; he was being carried down the slope to the aid station.

Everyone was mystified as to what had happened to Sheahan. I told Tom Fitzsimmons he had been in that hole, because I had spoken to him only a few minutes before the shell exploded. At dawn we started to look around and soon came across what appeared to be a piece of roast beef strapped by a web belt, and the initials 'W.S.' were burned into the belt. That was the mortal remains of Bill Sheahan.[23]

By 16 October the doughboys had carried most of this section of the Hindenburg line, and after considerable effort had reached the objective originally set for 26 September. Most of these positions were taken the hardest way of all – by frontal assault, pushed home with desperate grit and determination by infantry who had the temerity to be unaware of the possibility of being beaten. On 17 October the 42nd and 32nd Divisions were pulled out of the line to rest; their positions were taken over by the doughboys and marines of the 2nd Division on the left and the 89th Division on the right flank.

During this period of intense combat right across the Western Front, the Germans made peace overtures to President Wilson through the Swiss government. The new German chancellor, Max, Prince von Baden, requested an armistice on the basis of Wilson's message to Congress of 8 January. Wilson's reply of 8 October called on Germany to withdraw all its forces from occupied territory before any such negotiations could start. The Germans replied on 12 October, calling for a 'mixed commission' to make 'the necessary arrangements concerning the evacuation'. This did not sound like the sort of defeat the Allies would accept, as Wilson well knew. On 14 October he replied more emphatically:

It must be clearly understood that the process of evacuation and the conditions of an armistice are matters which must be left to the judgment and advice of the military advisers of the Government of the United States and the Allied Governments, and the President feels it his duty to say that no arrangement can be accepted by the Government of the United States which does not provide absolutely satisfactory safeguards and guarantees of the maintenance of the present military supremacy of the armies of the United States and of the Allies in the field. He feels confident that he can safely assume that this will also be the judgment and decision of the Allied Governments.[24]

Wilson also called for the end of the sinking of passenger vessels and smaller boats, and hinted very heavily that an elected and representative system of government would be needed in Germany before there could be much dealing. This diplomatic poker-game persisted until on 23 October Wilson stated (in fairly blunt terms by his standards) that what was wanted from the Germans was not offers of 'peace negotiations, but surrender. Nothing can be gained by leaving this essential thing unsaid.'

Despite this flurry of activity on the diplomatic front there was scepticism among the doughboys that the war would soon be over, or that the Germans were about to collapse. Brigadier-General Hagood's hopes on 10 October were no more than that the war would end in 1919. He made a realistic assessment:

[...] transportation difficulties and the weather will soon stop the advance of the Allies and [...] Germany will be able to withdraw her forces to a relatively secure line near her own frontier, for the time being. My prediction is that before spring Germany will be entirely out of France and Belgium; that during the spring and summer an aggressive campaign will be waged resulting in a complete military victory.[25]

The AEF's advance in the Vosges region had almost ground to a halt, largely due to a lack of transport but also because of the totally choked roads. No horse transport had been shipped from America for almost five months, and the Motor Transport Corps had been allowed, as Hagood put it, 'to slumber almost a year without proper organization and without proper support'. The AEF's transport problem was now so desperate that by 23 October Hagood recommended to a junior officer of the SOS that he should rent some taxi cabs, or even issue taxi-cab tickets, as a means of transporting troops closer to the front. Life was not so hard, however, that it prevented Hagood from going wild boar shooting near Tours on Sunday, 27 October.

In the midst of all this Pershing sent a note (dated 17 October) to his corps and division commanders in which he set out his view of how best to bring about the *coup de grâce*:

Now that Germany and the Central Powers are losing, they are begging for an armistice. Their request is an acknowledgment of weakness and clearly means that the Allies are winning the war. That is the best of reasons for our pushing the war more vigorously at this moment. Germany's desire is only to gain time to restore order among her forces, but she must be given no opportunity to recuperate and we must strike harder than ever. Our strong blows are telling, and continuous pressure by us has compelled the enemy to meet us, enabling our Allies to gain on other parts of the line. There can be no conclusion to this war until Germany is brought to her knees.[26]

This kind of morale-boosting stuff cut little ice with Clemenceau, who would not rest until he had managed to have Pershing removed and replaced by someone a little more malleable. On 21 October Clemenceau wrote to Foch 'a letter which had in view nothing less than to effect a change in the chief command of the American Army'. The contents of this letter were so muddle-headed and so motivated by personal malice, so ignorant of the astonishingly tough fight being waged right across the AEF's front at that moment, it is a wonder that the war was ever won. Clemenceau informed Foch that there was a 'crisis' in the American army, and, he said, 'I would be a criminal if I allowed the French Army to wear itself out indefinitely in battle, without doing everything in my power to ensure that an Allied Army which has hurried to its aid was rendered capable of fulfilling the military role for which it is destined.' What Clemenceau sought was the end of Pershing as head of the AEF:

[. . .] our worthy American Allies, who thirst to get into action and who are unanimously acknowledged to be great soldiers, have been marking time ever since their forward jump on the first day; and in spite of heavy losses, they have failed to conquer the ground assigned to them as their objective. Nobody can maintain that these fine troops are unusable; they are merely unused [...]

If General Pershing finally resigns himself to obedience, if he accepts the advice of capable Generals, whose presence at his side he has until now permitted only that he might reject their counsels, I shall be wholly delighted.

But if this new attempt to reconcile two contrary points of view should not bring the advantageous results you anticipate, I must say to you that, in my opinion, any further hesitation should be out of the question. For it would then be certainly high time to tell President Wilson the truth and the whole truth concerning the situation of the American troops [...][27]

It must have been galling in the extreme for Pershing and his senior staff to learn that the prime minister of France, a country which might by the same token be accused of 'marking time' for more than four years of conflict against the Germans, had accused the inexperienced, scarcely trained, under-resourced and courageous heroes of Grandpré, Châtillon and Romagne of slacking. Pershing sacked more officers than all the rest of the combatant armies put together; in his army it was a question of get on or get out. The doughboys were halted not because of inept leadership (though there were no doubt as many incompetent officers in the AEF as elsewhere) but for precisely the same reason that British and French armies had been stopped through much of the war: a determined opponent resisting from exceptionally well-formed defensive positions. Even Clemenceau's fit of pique could not do much about that. Foch, a greater realist, merely replied to Clemenceau that

[...] there is no denying the magnitude of the effort made by the American Army. After attacking at Saint-Mihiel on September 12th, it attacked in the Argonne on the 26th. From September 26th to October 20th its losses in battle were 54,158 men – in exchange for small gains on a narrow front, it is true, but over particularly difficult country and in the face of serious resistance by the enemy.[28]

Thanks to the sheer bulk of the ever-increasing AEF, the balance of power was beginning to swing more in Pershing's favour. By 23 October the AEF's combat strength was 1,256,478 men and officers, 592,300 of whom were in the First Army (as were another 100,000 French combat troops).[29] This kind of muscle, this sheer weight, gave him renewed confidence to withstand the pressure Clemenceau was exerting at every opportunity. Yet as October drew to its inconclusive end, Pershing was growing weary; so were most of his doughboys, now increasingly lacking in the mental and physical energy which had made them seem such gods to Vera Brittain. At the Meuse–Argonne in late October Private Arthur Yensen was driving his mule team to follow up the advance of his 5th Division:

Jack rode with me; and, as usual, we had to have an argument. He said it was wrong to take anything off a dead soldier for a souvenir; I said it was all right and just about had the argument won when I heard a popping noise. I looked down and saw I'd run over a dead Yank and broke his legs! Later we saw lots of dead men. Half a man here and another half across the road, bled white and spattered with mud. I felt sorry for the poor boys; they looked so pitiful! My heart melted within me as I turned to Jack and said, 'You Win! I'd shoot anyone who touched them!'[30]

17

11 November 1918

They stopped fighting at 11 o'clock this morning. In a twinkling, four years of killing and massacre stopped as if God had swept His omnipotent finger across the scene of world carnage and had cried 'Enough.'
Edwin L. James, *New York Times*, 11 November 1918

They never knew they were beaten in Berlin. It will all have to be done all over again.
General Pershing[1]

On the last day of fighting of the First World War, Battery D of the 129th Field Artillery, 35th Division, a National Guard unit, was situated east of Verdun. On that morning the battery fired 164 shells into the German lines, the last of about 12,000 delivered by the same unit of 194 men and four guns since it arrived in France on 13 April 1918. The battery's commander – Captain, later President, Harry S. Truman – heaved a sigh of relief. He had survived, and so had every single one of the men in his charge. He had shown nothing but the most exemplary courage, endurance, and care for his men, but he had sometimes hidden just how scared he was: 'The men think I am not much afraid of shells but they don't know I was too scared to run and that is pretty scared.'[2]

In the final days of the war the whine of the shells and the stuttering of the machine-guns reached a pitch of ferocity scarcely previously seen. The AEF's line – now beyond the Hindenburg line – extended from the Meuse in the east to Landres-St-Georges in the centre and to the Bois de Bourgogne in the west. The First Army was again to bear the main brunt of what proved to be the final assault, a straight drive towards Buzancy and Barricourt; beyond them, to the north, was the lure of one of the greatest prizes of all – the city of Sedan.

From the left of the First Army's line, the 1st Corps (still under Dickman) had the 78th, 77th and 80th Divisions; next in line to the right was the 5th Corps, which with the 2nd and 89th Divisions, commanded by Summerall, was to take the heaviest role in the direct assault upon Barricourt; to the right of this was the 3rd Corps, commanded by General Hines, with the 90th and 5th Divisions, which was intended to play a supportive role to the 5th Corps in the main thrust. In reserve of the 5th Corps were the battle-hardened 1st and 42nd Divisions, ready to be passed up through the ranks of the 2nd and 80th when reinforcements were needed.

The toll of the preceding weeks' savagery was beginning to be felt. Instead of the small quota of tanks that might be expected for any serious assault – anything between 100 and 200 – only eighteen were now available to the First Army. As Pershing later commented laconically:

It seems strange that, with American genius for manufacturing from iron and steel, we should find ourselves after a year and a half of war almost completely without those mechanical contrivances which had exercised such a great influence on the Western Front in reducing infantry losses.[3]

Yet when the end came it did so abruptly, taking by surprise many of those actually doing the fighting. For Private Malcolm Aitken,

From November 1st until 9th it was one continuous scrap. We would clean up one nest and then find another twice as bad. Woods and brush and individual spots hid these machine guns and they were very difficult to dislodge. You see there was so much cross-fire from the riflemen and other machine guns, that you didn't know which one to get first [. . .] Of course, strong rumor was around on the 9th and 10th as it had been ever since Champagne that the Armistice would be signed at 11 o'clock the 11th of November; but definite rumor setting the time did not show up until the evening of the 10th and just before we hopped off everyone was thanking his lucky stars that this was the last battle. It was for a large percentage [. . .] We had about completed our first consolidation and most of us were taking pot-shots at anything we thought we saw up ahead, when the order Cease Firing but Stand-to came hurling down the line, passed by word of mouth [...] We built a roaring fire, salvaged some wine and other rations that we had staked out; and saw the old year out and the new one in, in appropriate fashion. There was plenty of yelling and dancing around as we made bets as to who had fired the last shot.[4]

The final eleven days of the Meuse–Argonne saw some astonishingly fierce combat, and yet there was an unreal feeling about much of it. After all, it was well known that Ludendorff had fallen from power and that the Germans were suing for peace. Strange rumours – such as the end of the war, of Germans chained to their machine-guns, of women in uniform – were everywhere, the stock-in-trade of the front lines. Captain Charles Donnelly and his comrades thought they

could smell victory. Rumors spread over the area like fluff from ripe milkweed. Some soldiers swore that they had seen German machine gunners, dead, chained to their guns. What they had actually seen were machine gunners who had become entangled in the chain used to keep the water-cooling tank from becoming lost when the gun was moved. Others were dead sure they had seen evidences in abandoned dugouts of the presence of women. They may have been right. Many of the dugouts back of the Kreimhilde Stellung were almost luxurious with pianos, stocks of wine and champagne, cigars, gasoline lanterns, good heaters and comfortable chairs and beds.[5]

At 5.30 a.m. on 1 November, the AEF's last great battle of the First World War commenced, with an artillery barrage in a zone 1,200 yards deep. The total strength of the AEF was now 76,800 officers and 1,790,823 men. North of St-Mihiel General Bullard's Second Army had crossed the Moselle. The objective for General Liggett's First Army was to break through the final German defensive line, the Freya Stellung, and threaten the strategically vital railway yards at Sedan, from where the Germans were still capable of reinforcing the more northerly battle areas where the French and British were coming under severe pressure. By this stage the British under Haig were still about 200 miles from the Belgian city of Liège, and the French under Pétain were some considerable distance from Luxemburg. The closest and symbolically most important target within reach of any of the

Allies was undoubtedly Sedan, humiliatingly in German hands since 1871. Despite the resignation of the German joint commander, Ludendorff, on 27 October (his replacement in the field was General Wilhelm Groener, director of railways, a crucial aspect of the juggling of German forces now necessary to fend off the Allies), the Germans were at this stage not prepared to concede anything more than a stalemate.

By now the AEF had belatedly learned that the rifle was not in itself sufficient to defeat a powerful opposing force. Thanks to the careful planning of Allied generals like Monash, there was greater emphasis on combining all forces – artillery, aircraft, tanks and infantry – but the doughboys were still starved of the necessary equipment. In his attack Liggett had the resources of 650,000 men, including 100,000 French troops, but only nineteen light, French-made Whippet tanks. On Friday, 1 November Private Francis went over the top yet again:

It had been raining so the ground was soft. I was thankful for that for I would surely have been killed; a shell went a few feet over my right shoulder and hit only a little distance behind me, it buried itself in the soft earth and only kicked mud over me [. . .] I hadn't any more than laughed over this (for now, in a way, I did not care whether I was killed or not) when another shell went a few feet over me. Gee, I thought it was going right through me.

In Francis's company almost all his buddies were to die in this final assault, but for the first time the German lines genuinely fell apart, and the 2nd and 89th Divisions burst five miles through them; on the first day the 5th Corps positively galloped the five miles to reach its primary objective, the heights of Barricourt. By 4 November the Germans were in retreat from the doughboys all along the First Army front, though with strong rearguard protection from concealed machine-guns.

The end, when it came, was marred by a piece of crass behaviour on the part of Pershing. He coveted Sedan as a symbolic trophy for the AEF, when it was obvious that the honour of recapturing the city should be left to the French. Pershing, however, suggested to the French that the boundary line between the AEF First Army and the French Fourth Army be ignored in case the doughboys made faster headway than the French troops. Sedan was to the north-west of the extreme boundary on the left of the First Army, some eighteen miles beyond Barricourt. Pershing issued an order stating that he wished the 1st Corps (the 42nd and 77th Divisions) to take Sedan, 'assisted on the right by the 5th Corps'. The 1st Division, part of the 5th Corps, commanded by General Charles P. Summerall, decided to march straight across the path of the 42nd and 77th Divisions and beat them to Sedan, causing immense confusion and chaos to supply lines. The resulting mess caused some last-minute farces, including the brief arrest by some elements of the 1st Division of Colonel Douglas MacArthur of the 42nd Division, on suspicion of being a German spy. Marshal Foch, meanwhile, re-drew the boundaries separating the First Army from the French Fourth Army, ensuring that the honour of liberating Sedan fell to the French. By dawn on 7 November – when a group of German Reichstag members, led by Matthias Erzberger, reached Marshal Foch's railway car in the forest of Compiègne to discuss peace terms – the men of the 42nd and 1st were on the outskirts of Sedan, taking potshots at the German defenders and throwing occasional punches at each other. General Dickman, commander of the 1st Corps, was furious at such a shambles but Pershing, normally a fierce disciplinarian, indulged his boys in the Big Red One:

Under normal conditions the action of the officer or officers responsible for this movement of the 1st Division directly across the zones of action of two other divisions could not have been overlooked, but the splendid record of that unit and the approach of the end of hostilities suggested leniency.[6]

This kind of croneyism did not serve Pershing well in later years, when it has come to be seen as an example of the kind of favouritism a truly efficient commander-in-chief would have avoided. General Liggett, not a disloyal man, called the mess an 'atrocity'.

But despite this embarrassing incident, in less than a week from 1 November the First Army had swallowed twenty-four miles of territory previously in the hands of the enemy. This was a remarkable achievement. The AEF's Second Army (the 33rd, 28th, 7th and 92nd Divisions) turned its attention towards the Brier iron basin and set its sights on the capture of Metz, less than twenty miles to the east along the river Moselle. Between 26 September and 11 November twenty-two

American and six French divisions – about 500,000 men – fought against forty-three German divisions (470,000 combatants) on a front extending from Verdun in the south to the Argonne forest. The First Army suffered about 170,000 casualties, inflicted some 100,000 on the Germans, and captured 26,000 prisoners, 874 cannon, and 3,000 machine-guns.[7]

The First Army launched yet one more general attack just seven hours before the Armistice. The 89th Division had been in the midst of the final days' struggle, frequently existing on starvation rations. Company A of the division's 342nd Machine Gun Battalion spent four days without any food except the beech nuts they could find at their feet.[8] Right up to the last minute Francis Jordan of Company H, 356th Infantry, 89th Division, was in the thick of the fighting. The 356th was officially the last unit to be informed of the Armistice and in fact kept firing until midday, an hour after the official cease-fire.[9] In the early hours of 11 November Jordan's unit was ordered, along with many others, to cross the Meuse by means of some flimsy bridges. It was a senseless order which needlessly cost the lives of many doughboys, but regimental colonels and battalion majors were too insecure in their positions to do anything else but keep the pressure on right to the end; anything else might have meant their career was forever blighted. General Liggett attempted to justify the decision to continue to press home the attack by arguing that Foch had appealed for it on the evening of 9 November, while Berlin considered the terms of the proposed Armistice:

As a result of this appeal, I received orders on November 10 for a general attack by the First Army the following morning. We went into battle knowing that the terms of the armistice were being discussed with higher authority, but with no assurance that the enemy would accept those terms in the few hours that remained before the offer would expire. Fighting was our concern and our only concern until we were ordered to stop.[10]

The result for Lieutenant Jordan was a flesh wound:

We were then ordered forward and came under close machine gun fire not more than fifteen or twenty feet on our left. I received a minor flesh wound

Western Front manpower, 11 November 1918 (million)

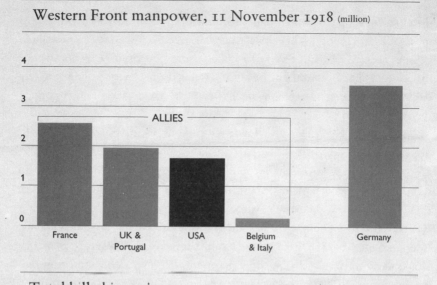

ALLIES

| | France | UK & Portugal | USA | Belgium & Italy | Germany |

Total killed in action including those who died of wounds (million)

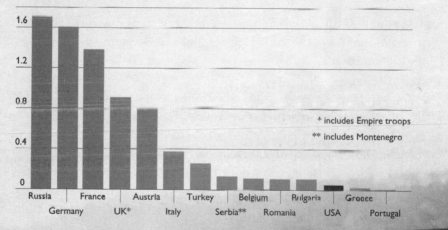

* includes Empire troops
** includes Montenegro

Russia   France   Austria   Turkey   Belgium   Bulgaria   Greece
   Germany   UK*   Italy   Serbia**   Romania   USA   Portugal

P.O.
Kx 739

through the shoulder, which bullet continued on to hit my pack which was filled with cans of food. The impact tipped me over backwards, and, in falling, I threw up my hand and received a bullet at the base of my left thumb. The machine gun had been shifted quickly and killed the first sergeant immediately behind me and the sergeant immediately behind him. Our advance was stopped for the time being.

Corporal Wicker crawled up beside me and put his rifle across my chest to fire in the direction of the German machine guns. The return fire was so accurate that the wood on the corporal's rifle was splintered. Those of us who had been wounded remained there for some time, while those who were unwounded took up the advance to locate and kill the German machine gunner. [He travelled by ambulance to Beaumont where] At 11 o'clock someone came into announce that the war was over, but there was little cheering. Someone was able to play a hymn on the pipe organ, however, and somehow that helped us to realize that the war was over.[11]

For Sergeant Rudolph Forderhase this last attack was possibly the worst of all. The Barricourt Heights had been taken, but the pursuit must continue:

Division Headquarters had been dissatisfied with the slow progress made after the Heights of Barricourt had been taken. They seemed unable to visualize the effectiveness of the enemy's rearguard tactics [. . .] Captain Arthur Y. Wear was now in command of the Battalion. He had orders to get men across the [Meuse] river. He now called for men to volunteer to swim across the river and attempt to get information as to the strength, and disposition, of the German troops. The stream was near bankfull, due to the fact that the enemy had placed obstructions on the upstream side of bridges, which hindered the normal flow of the stream. The water was cold and deep. Only about half of those who volunteered were selected. Of these, only a few succeeded in getting across. About half were killed by the enemy, or drowned in the cold water. Only about half of those who got back were able to give information of any value [. . .]

When the surviving swimmers returned and informed Captain Wear of what had been accomplished, he walked a short distance into the dark and somber woods and shot himself in the head with his service pistol.[12]

On the night of 10 November Forderhase's unit marched under cover of darkness to the river bank to set off in a pontoon boat across the river. His battalion crossed unscathed, though others nearby were badly shot up. When across the river the 356th formed open extended order and marched up higher ground towards the village of Pouilly, through a blanket of dense fog. Suddenly Forderhase was called over by an officer who had stumbled across a machine-gun pit with two young German soldiers in it, their hands held high in surrender:

I was quite surprised to see them. The Captain knew I could speak a bit of German and told me to ask them why they had not fired on us. They informed me that all fighting was to end at eleven o'clock that morning and they saw no reason to sacrifice their lives, or ours, needlessly. Neither the Captain, nor I, knew whether to believe them or not.

Forderhase and his unit took the two Germans prisoner and pressed on, coming under sniper fire:

We were somewhat concerned about this when suddenly the sniper's firing ceased – everything became perfectly quiet. I then remembered what the two German prisoners had said earlier that morning. I took a look at the cheap wrist watch that I had been wearing. It had stopped at eleven o'clock and I never did get it to run again.[13]

Elsewhere on Monday, 11 November Corporal Harry Wright, with the 104th Infantry Regiment, 26th Division, was waiting to

push them over a hill that was in front of us. We were froze, tired and hungry as the zero hour approached. But just before we started our last drive, which would have meant many more lives, an order came through to cease firing, an armistice had been signed for 11 o'clock. It is now 10.30, one half [hour] more of this hell on earth with us on the verge of going over the top again.

The next day Wright and his comrades

got the toughest job of all our service a job for other men than tired doughboys. There wasn't a man in our lot could speak from hoarseness but we had to move back over the ground we had just captured the last week and bury the dead, hundreds of them who got bumped off in that drive through Argonne. Gee what a rotten job to bury bodies a week or two dead. We finished our burial detail in 2 days, burying the Americans in one group and the Germans in another.[14]

Albert Ettinger of the 42nd Division was perhaps fortunate to have taken a whiff of gas a few days before 11 November; he spent the final days of the war in a hospital bed:

We heard a lot of singing and shouting outside. Raising myself in the bed, I could see out the window, and there was a rag-tag parade coming down the street with this tall, lanky guy leading it with an American flag. It was Rubin Bernstein, my old buddy from the Pioneer Platoon! [. . .] It turned out that the Armistice had been signed, and everybody started to celebrate; but at that moment all I cared about was rejoining my buddy.[15]

Peace arrived, but what sort of peace? Pershing was alarmed that the doves had been prematurely set loose. He had already indicated as early as 30 October (in a message to the Allied Supreme War Council and copied to Washington) that he was opposed to every peace gesture save one – unconditional surrender by Germany. He has since been criticized as being unjustifiably hawkish for this, though his reasoning was motivated not by bloodthirstiness but a fear that peace on terms any less harsh than complete and unconditional surrender would render it almost impossible to get the exhausted soldiers back to battle again, should that prove necessary. In his message to the SWC, points 10 and 11 (of a total of thirteen) cover this issue:

10. An armistice would lead the Allied armies to believe this the end of fighting and it would be difficult, if not impossible, to resume hostilities with our present advantage in morale in the event of failure to secure at a peace conference what we have fought for.

11. By agreeing to an armistice under the present favorable military situation of the Allies and accepting the principle of negotiated peace rather than a dictated peace the Allies would jeopardize the moral position they now hold and possibly lose the chance actually to secure world peace on terms that would insure its permanence.[16]

In retrospect this seems a remarkably prescient view of what was to happen in the two decades following the end of the First World War. As he remarked in his memoir, the Armistice was, in military terms, a disaster:

If unconditional surrender had been demanded, the Germans would, without doubt, have been compelled to yield, and their troops would have returned to Germany without arms, virtually as paroled prisoners of war. The surrender of the German armies would have been an advantage to the Allies in the enforcement of peace terms and would have been a greater deterrent against possible future German aggression.[17]

Pershing may have had his doubts, but throughout France doughboys celebrated the end of the fighting as best they could. Millions of civilians in the United States also danced in the streets that night, though some were not able to. A stubborn conscientious objector, Howard Moore, had been cast into Fort Leavenworth Disciplinary Barracks, where he was immediately placed in solitary confinement for refusing to work in the prison. There he was shackled to the bars of his cell for nine hours a day, on a bread-and-water diet. He had by this time lost ninety pounds.[18]

I soon learned that I was not alone. The cell was alive with bedbugs, which furnished an uneasy diversion as I watched them crawling up my manacled arms and dropping into my hair from the ceiling. By twisting and pressing my body against the bars I could crush some, but not all ... At night the bedbugs were more numerous and more active and were joined by rats, which kept pouncing on my chest as they played around my cell.[19]

Moore found a way of slipping out of his shackles and rested on the floor of his cell. When he refused for the third time to get up, an officer ordered guards to beat him with their clubs.

When I regained consciousness my head was in the lap of the regular guard on the wing. He was soaking up the blood from my hair and face with a handkerchief and saying as though to himself, 'Jesus, if he can stand that, he'll win.'[20]

He spent thirty-one days in solitary, by which time he was diagnosed as having TB and his weight was down to ninety pounds from 150 when he entered the prison. Then the authorities relented and declared that the harsh punishment meted out to him and other conscientious objectors would now cease.

For some, the end came a fraction too early. Brigadier-General Johnson Hagood had just managed to escape the career dead-end of his job as chief-of-staff of the Service of Supply, and on 11 November he found himself in Paris *en route* to take over command of the 30th Brigade of heavy artillery, a combat role which, he hoped, would eventually secure him the major-generalship he craved. He could summon up no enthusiasm for the end of the war; he could only see it as the end of his career:

Early in the morning news of the signing of the armistice was circulated. It was signed at 5.40 a.m. and at 11 a.m., firing would cease. Paris went wild. I suppose it was the most remarkable day in the history of the world. The streets soon became so crowded that it was impossible to move. The crowds were cheering, young girls were being carried on the shoulders of the soldiers, soldiers were being carried in the arms of civilians [. . .] I had played my cards badly and had had the most execrable luck.[21]

Hagood immediately set about lobbying to have himself given something rather more important than the 30th Brigade, which was to be returned to the United States as one of the first contingents to be sent home. He pulled strings and got an interview with General Hinds, Chief of Artillery, who told him that as he had had no active front-line experience he could not recommend Hagood for any of the three brigades that might be considered. But Pershing backed Hagood, and he got his command, of the 66th Brigade of Field Artillery, which had been under Colonel Lanza.

For army chaplain Samuel Devan the Armistice was a blessed relief:

Nov 11th [. . .] Tonight we had quite a grand dinner at our mess in celebration of the Peace. Some good goose was eaten, some speeches were made, some champagne was drunk. Everybody was toasted who ought to have been [. . .] Colonel Carpenter relaxed for a moment a degree or two of his military stiffness. He is striking terror into the heart of the regiment. His latest & crowning act of injustice is to order Franklain and Welsh to Blois – that one act is enough to want to have done with the Army forever.[22]

Some had seen the end of the war, and how it would finish, long before the end itself. Writing in his diary on 26 August 1917, soon after he landed at St Nazaire, Charles Dawes predicted that Germany would ultimately be brought low not by military action but internal collapse:

The French have been fought until they feel the war in every phase of life, but one realizes that this cannot be so in France and England and not be so in even greater degree in Germany. There being in Germany a military aristocracy against which the inevitable psychological reaction against continued war can find an outlet in attacking, I feel that the war will be ended by the internal revolt of the people of Germany. If that does not come, the end of the war now seems several years off.[23]

On the battlefield, the AEF was probably fortunate that the fighting stopped when it did. Shipments of supplies from the States destined for the AEF had fallen by October to twenty-two pounds in weight per man per day; horses and mules were now so scarce that in the 6th Division they harnessed men to pull wagons and guns. The Transport Corps was complaining that it had only 61 per cent of its necessary personnel, 73 per cent of the required locomotives, and only 32 per cent of cars. It is evident that if the Germans had not caved in when they did the AEF would very shortly have faced a logistical disaster.

The Armistice was thus a relief at a strategic level, and a joy on the personal. Private Arthur Yensen could not believe he had come through it alive:

About 10 o'clock, while we were standing around in the sunshine eating cabbage from a nearby garden, a man on a motorcycle came by and told us that an armistice had been signed and that the war would be over at eleven. It sounded like good news to us all right; but we didn't believe him [. . .]

At eleven o'clock there was a lull in the firing. However, we all said, 'Don't worry, it'll soon start up again.' Nevertheless, the afternoon passed and the lull continued. Then that night they let us build fires. Thousands of camp fires flared up all over the country. Not till then did we really begin to realize that maybe the war was really over and that we'd soon be going home. The thought of going home made us noisy and hilarious! We laughed and yelled and whooped it up till about midnight [. . .] Everyone was a friend to everyone else. At supper that night the cooks opened a barrel of captured sauerkraut and a sack of captured sugar and let us help ourselves. This was the first time sugar had ever been served to us – thanks to the Germans for leaving it behind [. . .]

Good times have come at last! We'll soon turn in our mules and go home where we can eat sugar, sleep in beds, get rid of cooties, ditch our wrap leggings, see our folks, chase around with girls, and maybe rate a little importance since we've been to war![24]

Yensen had to wait another ten months to see his 'folks'; by the time he arrived back in America the influenza epidemic had long displaced the war from the newspaper headlines, and the AEF's 4 million were already on course to become a historical footnote. The presence of thousands of unburied and semi-burned corpses added to the nightmare. Three days into the Armistice Private Yensen was camped on the banks of the Meuse at Brandeville. He decided to go scavenging:

Out of town a ways, it dawned on me to take home a German helmet; so I sent Palmer, who rode with me, after one lying along the road. He picked it up, and inside was the upper half of a German's head – all blood and brains. I told him I guessed I didn't want that one.

The next morning after feeding our donks I struck out to explore the heights along the Meuse River. Here I found several machine-gun nests, lots of dead Germans, and a few dead Yanks. In some places the men had been killed by bullets; but in others they were blown to pieces by shells; an arm here with the hand gone, and a leg there with the genitals hanging to it, or a solitary head which seemed to accuse civilization with its silence!

In one place I found a stomach lost in the grass, while wound around the limbs of a nearby tree were the intestines. The whole ridge had a stench so horrible and so repulsive that all the ghastly sights seemed indescribably worse!

Another place I found four Germans shocked together. Their stinking flesh had turned green and presented a spectacle so gruesome that I could see, smell, and taste them all at once! Sickening as it was, I s'pose history will say this battle was a glorious victory for American arms, which it is, without a doubt. Yet if those poor abandoned human carcasses could talk, they'd probably say:

'We are the dividends of war;
We're what you came to Europe for.
Our cause is lost; we died in vain,
And now we're rotting in the rain!'

But I hadn't seen anything yet. A little farther on was an American soldier stamping a dead German's face into a pulp. I suppose the Germans had killed one of his buddies; because, as he stamped, he ground his teeth and mumbled, 'You dirty Dutch[25] son-of-a-bitch!'[26]

In the final days of the conflict many began to take stock and try to assess how well they had done. In the welter of inter-divisional rivalries, of which the race for Sedan was but the most flagrant example, few bothered to ask how the black doughboy regiments had fared. The truth was that they had acquitted themselves extremely well, given the rotten treatment and lousy training they had received. The four regiments of the embryonic 93rd were never formed into a division but served entirely with the French army, apart from the 371st, which rejoined the AEF late in the war. The 93rd's regiments suffered 3,166 casualties, including 584 men killed in action; the total figure meant that 32 per cent of the division were casualties of one kind or another. As for the 92nd, which was a complete division and served in the AEF, it had the misfortune to be part of the AEF Second Army and thus under the command of General Bullard. On 5 November he toured the lines of the 92nd and commented:

Poor Negroes! They are hopelessly inferior [. . .] Altogether my memories of the 92nd Negro Division are a nightmare. When all my thought, time, and effort were needed to make war against a powerful enemy, they had for a week to be given over entirely to a dangerous, irritating race question that had nothing to do with war-making, the paramount matter of the time. I fear that it will always be so with Negroes wherever they are in contact with whites. This thought and my experience led me to this conclusion: If you need combat soldiers, and especially if you need them in a hurry, don't put your time upon Negroes.[27]

Bullard's view was, unfortunately, almost universally shared by the AEF's general staff. Yet the facts paint a very different picture from that Bullard sought to present. The 92nd, for example, represented 2 per cent of all the AEF's combat troops and took 1,700 casualties, about 1.5 per cent of all American casualties. Twenty-one members of the division were awarded the Distinguished Service Cross; not bad for a bunch of so-called cowards.[28]

18

The Cost

All of the Allies had a high respect for the enemy but a rather low
regard for each other, and the longer that the Allies were associated
with each other the worse this condition seemed to grow. We did
not reap the full hatred of our Allies, however, until the time came
for them to pay their war debts. Then we became much worse
even than the Belgians.   Major-General Dennis Nolan[1]

One of the most useful tasks performed by the War Department
in Washington in 1918 was the appointment of a civilian, Leonard
Ayres, chief statistician for the Russell Sage Foundation, to the rank
of major (and later colonel) as part of the General Staff.[2] Ayres's
war-time job was to collect and collate statistics related to America's
military contribution to the war. He performed a remarkably useful
service by ensuring the publication in 1919 of a slim volume of
unadorned statistical evidence demonstrating how heavily the Allied
victory depended on the United States in the final months of the
war.[3]

Out of every three American soldiers who reached France, two
took part in action of some kind; 2,084,000 landed in France and
of those 1,390,000 saw active front-line service.[4] In January 1918
the AEF held just 10 kilometres of the front line, but by October,
when the Western Front had shrunk from 854 kilometres (in July
1918) to 712 kilometres, the AEF held a front of 162 kilometres, or
23 per cent of the entire Western Front – and 29 kilometres more than
were held by the British.[5] The AEF's combat divisions were in battle
for a total of 200 days between Thursday, 25 April 1918 – when the
1st Division entered the front line in Picardy – until the Armistice. The
29 combat divisions (out of a total of 43 in France) captured 63,079

Total Americans killed in action per thousand men

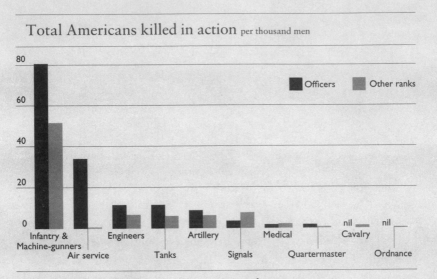

Officers ■   Other ranks ■

80
60
40
20
0

Infantry & Machine-gunners
Air service
Engineers
Tanks
Artillery
Signals
Medical
Quartermaster
nil Cavalry
nil Ordnance

Americans killed in action per week, 1918 (thousand)

MEUSE–ARGONNE

CHÂTEAU-THIERRY

CANTIGNY

6
5
4
3
2
1
0

Jan Feb Mar Apr May Jun Jul Aug Sep Oct Nov Dec

German soldiers but lost just 4,480 of their own men as prisoners.[6]

In numbers of dead the AEF got off lightly compared with other nations, in this bloodiest of all wars up to that time; between 1793 and 1914 total battle deaths across the world were under 6 million, whereas in the 1914–18 conflict the figure was perhaps 7.5 million. Ayres calculated that:

Of every 100 American soldiers and sailors who took part in the war with Germany, 2 were killed or died of disease during the period of hostilities. In the Northern Army during the Civil War the number was about 10. Among the other great nations in this war, between 20 and 25 in each 100 called to the colors were killed or died. To carry the comparison still further, American losses in this war were relatively one-fifth as large as during the Civil War and less than one-tenth as large as in the ranks of the enemy or among the nations associated with us.[7]

Ayres estimated that, of the leading powers, Germany lost 1.6 million men in battle deaths during the whole war; Russia, 1.7 million; France, 1,385,300; Britain, 900,000; Austria-Hungary, 800,000; Italy, 364,000; and Turkey, 250,000. Set against this, the 50,300 battle deaths he gives for the AEF may seem a relatively small figure.[8]

Yet if the calculation is made differently the doughboys indeed suffered badly. Between 4 August 1914 and 11 November 1918 there were 1,560 days of potential battle. According to Ayres, on each of those days Germany suffered an average of 1,025 killed in fighting; France, 888; and Britain, 577. Two of the participants, Serbia and Montenegro (an average of 80 men killed each day) and Belgium (65 daily battle deaths), were – if the tally of deaths is calculated in this way – less badly mauled than the AEF, which suffered an average of 251 battle deaths each day during which the AEF was in combat.[9]

This is still a significantly lower daily death rate than the other main combatants on the Western Front. This could imply one of several things. It may be that in the final 200 days of the war the AEF encountered weaker resistance than the British or French faced at earlier periods of the war; or that the average doughboy was more adept at avoiding death; or that he was simply more fortunate; or that the Germans' skill at killing its enemies diminished towards the end

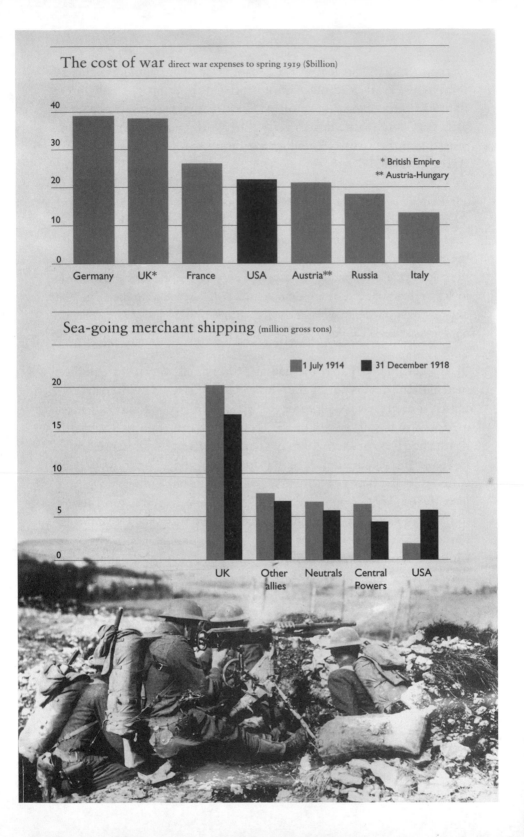

The cost of war direct war expenses to spring 1919 ($billion)

* British Empire
** Austria-Hungary

Germany | UK* | France | USA | Austria** | Russia | Italy

Sea-going merchant shipping (million gross tons)

■ 1 July 1914   ■ 31 December 1918

UK | Other allies | Neutrals | Central Powers | USA

of the war. These possibilities do not really stand scrutiny; if any-thing, German resistance initially grew stronger before fading in the final few days, and the typical doughboy was probably rather less skilled at avoiding death than his British or French comrades. The most plausible reason for the relatively lower death rate of the AEF is that the peak of the killing on the Western Front had passed before the AEF arrived in significant numbers. The three gigantic battles of the British – the Somme (July–November 1916), Arras (April–May 1917) and Passchendaele (June–November 1917) – in which collec-tively they probably suffered more than 800,000 casualties[10] (dead and wounded) all pre-date the AEF's arrival in force. So too does the bloodiest engagement for the French, Verdun (spring–autumn 1917), in which they are estimated to have lost some 300,000 dead. The Germans lost similar numbers of men in each of these vast, bloody engagements.

What Ayres did not calculate, however, is the numbers of battle deaths each day in the final 200 days of the war, when the front line of the Western Front was never without one or more AEF divisions taking a front-line position. If we try to compare the casualty figures of the British, French and Germans with those of the AEF from 25 April 1918 (when the 1st Division of the AEF first went into the front line) until 12 November 1918 (the final 200 days of the war), then we begin to get a clearer picture of the American sacrifice of human life.[11]

According to contemporary German government analyses an aver-age of 952 German soldiers died in action each day on the Western Front between March and June 1918, against a daily killed-in-action figure of 973 for the German army during August–November 1914. During March–June 1918 the daily figure for the British army was 495 killed in action. The figure for France is more difficult to calculate because it combined the figures of killed, missing and captured, yielding an average daily loss rate of 1,391 during March–June 1918. But given the proportion of the front line occupied by French troops during those four months – 71 per cent of the total, with just 17 per cent by the British – it is likely that no fewer than 1,000 French soldiers died in action each day in this period. During July–November the respective daily killed-in-action figure was 584 for Germany (thus demonstrating

Health: draftees in the United States passing their physical examination

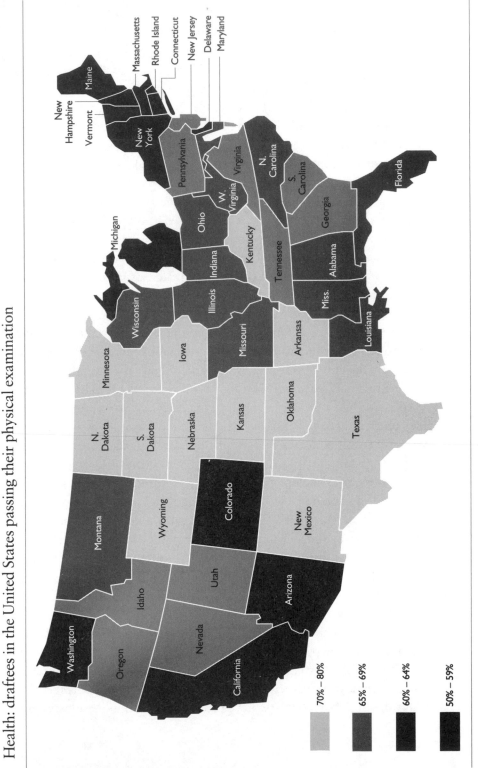

Massachusetts
Rhode Island
Connecticut
New Jersey
Delaware
Maryland

New
Hampshire
Vermont

Maine

New
York

Pennsylvania

Virginia
W.
Virginia

N.
Carolina

S.
Carolina

Florida

Michigan

Ohio

Kentucky

Georgia

Indiana

Tennessee

Alabama

Wisconsin

Illinois

Miss.

Louisiana

Minnesota

Iowa

Missouri

Arkansas

N.
Dakota

S.
Dakota

Nebraska

Kansas

Oklahoma

Texas

Montana

Wyoming

Colorado

New
Mexico

Washington

Idaho

Utah

Arizona

Oregon

Nevada

California

70% – 80%

65% – 69%

60% – 64%

50% – 59%

the less costly nature of defence over attack); Britain at 536 rather higher than previously, as a consequence of taking the offensive; and France (again complicated by being a figure for killed, missing and captured), 1,216 per day. Thus, combining the daily average for March–June with that for the period July–November, we reach the following tallies of daily killed-in-action figures for the final 200 days of the war: Germany, 681; Britain, 510; France, 908 (estimated); and the United States, 251. This gives a ratio of 2.7:1 for German/US deaths in action; 2:1 for British/US; and 3.6:1 for French/US. Given that the AEF through almost six months (from April–November 1918) held on average 14 per cent of the front line while the British accounted for 18 per cent, it is evident from these admittedly highly approximate calculations that the AEF certainly pulled its weight.

For the families and friends and an estimated 40,000 widows of those doughboys who were killed in action or died of their wounds, it was scant comfort to know that US losses amounted to only about 1 per cent of total war casualties. Total US deaths resulting from combat wounds, gas, and other forms of warfare in the army and navy combined were put at 125,000 by 1 July 1919; by 1930 that figure had crept up to about 130,000, with deaths resulting from injury and illnesses traceable to war service obviously continuing long after the war had ended.[12] 'Normal' mortality from 1917 to 1930 would in any case have accounted for perhaps 20,000 American males, leaving some 110,000 as the true number of deaths caused by the war.[13] The Veterans' Bureau estimated that by 1930, 460,000 deaths had resulted from all causes related to service in the war:

For those who escaped battle casualties, the War was still from three to four times as dangerous as staying at home and earning one's bread and butter in the usual way. Charging the aftermath of war-caused deaths against the period of service, it was probably six or seven times as dangerous.[14]

What was a human life worth in the decade of the First World War? For a true economist this figure 'is not so much the value of life [. . .] as the cost of death'.[15] The economic cost to the federal government of disabled war veterans was substantial, and the business of determining and administering the compensation gave rise to a whole new bureaucracy. By 1930, 900,000 disability claims had been filed and more than half of them were granted – about one for every ten men who joined up. Men who were deemed to be permanently and totally disabled received a basic rate of $100 a month while those who were temporarily totally disabled got a basic $80, with additional payments for dependants. A decade after the war ended, in 1928, there were 257,536 American veterans receiving compensation at a cost of $139 million a year, with the average disability being 43.7 per cent and the average award $540 a year.[16] The majority – 156,000 – were receiving support for 'general medical and surgical conditions', while 56,000 were suffering from tuberculosis and another 56,000 from 'neuro-psychiatric disabilities'. Those deemed to have had their earning capacity reduced by less than 10 per cent were, however, shown the door. Many veterans and their surviving dependants were grateful that they had taken up the federal government's offer of insurance policies from $1,000 to $10,000; more than 4.5 million service personnel had taken out such policies to an average amount of $8,756, the full $10,000 policy paying out $57.50 a month for twenty years. Such insurance was not self-supporting but subsidized by the federal authorities to the tune of an estimated $951 million over and above what the premiums brought in.[17]

The number of hospital patients under government care reached a peak in March 1922, when nearly 31,000 were being treated. The Veterans' Bureau after the war became an important body, administering vast funds. J. M. Clark estimated in 1930 that the total bill for the care of dependent war veterans would be as much as $25 billion, until the last dependant had died, and that this sum would roughly be balanced by the war-debt repayments made to the United States out of German reparations, the bulk of which would in fact go towards that war debt. Payments to dependants (widows, children and parents) were running at a monthly bill of $2.5 million in 1930; a widow with two children received $45 a month, one without children $30 a month: not riches, but 'compared to the French widow's pension of $67.60 a year, ours is munificent'.[18]

One projection of the future economic burden of the veterans and their dependants was that it would 'go on growing until 1940 or 1945, after which it will taper off, and will have reached vanishing proportions by 1975–80'.[19] This was not as absurd as it sounds, given that the Civil War pension list

grew from 123,000 in 1875 to a peak of 419,000 in 1891. If our present roll grows in the same way, we should in 1945 be compensating 875,000 disabled veterans and spending, at present rates of compensation, some 475 million [of dollars] a year for this alone [. . .] But the total list of Civil War pensions kept growing until 1902, when it was just short of 1 million. And the money payments kept on growing until 1921, when they were just short of 250 millions. We were then paying over twice as much for Civil War pensions as for death and disability compensation for the World War. In 1926 we were still paying more in pensions for a war ended sixty-one years before, than for the World War, only eight years in the past.[20]

In financial terms America certainly paid dearly for this first attempt at playing global policeman. But many in the administration tried their best to recover what costs they could. General March should have been awarded a medal for his tightfisted housekeeping at the War Department in Washington, particularly concerning his effort to knock down the price charged by the Allies for ferrying 2 million doughboys to Europe. It might be thought that Britain was only too pleased to put its massive merchant fleet gratis at the service of the AEF to transport its American rescuers to France. Not at all. After the war the British put in their invoice to Washington for the cost of shipping. They had not reckoned, however, on dealing with some of the hardest bargainers in the business:

When Great Britain presented her bill for transporting the troops to France [. . .] the transportation of the soldiers was charged for as if they had been passengers, at a flat rate of $150[21] a man. The men were packed in like sardines, and we declined to pay at this rate, which we considered exorbitant [. . .] Secretary Baker and General Hines, Transportation Chief, went to a meeting in London, where [Lord] Reading agreed that the settlement should be made on the actual cost of the service rendered [the price was then reduced to $81.75 per man, which given the conditions on board most troop transports was still exorbitant]. General Hines's services in this matter were noteworthy, and the acceptance by Lord Reading of his figures saved the United States $67,753,698.70.[22]

From saving the US taxpayer millions the War Department stooped to picking up pennies. Corporal Frederick Fear, a chemist who specialized in leather and spent all of his wartime conscription testing leather materials for their ability to absorb or deflect poison gas, received as part of his discharge papers his final payroll cheque, which totalled $20.22, minus four cents' 'deduction for clothing [. . .] for two pairs of wornout shoelaces'.[23]

The British tried hard to recover the financial costs of their staggering war bill. Eight Dreadnoughts at full steam for twenty-four hours, firing each gun and torpedo tube once, cost $200,000, and Britain had thirty-six ships of the Dreadnought class. Even a simple rifle cartridge cost a halfpenny at the start of the war; a million men firing away in two big engagements got through £1 million pounds' worth of rifle ammunition.[24] Britain's spending on its armed forces rose from £87.6 million (29.9 per cent of government expenditure) in 1913 to almost £734 million in 1915 (74.8 per cent of the total) and more than £2.33 billion (80.6 per cent) in 1918. Britain's war costs were of the order of £1 million a day; those for France, Germany and Russia were even greater.[25] One French assessment anticipated in 1927 the payment of war pensions to veterans until 1990, and commented that the French spending on the war was far in excess of 44 billion francs a year, at a time when the exchange rate was 5 francs = $1.[26] France's military spending alone during 1914–18 was 110 billion francs.[27]

The US war effort had been equally financially burdensome. By the Armistice the United States had mobilized fifty-eight divisions; forty-two had been shipped overseas. Twelve of them were not functioning as combat units, but were kept for replacements and other uses in France. Of the sixteen divisions still in the United States, nine were at less than half strength at that time. Such mass mobilization did not come cheap. Some US officials after the end of the war tried to calculate the total cost of running the AEF. They first came up with a figure of $16,669,825,654.31 as the net amount available to the War Department from war appropriations, i.e. federal finances of one sort or another. By 17 April 1920 the actual expenditure of the War Department had reached $16,276,288,337.19, the final nineteen cents presumably being the cost of the cable ordering Pershing to bring the boys back home. Receipts from the sale of AEF equipment overseas brought in $757 million, and $450 million came from the fire-sale back in the States. The net costs in other words were some $8,885 billion, which 'represents what the Government paid in transporting the 4,000,000 men of the Army, in feeding them, clothing them, and providing them with all other sorts of expendable supplies which they actually consumed, and in paying the troops their wages'.[28] The 'expendable supplies' included the 1,373,300 pounds of sweets (40 per cent assorted chocolates, 30 per cent stick candy and 30 per cent lemon drops) consumed each month by the doughboys.[29]

But this was just the immediate cost; there were longer-term financial implications, too. In the final year of the war the United States was drained of the equivalent of some 25 per cent of its goods and services, about $16 billion of the total national income of around $60 billion, which was ploughed into the war effort.

Leonard Ayres put the longer-term total federal cost at $21.85 billion up to April 1919, deducting $1.65 billion as normal expenses for the period April 1917 to April 1919. In June 1920 the US Treasury gave its own estimate as $24 billion. On top of this must be added $9.5 billion of loans to the Allies, making a grand total of some $33.5 billion. During the war the federal government raised some $23 billion in war loans and a further $10.7 billion by extra taxes, above the normal budget.[30] The National Bureau of Economic Research offered a 'conjectural' estimate that in 1918 the maximum war expenditure was $14.6 billion out of a total national income of $62 billion, or 23.5 per cent of the total. From the $31 billion of resources devoted to the war effort between 1917 and 1919, 'possibly 18 billions came out of decreased consumption as compared to the 1915 rate per capital, some $5\frac{3}{4}$ billions came out of increased personal real income beyond the 1915 per capital level, which leaves $7\frac{1}{4}$ billions to come out of increased productive effort represented in undivided corporate income, either borrowed or taken as taxes'.[31]

The range of goods and services which had to be paid for was vast: 'First, there are the governmental expenditures for goods and services;

the goods including food and clothes for soldiers as well as ships, guns, and explosives, and the services including the cooking of meals in company kitchens as well as the storming of hostile machine-gun nests.'[32]

Then there were loans to the Allies, interest on government debt issued to finance the war, cost of the care of veterans and the dependants of those killed or disabled, the cost involved in the extra consumption of raw materials, and the cost of paying 4 million men $30 a month and more to serve in the armed forces.

The fiscal burden imposed was vast. In 1916 the expenses of the federal government were put at less than $0.75 billion, growing to more than $2 billion in 1917, soaring above $13 billion in 1918, and $19 billion in 1919. In 1920 that huge burden had shrunk to slightly more than $6 billion, falling to $3.5 billion by 1922,[33] much of it financed by increased borrowing. The federal fiscal outlays amounted to about $37 billion by the end of June 1929, calculated as $27 billion to the end of the fiscal year 1921 (the official termination of hostilities was on 2 July 1921), and another $10 billion since then in the form of interest on the public dept and the expenses of the Veterans' Bureau; this $27 billion was an estimate of the additional costs of the war, over and above normal peacetime expenditure. In terms simply of goods and services paid for by the government and devoted to use in the war, the bill was probably around $31 billion.[34]

But if we include loans – there were four Liberty Loans and a final Victory Loan at the end of the war, all of them enthusiastically purchased by the majority of Americans – the figure balloons to about $34.5 billion up to 30 June 1921, and explodes to more than $50 billion before all war debts were settled. As J. M. Clark estimated: 'Within a period of something over thirty years, from 1917 to 1950, the total burden on taxes will be over 52 billions and probably in the neighbourhood of 54 billions, by which time our own war debt will be wiped out or nearly so, and the payments on foreign debt settlements will be reaching their full magnitude.'[35]

In November 1928 President Calvin Coolidge calculated that the sequel of maturing War Bonds would raise the total cost to almost $100 billion, before the final bond was redeemed and the last veteran or dependant off the books. America's debt burdens following the First

World War were eventually swallowed up in those of the Second; those of the Second were subsumed into those incurred through the Korean War; and so on until they have all become lost, mere droplets in the vast ocean that is the US federal debt burden, which, at the end of the twentieth century, was estimated at more than $5,000 billion.

These calculations are all too neat. An economist would want to argue that as well as costs, there were also benefits, though gathering those together in a tidily packaged fashion is considerably more difficult. The costs of the war were perhaps offset by greater employment (and thus higher tax returns) in the expanded wartime industries, such as Du Pont and Ford.

The effects of our own belligerency cannot be fully separated from the effects resulting from the existence of a war in Europe, whether we entered it or not. We profited greatly as a neutral country, and after the War we profited by serving the needs of Europe's reconstruction [. . .] How much of our post-war prosperity was due to Europe's needs and how much to the impetus of our own reconstruction demands and activities? No one can say. The profits of neutrality were swallowed up in the costs of belligerency.[36]

The United States was in a powerful economic position when war erupted in Europe in 1914. The richest nation in the world, both in terms of *per capita* and aggregate output, its national wealth was officially estimated in 1912 at $188 billion and was growing at a rate that would show as much as $210 billion for 1914. In 1913 annual *per capita* income was $344, growing to $385 by 1917. For the two decades before 1914, American industry had enjoyed an unprecedented boom. Production of pig iron had increased by more than 400 per cent, steel by almost 800 per cent, tinplate output had grown by fifteen times, copper production by 270 per cent, lead by 150 per cent, cement by 1000 per cent, coal by 212 per cent and petroleum by 400 per cent.[37] By 1914 America had become the world's leading industrial power.

But in 1914 the initial impact of war on the US economy was severely depressive, as demand for American goods fell sharply. US farmers produced record harvests of wheat and cotton but suddenly found that some of their most important markets, in Europe, were cut off. Prices for staple commodities fell; cotton from $62.50 a bale at the end of July 1914 to $36.25 in December. Steel production dropped to 30 per cent of capacity, slowly recovering to 50 per cent by January 1915: 'First expectations of war profits were apparently disappointed, and few observers at the end of 1914 could have confidently predicted the prosperity which was on the point of materialising.'[38]

That initial collapse was short-lived. As it became clear that the war was not going to end quickly, orders for essential war material began to flow in to US suppliers, with a vastly increased demand for steel, tin, iron, machine tools, wire and other essential items; US pig iron production alone in 1916 was 70 per cent greater than in 1914. Many US companies laid the basis for their twentieth-century dominance at the time of the First World War. The chemical manufacturer Du Pont increased its production of explosive powder from half a million pounds a month to almost 30 million pounds a month during the days of US neutrality. In the last year of the war the Du Pont Engineering Corporation – a special entity established to build and manage a new plant, called Old Hickory, to keep Pershing's AEF fed with munitions – took gross profits of $2 million. Old Hickory, seven miles from Nashville, cost the US government more than $85 million to build – twice as much as the Panama Canal. It included a new city complex to accommodate its 30,000 workers:

This was one of the most gigantic construction feats in the history of the nation. To run the plant at capacity each day, there was needed 1,500,000 pounds of nitrate of soda; 675,000 pounds of sulphur; 4,500 tons of coal equivalent to 100 carloads; 100,000,000 gallons of water, or as much as was used by a city of 1,000,000 inhabitants.[39]

Old Hickory was something of a white elephant. It started production on 1 June 1918, two months early, but still too late to contribute much to the defeat of Germany. Had the war gone on for another year, as everyone expected it would, it would have been invaluable. In other industries the war laid the foundation for future economic strength. In April 1917 America had just 37 steel shipyards with 162 slipways, and 24 wood shipyards with 72 slipways. By 11 November 1918 there were 223 yards with 1,099 slipways, 40 per cent of them devoted to building steel-hulled vessels. In 1913 the United States produced just 276,000 tons of merchant shipping; in 1917, the most devastating year of the war for U-boat sinkings, more than 6.6 million tons of shipping went to the bottom. By the end of 1918 America was annually churning out more than 3 million gross tons of shipping and 4 million in 1919, an astonishing growth but too late to make any difference to the war.[40]

The mobilization of industry was accompanied by a mobilization of manpower. Between 1915 and 1918 some 3.25 million workers left their traditional employment in construction, domestic service, the professions, and various specialized crafts and trades, while over the same period the working population increased by 1.5 million. Another 800,000 left other sectors of the economy for jobs in industry. These groups together enabled an increase of 3.2 million in government service and more than 2.25 million additional workers in industry.[41]

The Du Pont company, which already dominated the production of military and sporting smokeless explosive powders, was transformed by the war into a powerful economic dynasty; its early success in supplying explosives to the Allies paled into insignificance when it came to being awarded lucrative US government contracts. Du Pont sold to the Allies some 40 per cent of all the munitions they used in the war. Before the war Du Pont's military production had been about 5 per cent of its total output; once war came, the company was almost entirely identified with military production. It expanded production and its workforce by more than ten times and the company's shareholders enjoyed dividends totalling the staggering sum of $141 million during the years of the war, on revenues of almost $1.05 billion. The company produced 1,466,761,219 pounds of military explosives for the Allies and the United States during the war. Enough, of course, was never enough: the company's president at the time, Pierre S. duPont, wrote that 'taxes paid to the United States Government not only absorbed the entire profit of the company on powder sold to our Government, but, in addition, they wiped out all of the profit made on these powders during the preceding twenty years.' The shareholders, however, saw no reason to complain.[42] Indeed, Du Pont did well enough from the war to be able to fund the purchase of controlling interests in General Motors.

The economics of the situation were not a terribly immediate concern to those who served in the trenches, many of whom must have shared the view of Corporal Charles Bishop, 26th Division: 'After about 2 wks home [. . .] our great government forgot all about us esp. the ones that did the fighting and survived.'[43]

Besides the economic, there were, of course, many intangible costs to American society. The leading socialist writer of the time, Max Eastman, wrote with remarkable prescience when war was declared: 'It is not a war for democracy [. . .] We will Prussianize ourselves and will probably not democratize Prussia.'[44]

Once war broke out, dozens of xenophobic private institutions and organizations whipped civilian society into a frenzy of anti-German hysteria, in which the demonstration of anything less than rabid patriotism was often met with a bucket of hot tar and a sack of chicken feathers. This domestic upheaval created some of the most embarrassing and shameful episodes in US history. A form of back-door censorship, operated through the US Mail, enabled the federal government to quash any periodical it chose. Eastman's journal, *Masses*, was one of the first to come under the hammer of the zealous Postmaster-General, Albert Sidney Burleson, who was given far-reaching powers to ban from the US Mail any publication deemed to infringe draconian laws barring criticism of America's war effort. Small-circulation publications depended on being allowed to travel by second-class mail; without that privilege their generally low-income readership could ill afford to subscribe. Burleson denied the August 1917 issue of *Masses* access to second-class mail. By November 1918 some seventy-five US magazines and journals, forty-five of them socialist, had gone under. The German-language press also suffered, though as much through commercial collapse as government interference; of the 554 German-language newspapers and periodicals in the United States in 1910, just 234 were still around in 1920.

Conscientious objectors who chose to stand aside on pacifist rather than religious grounds found themselves particularly harshly treated. Howard Moore, aged twenty-eight, was held in 1919 at Fort Douglas, near Salt Lake City, along with a number of other conscientious objectors. Most of these men had already suffered appalling torture and deprivation, sufferings as bad as any doughboy ever faced, yet when Pershing inspected them he was unable to see them as anything but cowards:

He came to our compound with the fort commandant and other officers and entered the barracks that we used as a library. Many of us were reading or lying on cots, and no one moved when the post officer called 'Attention!'

I was near the entrance and heard Pershing say to the commandant, 'Don't these men stand at attention?'

The reply was, 'If they did, they would have to be held up.'

The general walked over to a table on which lay an assortment of magazines such as *The Nation, The New Republic,* Lydia Pankhurst's *Dreadnaught, The Survey,* and *The Liberator.* Picking up one and turning to the commandant, he exclaimed, 'Do you mean to say that these men are permitted to read such stuff?'

The commandant answered, 'You ought to see what they *write!*'

Pershing stamped out of the building, saying, 'These men are dirt beneath my feet!'[45]

Between May 1917 and November 1918, 64,693 drafted men filed claims for exemption on grounds of conscience.[46] Local draft boards accepted the claims of 56,830; objections on religious grounds were generally accepted. The most recalcitrant non-religious objectors found themselves facing a court-martial; 540 were tried and only one acquitted, with 17 death sentences (all later commuted to life), 142 life sentences and 345 punishments averaging 16.5 years.[47] Even religiously motivated objectors practising unusual religions, outside the mainstream of American conventional life, found themselves being severely treated; forty-five Mennonites from Oklahoma were each given twenty-five years' imprisonment for refusing to wear army uniform.[48] Those who objected to joining the army on political or humanitarian grounds were either forcibly inducted or tried and imprisoned. Moore had been classified 1-A fit on 22 January 1918 by his local draft board, no. 130, in New York City, even though he had sent the board a formal deposition on 28 December announcing his determination to be treated as a conscientious, though non-religious, objector. A fiercely independent-minded young man, Moore was soon jailed and sentenced to five years' imprisonment, the shortest sentence any of the conscientious objectors received, though he was the last to be released, on the day before Thanksgiving, 1920.

The erosion of civil liberties started at least several months before America joined the war, and may be said to have formally started on 14 February 1917, when Congress passed a bill promising a $1,000 fine and five years' jail to anyone who 'knowingly and willfully' wrote or spoke in a manner which threatened the life of the President. This unnecessary law was vigorously implemented, and the country sank into a mood of low-browed, white-knuckled thuggishness:

From the Atlantic to the Pacific the call was answered and obeyed [. . .] Pacifism, indifference, dissent, were swept from the path and fiercely pursued to extermination; and with a roar of slowly gathered, pent-up wrath which overpowered its every discordant yell, the American nation sprang to arms.[49]

With the excuse of the need to rally the nation to the flag, the Wilson administration often turned a blind eye to reigns of local terror which blighted the lives of many thousands of ordinary citizens, as vigilantes and sadists of all types used the war to justify their depredations. Free speech, the rights to a fair trial and independent thought were shunted aside in a hurricane of mass hysteria and violent conformism. To stand out from the crowd in the years 1917–19 was highly dangerous. Even the right to determine how to spend one's own hard-earned cash – the quintessence of 'the American way' – was removed, as mobs forced individuals to buy Liberty Bonds. Liberty Loan advertisements accused any who did not buy them of being 'an enemy to humanity and liberty, a traitor and disgrace to his country'.

Across the country in the months of the war those found not to have bought bonds, or too few, were tarred and feathered, daubed in yellow paint, beaten, scalped, dragged through the streets and subject to the forced auction of their property, the proceeds being used to buy them Liberty Bonds.

In the wartime drive to sell Liberty Bonds, the Hutterites [Anabaptists who had fled Russia in the late nineteenth century to avoid enforced military service] in their community near Alexandria, South Dakota, refused to buy the bonds but offered to contribute to the Red Cross instead. This did not satisfy their patriotic neighbors, who rounded up the Hutterites' cattle, sold them at auction, bought Liberty Bonds with the proceeds, and threw the bonds into the Hutterite church building.[50]

In the American hinterlands mob rule took over, while the judicial authorities often proved themselves vicious, cowardly and morally corrupt. Woodrow Wilson had recognized this possibility, though he did little to prevent it:

Once lead this people into war and they'll forget there ever was such a thing as tolerance. To fight you must be brutal and ruthless and the spirit of ruthless brutality will enter into the very fiber of our national life, infecting Congress, the courts, the policeman on the beat, the man in the street.[51]

Wilson enjoys a reputation of being a high-minded democrat but this ignores his ability to indulge in rabble-rousing speeches when he thought them useful, as in his State of the Union message on 7 December 1915:

There are citizens of the United States, I blush to admit, born under other flags, but welcomed under our generous naturalization laws to the full freedom and opportunity of America, who have poured the poison of disloyalty into the very arteries of our national life; who have sought to bring the authority and good name of our Government into contempt, to destroy our industries wherever they thought it effective for their vindictive purposes to strike at them, and to debase our politics to the uses of foreign intrigue.[52]

Two years later the implicit jingoism of this speech burst out in a stream of national vitriol, directed at anything German. Sauerkraut was renamed 'Liberty cabbage', the hamburger became the 'Liberty sandwich', the German names of towns were changed, German composers were reviled, and across the country individual towns and states issued edicts banning the use of the German language. In several towns – Lewiston, Montana; Shawnee, Oklahoma; and Spartanburg, South Carolina – German-language books were publicly burned. The Kaiser-Kuhn wholesale grocers of St Louis became the Pioneer Grocery Company.[53]

The federal government vigorously employed the 1798 Alien Enemies Act to give the Justice Department wide-ranging powers over the more than 500,000 German aliens and 3 million Austro-Hungarian aliens living in the United States.[54] Respect for life, liberty, free speech and independence of thought was breached so widely and so often that many Americans, particularly on the left, came to believe they were living in a police state. The day Congress declared war Wilson issued his first twelve regulations restricting the movements of enemy aliens. Regulation 12 said (in part):

[. . .] an alien enemy whom there may be reasonable cause to believe to be aiding or about to aid the enemy [. . .] or [who] violates any regulation promulgated by the President . . . will be subject to summary arrest [. . .] and to confinement in such penitentiary, prison, jail, or military camp.

One month later Thomas Gregory, the Attorney-General, announced that 125 enemy aliens had been detained and interned; by November 1918 the figure was above 4,000, crowded together in three camps – called the War Prison Barracks – established for civilian internees and prisoners-of-war.[55]

Other legislation in 1917 and 1918 extended these sweeping powers. The 1917 Espionage Act[56] and 1918 Sedition Act were used to stifle the merest indications of dissent and protest. The Espionage Act was framed so widely as to permit the legal punishment of anyone found guilty of disagreeing with official policy. Its key paragraph stated:

Whoever, when the United States is at war, shall willfully make or convey false reports or false statements with intent to interfere with the operation or success of the military or naval forces of the United States, or to promote the success of its enemies, or shall willfully make or convey false reports, or false statements [. . .] or incite insubordination, disloyalty, mutiny, or refusal of duty, in the military or naval forces of the United States, or shall willfully obstruct [. . .] the recruiting or enlistment service of the United States, or [. . .] shall willfully utter, print, write, or publish any disloyal, profane, scurrilous, or abusive language about the form of government of the United States, or the Constitution of the United States, or the military or naval forces of the United States [. . .] or shall willfully display the flag of any foreign enemy, or shall willfully [. . .] urge, incite, or advocate any curtailment of production [. . .] or advocate, teach, defend, or suggest the doing of any of the acts or things in this section enumerated and whoever shall by word or act support or favor the cause of any country with which the United States is at war or by word or act oppose the cause of the United States therein, shall be punished by a fine of not more than $10,000 or imprisonment for not more than twenty years, or both.[57]

Courts tended to interpret this guideline with maximum severity. In a test case on 28 August 1917 under the Espionage Act, Charles T. Schenck, general secretary of the Socialist Party, was sentenced to six months in jail for possessing a pamphlet criticizing America's entry into the war. The Supreme Court gave an ominous ruling:

When a nation is at war many things that may be said in time of peace are such a hindrance to its efforts that their utterance will not be endured so long as men fight and that no Court could regard them as protected by a constitutional right.

Walter Matthey got a sentence of twelve months simply for attending an anti-war public meeting in Iowa.[58] In total some 1,500 people were arrested and jailed on charges under the Espionage and Sedition Acts, including Eugene Debs, who in standing for the presidency as the Socialist candidate against Wilson in 1912 had polled more than a million votes, and Roger Baldwin, director of the National Civil Liberties Bureau.

State laws could be even harsher. In Minnesota it was declared illegal to say 'that men should not enlist in the military or naval forces of the United States'. In the same state, Abraham L. Sugarman, state secretary of the Socialist Party, was accused of denouncing the Selective Service Act; a secret service official testified that Sugarman had said: 'This is supposed to be a free country. Like hell it is.' Sugarman spent three years in Leavenworth penitentiary.

Vigilante groups sprang up everywhere, with the avowed aim of finding and beating up anti-war protesters. The Knights of Liberty, the All-Allied Anti-German League, the Anti-Yellow Dog League and the Boy Spies of America – along with many others – patrolled the streets of towns and cities, on the watch for traitors. The Department of Justice sponsored its own organization to attack anti-war demonstrators. For a dollar anyone could join the American Protective League, which by June 1917 had almost 100,000 members in 600 locations; by 1918 its membership had grown to 250,000. On Sunday, 1 July 1917 these state-licensed bullying thugs had a field day; 8,000 socialists, trades unionists, pacifists and others marched through Boston in protest against America's involvement in the war. They were attacked by several hundred uniformed soldiers under the command of non-commissioned officers; more than 10,000 vigilantes joined in, as the police stood by and watched.

This untrammelled mayhem wreaked havoc in many individual lives. Robert Praeger, a 45-year-old unemployed coal-miner, lived in Colinsville, ten miles north-east of St Louis. Designated an enemy alien, Praeger had applied for naturalization and had even tried to join the US navy; he was rejected because he had one glass eye. On the night of 4–5 April 1918, at a gathering of socialists, he allegedly offended Colinsville's pro-war activists by speaking against President Wilson. The police put him in Colinsville's jail for his own safety, but a large rowdy mob dragged him out, made him kiss the Stars and Stripes, permitted him to write a farewell note to his parents in Germany, and then hanged him. It is difficult to believe, but the *New York Times* on 11 April reported Praeger's dying wish that he should be buried wrapped in the Stars and Stripes. As the jury acquitted the eleven accused of Praeger's murder, a band of draftees played outside the courtroom the theme tune of America's commitment to the war, 'Over There'. On 3 June New York's *Evening Post* described the verdict as a 'gross miscarriage of justice'; but New York fastidiousness counted for little in America's heartland of darkness.

The nationwide war mania ensured the destruction of the country's leading radical political force of the time, the Industrial Workers of the World (IWW), the 'Wobblies'. The IWW claimed a paid-up membership of 60,000 by 1917, drawn from among the poorest-paid and least skilled of the country's industrial and agrarian labour force. For many hard-working poor people the IWW was the only defence they had against the extremes of capitalist exploitation. The IWW regarded the war in Europe as a capitalist adventure in which the working man and woman was merely a passive victim:

You ask me why the IWW is not patriotic to the United States. If you were a bum without a blanket; if you had left your wife and kids when you went west for a job, and had never located them since; if your job had never kept you long enough in a place to qualify you to vote; if you slept in a lousy, sour bunkhouse, and ate food just as rotten as they could give you and get by with it; if deputy sheriffs shot your cooking cans full of holes and spilled your grub on the ground; if your wages were lowered on you when the bosses thought they had you down [. . .] how in hell do you expect a man to be patriotic? This war is a businessman's war and we don't see why we should go out and get shot in order to save the lovely state of affairs that we now enjoy.[59]

Wobblyism caused serious problems for the US war effort, particularly in the timber industry; the construction of cantonments to house the draftees in the United States, the building of aircraft, the need for everything from trench props to railway sleepers meant an insatiable demand for lumber. Most of the AEF's timber requirements had to be imported from America because the French were extremely hostile to any suggestion that more French trees should be chopped down. But conditions in America's timber plantations were so appalling that skilled workers, any workers, rarely stayed long. In October 1917 there was estimated to be a shortage of 7,000 skilled timber workers in America's spruce districts; at that time the production of spruce for aircraft manufacturers was not more than 1.5 million feet a month, 70 per cent of which was already allocated to France, Italy, and Britain. 'It not only was necessary to increase the monthly production to 10,000,000 feet at once but to improve greatly the quality of the product. It was one of the great problems of the war.'[60]

The loggers in the great timber forests of the states of Washington and Oregon had genuine grievances, as the high turnover of the labour force – more than 600 per cent a year – indicated:

The operators were in the habit of saying, in bitter irony, that three men were necessary for every job – one going, one on, and one coming [. . .] The ten-hour day was the general rule in the camps and mills, and the employers clung to it stubbornly. Living conditions were atrocious. The camps too obviously were temporary, and the abode of any one man in them was even more transient [. . .] a sinkhole of discontent in which the IWW delegates and agitators could spawn their anarchistic ideas and ideals, with splendid hope of an excellent breeding ground [. . .] The Wobbly delegate was undoubtedly inflammatory, but he possessed, unfortunately, the additional advantage of having plenty of inflammable material.[61]

These labour problems in the timber industry were solved by an intelligent use of conscripted soldiers to supplement, not replace, the civilian workers. Colonel Brice P. Disque was placed in charge of the newly formed Spruce Production Division, which eventually mustered 30,000 officers and men in 234 camps in Oregon and Washington, across an area of 25,000 square miles.

[L]iving conditions were investigated, the food question was looked into, and in general all matters pertaining to the welfare of the men. Where these were found satisfactory, or made satisfactory to an Army inspector, the troops were sent [. . .] The soldier received his military pay and the operator paid him the going rate for his work, minus the military pay, which sum the operator paid to the Government.

The army also came up with the clever idea of creating a 'Loyal Legion of Loggers and Lumbermen', the aim of which was to be a unitary (and uniting) organization for employers, civilian employees and soldiers sent to work in the forests and lumber camps. The deal was that if the workers abandoned Wobblyism and concentrated on producing lumber in the needed quantities, then the military would ensure that they had satisfactory working and living conditions. In its first month 10,000 members enrolled in the Loyal Legion; after six months there were more than 80,000, and by October 1918 its total membership was about 125,000. An eight-hour day was introduced on 1 March 1918, ending a 25-year-old conflict, and labour turnover in the lumber camps dropped to 30–50 per cent; timber production shot up from 1 million feet in October 1917 to 20 million feet in the month of October 1918.

The timber industry was a relatively successful example of how the newly coercive United States could imaginatively solve industrial conflicts to the benefit of both workers and the state. But its imagination ran dry when it came to the copper industry, the focus of an equally bitter, long-running dispute between workers and employers. On 26 June 1917 the IWW called for strikes in the copper extraction and refining industries in Arizona; there was nothing new in the dispute – long hours and poor wages were at its heart. In Bisbee, Arizona, on the night of Wednesday, 11 July 1917, local vigilantes met with senior officials of the Copper Queen and Consolidated Mining Company (now the Phelps-Dodge Corporation). Next morning they grabbed their shotguns and rifles and marched on the strikers' homes, collecting 1,186 of them and herding them into a baseball park. The vigilantes and company officials then forced the kidnapped workers and their families at gunpoint onto cattle trains and sent them on their way into the desert of New Mexico. This completely illegal act went utterly unpunished and largely uncriticized. On 1 August Frank Little, a small, physically handicapped man who had lost the sight of one eye, was lynched in Butte, Montana, after being dragged behind a car through the streets until his kneecaps were torn off. His crime was to be an IWW organizer and member of the IWW's general executive board. Little had travelled to Butte to help organize a general strike of 15,000 copper workers who were protesting against the lack of safety standards at the Anaconda Copper Company, which had led to a fire that killed 160 miners on 8 June.[62] No one was punished for this foul crime; local newspapers, businessmen and politicians all saw the war as a good opportunity to break the power of the IWW.

What was good enough for Butte and Bisbee was good enough for America. On 5 September 1917 federal agents raided IWW offices in thirty-three different cities; it was the start of a mass trial of 113 IWW officials on a general charge of conspiracy to undermine the US war programme. The trial started on 1 May 1918 and dragged on laboriously – the government called 144 witnesses and the defence 184 – until Friday, 30 August when, after considering their verdict for just fifty-five minutes, the jury decided that ninety-six of the accused were guilty on all counts. The charges were trumped-up and politically motivated, the sentences savage. Bill Haywood, the tough, energetic leader of the IWW, was sentenced to twenty years and a fine of $30,000, while another fourteen got twenty years and fines of between $20,000 and $30,000. Further mass trials against the IWW continued through 1919.[63] The federal onslaught against the Wobblies signalled to the mobs that it was open season on pacifists, ethnic minorities, black Americans and indeed anyone who was remotely different. The final political prisoners held under US wartime emergency legislation were not amnestied until 15 December 1923, when the last thirty-one still in jail had their sentences commuted by President Calvin Coolidge.

The war also proved a catalyst for race relations in the United States, where segregation was the rule in both civil and military spheres. The summer of 1917 saw some of the worst racial clashes in US history. On Monday, 2 July rioting broke out in East St Louis, with the deaths of at least 38 black and 8 white Americans. On Thursday, 23 August black enlisted soldiers quartered near Houston were raided by white police, sparking a riot in which 15 people died. Forty-one of the black soldiers were given life sentences and another 13 were hanged on the morning of 11 November 1917. The response of one black newspaper, the *San Antonio Inquirer*, was to publish an article by C. L. Threadgill-Dennis in which he said: 'We would rather see you shot by the highest tribunal of the United States Army because you dared protect a Negro woman from the insult of a southern brute in the form of a policeman, than to have you forced to go to Europe to fight for a liberty you cannot enjoy.'[64] Following this, the newspaper's editor, G. W. Bouldin, was indicted for 'attempting to cause insubordination, disloyalty, mutiny, and refusal of duty'. He got two years in jail.

Black Americans had been deeply divided over the war. They lived in a society where segregation was an unquestioned fact of life and lynching a regular hazard. For many black intellectuals this was a white persons' war. Yet the official propaganda line, that the war was being fought for democracy, liberty, freedom, hit precisely at the most passionately held aspiration for all black Americans. Who did not yearn to be free? How could repressed, segregated, frustrated and politically corralled black Americans contemplate opposing such an event? Yet to join up meant, surely, throwing in their lot with whites – the very people responsible for their lack of freedom.

Racism coursed through the veins of the US regular army, running at levels deeper than was generally the case in the rest of American society. Nor was it merely directed against black Americans. Private Pablo Garcia felt his military experience was

quite strange, with complete loss of my personal freedom and privacy. Fortunately, I was not entirely among strangers, as there were some men serving alongside of me whom I had known quite well. Hispanos were regarded with disdain by the Anglos, or those who passed for 'Anglos' although they may have been from one or another of many nationalities.[65]

Many of the US regular army's leading officers were incorrigible bigots. When they were promoted to leading positions in the AEF their hatred of black Americans was perpetuated. General Bullard was particularly outspoken in his antagonism towards the very idea of black combat soldiers. Even members of the AEF who might be expected to have exercised greater tolerance and humanity, such as Samuel Arthur Devan, chaplain to the 58th Field Artillery Regiment, thought nothing of disparaging black American troops in the kind of patronizing remarks he never used of white soldiers:

There are lots and lots of darkeys in the big camp where I am now located. They are the most interesting soldiers you could ever hope to find – always cheerful and respectful. A darkey soldier will never fail to salute if he can possibly disengage a hand to do it without incurring [sic] serious consequences. One lost his mess kit today in his eagerness to salute me as he passed.[66]

On 1 July 1918, W. E. B. Du Bois, one of the black community's most widely respected leaders, called on black Americans temporarily to suspend their struggle against white injustice, and to throw their weight behind the Allied cause.[67] Du Bois wrote in the July issue of Crisis, the leading black intellectual monthly:

This is the crisis of the world. For all the long years to come men will point to the year 1918 as the great Day of Decision, the day when the world decided whether it would submit to military despotism and an endless armed peace –

if peace it could be called – or whether they would put down the menace of German militarism and inaugurate the United States of the World.

We of the colored race have no ordinary interest in the outcome. That which the German power represents today spells death to the aspirations of Negroes and all darker races for equality, freedom and democracy. Let us not hesitate. Let us, while this war lasts, forget our special grievances and close ranks with our own white fellow citizens and the allied nations that are fighting for democracy. We make no ordinary sacrifice, but we make it gladly and willingly with our eyes lifted to the hills.

This was a fairly remarkable volte-face by Du Bois, who when the war started in 1914 called it a conflict between two sets of colonialists, adding that the best that could be said for the Allies was that they were less vicious. Du Bois was no mealy-mouthed Uncle Tom; just one month earlier he had written a ferocious editorial in *Crisis* in response to the hanging of the thirteen black soldiers of the 24th Infantry Regiment who had rioted in East St Louis in July 1917. But his call to close ranks with that section of US society responsible for the lack of black liberty, in order that liberty should be brought to other whites in Europe, badly damaged his standing among more radical black Americans, who accused him of being 'accommodationist' with white segregationists. When it was discovered that Du Bois was also seeking a commission as a captain in the Military Intelligence Branch, a notoriously racist section of the US army General Staff, his previous high standing in the black community imploded. He had applied for the job at the suggestion of the white chairman of the National Association for the Advancement of Colored People (NAACP), Joel Spingarn, himself then serving as an intelligence officer with the MIB.[68] Du Bois denied that his counsel of closing ranks and his own job application were linked, but it left a bitter taste in the mouths of many black Americans.[69] Not only did Du Bois lose credibility within the black American civil rights movement; he also failed to get his commission. Young black radicals took to referring to him as 'Der Kapitan'.

Du Bois had also supported Spingarn's call for a segregated officers' training camp, soon after America declared war in April 1917. Spingarn's training camp, for blacks only, split the black emancipatory movement down the middle. By May 1917, 470 black college students had applied for admission to the camp at Des Moines, Iowa; a total of 1,400 black officers served during the war. Du Bois wrote of this camp: 'We must continually choose between insult and injury. We must choose then between the insult of a separate camp and the irreparable injury of strengthening the present custom of putting no black men in positions of authority.'[70] The flaw in this reasoning, of course, was that no one in Woodrow Wilson's southern-dominated administration had any intention of placing even skilled, highly trained black officers in positions of authority over *white* soldiers, the only position of power worth having in the eyes of most white officers.

While those who wished to protest or demonstrate their opposition to war were stifled, those who were merely indifferent had their feelings whipped up by a bombardment of brain-washing. Wilson's chief domestic propagandist was George Creel, a muckracking newspaper journalist of Irish descent. Creel, who adored statistics, had long been a Wilson acolyte, having tried to persuade him to run for president in 1905. Creel was the son of a Confederate officer from Independence, Missouri, but he was no reactionary, having fought for female suffrage, the end of child labour and other issues that had gained him considerable notoriety. Nevertheless, he would have remained a relatively obscure individual but for the war, which he used to thrust himself onto the centre stage of US life.

Creel persuaded Wilson to establish a Committee on Public Information (CPI), which sold to the nation the government's view on the war. The Trading with the Enemy Act permitted the censorship of all communications with foreign countries; Creel used this Act to justify the establishment of a national board of censors, with himself as its chairman. Theoretically the CPI had three cabinet members and was chaired by Creel; in fact they met as a body only once, when Creel listened to the cabinet members' advice and never spoke to them again. The CPI *was* George Creel, who came perfectly to embody the crude dictatorial values of Wilson's domestic wartime policies. Creel later said that his ambition for the CPI was to establish 'a passionate belief in the justice of America's cause that would weld the American people into one white hot mass instinct with fraternity, devotion, courage and deathless determination'.

His successes were many, but probably the most important was the energetic fashion with which he laid the groundwork for conscription. On 5 June 1917, all American men were to register for enlistment. Senator James Reed of Missouri had warned Newton Baker that the streets of American cities would 'run red with blood on registration day', but largely thanks to the CPI there was no such protest. The secret of Creel's success was his invention of the Four Minute Men, an idea he took from a friend, Donald Ryerson, who told Creel he had inspired a number of pro-war friends to make speeches in cinemas. As it took about four minutes to change the reels of film at movie theatres this was just enough time for a snappy speech. Creel turned that concept into a national programme, gave the volunteers their no-nonsense name, and appointed Ryerson their director. Soon, in cinemas across America, Four Minute Men popped up to air their potted puerility. The CPI supplied the Four Minute Men with material but urged them to add a personal touch whenever possible. Their first topic was 'Universal Service by Selective Draft'. From 12–21 May 1917, 75,000 orators deluged moviegoers with the idea that registration day should be a festival of honour for the future draftees. The country responded ecstatically. On 5 June, 10 million men signed up with scarcely a murmur of protest. The Four Minute Men spoke on such topics as 'Why We Are Fighting' and 'What Our Enemy Really Is'; they tried to develop memorable catchphrases, such as 'If you don't come across, the Kaiser will.' In order to join the ranks of the Four Minute Men, a man needed endorsements from three prominent citizens in his home town. But if it turned out that a man could not get the crowd going he was swiftly sacked by Creel. The Four Minute Men spoke everywhere: at lodge and union meetings, lumber and army camps, and even Indian reservations. College Four Minute Men operated in 153 higher education institutions. Creel claimed they gave 755,190 speeches to a total of 314,454,514 Americans, and that newspapers gave them more than 900,000 lines of coverage.

Creel also organized and financed propaganda movies, including *Pershing's Crusaders* and *Under Four Flags*. The producer and director D. W. Griffith helped to distribute the films, which managed to earn the CPI $852,744.30 – a vast sum considering the price of a cinema ticket at the time was just one nickel. When the government staged a second programme of registration for conscription the CPI was a very slick, highly professional organization. Its advertising division placed full-page advertisements in 18,000 newspapers; 20 million copies of a pamphlet called the *Selective Service Register* (a set of questions and answers about the army and conscription as well as a subtle blend of instructions, exhortations and appeals) were delivered by mail to homes across the United States. On 12 September 1918, 13,975,706 men registered, again without protest. Creel never tired of pointing out that his massive propaganda efforts cost the American public slightly more than $4.9 million, though as well as that sum he had unlimited access to a $50 million 'president's fund' that Congress had given Wilson early in the war to spend, with no questions asked.

One of the intangible legacies of its involvement in the Great War is America's knowledge that, deep in its soul, there is plentiful evidence that – for all its proud boasts of defending the rights to life, liberty and free speech – the country is as prone to mass neurosis and mob rule as anywhere else:

During the First World War freedom was taken away from the American people and placed in the hands of the lawyers. It ceased to be a constitutional right and became a personal concession of rulers and judges. Here was found a return to the idea of government by men rather than by laws. One judge might permit certain views to be expressed while another might prohibit all ideas not pleasing to him. What one had a right to say or print became a vague and unpredictable thing. A citizen without legal advice certainly could not tell. His only safety lay in silence.[71]

By the end of the war those Americans who imagined they had a democratic right to oppose US participation had learned how mistaken they were, and that while Wilson said the war had been fought 'to make the world safe for democracy', that resounding high-mindedness fell short of extending to US democracy. This was a profound, if unquantifiable, cost not just to America but the world as a whole.

19

Falling Apart
in Russia

I am trying to impress my men with the feeling that the Russians are our friends and to help them as much as possible. The Bolsheviks are only 3% and are losing power. If we could give the people bread there would be no Bolshevism and they would be grateful to the limit.   Captain Edward MacMorland[1]

The war might have ended for the doughboys in France, but for those unfortunate souls marooned in Russia there were many more months of hardship and risk. Towards the end of 1918 much of the Trans-Siberian railway line was under the control of Czechoslovak soldiers. The British, French, Japanese and Americans drew up an Inter-Allied Railway Agreement designed to allocate zones of control; in November 1918 the United States set up a plan for a commission, with representatives from each Allied government participating in the Siberian intervention. This commission would operate the Trans-Siberian railway until a settled Russian authority could take over. Under the eventual Railway Agreement of March 1919 the Czechs were given the long section between Omsk and Lake Baikal; the Chinese took over the Chinese Eastern; the Japanese received the Amur section; the United States got two sections close to Vladivostok and a third 1,500 miles to the west, in the Trans-Baikal region. But the rule of law had long ended in Russia. In April 1919 Admiral Kolchak decreed that all captured Red soldiers or deserters would be forcibly incorporated into his White army. In practice, he thereby gave *carte blanche* for mass executions, torture, and cruelties of all description, under a system of summary justice without trial or appeal. Some doughboys found to their surprise that the most honest and straightforward relationships in this appalling place were not with their supposed allies but former enemies – the German prisoners-of-war held in the vicinity. Private Russell C. Swihart, of E Company, 31st Infantry, was sent along with twenty or so others from his company on 15 October 1918 to Russian Island, south of the Vladivostok peninsula, to act as guards of about 150 German POWs who were to collect some wood. The barge in which they sailed was so slow that they did not reach the island until after dark. The Americans expected to reach their destination much earlier and had not taken any food or drink with them; they found themselves depending on the Germans for sustenance:

As I look back [. . .] I can only admire the high type of men these German Prisoners of War seemed to be. There was no rigid enforcement of rules against talking to the Prisoners and, as several of us could speak some German, a spirit of friendliness prevailed.[2]

Into this turbulent political nightmare were pitched several thousand young American males, including Major Sidney C. Graves, the general's son, who volunteered for duty in Siberia after earning himself an American DSC, a British DSO, and a French Croix de Guerre for his efforts on the Western Front as an infantry captain. The already hopelessly tumultuous political and social conditions inside Russia were rapidly deteriorating. The mood of the doughboys began to sour as they entered their first Siberian winter, still without proper clothing:

Day after day, week after week, we waited but the Siberian weather didn't. It rained, it snowed, it frosted, reached 60 degrees below zero, and still no woolens [sic] or furs [. . .] When on patrol and/or sentry duty, outside, it was a common thing to wrap rags on the feet and legs and to wear a blanket over the uniform [. . .] This went on until just before Christmas when we finally received the woolens, and the furs arrived about 10 days later.[3]

It was clear to 2nd Lieutenant Alf Thompson, in charge of a machine-gun company, that this expedition was a terrible muddle:

Our barracks about a mile from the city [Vladivostok]. Barracks around this place for a quarter of a million men and every hill has a fortification on it. Millions of dollars worth of supplies all about going to waste. Barbed wire, railroad supplies, autos etc [. . .] News from the Western front very encouraging. From the Volga front, not so good. The Tjecks [*sic*] are being driven back by the Bolsheviks. Why can't we get into it. The Russians (White remnants of the empire) are praying for us to help them and Washington holds us here doing routine guard duty while the Japs are fighting through and taking the credit and irking the Russians. 27th [Infantry] spread out on the way to Irkutsk. Three thousand Canadians arrived yesterday. Wonder if they will be taken to the Volga front.[4]

Thompson can be forgiven for being puzzled as to precisely what his mission was in eastern Siberia; after all, he was only sharing the profound confusion of his president. Technically, Thompson and his colleagues were there not as soldiers but policemen, with the job of guarding their sections of the Trans-Siberian railway against guerrilla attacks. But he was at least fortunate in being in Vladivostok, where there were voluntary organizations showing movies, and where it was relatively easy to meet Russian women. Guard duties were not too onerous and there were plenty of bars and restaurants selling good food and hard liquor, now banned in the States. Other doughboys, based in the North Russia campaign around Archangel and in the interior near Lake Baikal, had none of these luxuries. At the end of March 1919 a company of US soldiers, sick of their poor food, their infestation with lice, and the apparent pointlessness of their being stationed in such an appalling part of the world when everyone else was going home after the end of the war, refused to load sledges. Their gripes threatened to spill into outright mutiny.

Against this misery, however, some professional soldiers were having the time of their life. In Murmansk Major Edward MacMorland (who ended up as a major-general) was 'too tickled for words' to be in charge of a contingent of 32 officers and 688 men, all volunteers sent to maintain and run the Murman railway line south to Petrograd, an important communications link for the British forces. He and his unit had arrived towards the end of March 1919. By 27 April 1919 he was confident enough to write to his (somewhat long-suffering) wife Lucy, who had given birth to their first child in her husband's absence of almost two years on overseas duty, that my men are doing splendidly and [. . .] their morale is good. Further, the conditions of hardship headlines in the press are all 'bunk'. My worst hardship is the infrequency of a bath. The food is good for both officers and men and I have a fine Russian steel coach for headquarters. There is still a little fighting [. . .] Lucy, dear, if you hear any groaning of the hard lot of our men on this Front, which is the *Murman* Front as distinguished from the Archangel Front, where things are bad, just set them right from me, as Commanding Officer of the US troops here [. . .] There is nothing to worry about here; the Bolsheviks are poor fighters and dislike thoroughly our machine guns and 75m. My men look upon it as a splendid adventure in the Arctic spring [. . .][5]

It was a different story just three months later, when MacMorland sailed for France, his Siberian adventure over. One of his less pleasant duties on the journey back was to keep watch, along with medics, over one of his men who had gone mad: 'The doctor diagnoses it as Dementia Praecox, paranoid stage [. . .] His obsession is that everyone is trying to kill him, and that everyone believes him a Bolshevik. He tried to kill himself today with a hammer, but was not successful.'[6]

Mental illness was not commonplace among the Russian doughboys, but physical sickness was. A typhus epidemic had erupted in Omsk, and spinal meningitis was scything through Thompson's company. In January he wrote, with an air of desperate hope, 'the latest dope is that we leave here on or about March 5th'. No such luck. On 20 March he spent the evening

out all night on midnight patrols in Vladivostock to prevent trouble between Jap and American troops. Relations very strained between Jap and American Hdq. over our non-interference [. . .] at Blagoveshchensk. Call us helpers of the Bolsheviks. Great deal of robbing and killing in the city every day and night. Was attacked myself the night before but knocked the ring leader down and then beat it. Japanese continuing to send delegations of officers about twice a week to visit our barracks and learn what they can of our methods.[7]

Thompson managed to flee on the *Logan* on 1 April, the same ship which on 27 March 1919 had brought 2nd Lieutenant Douglas Osborn of the 31st Infantry Regiment to Vladivostok, one of a batch of replacements that also included 2nd Lieutenant Leroy Yarborough, a military intelligence officer whose Russian escapades gave him useful early training for his later espionage career.[8] Osborn recorded his initial impressions of Vladivostok:

Here at last. We sighted land at 2.30 p.m. and turned into the harbour at about 4.30. Docked at 6.00, American soldiers were certainly good to see. Some of these Dirty as Hell! Barracks all over the county & plenty of big batteries all over the hills [. . .] Everybody has a uniform on whether he is a soldier or not. There are Americans, Japs, French, Canadians, and Szecko-Slovak [sic].[9]

Yarborough quickly found himself a billet, the 'kitchen of old Russian officer quarters part of which is occupied by a Russian family and much of it by cockroaches'.[10] By 9 April he was in bed with dysentery, having the day before 'delivered a flank attack with my platoon' against an unknown enemy. Yarborough's diary entries casually record 'mixing it' in fights, sitting on 'special' courts, 'invading' Russian arsenals and generally flouting the US promise not to intervene in internal Russian affairs. But in doing all this he was far from alone, and what the Americans were doing paled into insignificance when compared with the illegal activities of the Japanese and others of the Allied contingent.

Many of these young Americans could not cope with the unbridled licentiousness of their new surroundings, a world away from the rather puritanical atmosphere of their childhood homes. They often had only a few things on their mind – booze, sex, and having a good time. On 26 April Osborn recorded how 'lonesome' he was, and that he took comfort from having received a photograph of his girl, Helen. However, by 5 May he took dinner at his regular spot, the Olympia, where he picked up a Russian girl called Vera: 'She took me home! It was a better-class place that she had and everything was very nice and clean. She herself was of a better nature. I got home at 3.00 a.m.'

Osborn spent his days playing at soldiers and his evenings indulging himself in various minor debaucheries, which seemed to him to be very daring. On Saturday, 10 May he went with some pals to try a new restaurant where we had the head man make us up a cocktail that beat anything I ever tasted. It was:

4 parts champagne
2 parts liqueur
4 parts wine
& fruit.

I [had] two big tumblers full & believe me it had some kick. I came right home after that – I didn't want to take any chances.

He was wise to be cautious after dark on the rough streets of Vladivostok. The random exchange of gunfire was a nightly affair and the city was no place for the unwary. Colonel Homer Slaughter recalled the night a Japanese and an American patrol clashed:

The American officer in charge warned the Japanese before dark that American patrols would have orders to fire on anything that moved on the American side of the railway. He further warned the Japanese about making contact along the railway and for them not to cross into the American sector. Notwithstanding the warning a 12-man Japanese patrol came into the American sector where it ran head on into a 3 man American patrol. Both sides dropped to the ground on opposite sides of the street and commenced firing. The American patrol fired 8 rounds, killing and wounding four Japanese. The Japanese patrol fired 72 rounds, killing and wounding none of the Americans.[11]

Undaunted by his fruit cocktail, Osborn the next evening was back on the town:

Met Darling [a fellow officer] and we went down to 'Shum's' (last night) and got another cocktail. They made so much of it that I filled two bottles of it and took it along. We met the girl that Tunnell [another fellow officer] and I met before and her friend. I grabbed the friend, Darling the other. We walked around & then went to a cabinet up the end of the street. We got a big dinner, drank the cocktail & got some more wine, until we began to feel mighty tipsy. Darling's girl was wild. Mine is the best-looking and is much the most reasonable and sensible. She is 18, from Petrograd and is very cute. Moore had her I think. Her name is Katy. Darling got what he wanted. Date for tomorrow.

The 'opportunities for meeting prostitutes' in Vladivostok 'were plentiful', according to Joseph S. Loughran, an army chaplain who served there. One notorious street 'frequented by the men was called "Shanker Alley".'[12] In Archangel by the end of March 1919 the doughboys' hospital had treated 54 cases of syphilis and 129 of gonorrhoea.[13]

Some of the American expedition at least took their work seriously, none more so than Yarborough, who was eventually based at Shkotovo, where he kept a close eye on the more shady goings-on of the local populace and also of his fellow soldiers. From Yarborough's reports to the commanding officer of the 31st Infantry it is clear that cocaine and opium abuse was a serious problem among the doughboys stationed in Siberia: 'It has been known for a long time that cocaine was being sold illegally to American soldiers from several places in Shkotovo. The local drug store was suspected as one of the places [. . .]'[14]

On another occasion Yarborough handed over to the 31st's Unit Supply Officer

    1 one-quart black bottle, $\frac{1}{3}$ full, liquid opium
    1 half-pint tin can, $\frac{3}{4}$ full, powdered opium
    1 one-pound tin coffee can, containing opium gum
    1 china plate, containing 4 small packages, opium gum[15]

all of which had been captured by a 'mounted patrol' led by Major Cutrer of the 31st Infantry.

Yarborough was clearly loving every moment of his tough-guy role. On 10 August 1919 he put in an official request for the delivery 'as soon as possible' of '6 shot guns, trench' and '600 rounds, shot gun ammunition (buckshot)' with the plea that 'in case this number of shot guns is not available please send any lesser number on hand and 100 rounds ammunition per gun'.

Yarborough's request for some heavy-duty close-order weaponry was approved by his immediate superior, Colonel Frederic Sargent, the commanding officer of the 31st Infantry based in Vladivostok, but turned down by the chief ordnance officer partly because the 'proper channels' had not been gone through but also because he could not believe such equipment was really necessary. The demand for shotguns was no mere posturing on the part of Yarborough; American soldiers were increasingly becoming drawn into large-scale gunfights with Russian criminals, Bolsheviks, and 'partisans', a generic term for anyone who simply liked to take pot-shots at passing doughboys.

The worst such engagement, which rather exaggeratedly became known in the regimental history of the 31st Infantry as the 'Romanovka massacre', took place early on the morning of 25 June 1919. Romanovka was a large village situated on the broad-gauge railway link between Vladivostok and Kanghaus, the latter being a terminal in the mountains leading to the Suchan coal-mining district. The Suchan coal-mines, upon which the locomotives depended for fuel, was one of the more important sites under American authority.

Two platoons of the 31st Infantry were stationed at Romanovka, the first from C Company (under the command of 1st Lieutenant Norval D. Hellworth) and one from A Company (commanded by 2nd Lieutenant Lawrence D. Butler). On the morning of the attack, which started just after 4 a.m., only Butler's platoon was still in position, the other having entrained for Kanghaus. It seems that a fair amount of trust had built up between the local Russians and the doughboys, for only one guard was posted over the doughboys, asleep inside their tents. They were surrounded and taken by surprise; most of the casualties occurred in the first minute of gunfire, as those who were able ran to some nearby log houses which gave greater protection against the sporadic shooting. Butler was shot in the jaw but continued to exercise command by writing his orders on pieces of paper.

One of Lieutenant Yarborough's duties was to conduct an investigation into the Romanovka incident; the intelligence section had a breakthrough when E Company of the 31st Infantry captured several Russian documents near Korvolets in late July. One was a report on what happened at Romanovka. By 3 August Sergeant F. K. Zitzer had produced an adequate translation of the document:

At dawn the 625 [25 June] the telegraph line was cut all along R.R. [railroad] line, at the same time as the wooden bridge across the Loobchinskey Key was set on fire and destroyed, at that time, the attack against the American forces in Romanovka started. The Americans numbered from 60 to 70 men they occupied tents on the Eastern outskirts of the village [. . .] no outposts were posted [. . .] As soon as fire was opened on the tents, amongst the Americans was noticed confusion. Part of them grouped together with raised hands, on account of which firing was almost stopped right after which the Americans opened fire from their Automatic rifles. To this time it has not been estimated whether the Americans really ever intended to surrender or were merely playing for time. Most likely that part of them intended to surrender, which was foiled by the other group, who took advantage of the lull by preparing their Automatic rifles, from which they opened fire immediately. On account of the poor discipline amongst part of the Partisans, our left flank, which was subject to a heavy well delivered fire from the Americans, took to their heels in panic. The more hearty ones made the Americans leave their tents. The Americans took possession of a house, and part of the shore along the river. Firing continued until 9 a.m. after which our forces left Romanovka [. . .] Our losses were never definitely established, at present it is known that seven are killed and eight wounded, amongst the killed was Commander of the 2nd Vladivostock Company Semenoff. The American losses are estimated at about 40 killed and wounded.[16]

Failure to place several guard posts around the tended encampment at Romanovka should have been a court-martial offence, but Butler had only taken over command of the post the previous evening, and his serious injuries probably prevented his being held to account for such a major error. Instead, he and Corporal Louis Heinzman, who ran to get reinforcements, both received the Distinguished Service Cross.[17] On 25 June, after the attack, Osborn recorded his version of the incident:

Nothing much doing until about dinner time (6.00) and then the fun began. Sergeant Mills blew in. He had left early for Romanovka where his platoon was located, had gotten as far as Ugolnia & found a bridge burned out & telegrams coming thru stating that his platoon had been all shot up and that the dead and wounded were being brought in then. They arrived at the Base here at about 6.00 just ahead of Sgt Mills. There were at the time 20 dead and 26 wounded – some total out of 53 men. Some are missing and unaccounted for. Some are in frightful condition and they expect 3 to die tonight. We can't get the details of the fight yet. The Col's just raising hell. Lieut Buttler was shot thru the chin.

PS – about 10.30 Capt Boon called up & had me get 4 men ready including Sgt Mills to go to the Evac Hospital to identify the dead. They were operating on them then and preparing the dead. Lieut Buttler was shot thru the cheek & chin losing part of his face and a set of teeth. Other men lost arms and legs and were blown to hell.

The detachment was jumped at 4.30 in the morning with high explosive shells and rifle fire and grenades. They fought them off till 11 o'clock in the morning when train guards arrived and drove them away.

The anti-Bolshevik forces were breaking down into an ill-disciplined rabble, with marauding Cossacks and criminals using the cover of anti-Bolshevism to justify their terrorism and theft. Generals Semenoff and Kalmykoff had been indiscriminately killing people up and down the railway line. White forces committed atrocities, as did the Red Army, and also the Japanese, who without proper legal authority arrested Russians and on the merest whim executed them, usually by chopping their heads off with swords.

General Graves recalled a report dated 27 July 1919 in which a company of Japanese soldiers arrested nine Russian men at the town of Sviagina, which was in that sector of the railway line designated as under US control. The Japanese told the local US officer in charge that these men were Bolsheviks; four were released but the other five were first beaten, then blindfolded and killed by decapitation and stabbing with sabres. Graves was infuriated:

I felt so strongly about this murder that I brought the commanding officer of Sviagina to American Headquarters at Vladivostock and, in the presence of the Japanese Chief of Staff, told him he should have used force to prevent it. I also told the Japanese Chief of Staff that if such a thing was ever attempted again in American sectors of the railroad, it would bring on a conflict between Japanese and American troops.[18]

These were brave words from an officer whose contingent was outnumbered by the Japanese by at least ten to one.

General Graves despised and loathed the Japanese behaviour in

Siberia, but he reserved a special detestation for Admiral Kolchak and his methods of suppressing opposition. Kolchak, however, had the backing of the Allies, who saw in him their greatest hope for a strong Russian opponent of Bolshevism. Graves eventually searched out Kolchak in Omsk, to see for himself if he was a man who was worth supporting. Following his visit Graves dismissed the admiral as a butcher lacking any credibility or genuine popular support. This did not prevent Woodrow Wilson from declaring on 12 June 1919 that the US would 'assist the Government of Admiral Kolchak and his associates with munitions, supplies, and food'.[19] How Wilson squared this policy with his *Aide Mémoire* is difficult to understand. What is more disturbing was his ability simply to ignore the observations of his field commander, General Graves, who said: 'I doubt if history will show any country in the world during the last fifty years where murder could be committed as safely and with less danger of punishment than in Siberia during the regime of Admiral Kolchak.'[20]

In September 1919 President Wilson's promise to ship aid to Kolchak began to bear fruit; rifles and ammunition began arriving on US ships in Vladivostok. But General Graves refused to hand them over, and refused to accept as payment from Kolchak's representatives $1 million in gold bars. What, he asked, was the point of handing over guns to those who might one day soon be using them against American soldiers? Enormous political pressure brought to bear by the British and Washington eventually forced Graves to conclude the deal.

Among the criticisms Graves levelled against these licensed bandits working on behalf of Kolchak was that they took hostages and executed them; however, it is evident too that American junior officers in the field were not averse to taking hostages – and indeed shooting them if they attempted to flee. By the middle of 1919 Leroy Yarborough was fully into his stride. He received word from Captain Frank A. Paul, the 31st's Regimental Intelligence Officer, back in Vladivostok: 'I am very very pleased with the completeness of the reports and with the character of the work turned in by your section.'[21]

And what was Yarborough's work? Why, nothing but wholesale intervention, in direct contradiction of Woodrow Wilson's so carefully framed *Aide Mémoire*. From Yarborough's reports he clearly enjoyed an almost completely free hand in rounding up, interrogating and jailing Russians, such as Dmitri Gimchutka, thirty-one years of age, who was 'captured at Novo Rosskaya by Co D July 30. Examined by Lt Yarborough Aug. 1':

Associated with Bolsheviki but stoutly denies that he was one of them. Works as a woodsman, for wages, when not working on his farm, and never carried a rifle or served as an outpost with Reds. No record of his examination by Co D officers and no check possible on the accuracy of his statements. Said to interpreter that he had been threatened by American officers when first captured but the threat turned out to be only a bluff, and he guessed he could tell this officer now just what he wanted to tell. Surly and defiant. Russians have him in their suspect book but have nothing on him.[22]

The years have long buried Dmitri Gimchutka; we have no idea what befell him and the dozens of others interrogated by Yarborough and his colleagues. Their fate was unlikely to be pleasant; though they probably were released unharmed by the Americans, the Japanese, the Kolchakites, the bandits, and any number of other armed murderers were ready to snuff their lives out. In one mission, on 26 May 1919, several companies of the 31st Infantry marched against two villages, Knevichi and Korlovets, looking for Bolsheviks suspected of attacking the railway line. A squad of eight men under Yarborough

searched houses and brought out all men. Also found three guns, in poor shape. Mail and telegrams of town [Knevichi] seized, and receipt given to postmaster. There were about 80 prisoners in all. One man, Georges Hoplik, was killed by rifle fire when attempting to escape in direction of Korlovets. Only casualty. People gave little trouble [. . .] After men had been examined, all were released except ten, who were kept as hostages. They were allowed to be relieved and replaced by others every three hours.

Occasionally the boot was on the other foot, and the hostage-takers themselves became hostages. Sergeant Bachelor of F Company, 27th Infantry, and others of his unit were taken prisoner by a 300-strong Bolshevik band and held for two weeks in June 1919. Bachelor later wrote a report of his capture:

Their leader [. . .] goes by the name 'Gorko'. His right name is 'Balanuzstea'. He speaks perfect English and was educated in America [. . .] Instead of being tried as Spies, they voted on us. The first vote was 295 to 6 in favor of shooting us, but then as all decisions must be the unanimous vote of the detachment, several of the men made speeches and another vote was taken. The result this time was a tie. Then ['Gorko'] made a talk in which he violently argued in our favor and the third vote was not to shoot us, but to keep us as prisoners[23] [. .]

I always accompanied Gorko, who thought that if I were left with the other Bolsheviks they would kill me when reports came in of Bolshevik losses.

Their spy system is excellent and they are acquainted with all our movements.

At the town of Timerofka, two stylishly dressed girls reported to Gorko. These girls were employed at Vladivostock and Habarovsk doing propaganda work. One of the girls said she knew many American soldiers.

I was very well treated by the Bolsheviks and they tried to prepare food that I could eat. Their food consists of black bread, milk, and a soup made from some grass. Occasionally, they have tea and cabbages. Sugar is unknown. They are very filthy and during the 14 days I did not see one man wash or bathe. They have no soap [. . .]

At one place they showed me their arsenal, where they claim they make from fifteen to eighteen thousand rounds of ammunition daily. They have plenty of sheet copper, but no brass. Most of their rifles are of Japanese make.[24]

By the time Lieutenant-Colonel Alvin Gillem, a career soldier, arrived with a fresh replacement batch of 1,200 men towards the end of August 1919, he was entering bandit country. Morale among the doughboys was plummeting. Rowdiness and insubordination were becoming problems:

Most of them were replacements, and their training had not been adequate, and they would get out in the Russian villages and, of course, a great many lived with Russian women in those days, and the vodka was of a very poor quality with the result that we had quite a disciplinary problem [. . .] they sought refuge with the Russian women and venereal disease was of a high incident.[25]

As Yarborough and his colleagues became increasingly busy in the winter of 1919–20 this degeneration into anarchy gathered pace. The Czech Legion began to abandon their sector of the railway and to show greater determination to leave Siberia; Kolchak's army was smashed on the Volga front; typhus became endemic, and the unburied dead lay in their thousands across the Russian steppes. Pressure began to build on the Wilson administration to extricate the US troops from what was clearly an impossible position. News of the Romanovka incident was beginning to filter back to the United States, and a strong reaction was setting in against this futile involvement in Russia's internal affairs. On 8 October 1919 the *San Francisco Examiner* reported the return of 600 doughboys from Siberia:

Some of them had to be carried down the gangplank on stretchers. Others had memories of 'bunkies' [pals] who have filled graves in the frozen soil about Vladivostock. Somewhere in the hospital of the transport were eight men, sent away months ago on this devil's errand, and these eight WERE INSANE!

Is it not about time to stop this madness of meddling in an affair which is absolutely no concern of ours? [. . .]

The fact is that by our participation in the Siberian squabble – as sordid a squabble involving 'concessions' for British lumber syndicates, concessions for Japanese commercial corporations, and 'hopes' for Russian militarists and reactionaries – we are participating in a civil war that rightfully belongs for settlement to Russians. We will grant that Britain has something to gain from the victory of the Kolchak–Denikine end of this civil war. Japan has much to gain too.

But AMERICA HAS NOTHING TO GAIN.

And most decidedly America should not be lending its aid, in money, arms and, most precious of all, America's sons, to the commercial ambitions of Britain and Japan in the undeveloped resources of Siberia. Let Russia's factions fight out their fight. It's their quarrel, not ours.[26]

In the second week of December 1919 there were food riots in Vladivostok. The city's normal population of about 80,000 was swollen to more than 300,000 by the influx of refugees fleeing the Bolsheviks as the Kolchak regime began to crumble. MacMorland wrote: 'There is practically no fuel and no food – the suffering this winter is going to be terrible. When I came here two months ago the ruble exchange was 85 for $1.00. Today you can get 320 for $1.00. Normally 2 rubles equal $1.00.'[27]

It was time for the doughboys to get out while they still could. The 339th Regiment, which had been stationed in Murmansk as part of the North Russian expedition, returned to the States via Europe in the summer of 1919, the last to leave being their commanding officer, Brigadier-General W. P. Richardson, who sailed on 23 August 1919. By 1 April 1920 the last of the doughboys had sailed from Vladivostok; most of the Czechs were out by August; the Japanese held on in Vladivostok for another two years but finally left in October 1922, as the Red Army relentlessly pushed through. The last US personnel to leave Russian soil – intelligence officers, diplomatic staff, some guards looking after the German and Austro-Hungarian prisoners, and radio operators – evacuated Russian Island on 19 November 1922.[28]

Woodrow Wilson made a clumsy error by intervening in Siberia, but at least he got one thing right: in January 1920 he ordered the final evacuation of the American forces, which certainly helped make up the rather confused mind of Douglas Osborn, who was clearly smitten with Russian girls. On Tuesday, 13 January 1920 – which he tells us had the 'worst blizzard in the history of Vladivostok' – he married one, Mary, in a service conducted by a Lutheran pastor, Mary wearing a dress which cost $72 ('Wow!' commented the happy husband; 'Woe!' was the probable but unrecorded sentiment of the spurned Helen). It must have been a hell of a wedding party at the Golden Horn restaurant: the total bill was $100 (including $20 for a bottle of Canadian Club whiskey). Finally 'the Military Police were called in to quell the disturbance'.

Did all the doughboys who lived come home safely from Russia? It is not certain. In 1930 the US Justice Department took an affidavit from an anonymous Russian seaman who claimed to have been in the Lubyanka jail in Moscow on 1 March 1927, where he allegedly met several American former doughboys, including four officers and fifteen enlisted men who had been there since 1919. This seaman then claimed to have been transferred to Solovetz island prison where he supposedly met many more American soldiers and civilians; he recalled the names of three of them, Mr Martin or Marten, Mr G. Heinainkruk, and Roy

Molner, the last an army sergeant. An internal government memo commented on this information:

[...] at least one case that has an important bearing on it, namely the case of William J. Martin, Company A, 339th Infantry, which regiment served in Archangel or North Russian Expedition. Under date of Feb. 3, 1919 a report from Archangel showed Martin missing in action. Under date of March 14, 1921 we made a determination showing: 'Was killed in action January 19, 1919.' This determination was no doubt predicated on the unexplained absence of the soldier for about two years [until the KIA-BNR – killed in action, body not recovered – determination was made].' I also found another case which may possibly be involved, it is of Lindsay Retherford, up in my mind because of the mention by the Russian sailor of Alfred Lindsay. Lindsay Retherford was reported missing and a similar determination [KIA BNR] was made in his case.[29]

In April 1921, the *New York Times* reported that the American prisoners held by the Soviet government of Russia had been told by the Bolsheviks that they were held because the US government had failed to make strong demands for their release.[30] The Soviet government attempted to barter US prisoners-of-war held in their prisons for US diplomatic recognition and trade relations with their regime. The United States refused, even though the *New York Times* article reported that the Soviets were threatening that 'Americans held by the Soviet government would be put to death'. In August 1921 America signed the Riga Agreement with the Soviet Union, which offered humanitarian relief in exchange for US POWs. The US government was expecting no more than twenty prisoners to be sent home, but was astonished when on 1 September more than 100 Americans were freed.

The official casualty figures for the Siberian side-show stated that 137 doughboys had been killed in action (including 28 presumed killed); 43 died from their wounds; 122 died from disease; 46 died from accidental causes; and 5 committed suicide, giving a total death toll of 353. But these figures are controversial in that they

conceal the fact that out of the 144 combat deaths of American soldiers officially reported in 1919 in Northern Russia, 127 of those deaths, or 88 per cent of those official combat death figures were made up of some 70 MIAs declared dead, and another 57 soldiers who were declared KIA-BNR.[31]

In other words, 127 men were never properly accounted for; in 1929, eighty-six sets of human remains were identified by a US Graves Registration expedition, though how well the task was carried out, given the contemporary forensic skills and the lapse of a decade, is open to question. Equally controversially, when US soldiers in this theatre were declared missing in action it was simultaneously registered in their service record that they were *killed* in action, even if there had been no evidence in support of this. There lingers a suspicion that some doughboys who were taken prisoner by Bolshevik partisans never made it back to the United States. Certainly the Bolsheviks used their American captives as bargaining chips.

There was plenty of scope for individuals simply to disappear in such a vast landscape, where such principles as *habeas corpus* were mere chimeras. Among the captured partisan documents mentioned earlier was one which gave a report into conditions in the Suchan district in June 1919, which mentioned that on 22 June 'five Americans were captured, two of which are officers'. Did they ever make it back to their homes or were they simply reported as KIA-BNR?

As for those doughboys who managed to escape with their lives, they were happy to leave behind that grisly, surreal world in which distance was measured in hundreds of miles, where any idea of a front line was a fantasy, and where their greatest achievement was perhaps the successful repatriation of the Czechoslovak soldiers.

Now did we do the right thing in Siberia? As far as we were concerned while we were there, certainly [. . .] I wouldn't say it was exactly a success, but it represented exactly what the General's mission told him to do [. . .] yet I would think it was typical of the patch that we wore on our shoulder which was a bear sitting and the men said they did nothing but sit on their butts, and I think strictly speaking, we did that for about two years.[32]

In January 1919 a by now broken Admiral Kolchak placed himself and the Russian imperial treasure trove – estimated to have been worth at the time $325 million (perhaps twenty times that today) – in the care of the Czechs, who fled eastwards from Omsk to Irkutsk. On 13 January the miners in the city of Cheremkhovo demanded that the Czechs surrender the admiral to them. The Czechs promised to hand him over to the authorities next day in Irkutsk, where the Czechs bartered Kolchak and his treasure for their freedom. After a show trial and a death sentence, Kolchak's brains were blown out by an automatic pistol on 7 February 1920. Two weeks later Irkutsk was in the hands of the Red Army.

20

Aftermath

The behavior of our soldiers in Europe, whether in England, France or Germany is really something to be proud of, and has astonished the world. Sturdy and docile as a Newfoundland dog, with a kindly word and deed for everyone, he fought like a lion. He poured out his blood like water, and simply swept the trained soldiers of Europe off the map.

Brigadier-General Johnson Hagood[1]

My present ambition is to get out of the army at the earliest possible moment. It is an awful thing to be in. The war isn't so bad, but the army – O my!   Samuel Arthur Devan[2]

In the bleak winter days of mid November 1918 the AEF decided to try to see for itself just how thoroughly defeated the Germans were, through a discreet exploratory mission into Germany. Nominally it was a humanitarian trip aimed at discovering the welfare needs of the local populace, though it was designed more to glean detailed information concerning military and civilian morale. Bishop Brent, senior chaplain of the AEF, together with Lieutenant-Colonel M. C. Maddox, chief medical officer of the Third Army, accompanied a senior AEF intelligence officer on a trip through Luxemburg to Treves in Prussia. What they saw surprised them:

The party caught up with the retreating [German] Army at Remach on the Moselle. The discipline and morale were perfect. From Remach to Treves by way of Wasserbillig there was an almost unbroken column [. . .] There was not a straggler nor a symptom of disorder [. . .] The troops seemed happy and full of spirits [. . .] A triumphal arch was erected at the entrance to Treves, with the inscription, 'Welcome to our Unconquered Heroes'.[3]

German soldiers had done with fighting for the Kaiser but their self-esteem was far from crushed. The terms of the Armistice were harsh, but they took so long to implement that initially many of those in the Allied camp wondered what had been gained. Could this really be victory? Soldiers on the field of battle know what victory is; it can be smelled, touched and seen, and is made manifest by the fleeing enemy, the rounding-up of crestfallen prisoners, the fanfares of public acclaim. But what kind of victory was it where the defeated walked calmly from the battlefield, bearing arms and flags held aloft, greeted as victors by the families they returned to? The scurrying off into exile in the Netherlands by Kaiser Wilhelm indicated a degree of internal collapse, but by the end this was a fairly nugatory gesture.

Among many of the front-line troops in the Allied armies there was therefore an ambivalent mood, elation at the end of hostilities yet frustration that the victory was somehow muddied by a sense that Germany was still on its feet, bloodied but unbowed. Among the AEF there was a widespread sense of having been cheated of real triumph. Many doughboys could not understand why the ceasefire happened when it did, without a clear breakthrough on their part of the front. After all, by 11 November the AEF was 3,703,273 strong, a massive army which, given time, might have been able to deliver a knock-out blow.[4] Genuine victory surely meant pursuing the enemy and laying waste to his country, much as that enemy had done to Belgium and France? General Johnson Hagood expressed the thoughts of many when he said the Germans were 'still a terrible menace to the world'.[5] He believed it would be

a good thing if the [German] nation could be dissapated [sic] like the Jews. Somebody has got to suffer the consequences of the war, and it seems to me that the Germans should be sold out bag and baggage and the proceeds turned over to the Belgians, the French and the others who have suffered by Germany's bringing on the war [. . .] I do not see why any peasant of France should go without a horse as long as a German peasant has a horse. I do not see why the Comtesse of Beaumont should see her chateau in ruins when there is a chateau left standing in Germany.

Above all there was considerable anger among the Americans that the arch-villain, the Kaiser, had got off scot-free. A handful of swashbuckling doughboys from the 114th Field Artillery Regiment decided to bring him to justice; on 1 January 1919 they set off by car to kidnap the Kaiser. The expedition was led by Colonel Luke Lea, former US senator, former publisher of the Nashville newspaper the *Tennessean*, and now commander of the 114th regiment of Field Artillery in the AEF. Lea managed to persuade Brigadier-General Spaulding, in charge of the 55th Brigade of Field Artillery, to allow him (Lea), three other officers and three enlisted men to have five days' leave. They drove in two cars from their base in Luxemburg first to Maastricht, to get the necessary passports to enter Holland; they planned to continue to Amerongen, where the Kaiser was living in luxurious exile. Lea was an angry man:

Why should those not responsible for the war and against whom we had not waged war – the German people – be killed, wounded, and imprisoned and the only person against who we had really waged war, the Kaiser, escape punishment, not ever being brought to trial but permitted to live in luxurious pomp and glory with all his fabulous fortune untouched? [. . .] The capture, trial and punishment of the Kaiser was to the American doughboy the object which inspired him to leave home, to cross submarine swept seas, to surrender the freedom of a citizen of a republic to become a cog in the best disciplined fighting machine in any war and finally to give his life, if need be.[6]

Lea had a point, and many American officials along the way, including Brand Whitlock (who had been appointed by President Wilson to the important foreign diplomatic post of Minister to Belgium), connived at assisting Lea and his cronies to obtain the correct documents for the journey. The desperadoes arrived at Amerongen just before 8 p.m. on 5 January, and after getting directions from a local Dutch inhabitant of the village they were soon at the Kaiser's residence. Astonishingly, the German guard at the front gate (dressed in Dutch military uniform) instantly obeyed Lea's guttural German command to let them in. They were ushered into the library where they were received by the Kaiser's son, Count Bentinck, who asked them their business. Lea declined to reply, except to say that they would answer that question only to the Kaiser, in person. The situation was formally polite but extremely tense. Bentinck left the room and a butler served the Americans cigars and, oddly enough, water: 'Our guess was the Count believed not only was America prohibition [sic], but all Americans, even soldiers while in Europe, were teetotalers, and did not want to offend or shock his uninvited guests by offering them liquor.'[7]

Soon the perspiring burgomaster of Amerongen, in full evening dress, arrived in the library and started questioning Lea and his colleagues. Lea tried speaking German but the burgomaster quickly put a stop to that and said, 'I am sure we will progress more rapidly speaking in English. I am a graduate of Harvard University.'

The verbal sparring continued but it was becoming evident that, unless they were prepared to use force, they were not going to see Wilhelm Hohenzollern. With their tails between their legs the Americans left, to find their cars surrounded by two companies of Dutch infantry, heavily armed and looking threatening. Lea and his men were permitted to leave, but on their return the colonel was officially hauled over the coals – and privately cheered to the rafters. Lea dined out on this farce for many years afterwards. When he got back to America, Lea had lunch with General Bullard.

Suddenly General Bullard turned to me and said: 'Luke, what did John Pershing say to you about your trip to see the Kaiser?'

'General Pershing,' I replied, 'wrote the trip was "amazingly indiscreet".'

'Oh hell! I don't mean what General Pershing said officially. What I want to know is what did John Pershing say to you personally about the trip?' interrupted General Bullard.

'General Pershing never spoke to me about it personally,' I answered.

'Well I'll tell you what John Pershing really thought about the trip,' were the final words of General Bullard on the subject. 'John Pershing said to me, "Bullard, I'm a poor man, but I'd have given a year's pay to have been able to taken Lea's trip into Holland and to have entered the castle of Count Bentinck without invitation."'[8]

This kind of buccaneering spirit had no place in the heart of General Peyton March. He was determined to demobilize the AEF immediately the last shot was fired. As well as being cost-effective – a factor never far from March's mind – a rapid dismantling of the AEF would have the pleasing side-effect of cutting the hero of the hour, Pershing, down to size. Pershing's unsteady start and the logistical chaos into which the AEF had sunk by the end of the fighting were now all but forgotten in the post-war euphoria sweeping the country, where rumours were rife that Pershing would run for the presidency. Talk of his seeking the highest office refused to die, despite Pershing's own silence on the matter. The possibility of having to answer to Pershing as his ultimate commander-in-chief must have given March dyspepsia. Thus on 16 November March ordered the immediate demobilization of the AEF. He took a smug pride in its smooth accomplishment, believing each individual soldier leaving the AEF was hale and hearty:

In health he was in general at least as good as when he entered the service; if wounded or in worse health, he was entitled to compensation. No officer or enlisted man was discharged, even on his own desire, until he had received the full benefit of army medical treatment. Every man was also given a uniform, shoes, and an overcoat or a raincoat. In the case of overseas men, helmets and gas masks were issued as souvenirs. All men who had taken out war-risk insurance were informed of the right to convert it to a five-year-term insurance; and all were furnished with records of their service.[9]

Individual servicemen were rather less satisfied with their treatment. Many felt the country was neglectful of their sacrifice and was letting them drift back home to a future at best uncertain and at worst blighted by unemployment and emotional and physical scars.

Despite March's best efforts demobilization proceeded slowly, not least because technically the Allies remained at war with Germany until the final peace settlement was signed in 1920. By 1 May 1919, 1,936,011 doughboys had been discharged. Those who found themselves reluctant participants in the messily complicated post-war settlement, as part of the AEF's Third Army (which was not dissolved until 2 July 1919), formed part of the Allied army of occupation, designated the American Forces in Germany (AF in G). An exasperated Lieutenant Clark found this a mixed blessing:

Again it seems the 2nd Division is indispensable, and, instead of being relieved, we are marching to Germany as part of the army of occupation. Quite an honor and a most interesting experience – but I should like to have had a couple of free weeks in France.

We crossed the line on the 17th and since then have been closely following the evacuating Germans. Belgium and its people were splendid! Their reception of us was gloriously enthusiastic, for we were their deliverers and liberators, the conquerors of the Hun for whom they have only the bitterest hatred.[10]

As late as 5 July 1919 the 1st, 2nd, 3rd, 4th and 5th Divisions were still in Germany, as well as various air service personnel, engineers, medics, police, quartermaster, signals and miscellaneous other units. The 1st and 2nd Divisions were in the Coblenz bridgehead; the 3rd was on the left bank of the Rhine; the 4th and 5th were preparing to head back to Brest to debark. The 1st Division was the last division to leave Europe: but not the last doughboys – a few small contingents were the last to go. By the end of 1919 the AF in G's actual strength was 842 officers and 17,986 enlisted men; even at the end of 1920 there still were 622 officers and 15,887 men. By 11 January 1923 the token force, now down to a few hundred, received orders for the final withdrawal; on 25 January they sailed home from Antwerp.[11]

The doughboys had very varied responses to their role as part of the AF in G. Some relished the prestige gained by their relative financial wealth, but others found the whole experience tedious. It very much depended on the kind of unit in which the doughboys found themselves and the nature of the officers. In an outfit run by incompetent bullies, the end of the war meant little or no change. Private Yensen titled his diary entry of 13 January 1919 'In the same old hell hole':

Life has been worse than anything we have ever known. For twenty-one meals all we've had to eat is terrible slum, coffee and bread. We've crabbed at the cooks; but they say they cook all the rations that come. Yesterday we heard that $1,500,000.00 worth of our chow had been sold by our officers to the Germans. Yet we have to salute such – Oh what words can describe them? The worst words I know are too complimentary!

Some days it rains and some days it snows. On the rainy days the mud is halfway to our knees; and since the soles of our boots are worn out, the mud gets in and squirts around when we walk. On other days, when the ground is frozen, the rough clods make our feet bleed. We try to keep the holes patched up with chips of wood or pasteboard. We can't get any more boots or shoes because our supply sergeant doesn't have any.[12]

But in the letters and diaries of a number of soldiers it is clear that life as part of the occupying forces in Germany was, on the whole, infinitely preferable to what they had experienced as defenders of France. Once the shooting ended a barely suppressed mutual antipathy between the doughboys and the French broke out in a hundred different ways. Much of it boiled down to money. According to a report by Captain Stuart Benson, Liaison Officer, Combined Allied Forces (CAF), dated 3 February 1919, on conditions in Coblenz, which was occupied jointly by the AEF and French forces, the enlisted doughboy felt little short of hatred for his French allies:

The French mission at Coblenz had caused a considerable amount of friction, by butting in where it has no business, by spying and criticism of our methods [it] is top-heavy, completely over-manned, like most French missions [. . .] The almost hatred of the enlisted men for the French is actuated by many of the foregoing conditions [. . .] but there is another reason, of much earlier origin, which is growing rather than diminishing with age. Practically every enlisted man one talks to, speaks of how much more comfortable he is in Germany than in France, of how much more like America German towns and people are and therefore how much more at home he is, and *how much cheaper everything is in Germany*. This last is the big cause, the wail of the squeezed pocketbook. And there's a lot of truth in it all [. . .] The great fact stands out that he can buy very much more cheaply here and *that he was stung in France*, which is true and very bad if one does not take into account the extenuating circumstances.[13]

Private Yensen certainly supported Benson's argument. In late September 1918 Yensen's 5th Division had been camped near a French village during the first stage of the Meuse–Argonne offensive.

In the village where we water our animals, all we can buy is Vin Blanc (white wine), sour grapes and jam. And take it from me, it's like open robbery! The grapes sell for one franc a bunch [about 20 cents] and the jam sells for five francs a can [about $1] (cans about the size of an ordinary glass tumbler). The saleswoman acted big-headed and cross, even refusing paper money and growling at everyone who flashed it. I finally broke my vows to quit swearing and gave her a good American cussin'!

As a group, we were sure disgusted with France! Walt [his brother] said they could shoot him if they ever caught him saying anything good about France again. They can do the same to me, because if this isn't a no good country there never was, or never will be one. Their towns, dizzy as barber poles, used to amuse me, but now I'm weary of them.[14]

The presence on the soil of France of a large American army was, after the war ended, an uncomfortable reminder to the French that their military had not covered itself with glory; the rescued are often rather graceless to their rescuers. Even worse for the French, the peace negotiations in Versailles revealed the Americans to be utterly bereft of the sort of lust for revenge France expected from her allies. French civilians and American soldiers rapidly developed mutual contempt, and the treatment the doughboys received in Germany was in stark contrast:

French magazines began to jibe at the AEF for posing as the saviour of Civilization, indicating the while that it had played a very small part in the War after all [. . .] the AEF was [. . .] busily engaged in building up an anti-French animus of its own, based largely upon comparisons between conditions found in occupied Germany as contrasted with those which they had experienced, and were still experiencing, in France. Reports began to filter back from the Rhineland as to the courtesy and cleanliness of the natives, the neatness of their homes and villages, the modest prices charged for luxuries and necessities alike, the fine foods and choice wines [. . .][15]

The AEF 1st Division reported on 25 May 1919 that, among its troops, 'whenever they [the French] are mentioned [...] it is in a disparaging manner', for 'three basic reasons [...] Profiteering, Ingratitude, and Inhospitality'.[16]

Allegations of profiteering were nothing new. Doughboys had felt themselves subjected to merciless financial exploitation ever since they first landed in France. To some extent they had only themselves to blame, as General Bullard pointed out. In France in 1917,

> Prices by themselves were growing, not lessening, and to this the Americans always and everywhere contributed in two ways: first, being used to plenty, unquestioningly they paid any price, however great, and often in a grand way demanded no change: second, supply being often small, they paid any price rather than, by refusing, let the thing to go another willing to pay [...] The resulting high prices became at last a source of bitter complaint and criticism against the French among American soldiers – upon whom, however, the conditions bore less hardly than upon the French soldier and civilian, who had far less money than the American soldier.[17]

French men – civilians and uniformed – quickly grew resentful of the doughboy after the Armistice:

> Troops arriving from overseas were hailed as knights-errant, come to erase from the soil of France the imprint of an iron heel. Old women mothered them; young women welcomed the opportunity to engage in sentimental exchanges with persons of their own age and opposite sex. Old men regarded them with indifference. Children adored them, for they always had a kind word and a smile – and frequently some more substantial token, for their small admirers [...] Kindly feelings were general, and reciprocal, until after the Armistice. Then changes soon became apparent. The French soldier, back at his fireside, resented the friendliness which existed between his womenfolk and the Americans. The shopkeeper, foreseeing the departure of the source of many a golden egg, began to urge that the entire AEF, or large elements of it, be retained in France indefinitely – to assist in rebuilding the devastated areas and lay the spectre of a revived and rearmed Germany. The rank and file of Frenchmen did not, apparently, share this sentiment. Rather did they feel that the Americans had done the job for which they came (having been none too speedy in the coming, though com-

mendably efficient in the doing), and the sooner they went back to their home-land, the better for all concerned. Indeed, these foreigners toward whom they had felt bursts of enthusiastic affection when they first appeared in France, and again at the signing of the Armistice, had now become more of a liability than an asset. They were a little too 'cocky' over the part they had played in the War, and seemed to have forgotten that it was *France* which had held the line for four long years against their tardy arrival . . . They bought the best of everything at prices which the native could not afford, and turned the heads of the mademois-elles with their breezy ways and fat pocketbooks. It was high time to put them in their place – and France was not the place for them.

As a result, the American soldier [. . .] began to sense that he was no longer an honored saviour from a hated oppressor, but an alien who had overstayed his welcome.[18]

Against their experience in France many doughboys in the AF in G found the locals to be extremely warm and friendly, while the cost of living was cheap. In 1919 the incidence of VD among AEF troops in occupied Germany was higher than during the AEF's time in France. This may have meant that proportionately more German women than French had VD, but more probably it revealed a far greater degree of fraternization with German than with French women:

The war was not technically ended, and 'fraternizing' with the Germans was forbidden, but the Germans seemed more like home folks than had the French; they were as war weary and glad to see Americans; they hoped for remote benefits from American good will and immediate benefits from American liberal spending. Their currency was becoming more and more worthless and the American soldier's pay was big money when converted into marks. The American himself was tired of war, keen to experience the sensations of a millionaire and to act like one, so he spent and he fraternized, he enjoyed wines and frauleins at ridiculously low figures, and his venereal disease rate surpassed that of the armies in the AEF or at home.[19]

Many ordinary soldiers shared the opinion of Private Frederick Wechmeyer, whose 89th Division was part of the AF in G: 'I said we was fighting on the wrong side.'[20]

*

Psychologically, many doughboys found it well-nigh impossible to adapt to civilian life once they were finally home. In December 1932 Private Yensen recalled the difficulties he and his brother Walt had experienced when they returned to America. Yensen's girlfriend Eva 'finally gave up on me and married her former boy friend'. The war had severely damaged both brothers:

It was a long hard job for Walt and me to adjust to civilian life. We were both partially deaf from exploding shells. My throat was damaged by gas, and Walt had a breaking out on his face from cootie bites. We had traveled so much that we had the wanderlust. Every time we heard a train whistle, we wanted to get on it and go somewhere. Every horizon beckoned. No matter where we were, we wished we were somewhere else.

However, our worst handicap was a callous indifference to everything and everybody.[21]

Yensen estimated it took him thirteen years to normalize 'somewhat'. Some never normalized. For many, this was the most significant episode in their life and nothing could ever again match its power, horror and fascination. The inevitable deflation set in very fast; most non-regulars could not wait to get out of the army, an institution whose petty rules and minor tyrannies were exposed to the full during the war. For such as Samuel Devan, the army jolted his confidence in human decency. He was particularly aggrieved at seeing various officers of his regiment 'busted' for no good reason. One major was relieved of command for performing a piece of heroism 'of the kind for which the hero never gets any decoration'.

Last week, while hostilities were still going on, he was ordered to move his battalion to a new and very advanced position. The new position was known to be very dangerous not only by theory because it was defiladed in two directions by enemy positions but in fact also, because the preceding outfit there had been shot up & forced to move, after many casualties. [He] protested & pointed out a new position, equal or better from an artillery point of view. He was still ordered to move as before. Knowing the penalty, he declined to obey the order, refusing to sacrifice his men's lives needlessly. He won his point; for the orders were changed & the position of his choosing adopted; but he has been relieved of command & disgraced for disobeying orders.[22]

Despite his best efforts to enhance his professional career, Brigadier-General Hagood fairly soon found himself back in command of the cantonment of Camp Eustis, Virginia, in a dull routine job, supervising the welfare and needs of four regiments:

The situation at Eustis was not good! The morale was low and the soldiers had been threatening the Secretary of War by anonymous letters. The general next above me – at Fortress Monroe – warned me of this and said that I might expect trouble.[23]

One of the most irksome things for the returned troops was the army's unsophisticated efforts to cheer them up:

On movie nights, one of the uplifters of the camp, a jovial song leader, would appear before the screen wreathed in smiles, and after making a survey of the audience, would open up with:

'Come on boys!! Let's make a night of it . . . You did not do so good last time . . . But this is going to be a date to remember.'

Raising his hands above his head with a baton poised between his thumb and forefinger, he gives the nod to the pianist, holds the boys in suspense for a moment, and then bursts forth:

'OVER THERE!! . . . OVER TH-E---R--e-e-e-.' (Stops music).

'Now, Now, Now! this won't do! . . . Open up! . . . Open up! . . . EVERY-BODY . . . What's the matter with you sergeant. Why are you looking so sad.'

The sergeant does not reply but he is looking sad because he has just had a letter from his wife telling him that someone else has gotten his job, or that the war is over and if he does not come home very soon the Johnson grass will destroy his crop.

I listened to this fellow a couple of times and then I fired him, saving the government two hundred dollars a month and greatly increasing the attendance at the show.[24]

One of the last soldiers in the AEF to leave Europe was Major Edward MacMorland who, after being withdrawn from Murmansk and hoping to be sent back to the United States, found himself escorting Major-General Cheney on yet another expedition, this time as executive officer for the American Section of the Inter-Allied Mission, based in Tilsit, to oust the Germans from Latvia and Lithuania. He and General Cheney left Berlin on 11 November 1919 but by the end of the month they were kicking their heels in Tilsit,

waiting patiently for the Germans to do something. They are displaying their bad faith and rouse our anger almost every day over one thing or another. We have pulled the Baltic countries off their backs and given them an opportunity to depart gracefully, but what they need is the utter defeat which the Letts are unable to administer. It's a devious path when you deal with the Boche![25]

What MacMorland and other American officers in various inter-Allied missions across the devastated central and east European nations discovered was that, as Pershing had warned, the Allies had merely scotched the snake, not killed it. MacMorland found marauding bands of drunken and aggressive German soldiers right across the Baltic countries, causing mayhem and terrorizing the local populations, while no one had either the will or the muscle to prevent them from doing whatever they wanted. The Germans had until 13 December 1919 to comply with an order to remove an estimated 30,000 troops from the Baltic provinces. MacMorland wrote to his wife:

Our greatest fear is the so-called 'Iron Division', an old Prussian guard Division with imperialistic tendencies. It is scheduled to begin its movement through Tilsit today and there is no predicting what may happen when they enter Germany. The German authorities fear this unit and will doubtless scatter it as soon as possible [. . .] I am thoroughly weary of Europe, after my sojourn of a month in Germany. Barring none, the Germans are the worst liars I have encountered. Their spoken and written words in relating to us are uniformly false. We laugh over the comedy of deception they are practising. They are coming out of the Baltic States now, 9,000 having passed, but when 15,000 more are gone we shall be satisfied. They have lived up to their old reputation for frightfulness – have very effectually burned, destroyed and murdered in their retreat. It makes our blood boil, but we are in their midst and, for safety's sake, must even endure insults. If we had a few thousand troops behind us we could club them into submission.[26]

By 17 January 1920 MacMorland was back in Paris, headed for home. All the AF in G had gone, save a few who, like himself, had been sent with particular missions. On 5 February 1920, twenty-one months after sailing for France, he boarded the forty-year-old USAT *Buford*, which took eighteen days to cross the Atlantic. MacMorland's discovery that post-war Europe was a viper's nest of sporadic armed banditry pushed him and other AEF officers into wishing they could turn their backs on the continent as fast as possible.

One remarkably frank account of how impossible it was to take on the role of Europe's post war policeman was written by Brigadier-General Harry H. Bandholtz, appointed the US representative on the Inter-Allied Mission to Hungary, stationed in Budapest, between August 1919 and February 1920. His experience left him utterly disenchanted with the notion that America should have a policing role in Europe – rather ironic, as he had spent most of his career as a policeman. Bandholtz had been in France as a brigadier-general with the SOS, where he was director-general of transport and the military police; he had formerly been a chief constable in the Philippines. Bandholtz's diary,[27] written during his stint in Budapest, moves rapidly from diplomatic niceties to an outright denunciation of almost everyone he has the misfortune to have to deal with – French, British, Italians, Hungarians and Romanians – above all, the Romanians. At sixty-one, Bandholtz was far too long in the tooth to tolerate the kind of duplicity he had to endure in Budapest. The catalogue of ghastliness which greeted him and his colleagues he found almost impossible to describe. He wrote on 19 August:

It is not possible to describe conditions in the city or country occupied by an enemy but it is an object lesson to us Americans that we should promptly take every possible measure to avoid any such catastrophe overtaking our own country. Universal training should be adopted without further parley.

The Romanians had taken advantage of the collapse of Hungary's drift into a post-war Bolshevik republic to invade and to loot everything of value, including all motor vehicles, railway engines and rolling stock, all armaments, munitions, farm implements, cattle, horses, clothing, sugar, salt, coal, foodstuffs – anything that was not nailed to the floor.

The Romanians were constantly lectured by the Inter-Allied Mission in Budapest that this would not be tolerated and was not permitted by the Supreme War Council of the Peace Conference, but the Romanians lied, wheedled, intimidated and – if necessary – killed to prevent the Hungarians from holding on to any property. They took 4,000 telephones from private houses, looted all the equipment from the Hungarian ministry of posts and telegraphs, stole the final few Hungarian breeding stallions, resorted to armed robbery of banks, and by 20 September 1919 had reduced Budapest to just five days' food supply. Bandholtz travelled to Bucharest on 6 September to register official protests with King Ferdinand of Romania, who spoke English 'fairly well but with a peculiar hissing accent probably due to false teeth'. On 8 September at lunch with the king and his queen – the rather vacuous British princess Marie, a granddaughter of Queen Victoria – Bandholtz listened to the monarchs' views:

During the conversation the Queen said that she felt keenly that Roumania had fought as an ally and was now being treated as an enemy; that all Roumania had been pillaged by the Huns, and why shouldn't they now retaliate and steal from Hungary, saying, 'You may call it stealing if you want to, or by any other name, but I feel we are entitled to do as we want to.' The King butted into the conversation and said that anyway the Roumanians had taken no food stuffs. As it is bad form to call a King a liar, I merely informed His Majesty that he was badly mistaken, and that I could give him exact facts regarding thousands of carloads of food stuffs that had been taken out of Budapest alone.

Bandholtz noticed that the French favoured the Romanian side, and various British liaison officers fell for the flirtatious charms of Queen Marie. With friends like this, Bandholtz felt the entire post-war settlement arrangements were one great fraud.

Not that the Hungarians under the proto-fascist Admiral Horthy (who took over following the eventual departure of the Romanians) were much better. On 15 September Bandholtz wrote, 'we have also heard reports about the Hungarians starting pogroms in several places'; four days later, 'reports from Western Hungary indicate all kinds of atrocities on the part of the Hungarians, who are butchering and torturing the Jews. These people in Eastern and Central Europe make Anninias [*sic*] look like George Washington.'

On 13 October 1919 representatives of the British Food Commission and the International Red Cross briefed him on the conditions in twelve Romanian-occupied Hungarian towns. They found

an oppression so great as to make life unbearable. Murder is common, youths and women flogged, people imprisoned without trial, arrested without reason, theft of personal property under the name of requisition [. . .] Last Friday Roumanians advanced suddenly to Boros-Sebes and two hundred fifty Hungarian soldiers were taken prisoners. These were killed in the most barbarous manner; stripped naked and stabbed with bayonets in a way to prolong life as long as possible.

Bandholtz protested long and often to General Marderescu, the Romanian senior officer in Budapest, to no avail. On 18 October the Supreme Council issued a final ultimatum to the Romanians, but in Bandholtz's opinion, 'if a duck should drop into the Mediterranean Sea it would have about as much effect on the tide in the Gulf of Mexico as would any such ultimatum on our Roumanian friends'. Three weeks later he reached almost the lowest point of despair: 'Despite their oft repeated and solemn promises, the Roumanians continue to steal property right and left. It is simply impossible to conceive such a national depravity as these miserable Latins of South East Europe are displaying.' The Romanians finally marched out of Budapest on 14 November 1919, once there was nothing left worth looting, and having achieved their main objective: the doubling, almost, of Romania's land area, largely at the expense of Hungary.

Just before General Marderescu left Budapest, General Gorton [the British member of the Inter-Allied Mission] and I went to see him and he promised faithfully to leave behind fifty-three motor trucks for the distribution of food. [By now there was severe malnutrition among the Hungarian populace.] When our men went to get the trucks, instead of fifty-three they found only thirty-six, not one of which was serviceable and most of which were lacking wheels, motors, or something equally important, and then when Marderescu left he even took these along.

On 29 November Bandholtz wrote:

I recently received a clipping from a Roumanian newspaper which with big headlines read as follows:

'A REPLY FROM GENERAL MARDERESCU.

'The conduct of the Roumanians in regard to the Hungarians and the Allies is best characterized by the reply of General Marderescu as given to the complaint of the Interallied Military Mission against requisitions: "Gentlemen, you have four telephones but I have 80,000 bayonets."'

Of course the old skunk never said any such thing, or we would have choked him on the spot. But the worst of it is that if he had said it, it would have been the truth, which further proves that he never said it.

Bandholtz gratefully, delightedly, departed from Budapest on 9 February 1920, by which time he was thoroughly disenchanted not merely with east- and central-European treachery, but the whole corrupt game of diplomacy being enacted at Versailles. His judgement was that the Allies had betrayed Hungary, and thus betrayed the cause of a just and lasting peace settlement:

Turning over portions of Hungary with its civilized and refined population will be just as if we turned over Texas and California to the Mexicans. The great Powers of the Allies should hang their heads in shame for what they allowed to take place in Hungary after an armistice. It would be just as sensible to insist also that Switzerland, on account of her mixed French, German and Italian population, be subdivided into three states, as to insist upon illogical ethnographic subdivision of the territory and people of Old Hungary. It is simply another case of the application of long-range theory as against actual conditions. The Hungarians certainly have many defects, at least from the American point of view, but they are so far superior to any of their neighbours that it is a crime against civilization to continue with the proposed dismemberment of this country.

At the end of the twentieth century, Bandholtz's words reverberate; he could have been writing about the Balkans in the 1990s.

The end of the war brought little but frustration for Pershing. As a reward for his service in France he was accorded the rank and title of General of the Armies, but this brought him neither real authority nor actual duties. The actual command of the US army passed to the Secretary of War. Pershing was given an office in Washington DC, with a secretary and the rump of his General Staff. He settled down with the assistance of his aide, George Marshall, to write his account of the AEF. He had tired of his relationship with Nita Patton and in 1919 wrote to her saying they ought not to announce their engagement until his feelings returned; callously enough, he did not send her a ticket to the victory gala held in Paris on 3 July 1919, where he was the guest of honour. Nita then returned the diamond ring he had given her in 1917.[28]

Pershing was bored; so bored that he decided to make a national inspection of the condition of the US army in 1919–20. One of the posts he visited was Camp Eustis, under the command of General Hagood, who 'did not expect to find the General in good humor', as the army was in a pitiful state. The camps were poorly equipped and shoddily constructed; morale was at rock-bottom. Hagood decided to try to cheer Pershing up by diverging from the stifling formality dictated by correct protocol for the visitation of a general, including the usually unbearably dull food:

The General finds his rank or the coat of arms of the United States done in cut flowers as a centerpiece for the table. He finds a little flag or perhaps a toy cannon at his place with his name on it. Canton china, with birds of Paradise, or big-eyed fish, is in evidence. Lamb chops and peas are as inevitable as reveille and retreat. At the time of which I speak, the latest fad in the culinary art was candied sweet potatoes with marshmallows. Word goes around that the General likes carrots, so the General not only has to have carrots, but the General has to eat carrots.

It was in the days of strict prohibition so that generals never got anything to drink, even though for ordinary occasions the host was accustomed to having a bottle shipped in by way of the kitchen.

Mrs Hagood decided to change all this. She cut out all rank and made up the luncheon party by inviting only the best-looking and most attractive young women that she could find on the post or elsewhere, politely requesting the husbands to stay at home, as Pershing's staff would furnish enough of the male sex.

On the table she had a very fine young turkey at one end and a Virginia ham at the other. There was rice and gravy, brandied peaches, little simlin squashes out of the garden, Jerusalem artichokes cooked in cream, palmetto cabbage pickle sent up from South Carolina [. . .]

There had been some very fine cider at the Post Exchange which had gone bad, that is it had fermented and would pop and foam when you started the cork. This was manifestly not a thing to be left in the hands of the soldiers, so I had several cases sent to my quarters. We had it put on ice and when the Pershing party arrived it was so cold that it frosted the glasses.

There was not room at the table for everyone to be seated, so some of the staff had to stand. But General Pershing had a place at the head, flanked by two of our best looking young women who were changed from time to time to give him variety [. . .]

It was a Pershing party for Pershing. No Oriental potentate could have received more attention or had more freedom. The cider business was a great success. Pershing thought it looked like champagne, tasted like champagne, was champagne.[29]

Hagood owed his wife much. On 30 June 1920, soon after Pershing visited Camp Eustis, more than a thousand officers, including Hagood, were booted back down to their pre-war ranks; in Hagood's case, lieutenant-colonel. But three days later Hagood was made a brigadier-general again, leap-frogging several hundred more senior officers, including some who had been major-generals during the war. He owed it largely, he felt, to his post-war work at Camp Eustis, not least the memorable lunch for the General of the Armies.

There was frustration too for black American doughboys. With the end of the war the US army had no intention of changing its attitude to black soldiers; they were to remain outsiders. In 1925 Major-General Hanson Ely, a war hero who was now commandant of the Army War College in Washington, commissioned and distributed a study entitled 'Employment of Negro Man Power in War'.[30] Prepared by a committee of the War College (comprising Colonel Bishop, Major Drain and Major Somervell), this was a fine example of the depth of prejudice which remained rooted in the US army. It is a piece of spurious research which prefers assertion to evidence. Among other things it states:

The negro does not perform his share of civil duties in time of peace in proportion to his population. He has no leaders in industrial or commercial life. He takes no part in government. Compared to the white man he is admittedly of inferior mentality. He is inherently weak in character [. . .]

The life of the nation is at stake in war. Neither the white man nor the negro should be given tasks they are not qualified to perform [. . .]

In past wars the negro has made a fair laborer, but an inferior technician. As a fighter he has been inferior to the white man even when led by white officers.

The negro officer was a failure as a combat officer in the World War

And the bottom line?

Negro soldiers as individuals should not be assigned to white units.

Racism against black Americans was institutionalized in the AEF, where segregation was total. But snobbish jingoism was also widely prevalent among the British leadership of the day, and many French senior officers and politicians expressed an insupportable arrogance towards not only the Americans but all their partners in the struggle to defeat Germany. Of course the doughboys themselves were also possessed of an arrogant swagger, a sense of coming to finish off what was clearly beyond their British and French comrades, a self-confident certainty that they would not commit the same mistakes. But they were, perhaps, entitled to a degree of self-confidence. They were on the whole fresh, strapping, well-fed and well-exercised young men, unaccustomed to taking orders from anyone, inordinately proud of being American, yet also rather in awe of everything European. Their morale usually touched the heavens, while that of their British and French comrades was often to be found cowering in a muddy trench. The doughboys' sheer enthusiasm, their relish for a fight, their earnestly expressed yet incorrigibly naive wish to hunt Germans derived from a deceptively casual readiness to fight and die – deceptive because it stemmed from a fierce sense of honour and a widespread determination not to appear cowardly. For most doughboys a coward was often synonymous with someone who ducked at the approach of a shell, which by late 1917 was an automatic and sensible response among British and French troops. The doughboys were not in the war long enough to develop the calloused cynicism of their British and French comrades.

Was the AEF responsible for bringing Germany to its knees? In purely battlefield terms its presence was necessary but not sufficient. It is in any case the wrong question. The important question, in assessing the part the United States played in the First World War, has a much broader focus: could the Allies have defeated Germany without the financial, economic, military, and psychological backing of the United States? Unquestionably not. Yet the AEF has been ignored,[31] and overlooked, even by American historians.

Debate over the precise turning-point of the war is endless. It is futile to enter into such a debate, which can only lead to an ultimately sterile regress. But America's true value to the Allied war effort should be understood as nothing less than vital. The process of transforming America's paltry regular army into the strongest army on the European continent within twenty months was nothing less than remarkable. By dint of careful planning, sheer determination and hard work, spiced with a willing suspension of some democratic principles and a lot of aggression, this small combat force was expanded until, by 11 November 1918, there were a total of 1,962,767 US troops in France, including 1,253,330 combatants.[32] Of the 709,437 non-combatants, by far the biggest group – 152,318 – comprised medical staff. Service of Supply troops – who laboured behind the front lines to keep the combat troops supplied and transported – amounted to 20 to 35 per cent of total AEF strength in different periods of the war. In the AEF's greatest battlefield effort – the Meuse–Argonne offensive of October–November 1918 – some 1.2 million AEF troops were engaged, though probably not more than 400,000 were in action at any one time. All these were backed up by 9 million civilian workers in France and the United States, engaged in war duties.

The war had tangible effects on American society. It shortened women's skirts, in a drive to save wool. It hastened the arrival of Prohibition, thus inadvertently incubating the careers of Al Capone and many other gangsters. The banning of alcohol was originally introduced as a wartime scheme to save allegedly scarce resources, although in reality it had been on the agenda of conservative political forces for years. The war spread jazz across America, and ultimately the world, by forcing this new form of music out from its ghetto in the red-light district of St Louis, which was closed down as part of an effort to prevent the vast influx of new army recruits from having their morals tainted and their bodies infected. It galvanized the soluble coffee industry; the presence of the AEF in France rocketed the demand for soluble coffee to thirty times more than pre-war production figures.[33] The war did its bit to help Americans become addicted to smoking: the monthly ration shipped to France for the AEF by the end of the war was 20 million cigars and 425 million cigarettes, all available at cost to the troops – not a cent of tax or profit was added. It brought ordinary Americans into first-hand contact – and in many cases actual combat – with Russian Bolsheviks thirty years before the outbreak of the Cold War, as US soldiers fraternized, fought and froze in Siberia. Most of all, the war cost America an enormous amount of money – more than $1,000,000 an hour over the twenty-five months from April 1917 to April 1919, enough to pay the entire costs of the US government from 1791 up to the outbreak of the First World War.[34]

The United States certainly learned one lesson: that efforts to help Europe sort out its problems carry big risks. Not only do you get precious little thanks; you never quite manage to extricate yourself from the mess. But despite the inevitable sense of deflation after the Armistice, most doughboys felt proud of what they had achieved, or helped the British and French to achieve, even though Uncle Sam said thanks and goodbye with a measly $60 gratuity, just two months' pay. Private Robert Glover recalled his service with pride:

In World War One the moral [*sic*] did not come down from the top. It came up from the bottom. The fighting men were of one mind. They came to fight a war. They meant to finish it. They were not going back until they had brought the enemy to defeat. Their General Pershing shared their sentiments and they accomplished what they set out to do. I feel honored to have been one of them.[35]

Private First Class Philip Foster (of the 356th Infantry, 89th Division) had joined up to 'save America from Germans bent on world domination' and by the end felt, with considerable justice, that 'if it hadn't been for us, they'd have whipped Europe'.[36] For American soldiers and civilians it had generally been a popular war. For the vast majority of the doughboys it would prove in many respects the most important experience of their lives. Yet in the 1920s, as economic decline set in, many Americans rejected what their country did in the Great War. A feeling grew that the United States had been duped into wasting money and men on behalf of a squabbling and thankless Europe.

John Maynard Keynes said that 'without the assistance of the United States the Allies could never have won the War'.[37] That word 'assistance' must be understood in a far broader fashion than simply that which was done on the field of battle. A more partisan view, but from one who was nevertheless a highly objective analyst of the progress of the war, comes from Major-General Hugh Drum, who went to France with Pershing's General Staff a mere major, but rose to become Pershing's chief-of-staff and a brigadier-general. Drum intended to write his own memoir of the war, but never completed it; the following was to be part of his introduction:

We have read of the strategical genius of Foch, the tactical superiority of Pétain, the dogged perseverance of Haig and King Albert, and the patriotic firmness of our own Commander-in-chief. And we have been told of the élan of the French infantry, and of the tenacity of the British, and of the intrepidity of our own troops, rushing to battle in the words of a French army commander 'as to a fire'. But nowhere do we find proper recognition given to Voltaire's precept that God is on the side of the heaviest battalions. Let the American people consider and reflect upon the facts that follow. Let them weigh these facts against the misinformation that has shrouded the glories of our armies since 1918; and let them be eternally proud of the fact that it was the preponderance of American manpower – and nothing else, that brought Germany to her knees on November 11, 1918.[38]

Appendix 1
First Arrivals in France

According to Pershing, 190 officers and other ranks sailed with him on the *Baltic* to France. They included:

Regular army officers	40
Marine Corps officers	2
Reserve officers on active service	7
Enlisted men	67
Field clerks	36
Civilian clerks	20
Civilian interpreters	5
Correspondents	3
Others	10
Total	190

Personal Staff (aides-de-camp)

Captain James L. Collins, later Colonel, Field Artillery.
Captain Nelson E. Margetts, later Colonel, Field Artillery.
1st Lieutenant Martin C. Shallenberger, later Colonel, General Staff.

Original members of the General Staff

Captain Arthur L. Conger, later Colonel, General Staff, and regimental commander.
Major Fox Conner, Assistant Inspector General (attached), later Brigadier-General and chief of Operations, AEF.
Captain Hugh A. Drum, later Brigadier-General and chief-of-staff, First Army.
Major James G. Harbord, later Major-General and chief-of-staff.
Major Dennis E. Nolan, later Brigadier-General and chief of Intelligence, AEF.
Major John McAndrew Palmer, later Colonel, Infantry.

Administrative and Supply Staff

Colonel Benjamin Alvord, later Brigadier-General and Adjutant General, AEF (invalided home).

Lieutenant-Colonel Walter A. Bethel, later Brigadier and Judge Advocate General, AEF.

Colonel Alfred E. Bradley, MC, later Brigadier-General and Chief Surgeon, AEF (joined in London; invalided home).

Colonel Andre W. Brewster, later Major-General and Inspector General, AEF.

Major Townsend F. Dodd, later Colonel and Chief of Air Service, AEF, until 3 September 1917.

Lieutenant-Colonel Merritte W. Ireland, MC, later Brigadier-General and Chief Surgeon, relieving General Bradley.

Colonel Daniel E. McCarthy (invalided home).

Colonel Edgar Russell, Signal Corps, later Brigadier-General and Chief Signal Officer, AEF.

Colonel Harry Taylor, Corps of Engineers, later Brigadier-General and Chief of Engineers, AEF.

Lieutenant-Colonel Clarence C. Williams, later Brigadier-General and Chief of Ordnance, AEF.

Appendix 2
Merchant and Military Shipping

The US view as to the distinction between merchant and military ships is set out in the following memorandum from the Department of State.

Department of State
Washington, 19 September
1914

A. A merchant vessel of belligerent nationality may carry an armament and ammunition for the sole purpose of defense without acquiring the character of a ship of war.

B. The presence of an armament and ammunition on board a merchant vessel creates a presumption that the armament is for offensive purposes, but the owners or agents may overcome this presumption by evidence showing that the vessel carries armament solely for defense.

C. Evidence necessary to establish the fact that the armament is solely for defense and will not be used offensively, whether the armament be mounted or stowed below, must be presented in each case independently at an official investigation. The result of the investigation must show conclusively that the armament is not intended for, and will not be used in, offensive operations. Indications that the armament will not be used offensively are:

1. That the caliber of the guns carried does not exceed six inches.

2. That the guns and small arms carried are few in number.

3. That no guns are mounted on the forward part of the vessel.

4. That the quantity of ammunition carried is small.

5. That the vessel is manned by its usual crew, and the officers are the same as those on board before war was declared.

6. That the vessel intends to and actually does clear for a port lying in its usual trade route, or a port indicating its purpose to continue in the same trade in which it was engaged before war was declared.

7. That the vessel takes on board fuel and supplies sufficient only to carry it to its port of destination, or the same quantity substantially which it has been accustomed to take for a voyage before war was declared.

8. That the cargo of the vessel consists of articles of commerce unsuited for the use of a ship of war in operations against an enemy.

9. That the vessel carries passengers who are as a whole unfitted to enter the military or naval service of the belligerent whose flag the vessel flies, or of any of its allies, and particularly if the passenger list includes women and children.

10. That the speed of the ship is slow.

D. Port authorities, on the arrival in a port of the United States of an armed vessel of belligerent nationality, claiming to be a merchant vessel, should immediately investigate and report to Washington on the foregoing indications as to the intended use of the armament, in order that it may be determined whether the evidence is sufficient to remove the presumption that the vessel is, and should be treated as, a ship of war. Clearance will not be granted until authorized from Washington, and the master will be so informed upon arrival.

E. The conversion of a merchant vessel into a ship of war is a question of fact which is to be established by direct or circumstantial evidence of intention to use the vessel as a ship of war.

Appendix 3
The Zimmerman Telegram

Berlin, January 19, 1917

On the first of February we intend to begin submarine warfare unrestricted. In spite of this, it is our intention to endeavor to keep neutral the United States of America. If this attempt is not successful, we propose an alliance on the following basis with Mexico: That we shall make war together and together make peace. We shall give general financial support, and it is understood that Mexico is to reconquer the lost territory in New Mexico, Texas, and Arizona. The details are left to you for settlement. You are instructed to inform the President of Mexico of the above in the greatest confidence as soon as it is certain that there will be an outbreak of war with the United States and suggest that the President of Mexico, on his own initiative, should communicate with Japan suggesting adherence at once to this plan; at the same time, offer to mediate between Germany and Japan. Please call to the attention of the President of Mexico that the employment of ruthless submarine warfare now promises to compel England to make peace in a few months.

Zimmerman (Secretary of State)

Appendix 4
President Woodrow Wilson's Fourteen Points

Washington, 8 January 1918

We entered this war because violations of right had occurred which touched us to the quick and made the life of our own people impossible unless they were corrected and the world secure once for all against their recurrence. What we demand in this war, therefore, is nothing peculiar to ourselves. It is that the world be made fit and safe to live in; and particularly that it be made safe for every peace-loving nation which, like our own, wishes to live its own life, determine its own institutions, be assured of justice and fair dealing by the other peoples of the world as against force and selfish aggression. All the peoples of the world are in effect partners in this interest, and for our own part we see very clearly that unless justice be done to others it will not be done to us. The programme of the world's peace, therefore, is our programme; and that programme, the only possible programme, as we see it, is this:

I. Open covenants of peace, openly arrived at, after which there shall be no private international understandings of any kind but diplomacy shall proceed always frankly and in the public view.

II. Absolute freedom of navigation upon the seas, outside territorial waters, alike in peace and in war, except as the seas may be closed in whole or in part by international action for the enforcement of international covenants.

III. The removal, so far as possible, of all economic barriers and the establishment of an equality of trade conditions among all the nations consenting to the peace and associating themselves for its maintenance.

IV. Adequate guarantees given and taken that national armaments will be reduced to the lowest point consistent with domestic safety.

V. A free, open-minded, and absolutely impartial adjustment of all colonial claims, based upon a strict observance of the principle that in determining all such questions of sovereignty the interests of the populations concerned must have equal weight with the equitable claims of the government whose title is to be determined.

VI. The evacuation of all Russian territory and such a settlement of all questions affecting Russia as will secure the best and freest cooperation of the other nations of the world in obtaining for her an unhampered and unembarrassed opportunity for the independent determination of her own political development and national policy and assure her of a sincere welcome into the society of free nations under institutions of her own choosing; and, more than a welcome, assistance also of every kind that she may need and may herself desire. The treatment accorded Russia by her sister nations in the months to come will be the acid test of their good will, of their comprehension of her needs as distinguished from their own interests, and of their intelligent and unselfish sympathy.

VII. Belgium, the whole world will agree, must be evacuated and restored, without any attempt to limit the sovereignty which she enjoys in common with all other free nations. No other single act will serve to restore confidence among the nations in the laws which they have themselves set and determined for the government of their relations with one another. Without this healing act the whole structure and validity of international law is forever impaired.

VIII. All French territory should be freed and the invaded portions restored, and the wrong done to France by Prussia in 1871 in the matter of Alsace-Lorraine, which has unsettled the peace of the world for nearly fifty years, should be righted, in order that peace may once more be made secure in the interest of all.

IX. A readjustment of the frontiers of Italy should be effected along clearly recognizable lines of nationality.

X. The peoples of Austria-Hungary, whose place among the nations we wish to see safeguarded and assured, should be accorded the freest opportunity of autonomous development.

XI. Rumania, Serbia, and Montenegro should be evacuated; occupied territories restored; Serbia accorded free and secure access to the sea; and the relations of the several Balkan states to one another determined by friendly counsel along historically established lines of allegiance and nationality; and international guarantees of the political and economic independence and territorial integrity of the several Balkan states should be entered into.

XII. The Turkish portion of the present Ottoman Empire should be assured a secure sovereignty, but the other nationalities which are now under Turkish rule should be assured an undoubted security of life and an absolutely unmolested opportunity of autonomous development, and the Dardanelles should be permanently opened as a free passage to the ships and commerce of all nations under international guarantees.

XIII. An independent Polish state should be erected which should include the territories inhabited by indisputably Polish populations, which should be assured a free and secure access to the sea, and whose political and economic independence and territorial integrity should be guaranteed by international covenant.

XIV. A general association of nations must be formed under specific covenants for the purpose of affording mutual guarantees of political independence and territorial integrity to great and small states alike. In regard to these essential rectifications of wrong and assertions of right we feel ourselves to be intimate partners of all the governments and peoples associated together against the Imperialists. We cannot be separated in interest or divided in purpose. We stand together until the end. For such arrangements and covenants we are willing to fight and to continue to fight until they are achieved; but only because we wish the right to prevail and desire a just and stable peace such as can be secured only by removing the chief provocations to war, which this programme does remove. We have no jealousy of German greatness, and there is nothing in this programme that impairs it. We grudge her no achievement or distinction of learning or of pacific enterprise such as have made her record very bright and very enviable. We do not wish to injure her or to block in any way her legitimate influence or power. We do not wish to fight her either with arms or with hostile arrangements of trade if she is willing to associate herself with us and the other peace-loving nations of the world in covenants of justice and law and fair dealing. We wish her only to accept a place of equality among the peoples of the world – the new world in which we now live – instead of a place of mastery.

Appendix 5
AEF Divisions in France, 1917–18

Divisions 1, 2, 3, 4, 5, and 6 = regular
Divisions 26, 29, 32, 35, 36, 37, and 42 = National Guard
Divisions 77, 79, 81, 88, 89, 91, and 92 = National Army

Division	*Date of Arrival of First and Last Units*
1st	26 June – 22 December 1917
2nd	20 September 1917 – 12 March 1918
3rd	21 December 1917 – 19 June 1918
4th	13 May – 8 June 1918
5th	2 March – 19 June 1918
6th	18 May – 26 July 1918
7th	11 August – 3 September 1918
8th*	10 November 1918 (HQ units only)
26th	20 September 1917 – 12 January 1918
27th	23 May–12 July 1918
28th	13–31 May 1918
29th	26 June – 22 July 1918
30th	23 May – 25 June 1918
31st* (replacement)	29 September – 9 November 1918
32nd	6 February – 26 March 1918
33rd	18 May – 27 June 1918
34th* (replacement)	29 September – 24 October 1918
35th	7 May – 8 June 1918
36th	30 July – 12 August
37th	22 June – 18 July 1918
38th* (replacement)	28 September – 25 October 1918
39th* (replacement)	18 August – 12 September 1918
40th*	17–31 August 1918
41st*	11 December 1917 – 6 February 1918
42nd	1 November – 8 December 1917
76th*	12 July – 8 August 1918

77th	12 April – 6 May 1918
78th	31 May – 12 June 1918
79th	15 July – 3 August 1918
80th	30 May – 18 June 1918
81st	11–25 August 1918
82nd	7 May – 10 July 1918
83rd*	15 June – 6 August 1918
84th*	9 September – 25 October 1918
85th*	3–11 August 1918
86th*	21 September – 9 October 1918
87th*	3–16 September 1918
88th	17 August – 9 September 1918
89th	16 June – 10 July 1918
90th	21 June – 26 July 1918
91st	17–26 July 1918
92nd	19 June – 12 July 1918
93rd*	4 March 1918

*Signifies did not serve in combat.

Of a total of 43 divisions, 29 saw combat.

(*Source*: US Army Center of Military History)

Bibliography

Note on Sources

This is not an exhaustive bibliography; it details only those materials which I consulted and found most useful. A complete bibliography of the topic would require a volume bigger than this book.

Paramount among archive sources for my purpose (which was to use, as far as possible, individual stories and accounts) were papers at the US Army Military History Institute (AMHI) at Carlisle Barracks, Pennsylvania. The AMHI has one of the world's largest collection of memoirs, letters, diaries and associated papers of doughboys who served in the Great War. The core of this collection is more than 7,000 individual responses to a survey called the Army Service Experiences Questionnaire (ASEQ) conducted in the 1970s and 1980s among surviving doughboys. The personal testaments used in this book have all been taken from this archive, which has only recently started to come to wider notice. Many of those who answered the ASEQ also submitted diaries, letters and memoirs. For simplicity's sake I have only referred in the Notes to the name of the soldier who is quoted, and where appropriate appended the abbreviation ASEQ. Where no ASEQ is specified but simply 'Carlisle', this indicates that the material has been taken from documents that are part of the AMHI but are not from the ASEQ.

The principle of selection for quotation was to focus on those divisions which saw most action, or which were involved in particularly memorable incidents; this was then refined to focus on individuals who seemed to me to have a good story to tell, or who told a representative story well.

Primary Sources

UNPUBLISHED MATERIAL

The following unpublished collections at the AMHI were particularly useful; but in emphasizing these it is not implied that the many others consulted were unimportant or irrelevant.

Adams, Griffith L.: Private, 105th Machine Gun Battalion, 27th Division.

Ahearn, Joseph P.: Private, 31st Infantry Regiment.

Aitken, Malcolm D.: Private, 5th Marines, 2nd Division.

Austin, Raymond: Major, 6th Field Artillery, 1st Division.

Bandholtz, Harry Hill: Brigadier-General, Services of Supply.

Bishop, Charles B.: Corporal, 102nd Field Artillery, 26th Division.

Bugbee, Frank: Colonel, commander of 31st Infantry.

Clark, John D.: 1st Lieutenant, 6th Field Artillery, 2nd Division.

Clark, Paul H.: Major, Pershing's liaison officer with the French GHQ. (Two unpublished volumes entitled 'Secret Letters to Pershing'.)

Conger, Arthur: Lieutenant-Colonel, G-2 GHQ, AEF.

Conner, Fox: Brigadier-General. (Lecture at the Army War College, 21 March 1933.)

Dattel, Clinton: Private, 1st Ammunition Train, 1st Division.

Devan, Samuel Arthur: 1st Lieutenant and chaplain, 58th Field Artillery Regiment.

Dexter, Benjamin D.: Private, 320th Machine Gun Battalion, 82nd Division.

Donnelly, Charles H.: Captain, 119th Field Artillery Regiment, 32nd Division.

Drum, Hugh: Major-General, General Staff, AEF.

Ettinger, Albert (with Churchill Ettinger): Private, 42nd Division ('Shamrocks Under the Rainbow – A Doughboy and His Buddies in World War I', unpublished manuscript.)

Fear, Frederick W.: industrial chemist, attached to the US army.

Forderhase, Rudolph: Sergeant, 356th Infantry Regiment, 89th Division.

Foster, Philip R.: Private First Class, 356th Infantry, 89th Division.

Francis, William A.: Private, 5th Marines, 2nd Division.

Garcia, Pablo: Private First Class, 356th Infantry, 89th Division.

Gillem, Alvin C.: Lieutenant-Colonel (later Major-General), 27th Infantry.

Glover, Robert Ellsworth: Private, 342nd Machine Gun Battalion, 89th Division.

Griscom, Lloyd; Colonel, Pershing's representative at the War Office in London.

Hagood, Johnson: Brigadier-General. (Manuscript of autobiography in Hagood family papers.)

Hochee, Nick: Private First Class, 27th Infantry Regiment.

Jordan, Francis N.: 2nd Lieutenant, 356th Infantry Regiment, 89th Division.

Korn, Otto H.: Private First Class, 27th Infantry Regiment.

Kyler, Donald Drake: Private, 16th Infantry, 1st Division.

Loughran, Joseph S.: Captain and chaplain, 31st Infantry.

MacMorland, Edward E.: Brigadier-General, 31st Infantry Regiment.

Mahan, Clarence L.: Corporal, 116th Infantry Regiment, 1st Division.

Mead, Forest R.: Musician Third Class, 356th Infantry Regiment, 89th Division.

Nash, Chester C.: Private First Class, Base Hospital No. 12.

Nolan, Denis: Colonel, General Staff, AEF.

Ogden, Hugh: Major (later Lieutenant-Colonel), Judge Advocate with the 42nd (Rainbow) Division.

Osborn, Douglas: 2nd Lieutenant, 31st Infantry Regiment.

Poorbaugh, Earl R.: Private, 26th Infantry Regiment, 1st Division.

Sargent, Daniel: 1st Lieutenant, 5th Field Artillery, 1st Division.

Slaughter, Homer: Colonel. (Speech given to the Army War College, Washington DC, 1934.)

Sterling, Francis M.: Private, 27th Infantry Regiment.

Swihart, Russell C.: Private, 31st Infantry Regiment.

Thompson, Alf R.: 2nd Lieutenant, 31st Infantry Regiment.

Wechmeyer, Frederick: Private First Class, 342nd Machine Gun Battalion, 89th Division.

Wilder, Fred Calvin: Corporal, 101st Infantry Regiment, 26th Division.

Winters, W. Fehr: Private First Class, Base Hospital No. 32, 89th Division.

Wright, Harry: Corporal, 104th Infantry Regiment, 26th Division.

Yarborough, Leroy: 2nd Lieutenant, 31st Infantry.

Yensen, Arthur: Private, 7th Engineers, 5th Division ('The War Log of an Underdog,' unpublished manuscript.)

PUBLISHED MATERIAL

American Armies and Battlefields in Europe, American Battle Monuments Commission, US Government Printing Office (1938).

The Americans in the Great War, illustrated Michelin Guides to the Battlefields, 1914–1918 (1919). vol. 1, the Second Battle of the Marne (Château-Thierry, Soissons, Fismes); vol. 2, the Battle of St-Mihiel (St-Mihiel, Pont-à-Mousson, Metz); vol. 3, Meuse–Argonne Battle (Montfaucon, Romagne, St Menehould).

Ashburn, Colonel P. M., *A History of the Medical Department of the United States Army* (1929).

Ayres, Colonel Leonard P., *The War With Germany: a Statistical Summary* (second edn., with data revised to 1 August 1919) US Government Printing Office (1919).

Baker, Newton D., *Why We Went to War* (New York, 1936).

Baruch, Bernard M., *American Industry in the War: a Report of the War Industries Board* (New York, 1941).

Bernstorff, Count Johann von, *My Three Years in America* (New York, 1920).

Bullard, Lieutenant-General Robert Lee, *Personalities and Reminiscences of the War* (New York, 1925).

Bullard, Robert Lee (in collaboration with Earl Reeves), *American Soldiers Also Fought* (New York, 1939).

The Causes of the German Collapse in 1918, sections of the officially authorized report of the Commission of the German Constituent Assembly and of the German Reichstag, 1919–1928, selected by Ralph Haswell Lutz (Stanford, Calif., 1934).

Chase, Joseph Cummings, *Soldiers All: Portraits and Sketches of the Men of the* AEF (New York, 1920).

The Chicago Daily News War Book for American Soldiers, Sailors and Airmen (no author) (1918).

Churchill, Winston S., *The World Crisis, 1911–1918*, 5 vols. (London, 1923–9).

Clark, John Maurice, *The Costs of the World War to the American People* (New Haven, Conn., 1931).

Clarkson, Grosvenor B., *Industrial America and the World War: The Strategy Behind the Lines, 1917–1919* (Boston, Mass., 1923).

Cobb, Irvin S., *The Red Glutton: impressions of war written at and near the front* (London, 1915).

Creel, George, *How We Advertised America* (New York, 1920).

Crowell, Benedict and Wilson, Robert Forrest, *How America Went to War*, 6 vols. (New Haven, Conn., 1931).

Dawes, Charles G., *A Journal of the Great War*, 2 vols. (Boston, Mass., 1921).

de Chambrun, Colonel, and Captain de Marenches, *The American Army in the European Conflict* (New York, 1919).

Enforced Peace, Proceedings of the first annual national assemblage of the Assemblage of the League to Enforce Peace, Washington, 26–27 May 1916, with a Preface by Charles Frederick Carter.

Fayle, C. Ernest, *History of the Great War Based on Official Documents: Seaborne Trade*, 3 vols. (London, 1924).

Fife, George Buchanan, *The Passing Legions; How the American Red Cross Met the American Army in Great Britain, the Gateway to France* (New York, 1920).

Friends of France, the Field Service of the American Ambulance Described by its Members, with an Introduction by A. Piatt Andrew (London, 1916).

Gough, General Sir Hubert, *The Fifth Army* (London, 1931).

Grattan, C. Hartley, *Why We Fought* (New York, 1929).

Graves, Major-General William S., *America's Siberian Adventure 1918–1920* (London and New York, 1931).

Hall, Norman, *Kitchener's Mob* (New York, 1916).

Harbord, Major-General James G., *The American Army in France, 1917–1919* (Boston, Mass., 1936).

Jerrold, Douglas, *The Lie About the War* (London, 1930).

Kendall, Harry, *A New York Actor on the Western Front* (Boston, Mass., 1932).

Lansing, Robert, *War Memoirs of Robert Lansing* (London, 1935).

Lauriat, Charles E., *The Lusitania's Last Voyage* (Boston, Mass., 1915). (The author was a survivor of the sinking.)

Liddell Hart, Basil, *The Real War* (London, 1930).

Liggett, Major-General Hunter, *The A.E.F. – Ten Years Ago in France* (New York, 1928).

Little, Arthur W., *From Harlem to the Rhine: The Story of New York's Colored Volunteers* (New York, 1936).

Lloyd George, David, *War Memoirs*, 2 vols. (London, 1936).

Majors, C. L., *World War Jokes* (Ramer, Tennessee, 1930).

March, Major-General Peyton C., *The Nation at War* (New York, 1932).

March, William, *Company K* (London, 1933).

Marshall, General George C., *Memoirs of My Services in the World War 1917–1918* (Boston, Mass., 1976).

McCain, George Nox, *War Rations for Pennsylvanians* (Philadelphia, 1920).

The Memoirs of Marshal Foch, trans. Colonel T. Bentley Mott (London, 1931).

Moore, Howard W., *Plowing My Own Furrow* (New York, 1985).

Mr Punch's History of the Great War (London, 1919).

The New War Encyclopaedia and Dictionary (London, n.d.).

The Occupation of the Rhineland 1918–29, with an Introduction by G. M. Bayliss (HMSO, 1987).

Palmer, Frederick, *John J. Pershing, General of the Armies* (New York, 1948).

Papers Relating to the Foreign Relations of the United States, Supplements for 1914, 1915, 1916, 1917 and 1918, US Government Printing Office (1929) (Foreign Relations Supplement).

Peel, C. S., *How We Lived Then: 1914–1918* (London, 1929).

Pershing, John J., *My Experiences in the World War*, 2 vols. (New York, 1931).

Salter, J. Arthur, *Allied Shipping Control* (Oxford, 1921). Salter was director of ship requisitioning and chairman of the Allied Maritime Transport Executive during the war.

Schauble, Peter Lambert, *The First Battalion* (Philadelphia, 1921).

Seeger, Alan, *Letters and Diary* (London, 1917).

—, *Poems* (London, 1917).

Seymour, Charles (ed.), *The Intimate Papers of Colonel House*, 4 vols. (London, 1926).

Seymour, James W. D. (ed.), *Memorial Volume of the American Field Service in France* (American Field Service, Boston, Mass., 1921).

Stallings, Lawrence, *The Doughboys* (New York, 1963).

Thomas, Captain Shipley, *The History of the AEF* (New York, 1920). Thomas was Intelligence Officer with the 16th Infantry, 1st Division, and fought at Cantigny and elsewhere.

Thomason, John W., *Fix Bayonets! With the US Marine Corps in France, 1917–1918* (New York, 1925).

The Times Illustrated History of the War 1914–1919, 21 vols. (London, 1920).

The Two Battles of the Marne, by Marshal Foch, Marshal Joffre, Marshal Ludendorff, and the ex-Crown Prince William of Germany (London, 1927).

Wharton, James B., *Squad* (London, 1929).

Wilgus, William J., *Transporting the AEF in Western Europe, 1917–1919* (New York, 1931).

Woodward, David R. (ed.), *The Military Correspondence of Field-Marshal Sir William Robertson* (Army Records Society, 1989).

Wooldridge, Jesse W., *The Giants of the Marne: A Story of McAlexander and His Regiment* (Salt Lake City, 1923).

Secondary sources

PUBLISHED MATERIAL

Adams, R. J. Q. (ed.), *The Great War 1914–1918: Essays on the Military, Political and Social History of the First World War* (Texas University Press, 1990).

Ambrose, Stephen, *Duty, Honor, Country* (Baltimore, Md., 1966).

Asprey, Robert, *At Belleau Wood* (New York, 1965).

Bailey, Thomas A., *The Policy of the United States Towards Neutrals* (Baltimore, Md., 1942).

Barbeau, Arthur E., and Henri, Florette C., *The Unknown Soldiers: African-American Troops in World War I* (New York, 1996).

Binneveld, Hans, *From Shellshock to Combat Stress* (Amsterdam, 1997).

Birnbaum, Karl E., *Peace Moves and U-Boat Warfare* (Stockholm, 1958).

British Vessels Lost At Sea (London, 1977). A reprint of the official publications *Navy Losses* and *Merchant Shipping (Losses)* first published by HMSO in August 1919.

Burk, Kathleen, *Britain, America and the Sinews of War, 1914–1918* (London, 1984).

Cecil, Hugh, and Liddle, Peter H. (eds.), *Facing Armageddon* (London, 1996).

Cottman, Edward M., *The War To End All Wars* (Oxford, 1968).

Cornebise, Alfred E., *The 'Stars and Stripes'. Doughboy Journalism in World War I* (New York, 1984)

Cuff, Robert D., *The War Industries Board* (Baltimore, Md., 1963).

Deighton, Len, *Blitzkrieg* (London, 1996).

D'Este, Carlo, *A Genius For War – A Life of George Patton* (New York, 1996).

Ellis, John, *The Social History of the Machine Gun* (London, 1993).

Evans, Martin Marix, *Retreat, Hell! We Just Got Here* (London, 1998).

Ferro, Marc, *The Great War 1914–1918* (London, 1995).

Fiebig-von Hase, Ragnhild, and Lehmkuhl, Ursula, *Enemy Images in American History* (Oxford, 1997).

Fowler, W. B., *British–American Relations, 1917–1918* (Princeton, NJ, 1969).

Frothingham, T. G., *The American Reinforcement in the World War* (London, 1927).

Gibbons, Edward, *Your Headline Hunter* (New York, 1953).

Gregory, Martin, *German Strategy and Military Assessments of the American Expeditionary Force, 1917–1918*, from *War In History*, 1 (1994).

Grieves, Keith, *The Politics of Manpower, 1914–18* (Manchester, 1988).

Griffith, Paddy, *Battle Tactics of the Western Front* (New Haven, Conn., 1994).

Hagedorn, Hermann, *Leonard Wood: A Biography* (New York, 1931).

Harries, M. and S., *The Last Days of Innocence* (New York, 1997).

Haws, Duncan, *Merchant Fleets: Anchor Line* (London, 1986).

Haythornthwaite, Philip J., *The World War One Source Book* (London, 1994).

Hobart, F. W. A., *Pictorial History of the Machine Gun* (London, 1971).

Huidekoper, Frederic Louis, *The Military Unpreparedness of the United States* (New York, 1915).

Jeze, Gaston, and Truchy, Henri, *The War Finance of France* (New Haven, Conn., 1927).

Kazin, Alfred, *On Native Grounds* (New York, 1942).

Kennedy, David M., *Over Here: The First World War and American Society* (New York, 1980).

Kludas, Arnold, *Great Passenger Ships of the World*, vol. 2, *1913–1923* (London, 1976).

Knightley, Philip, *The First Casualty* (London, 1982).

Kraft, Barbara, *The Peace Ship* (London, 1978).

Laffin, John, *British Butchers and Bunglers of World War One* (Stroud, Glos., 1988).

Link, Arthur S., *Woodrow Wilson: The Struggle For Neutrality 1914–1915* (Princeton, NJ, 1960).

—, *Woodrow Wilson: Confusions and Crises, 1915–1916* (Princeton, NJ, 1964).

—, *Woodrow Wilson: Revolution, War, and Peace* (Arlington Heights, Ill., 1979).

Lochner, L. P., *America's Don Quixote: Henry Ford's Attempt to Save Europe*, (London, 1924).

May, Ernest R., *The World War and American Isolation 1914–1917* (Cambridge, Mass., 1966).

McCullough, David, *Truman* (New York, 1992).

Meigs, Mark, *Optimism at Armageddon* (London, 1997).

Middlebrook, Martin, *The Kaiser's Battle* (London, 1978).

Millett, Allan R., and Williamson, Murray (eds.), *Military Effectiveness*, vol. 1, The First World War (Winchester, Mass., 1988).

Millis, Walter, *Road to War: America 1914–1917* (Boston, Mass., 1935).

Mitchell, Frank, *Tank Warfare* (Stevenage, Herts., 1987).

Nye, R. B., and Morpurgo, J. E., *A History of the United States*, vol. 2 (Harmondsworth, 1955).

Offer, Avner, *The First World War: an Agrarian Interpretation* (Oxford, 1989).

Paxson, Frederic L., *America at War 1917–1918* (Boston, Mass., 1939).

Peterson, H. C., and Fite, Gilbert C., *Opponents of War, 1917–1918* (Seattle, 1968).

Robb Ellis, Edward, *Echoes of Distant Thunder: Life in the United States 1914–1918* (New York, 1975).

Sanders, M. L., and Taylor, Philip M., *British Propaganda during the First World War, 1914–18* (London, 1982).

Schaffer, Ronald, *America in the Great War* (Oxford, 1991).

Shrader, Charles R., *Reference Guide to the United States' Military History 1865–1919* (New York, 1993).

Silverlight, John, *The Victors' Dilemma – Allied Intervention in the Russian Civil War 1917–1920* (New York, 1970).

Smithers, A. J., *Sir John Monash* (London, 1973).

Smythe, Donald, *Pershing: General of the Armies* (Bloomington, Ind., 1986).

Stewart, George, *The White Armies of Russia* (London, 1933).

Straubing, Harold Elk (ed.), *The Last Magnificent War* (New York, 1989).

Swettenham, John, *To Seize The Victory* (London, 1965).

Tansill, Charles C., *America Goes to War* (Boston, Mass., 1938).

Taylor, A. J. P., *English History 1914–1945* (Oxford, 1965).

Tennent, A. J., *British Merchant Ships Sunk by U-boats in the 1914–18 War* (London, 1990).

Terraine, John, *Business in Great Waters: the U-boat Wars 1916–1945* (London, 1989).

Thompson, John A., *Reformers and War* (Cambridge, 1987).

Trask, David, *The AEF and Coalition Warmaking, 1917–1918* (University Press of Kansas, 1993).

Tuchmann, Barbara, *The Zimmerman Telegram* (New York, 1958).

—, *The Guns of August* (London, 1962).

Vernon Gibbs, C. R., *British Passenger Liners of the Five Oceans* (London, 1963).

Ward, G. Kingsley, and Gibson, Edwin, *Courage Remembered* (HMSO, 1989).

Winter, Jay, and Baggett, Blaine, *The Great War* (Harmondsworth, 1996).

Zinsser, Hans, *Rats, Lice, and History* (London, 1935).

Papers and Journals

Benson, Colonel C., *A Study of Volunteer Enlistments, Army of the United States (1775–1945)* (September 1945) (copy in AMHI).

Brandt, Colonel Alfred, *Problems of Petroleum Supply to Mechanized Equipment in the Field* (August 1942) (copy in AMHI).

Collins, Major Charles H., *Conservation of Food in the United States Army 1917–1919* (February 1943) (copy in AMHI).

DeWeerd, Harvey A., American Adoption of French Artillery, *Journal of the American Military History Institute*, Summer, 1939, pp. 104–16.

Ellis, Mark, 'W. E. B. Du Bois and the Formation of Black Opinion in World War I', *Journal of American History*, March 1995, pp. 1584–90.

—, 'Closing Ranks and Seeking Honors in World War I', *Journal of American History*, June 1992, pp. 96–124.

Ely, Major-General Hanson, *Employment of Negro Man Power in War* (10 November 1925) (copy in AMHI).

Goddard, Lieutenant-Colonel Calvin H., *Transportation Problems of the AEF, World War I* (Army War College, Carlisle, March 1942).

—, *A Study of Anglo-American Relations and Franco-American Relations During World War I* (9 October 1943) (copy in AMHI).

Harbord, Major-General J. G., *Personalities and Personal Relationships in the American Expeditionary Forces*, lecture delivered at the Army War College, Washington DC (29 April 1933) (copy in AMHI).

Hayward, Colonel William, *Report on the performance of the 369th Regiment* (7 April 1919) (copy in AMHI).

Humber, Robert G., *Absences and Desertions during the First World War* (1942) (copy in AMHI).

Lanza, Colonel Conrad H., extracts from articles in the *Field Artillery Journal*, in the Drum papers collection in AMHI.

Lea, Luke, 'The Attempt to Capture the Kaiser', *Historical Quarterly*, September 1961.

Love, Colonel Albert G., *Probable Questions in War and Methods of Calculation*, written for the 10th International Congress of Military Medicine and Pharmacy, May 1939.

Martin, Gregory, 'German Strategy and Military Assessments of the American Expeditionary Force, 1917–1918', *War in History*, 1 (2), 1994.

McCleary, Major Oliver S., *The shortage of essential war materials in the lumber industry and the handling of the labor problem by the Army in connection therewith during World War I* (August 1942) (copy in AMHI).

McLendon, Idus R., 'The First Shot', *American Legion Monthly*, October 1931.

Nickerson, Major Hoffman, *The Lessons of the Armistice* (February 1944) (copy in AMHI).

—, *Preliminary Report on the Historical Method in Military Forecasting* (April 1944) (copy in AMHI).

Opperman, David R., *Army Transports and Navy Warships Participating in the Siberian Intervention, 1917–1922* (copy in AMHI).

Rhodes, Benjamin D., 'The 339th Infantry of Archangel', *International History Review*, VIII, no. 3, August 1986.

Yockelson, Mitchel, *The War Department: Keeper of Our Nation's Enemy Aliens During World War I*, paper presented to the Society for Military History Annual Meeting, April 1998 (copy in AMHI).

Notes

In these notes, references to works included in the bibliography of published sources are by author or editor. Where more than one work by an author is listed in the bibliography, a shortened title of the work referred to is also given.

1. No More Sleeping Treason

1. Palmer, p. 120.
2. Address to the 65th Congress, 1st Session Senate, Washington DC, 1917.
3. Robb Ellis, p. 325.
4. ibid., p. 330.
5. Peterson and Fite, p. 4.
6. Link, *Woodrow Wilson; Revolution, War, and Peace*, pp. 36–7. Link – who is always prepared to put the best gloss on Wilson's words and deeds – claims that Wilson's acceptance of the House–Grey Memorandum did not signal his abandonment of neutrality but actually reaffirmed his commitment to achieving a lasting peace as it 'seemed that the best, indeed the only, hope for peace at this time lay in Anglo-American cooperation [. . .] he gave the necessary assurances in the belief that the risk of American belligerency was insignificant as compared to the dangers of war with Germany if he did not bring the war to an end'. That is highly debatable. The British Foreign Office certainly did not think, as did Wilson, that a 'reasonable' settlement would be 'a return to the *status quo ante bellum*, with only minor adjustments and with no annexations and indemnities' (Link, p. 37). The French even less so.
7. Birnbaum, p. 40. Germany tried (unsuccessfully) in April 1916 to persuade the US government to place an embargo on the export of all munitions and war products; not surprisingly, given the profits being made by American industry, the US government rejected this request on the rather dubious grounds that any change in America's policy of neutrality during the war would be 'an unjustifiable departure from the principle of strict neutrality'.
8. Clark, p. 281.

9. Burk, p. 5.

10. The connection with J. P. Morgan came through David Lloyd George, then Chancellor of the Exchequer. He knew E. C. Grenfell, senior partner of Morgan Grenfell, and a director of the Bank of England. See Burk, p. 15.

11. Burk, pp. 21–7.

12. Millis, p. 221.

13. Burk, p. 6.

14. ibid., pp. 42–3.

15. ibid., p. 81.

16. ibid., p. 94.

17. ibid., p. 95.

18. Millis, p. 114.

19. Peterson and Fite, p. 4.

20. Foreign Relations Supplement, *1917*, pp. 24–9.

21. D'Este, p. 152.

22. Baker had taken over from Lindsay Garrison as Secretary of War on 7 March 1916.

23. Pershing, vol. 1, p. 16.

24. Stallings, p. 23.

25. Paxson, p. 16.

26. Conner, p. 1/Carlisle.

27. Millett and Williamson, p. 119.

28. Correspondence dated 13 February 1917; Woodward, p. 149.

29. *Causes of the German Collapse* (Lutz), pp. 62–3.

30. War Plan 'Black' cited in John A. S. Grenville and George Berkeley Young, *Politics, Strategy, and American Diplomacy: Studies in Foreign Policy, 1873–1917* (Yale University Press, 1966), p. 319.

31. Pershing, vol. 1, pp. 30–31.

32. ibid., vol. 1, p. 32.

33. Millett and Williamson, p. 216.

34. March, Peyton C., pp. 21–2.

35. Conner/Carlisle, p. 3.

36. ibid., p. 4.

2. Hearts and Minds

1. Robb Ellis, p. 266.

2. From a letter to Asquith dated 5 September 1914, quoted in *The World in Crisis*, vol. 1, pp. 293–4.

3. Donnelly/Carlisle.

4. Millis, pp. 43–4.

5. Cobb, p. 39.

6. ibid., pp. 58–9.

7. The strong temperance movement in the United States was particularly hostile to German-Americans, regarding German beer-drinking habits as a significant stumbling-block to prohibition. 'The prohibition issue was important, in that it helped to condition Americans to accept the wartime portrayal of German culture as bestial, deviant, and incompatible with Americanism [. . .] German resistance to temperance had prevented the passage of state prohibition laws in Pennsylvania, New York, Ohio, Wisconsin, Indiana, Illinois, and Iowa. Long before the United States itself declared war, the temperance movement began to exploit the European conflict to attack Germans and, by association, the trade in alcohol.' (Fiebig-von Hase and Lehmkuhl, p. 187.)

8. Cobb, pp. 64–5.

9. ibid., p. 80.

10. May, p. 36.

11. 'The Government of the United States readily admits the full right of a belligerent to visit and search on the high seas the vessels of American citizens or other neutral vessels carrying American goods and to detain them *when there is sufficient evidence to justify a belief that contraband articles are in their cargoes.*': Memo from William Jennings Bryan, US Secretary of State, to the Foreign Office in London on 26 December 1914. Foreign Relations Supplement, *1914*.

12. Birnbaum, p. 24.

13. Salter, pp. 98–9.

14. A good discussion of the complexities of this issue can be found in May.

15. Robb Ellis says she was designed to carry twelve six-inch guns (p. 208) – which would have made her one of the most heavily armed ships in the British navy.

16. Churchill, vol. 2, pp. 769–70; Terraine, p. 10.

17. Seymour (ed.), vol. 1, p. 435.

18. Contained in a telegraphed message dated 9 May by Wesley Frost, US consul in County Cork, to the US State Department; in Clark, p. 387.

19. Lauriat, pp. 10–11.

20. Millis, p. 164.

21. These figures are those given by Millis (p. 167), Link, *The Struggle for Neutrality* (p. 372) and other sources. *The Times History of the War* gave 1,225 deaths, while *Punch* in May 1915 said there were '1,200 victims' of whom 'about 200 were Americans'. Cunard archives at Liverpool University give 1,195 deaths, including 128 Americans.

22. The fates had clearly destined Vanderbilt to die in a famous shipping

disaster; he had cancelled a previous reservation three years earlier to travel aboard the *Titanic*.

23. Robb Ellis, p. 194.

24. ibid., p. 196.

25. Millis, p. 167.

26. Schwieger went on to command U-88 and died, along with all his crew, when it sank in September 1917 as a result, it is believed, of hitting a British mine.

27. Millis, p. 411.

28. Straubing, p. 168.

29. Robb Ellis, p. 217.

30. ibid., p. 207.

31. Seeger, *Letters and Diary*, p. 99.

32. This refers to the well-displayed statement carried in the morning editions of the New York City newspapers, next to Cunard sailing schedules, on Saturday, 1 May 1915, the day *Lusitania* sailed from Manhattan. It read: 'Travelers intending to embark on the Atlantic voyage are reminded that a state of war exists between Germany and Great Britain and her allies; that the zone of war includes the waters adjacent to the British Isles; that, in accordance with formal notice given by the Imperial German Government, vessels flying the flag of Great Britain, or any of her allies, are liable to destruction in those waters and that travelers sailing in the war zone on ships of Great Britain or her allies do so at their own risk.'

33. Robb Ellis, p. 205.

34. Seymour (ed.), vol. 1, p. 437.

35. Robb Ellis, p. 215.

36. Clark, p. 394.

37. ibid., p. 396.

38. ibid., p. 396.

39. In his memoir of his term in Washington, Bernstorff claimed that he frequently complained to Berlin about the inadequacy of the propaganda material it sent to him for dissemination in the United States. 'The outstanding characteristic of the average American is rather a great, even though superficial, sentimentality. There is no news for which a way cannot be guaranteed through the whole country, if clothed in a sentimental form. Our enemies have exploited this circumstance with the greatest refinement, in the case of the German invasion of "poor little Belgium", the shooting of the "heroic nurse", Edith Cavell, and other incidents [. . .] One thing that would have exerted a tremendous influence in America, if publicity had been handled with only average skill, was the suffering of our children, women and old people, as a result of the British hunger blockade – that they have made no attempt

to bring to the notice of the world' (Bernstorff, p. 53). This was entirely accurate, though it overlooks the remarkably skilled way in which Germany presented Britain with perfect sympathy-arousing incidents.

40. Robb Ellis, p. 211.

41. Millis asserts (p. 155) that the *Lusitania* had 'forty-two hundred cases of rifle ammunition in her hold'.

42. Clark, p. 437.

43. Birnbaum, p. 34.

44. Sanders and Taylor, pp. 143–4.

45. Bryce Report, 1915.

46. May, p. 180.

47. Once the United States joined in the war it became dangerous for Americans to voice such scepticism. On 24 July 1918 William Powell was charged under emergency wartime legislation (the Sedition and Espionage Acts); one of his 'crimes' was that he had questioned the truth of stories of German atrocities. A sentence of twenty years' jail and a $10,000 fine no doubt helped him to overcome his scepticism.

48. *The Times*, 7 September 1932.

49. Sanders and Taylor, p. 169.

50. ibid., p. 35.

51. 'By 1917, Reuters was sending about one million words a month abroad on behalf of the British government. Working in close collaboration with the News Department, the Agence Service Reuter was able to cable an average of 8,000 words a day in English and French to Europe, Morocco, Japan and Central and South America. On occasion, as much as 60,000 words was transmitted in a single day.' (Sanders and Taylor, pp. 37–8.)

52. Robb Ellis, p. 253.

53. *Mr Punch's History*, p. 66.

54. Lochner, p. 2.

55. ibid., p. 27.

56. Kraft, p. 86.

57. Lochner, p. 224.

58. Quoted in Sanders and Taylor, p. 183.

59. Wilson, 65th Congress, 1st Session Senate, doc. no. 5, serial no. 7264, Washington DC, 1917, pp. 3–8.

3. Easeful Death

1. *Friends of France*, pp. 61–2.

2. Columbia War Paper No. 4, Series 1: *Our Headline Policy*, an appeal to the press, by Henry Bedinger Mitchell (New York, 1917).

3. Prince was to die in October 1916, in a crash landing; Lufbery died when his aircraft burst into flames on 19 May 1918, having gained the Croix de Guerre (with ten palms), the Médaille Militaire and the Légion d'Honneur.

4. Hall, p. 45.

5. ibid., pp. 199–201.

6. Seeger is buried in Ossuaire No. 1 – a mass grave for individuals whose bodies were not identified at the time – at the National Military Cemetery, Lihons, in the Somme.

7. Seeger, *Letters and Diary*, p. 7.

8. ibid., p. 9.

9. ibid., p. 204.

10. Seeger, *Poems*, p. 161.

11. *New War Encyclopaedia and Dictionary*, p. 50.

12. Harvard accounted for 325 voluntary ambulance drivers; Yale, 187; Princeton, 181; Dartmouth, 118; and Cornell, 105.

13. *Friends of France*, p. 37.

14. ibid., pp. 136–8. Poem by Emery Pottle.

15. Birnbaum, p. 60.

16. Foreign Relations Supplement, *1916*, pp. 237–8.

17. The *Arabic*, a steamer of the White Star Company, was torpedoed without warning and sunk in that graveyard for transatlantic vessels, near Queenstown, at 9.30 a.m. on 19 August 1915. She went down in eleven minutes, and of the twenty-one Americans on board two died: Edmund F. Woods and Mrs Josephine Bruguiere. Moments before, the SS *Dunsley*, sailing with the *Arabic*, was sunk by the same U-boat. (Foreign Relations Supplement, *1915*, pp. 516–19.)

18. Foreign Relations Supplement, *1916*, pp. 233–4.

19. Birnbaum, p. 83.

20. Foreign Relations Supplement, *1916*, pp. 290–95; Birnbaum, pp. 177–201.

21. The following were the main incidents of merchant ships carrying Americans which were attacked without warning in this period (from Foreign Relations Supplement, *1916*, pp. 298–328):

3 September: the British vessel *Rievaulx Abbey*, sunk five miles off Spurn Point at the mouth of the Humber.

6 September: the British vessel *Strathay*, torpedoed and sunk 30 miles from Brest.

12 September: the Dutch vessel *Antwerpen*, torpedoed and sunk 25 miles south of the Scilly Isles.

12 October: the British vessel *Sebek* torpedoed; sank ten miles east of Malta.

20 October: in the English Channel the British coal freighter *Barbara*, carrying coal from Philadelphia to Hartlepool, torpedoed and sunk.

26 October: the 6,705-ton freighter *Rowanmore*, sailing from Baltimore to Liverpool, with a mixed cargo including munitions, sunk by U-boat gunfire and torpedo 140 miles south-east of Cape Clear; the ship carried among the passengers and crew (all of whom escaped unscathed) 7 American citizens.

28 October: the British steamer *Marina*, sailing from Glasgow to Baltimore, torpedoed in heavy seas 100 miles west of Cape Clear, was carrying 50 Americans, 9 of whom were killed or wounded.

28 October: the Philippine-registered, US-owned steamer *Lanao*, *en route* from Saigon to Le Havre and carrying rice, sunk by torpedo 30 miles off Cape Vincent, Portugal.

31 October: the Norwegian vessel *Delto*, sailing from Naples to Wales, sunk by gunfire from U-boat 55 miles off Cape Palos, Spain.

6 November: the P&O liner *Arabia*, carrying a 4.7-inch gun, torpedoed in the Mediterranean.

7 November: the American steamer *Columbian* torpedoed by U-49 while sailing from St Nazaire to Genoa; sank 50 miles north-west of Cape Ortegal.

11 November: the Norwegian steamer *Trippel*, sailing from Baltimore to Genoa, torpedoed and sunk 18 miles off Villarica.

11 November: the Norwegian ship *Lokken*, *en route* from Cardiff carrying coal to Philippeville, near Algiers, sunk by submarine gunfire 180 miles from the shore in the Bay of Biscay.

16 November: the British steamer *Trevarrick*, carrying grain from Buenos Aires to Hull, torpedoed and sunk 90 miles off Ushant Point.

22 November: the French ship *John Lambert*, sailing from Montreal to Le Havre and carrying coal, sunk by gunfire from submarine between Le Havre and Falmouth.

2 December: the Italian horse transport ship *Palermo*, sailing from New York to Genoa, torpedoed and sunk 25 miles off Cape San Sebastian, Spain.

22. Foreign Relations Supplement, *1916*, p. 308.

23. Terraine, p. 9.

24. ibid., p. 15.

25. Foreign Relations Supplement, *1916*, pp. 87–9: Hollweg made no mention of any terms for peace but was evidently in no mood for much compromise. He said, in part, 'With God's help our glorious troops have created a situation

which affords us full security greater than ever before. The western front stands [. . .] Now we are putting the human question of peace. We shall await the reply with the calmness which our internal and external strength and our clear conscience lend us. If the enemies decline, if they want to assume the world's heavy burden of the terrible things which will then come, then every German heart, even in the smallest cottage, will again flare up in sacred wrath against enemies who, for the sake of intentions of destruction and conquest, are still unwilling to call a halt to the slaughter of human beings.'

26. However, the British MP John Norton-Griffiths, who was sent to Romania on an intelligence mission, managed to destroy vast reserves of grain and a considerable amount of the country's oil-producing capacity before the arrival of the German occupiers.

27. Foreign Relations Supplement, *1916*, pp. 97–9.

28. Quoted in Terraine, p. 15.

29. Foreign Relations Supplement, *1916*, pp. 314–18. The memo was dated 7 November, but was only received on 4 December.

30. From the *Chicago Tribune*, 26 February 1917. Gibbons was later to spend time with the AEF reporting the war from France. He was with a company of marines at Belleau Wood in June 1918, where he took two machine-gun bullets, one through the shoulder and the other costing him his left eye; after being treated in the American Hospital in Paris he wore a black eye-patch.

31. Terraine, p. 40. He writes that 395 ships went down in April alone, totalling 881,027 tons, 545,282 tons of which were British; 96 per cent were sunk by U-boats.

32. See Appendix 3.

33. May, p. 425.

34. Foreign Relations Supplement, *1917*, pp. 177–84.

4. Enter the Doughboys

1. Quoted in Schaffer, pp. 167–8.

2. Poorbaugh/ASEQ/Carlisle.

3. *Stars and Stripes*, 2, no. 12, 25 April 1919. Lawrence Stallings in *Doughboys* is dogmatic about the derivation: 'There can be little dispute as to the derivation of the name. In Texas, US Infantry along the Rio Grande were powdered white with the dust of adobe soil, and hence they were called "adobes" by mounted troops. It was a short step to "dobies" and then, by metathesis, the word was Doughboys' (p. 5). This theory is a little tarnished when it is recalled precisely what adobe was – sun-dried brick. Strictly speaking, 'adobe soil' does not exist.

4. Lloyd George, vol. 2, p. 1833.

5. ibid., p. 1826.

6. See Chapter 7 for more on this topic.

7. There is no consensus as to the precise numbers of US regular army and National Guard troops at this time. Smythe (p. 8) says there were '127,588 Regular Army officers and men and 80,446 National Guard officers and men – a total of 208,034'. Smythe also states that the General Staff consisted of just forty-one officers at this time.

8. By 30 June 1917 there were 401 permanent recruiting stations, as well as numerous temporary ones. By the same date 160,084 men had enlisted. Another 206,059 were rejected, most on physical grounds, but also 14,229 as being too young, 4,798 because they were not US citizens, and 4,707 on grounds of illiteracy.

9. The House voted 397 to 24 in favour, the Senate 81 to 8.

10. Millett and Williamson, pp. 122–3.

11. Ayres, pp. 17–19.

12. ibid., p. 21.

13. Ely/1925/Carlisle.

14. Millett and Williamson, p. 123.

15. Wharton, frontispiece.

16. Liggett, p. 248.

17. Their names were: Albert Billy, Mitchell Bobb, Victor Brown, Ben Caterby, James Edwards, Tobias Frazer, Ben Hampton, Solomon Louis, Pete Maytubby, Jeff Nelson, Joseph Oklahombi, Robert Taylor, Calvin Wilson, and Walter Veach. (From *The Native American Almanac*, by Arlene Hishfelder and Martha Kreipe de Montano (1993), pp. 232–4.)

18. Clark, p. 16.

19. Austin, letter dated 8 June 1918, Carlisle. Austin was later promoted to major, but there was no new car for him, nor any *après la guerre*; he wrote his last letter home on 29 September 1918.

20. From *Fifteen Little War Stories*, no. 28 of *Patriotism Through Education*, a series of propaganda pamphlets published by the National Security League in New York City; no date, but probably 1917.

21. Quoted in Ellis, 'W. E. B. Du Bois . . .', p. 1585. Private Wilson was identified as the author of this and other letters in a similar vein. On 2 July 1918 he was court-martialled, sentenced to ten years' hard labour, dishonourably discharged, and he forfeited all pay due.

22. Majors, p. 2.

23. Cornebise, p. 115. Viskniskki's letter was dated 23 November.

24. Jordan/ASEQ/Carlisle.

25. Pershing, vol. 2, p. 97 (footnote).

26. Yensen/Carlisle: Yensen's writing is direct, forceful and impressive. It is,

however, quite wayward when it comes to spelling. I have corrected the spelling errors in order that the reader will not be slowed down by what might be thought to be mistakes or typographical errors.

27. Moan survived the war, despite being blown up in September 1918. Invalided to Grenoble, he was awarded the Croix de Guerre and the Distinguished Service Cross, and returned to the United States in July 1919.

28. Papers at Carlisle.

29. Papers at Carlisle.

30. *Current Biography*, 1946.

31. ibid.

32. ibid.

33. ibid.

34. ibid.

35. *Chicago Tribune* (Paris edition), 8 March 1919.

36. Kendall, pp. 9, 85.

37. *Current Biography*, 1946.

38. Yensen/Carlisle.

39. Yensen/Carlisle.

40. *La Main coupée* (1946); translated as *Lice* (London, 1973), p. 183.

41. All details from Ragueneau document, dated 6 March 1918, and contained in Box 15 of the Drum papers at Carlisle.

42. Ferro, p. 86.

43. *Stars and Stripes*, June 1918.

44. Details of the mail order from the Carlisle file of Private Griffith L. Adams, 105th Machine Gun Battalion, 27th Division.

45. The AEF First Army comprised the following divisions at different periods of its formation: 1st, 2nd, 3rd, 4th, 5th, 6th, 7th, 26th, 28th, 29th, 32nd, 33rd, 35th, 36th, 37th, 41st, 42nd, 77th, 78th, 79th, 80th, 81st, 82nd, 88th, 90th, 91st and 92nd.

46. By the end of the war 72 per cent of the almost 4 million who had joined up were draftees; more than 50 per cent of the AEF were draftees.

5. To France

1. Pershing, vol. 1, p. 48.

2. From the short story 'A Way You'll Never Be'.

3. Pershing, vol. 1, p. 37.

4. ibid., p. 18.

5. Harbord/Carlisle.

6. Millett and Williamson, p. 216.

7. Pershing, vol. 1, p. 28.

8. ibid., p. 27.

9. ibid., p. 28.

10. ibid., p. 27.

11. March, Peyton C., pp. 200–201.

12. Millett and Williamson, p. 96.

13. Nolan, memoirs, pp. 13–14/Carlisle.

14. Pershing, vol. 1, pp. 38–9.

15. ibid., p. 47.

16. Crowell and Wilson, vol. 3, pp. 225–38. In 1918 the Germans protested to the United States that its use of sawn-off shotguns was barbaric, but as they were not banned under the Geneva Convention the United States continued to use them.

17. Millett and Williamson, p. 35.

18. ibid., p. 94.

19. Pershing, vol. 1, p. 107.

20. A swift decision was made in the United States to adopt a modified version of the Enfield rifle, which was being manufactured at a number of US factories on behalf of the British.

21. Pershing, vol. 1, p. 113.

22. Millett and Williamson, p. 35.

23. Deighton, pp. 104–5. America started a programme to build the Liberty tank (based on the impressive 330 horsepower Liberty engine) but the first of these tanks 'was completed in the United States in November 1918, too late for the war [. . .] only some twenty Renault tanks made in America had been landed in France at the time of the Armistice'. (Mitchell, pp. 277–8.)

24. Millett and Williamson, p. 136.

25. Baruch, pp. 290–91.

26. Millett and Williamson, p. 35.

27. In fairness, it should be added that the AEF was in some instances no more technologically backward than the supposedly machine-like German armed forces. By 1918, despite the obvious usefulness of the tank, Germany had produced none; even by the end of the war it had manufactured only twenty or so of its own A7V tanks, all of them prone to breakdown.

28. Once war was declared various US administrators ordered vast numbers of items with little or no understanding as to whether they could be delivered on time or, indeed, at all.

29. On 18–19 June 1918 Companies A and B carried out the first gas attack of the AEF, firing a total of 1,333 shells of chlorine gas; on 13 July the regiment was renamed the First Gas Regiment of the Chemical Warfare Service. It served with distinction at St-Mihiel, suffered a total of 575 casualties, and gained 1 DSM, 15 DSCs and 45 Croix de Guerre.

30. Pershing, vol. 1, p. 45.

31. ibid., p. 45.

32. ibid., p. 54.

33. Smythe, p. 21.

34. Millett and Williamson, p. 95.

35. Drum papers/Carlisle.

36. Bullard, *Personalities*, p. 50.

37. Ferro, p. 184. Major Paul H. Clark, Pershing's liaison officer at the French GHQ, was informed on 17 November 1918 by General Duval that 13–17 men were executed. See Paul H. Clark/Carlisle, letter no. 249. Pershing says twelve French mutineers were executed (vol. 1, p. 97, footnote); Michael Hanlon (on the Internet web site Trenches on the Web) gives a figure of fifty-five. Precise numbers here, as in most aspects of the First World War, are always in dispute.

38. Smythe, p. 23.

39. Millett and Williamson, p. 126.

40. Drum diary/Carlisle.

41. Bullard, *Personalities*, p. 34.

42. Mahan/Carlisle, pp. 9–10.

43. Bullard, *Personalities*, p. 38.

44. Marshall, p. 8.

45. ibid., p. 8.

46. Kyler/ASEQ/Carlisle.

47. Pershing, vol. 1, p. 93.

48. Bullard, *Personalities*, vol. 1, pp. 51, 53.

6. Black Jack

1. Dawes, vol. 1, p. 20.

2. Bullard, *Personalities*, p. 43.

3. Yensen/Carlisle.

4. Pershing's love of the Sam Browne belt came to symbolize the bitter rivalry between himself and General March, who nonsensically considered himself Pershing's superior. March said the Sam Browne belt was a waste of a scarce resource, leather, and had his military police remove it, by force if necessary, from all AEF officers who returned home. While March had no superior in the United States, Pershing had none in the AEF.

5. Dawes recorded that one December morning it was 'freezing cold, and I was quite proud of myself for forcing myself through my morning gymnastic exercises. While I was so engaged I looked out of the window, and there was "Black Jack" clad only in pajamas, bathrobe, and slippers, his bare ankles

showing, running up and down in the snow outdoors. I never saw a man more physically fit at his age' (vol. 1, p. 65).

6. Dawes, vol. 1, pp. 22–3.

7. Smythe, p. 296.

8. ibid., p. 298.

9. ibid., p. 307.

10. ibid., p. 14.

11. Adams/Carlisle. Letter dated Friday, 27 July 1918.

12. John D. Clark/ASEQ/Carlisle.

13. Pershing also refused permission for officers' wives to accompany their husbands to France – such a scheme would have been deeply undemocratic had enlisted men been refused the same right, and there was in any case insufficient shipping tonnage without adding to the burden by transporting wives.

14. Poorbaugh/ASEQ/Carlisle.

15. Smythe, p. 10.

16. Harbord/Carlisle.

17. Nolan memoirs, p. 21/Carlisle.

18. Harbord/Carlisle.

19. According to General Hunter Liggett, 'only' 1,101 of the AEF's officers were thus 're-classified'. To put this in context, Liggett says that 'In the Northern Army from 1861 to 1865 more officers were cashiered than were killed in the field [. . .] An adverse report would bring an officer of the Inspector General's department. If he confirmed the report the officer went before an efficiency board and was sent to Blois, which was pronounced "Blooey" in the AEF. The same fate was the penalty of any discovered mistake in action, no officer was given an opportunity to make a second' (pp. 254–6).

20. Bullard said of this meteoric rise: 'Convinced of Pershing's efficiency and merit, notwithstanding the wide criticism of his promotion, notwithstanding the common assertion that it was due to the senatorial influence of his father-in-law, Mr Warren, Chairman of the Senate Military Committee, I wrote to him a sincere letter of congratulation – to which I received no answer.' (*Personalities*, p. 46.) Stallings puts the number of officers that Pershing overtook as 882 (p. 30), but it is likely that someone, such as Bullard, who was bitter about being passed over, would not make a mistake.

21. Smythe, p. 2.

22. Bullard, *Personalities*, p. 42.

23. ibid., p. 47.

24. Smythe, p. 3.

25. De Chambrun and De Marenches, pp. 41–2.

26. Griscom/Carlisle.

27. Robert Bacon (1860–1919) came from an old Boston family. A Harvard football hero, he was a contemporary there of Theodore Roosevelt. He went into banking with both J. P. Morgan and Drexel & Co. William Taft named him first as Assistant Secretary of State under Elihu Root and then ambassador to France. A francophile, Bacon loved his post in Paris but could not resist the offer of a Harvard fellowship in 1912. Like his fellow Republican Roosevelt, Bacon was impatient with the Democratic administration's reluctance to enter the war; his wife was active in fundraising for the American Ambulance Service and Bacon returned to France to direct its operations, only returning to America in 1915 to agitate for military preparedness.

28. When Dawes published his own two-volume memoir of his work in the AEF in France he demonstrated his veneration of Black Jack by having Pershing's profile, Roman-like, embossed on the front board.

29. 'Hell and Maria' came from some words Dawes spoke at a Congressional committee investigating charges of waste and extravagance in the conduct of the First World War. When a member of the committee asked Dawes if it was true that excessive prices were paid for mules in France, he shouted 'Helen Maria, I'd have paid horse prices for sheep if the sheep could have pulled artillery to the front!' 'Helen Maria' was an expletive in common usage in Nebraska, and it became corrupted by newspaper reportage as 'Hell and Maria'.

30. Dawes won the 1925 Nobel Peace Prize for chairing in 1923–4 a League of Nations committee investigating German reparations. Dawes was Vice-President from 1925 to 1929 and later ambassador to Britain (1929–32). He was an accomplished flautist and pianist.

31. Dawes, vol. 1, pp. 45–6.

32. Griscom/Carlisle.

33. ibid.

34. Instead, three of Roosevelt's sons sailed to France and fought there. One, Quentin, became a pilot in the US air force and was shot down and killed; he was buried on the battlefield of the Marne in 1918. Another, Theodore Junior, was a major and suffered relatively minor wounds.

35. March, Peyton C., p. 205.

36. Pershing, vol. 2, p. 50.

37. March, Peyton C., p. 207.

38. Griscom/Carlisle.

39. Tasker Bliss was appointed by Woodrow Wilson to be the US permanent representive at the Allied Supreme War Council at Versailles.

40. Dawes, vol. 1, p. 71.

7. Ships for Souls

1. Pershing, vol. 1,, p. 269.
2. Salter, pp. 109–10.
3. ibid., p. 149.
4. ibid., p. 152.
5. Nolan, memoirs, p. 5/Carlisle.
6. Fox Conner lecture, p. 13/Carlisle.
7. Pershing, vol. 1, p. 185.
8. ibid., p. 241.
9. Goddard, *Transportation*, pp. 1–2.
10. ibid., p. 9.
11. ibid., p. 18.
12. Drum papers/Carlisle.
13. Salter, p. 290.
14. ibid., pp. 8–9.
15. Salter, pp. 3–4. 1917 was the worst year for Allied shipping losses. Total Britain and the Dominions' ships sunk amounted to 252,738 gross tons during August–December 1914; 885,471 gross tons in 1915; 1.23 million gross tons in 1916; 3.66 million gross tons in 1917; and 1.63 million gross tons in 1918. (Salter, pp. 357–60.)
16. Salter, p. 7.
17. Conner, p. 4/Carlisle.
18. Peel, pp. 61, 82, 219.
19. Tankers could not ferry doughboys; but they did use scarce quayside space and labour that could be employed elsewhere.
20. Brandt/Carlisle.
21. In 1915, America constructed eighty-four ships, amounting to 177,000 gross tons, against the UK's 354,664,000 gross tons. The balance shifted slightly in 1916, when American constructed 211 ships, 504,000 tons, against Britain and the Dominions' 342 ships and 630,000 tons. In 1917 Britain and the Dominions produced 366 ships, with a gross tonnage of 1.23 million, against America's 326 ships with a gross tonnage of almost 1 million.
22. Salter, p. 361. (Total US shipping losses from enemy action from 1 August 1914 until the Armistice amounted to no more than 115 ships, totalling 322,946 gross tons, and valued at something below $100 million. Not only was this considerably less than losses due to ordinary marine risks – 278 ships totalling 405,400 gross tons, over the same period – it was far less than the rest of the Allies'. Total Allied and neutral shipping sunk was about thirty-six times greater than the US losses. The United States lost only twenty-one ships

to U-boats during its period of neutrality – a total of just 79,562 gross tons. Clark, pp. 247–8.)

23. 'Generally speaking we are in a position probably never foreseen. Ever since I can remember and years before then it has always been assumed that we would have command of the sea and everything was based upon that hypothesis, and if anybody had thought it should be based on any other hypothesis they would have been classed as fools. As a matter of fact we have not got command of the sea. In every theatre we are suffering from shipping shortages.' (Woodword, p. 177.)

24. Conner, p. 13/Carlisle.

25. Salter, p. 54.

26. ibid., pp. 66–7.

27. Conner, pp. 10–11/Carlisle.

28. Woodward, p. 169.

29. In fact just 20,120 American military personnel had arrived in France by 31 July 1917.

30. Pershing, vol. 1, p. 274.

31. ibid., p. 289.

32. ibid., p. 295.

33. Salter, p. 125.

34. Salter, p. 126.

35. Pershing, vol. 1, pp. 33–4.

36. Conner, p. 14/Carlisle.

37. ibid., p. 15.

38. ibid., p. 15.

39. March, Peyton C., pp. 82–3.

40. ibid., p. 86.

41. Conner, p. 16/Carlisle.

42. ibid., p. 17.

43. ibid., p. 17.

44. ibid., p. 17.

45. How big is a division? The US War Department used different figures at different stages of the war, but American divisions were consistently at least twice as big as those of the British, French or Germans, which all consisted (in theory – in practice far fewer in the final year of the war) of about 12,000 combatant troops. General Peyton March stated that US divisions were 27,000 strong, excluding all SOS and other non-combatants, or 40,000 including all such auxiliaries. But the War Department's own eighty-division programme by 30 June 1919 called for a total of 3,160,000 officers and men, less than 40,000 per division. Meanwhile General Fox Conner seems to imply a division

strength (all combat and auxiliary troops included) of 52,000. March's figure is probably nearer the reality of the time.

46. Conner, pp. 19–20/Carlisle.

47. Goddard, *Transportation*, p. 2.

48. Donnelly/Carlisle.

49. Others pointed out some of the more serious consequences of shipping the dougboys like sardines: 'In many instances three men were assigned to two bunks (thus requiring one to sleep by day); others were forced to sleep on table tops, exposed surfaces on deck, etc. During summer months such arrangements operated satisfactorily, but failure to curtail such overcrowding when cold weather arrived caused much discomfort, illness and some mortality [. . .] During the influenza epidemic (September–December 1918) over-crowding resulted in a terrifically high morbidity and mortality on vessels affected.' (Goddard, *Transportation*, p. 6.)

50. The *Leviathan* was the interned German ship *Vaterland*; the United States impounded a total of ninety-seven enemy ships during the war, with a gross tonnage of 700,000 tons, and spent $11 million to refit them; the *Northern Pacific* and the *Great Northern*, also interned ships, beat *Leviathan*'s turn-around record, notching up nineteen-turnarounds. (March, p. 78.)

51. March, Peyton C., pp. 76–7.

52. Conner, p. 18/Carlisle.

53. Pershing, vol. 2, p. 84 (footnote).

8. July–December 1917

1. Yensen/ASEQ/Carlisle.

2. Dawes, vol. 1, p. 13.

3. 'The actual construction of cantonments was not begun until nearly three months after we had entered the war, and even though the task of erecting them was accomplished in record time, some ninety days more had elapsed before they were ready to receive troops.' (Pershing, vol. 1, p. 30.)

4. Donnelly/Carlisle. This equipment is very similar to that described by Norman Hall as being the load carried by the British soldier in 1915: 120 rounds of .303 rifle ammunition, entrenching tool, waterbottle, haversack containing the day's and emergency rations, and a pack containing 'greatcoat, a woolen shirt, two or three pairs of socks, a change of underclothing, a "housewife" – the soldier's sewing-kit – a towel, a cake of soap, and a "hold-all", in which were a knife, fork, spoon, razor, shaving-brush, tooth-brush, and comb. All of these were useful and sometimes essential articles, particularly the toothbrush, which Tommy regarded as the best little instrument for cleaning the mechanism of a rifle ever invented. Strapped on top of

the pack was the blanket roll wrapped in a waterproof ground sheet; and hanging beneath it, the canteen in its khaki-cloth cover [. . .] A first-aid field dressing, consisting of an antiseptic gauze pad and bandage and a small vial of iodine, sewn in the lining of his tunic, completed the equipment.' (Hall, pp. 39–40.)

5. The AEF's Transportation Corps, which unloaded ships in French ports, comprised by the end of the war 760 officers, 1,970 white enlisted men, and 18,451 enlisted black Americans. Their working day was arduous. At St-Nazaire by the end of the war they were working a two-shift system, from 7 a.m. to 6 p.m. and 6 p.m. to 4 a.m., each with a one-hour break. One day out of seven was a rest day.

6. Yensen/Carlisle.

7. Korn/ASEQ/Carlisle.

8. Dawes, vol. 1, pp. 9–10.

9. Gough, p. 211. The battle was that of Polygon Wood, September–October 1917.

10. Pershing, vol. 2, p. 56 (footnote).

11. Pershing, vol. 1, p. 158.

12. ibid., p. 218.

13. Pershing, vol. 2, p. 58.

14. Bullard, *Personalities*, p. 79.

15. ibid., pp 86–7.

16. Ayres, p. 15.

17. Marshall, p. 13.

18. Smythe, p. 39.

19. Bullard, *Personalities*, p. 95.

20. A young battalion commander, Erwin Rommel, received Germany's highest military honour, the *Pour le Mérite*, at Caporetto, for taking 9,000 prisoners and eighty-one guns.

21. Pershing, vol. 1, p. 216.

22. Liggett, pp. 14–15.

23. Dawes, vol. 1, p. 30.

24. Dawes had to contend not only with British and French obstructiveness but also with the bureaucratic red-tape of the United States' own military powers. He suggested to Pershing, who endorsed the idea, that steamers from the Great Lakes in America should be converted for use as colliers, to help transport coal from Britain. Admiral Sims, in charge of the US navy, had earlier refused to give Dawes a collier from the navy; which entailed Pershing cabling the War Department in Washington, and in turn the War Department cabling Sims instructing him to give one or two colliers to the AEF to help transport coal from England. This nightmarish red tape was

ubiquitous; winning the war sometimes appears to have been almost an afterthought.

25. Dawes, vol. 1, p. 39.

26. Nolan papers, p. 11/Carlisle.

27. Poorbaugh/ASEQ/Carlisle.

28. Kyler/ASEQ/Carlisle.

29. McLendon, p. 17.

30. ibid., p. 58.

31. The gun was sent to West Point; the brass shell case was inscribed and presented to President Wilson.

32. McLendon, p. 61.

33. ibid., pp. 59–60.

34. Frank Coffman, *American Legion Magazine*, 13 January 1922.

35. Mahan, pp. 15–16/Carlisle.

36. At their graveside the following tribute was read; it was written by General Bourdeaux, who commanded the French unit they were attached to at the time of their deaths: 'The death of this humble corporal and these privates appeals to us with unwonted grandeur. We will, therefore, ask that the mortal remains of these young men be left here, be left to us forever. We will inscribe on their tombs, "Here lie the first soldiers of the United States to fall on the fields of France for justice and liberty". The passer-by will stop and uncover his head. The travellers of France, of the Allied countries, of America, the men of heart, who will come to visit our battlefields of Lorraine, will go out of their way to come here to bring to these graves the tribute of respect and gratitude. Corporal Gresham, Private Enright and Private Hay, in the name of France, I thank you.'

37. Dawes, vol. 1, pp. 59–60.

38. ibid., p. 62.

39. ibid., p. 25.

40. Conner, p. 13/Carlisle.

41. Conger papers/Carlisle.

42. Hayward/Carlisle.

43. Bullard, *Personalities*, p. 115.

9. Killing Time

1. Ogden, diary, p. 149/Carlisle.

2. Aitken/ASEQ/Carlisle.

3. Millett and Williamson, p. 215.

4. Mead/ASEQ/Carlisle.

5. Garcia/ASEQ/Carlisle.
6. Millett and Williamson, p. 149.
7. Ambrose, p. 251.
8. Harbord/Carlisle.
9. Ambrose, p. 258.
10. Bullard, *Personalities*, p. 64.
11. ibid., pp. 101–3.
12. Hagood, p. 15/Carlisle.
13. Ferro, p. 86.
14. Bullard, *Personalities*, pp. 102–3.
15. Crowell and Wilson, vol. 3, pp. 225–38.
16. Aitken/ASEQ/Carlisle.
17. Pershing, vol. 1, p. 151.
18. ibid., p. 153.
19. ibid., pp. 11–12.
20. Binneveld, p. 145.
21. Smithers, p. 197.
22. Aitken/ASEQ/Carlisle.
23. Smithers, pp. 212–21.
24. Millett and Williamson, pp. 100–101.
25. Austin, 31 July 1918/Carlisle.
26. ibid.
27. Millett and Williamson, pp. 143–4.
28. John D. Clark/Carlisle.
29. General Liggett commented that there was 'a lack of coordination between the field artillery and the infantry until toward the end'. (Liggett, p. 250.)
30. Bullard, *Personalities*, p. 70.
31. The nominal composition of an AEF division was: 8 men to a squad; 7 squads plus a sergeant and a lieutenant (58 men) to a platoon; 4 platoons plus a captain in command and an HQ detachment (250 men) to a company; 4 companies, commanded by a major, to a battalion (1,000 men); 3 battalions plus one machine-gun company, commanded by a colonel, to a regiment (3,850 officers and men); 2 infantry regiments plus 1 machine-gun battalion formed a brigade (some 8,200 men and 250 officers) commanded by a brigadier-general; 2 infantry brigades plus 1 artillery brigade (comprising two artillery regiments of French 75mm guns and 1 of French 155mm guns) plus a regiment of engineers, a machine-gun battalion, signallers, supply trains and sanitary trains formed a division under the command of a major-general. Altogether an AEF division could muster slightly more than 27,000 officers and men; in the last days of 1918 British, French and German divisions were

so badly depleted that they often amounted to little more than 5,000 rifles. An AEF corps was made up of 2 or more divisions, an army 2 or more corps, and an army group 2 or more armies.

32. Bullard (in *Personalities*, p. 75) gives a slightly different reason for the large size of the AEF's division: 'It was so made because, on account of unsuitable recruiting and replacement plans, it could not be hoped that a command once depleted or reduced below a proper fighting strength could be promptly filled up again.' This may have been true, but it does not quite make sense; once depleted to below a certain level the obvious thing to do, if replacements were hard to come by (and they were not), would have been to amalgamate divisions.

33. Smythe points out that doubling the size of divisions in order to alleviate the shortage of suitable officers could also be said to have imposed double the burden on those who were selected to run the various units of the division (p. 38).

34. 30 January–10 February: Drum diary, 1918/Carlisle.

35. Paul H. Clark, 'Secret Letters', vol. 1, pp. 11–12/Carlisle.

36. '[. . .] the French general staff tended to be a bureaucratic machine rather than a "brain". Staff officers spent much time in routine administrative duties to the detriment of their operational skills' (Millett and Williamson, p. 211). The AEF's staff officers tended to excess in the opposite direction, constantly seeking to ditch their routine tasks in an effort to get to the front line.

37. Brittain, *Testament of Youth*.

38. Smithers, pp. 196–7.

39. Martin, p. 173.

40. Foch, Joffre, Ludendorff, ex-Crown Prince William of Germany, *The Two Battles of the Marne*, pp. 246–8.

41. Martin, p. 164, note 20.

10. Filth, Food and Fornication

1. Zinsser, p. 132.

2. Yensen/Carlisle.

3. ibid.

4. Ashburn, pp. 319–20.

5. John D. Clark/Carlisle.

6. Poorbaugh/Carlisle.

7. Bullard, *Personalities*, p. 54.

8. Donnelly/Carlisle.

9. Dexter/ASEQ/Carlisle.

10. In 1914 the official British ration per day comprised the following: 20 oz.

fresh or frozen meat, or 16 oz. preserved or salt meat; 20 oz. bread, or 16 oz. biscuit or flour; 4 oz. bacon; 3 oz. cheese; $\frac{5}{8}$ oz. tea; 4 oz. jam; 3 oz. sugar; $\frac{1}{2}$ oz. salt; $\frac{1}{36}$ oz. pepper; $\frac{1}{20}$ oz. mustard; 8 oz. fresh or 2 oz. dried vegetables; $\frac{1}{2}$ gill lime juice, if vegetable not issued; $\frac{1}{2}$ gill rum (at discretion of commanding general); 20 oz. tobacco per week. Permitted substitutions were: 4 oz. oatmeal or rice instead of bread; $\frac{1}{3}$ oz. cocoa instead of tea; 1 pint porter instead of rum; 4 oz. dried fruit instead of jam; 4 oz. butter, lard, or margarine, or $\frac{1}{2}$ gill oil instead of bacon. The equivalent daily ration for German soldiers in 1914 included: $26\frac{1}{2}$ oz. bread or $17\frac{1}{2}$ oz. field biscuit, or 14 oz. egg biscuit; 13 oz. fresh or frozen meat, or 7 oz. preserved meat; 53 oz. potatoes, or $4\frac{1}{2}$ oz. vegetables, or 2 oz. dried vegetables, or 21 oz. mixed potatoes and dried vegetables; $\frac{9}{10}$ oz. coffee, or $\frac{1}{10}$ oz. tea; $\frac{7}{10}$ oz. sugar; $\frac{9}{10}$ oz. salt; 2 cigars and 2 cigarettes, or 1 oz. pipe tobacco, or $\frac{9}{10}$ oz. plug tobacco, or $\frac{1}{5}$ oz. snuff (at discretion of commanding officer); 0.17 pint spirits; 0.44 pint wine; 0.88 pint beer. By the time the AEF arrived in France the soldiers of all armies were accustomed to getting nothing like their full ration on a regular basis.

11. Collins/Carlisle.

12. ibid.

13. Aitken/ASEQ/Carlisle.

14. Collins/Carlisle.

15. Donnelly/Carlisle.

16. Yensen/Carlisle.

17. Not that all Americans were that enamoured of democracy, even then Bullard wrote in *Personalities* (p. 77) that the formation of the AEF was 'a mightly organization' and 'the product of many brains but of one will. Its like could be produced only where but one will governs, not ever in a democracy. Democracy means mediocrity. This was superiority.'

18. Collins/Carlisle.

19. ibid.

20. Pershing, vol. 1, p. 282.

21. Ashburn, p. 320.

22. Devan/Carlisle.

23. Little, pp. 104–5.

24. Ashburn, pp. 336–7.

25. Loughran/Carlisle.

26. Yensen/Carlisle.

27. Osborn/Carlisle.

28. Loughran/Carlisle.

29. Ashburn, pp. 208, 318–19.

30. ibid., p. 320.

31. Bishop/ASEQ/Carlisle.

11. January–June 1918

1. Aitken/ASEQ/Carlisle.
2. Drum diary, 29 January 1918/Carlisle.
3. Donnelly/Carlisle.
4. Donnelly/Carlisle. When fully loaded the typical doughboy carried about ninety pounds, excluding his rifle; soldiers of other nations carried anything between seventy and ninety pounds, plus rifle.
5. Terraine, p. 150.
6. Crowell and Wilson, vol. 2, p. 441 (original italics). That Crowell and Wilson overlooked the fate of the *Tuscania* may be due to their concentration on US vessels used to transport doughboys. Thus they point out that there were several U-boat attacks on American transports (the *Antilles* on 17 October 1917, and the *Covington* on 1 July 1918, were both sunk on their return journey to the United States, for example) but ignore British shipping losses and hence omit AEF casualties from those losses.
7. The official US figure for the total number of deaths of army and navy personnel at sea was 768, of which 381 were counted as battle deaths, as their loss was the direct result of submarine activity (see Ayres, p. 123). The sinking of the *Tuscania* by torpedo on 5 February 1918 is confirmed by Lloyd's Register of shipping losses, but sources conflict as to precise numbers of casualties. Kludas says it was sunk by U-77 and that there were '166 dead'. Haws is even less reliable, giving the date of the sinking as 2 February, with the same number of dead. Tennent follows the official HMSO publication (1919) and gives the death toll as forty-four. I suspect that the confusion has arisen because the Lloyd's Register may only have given the *crew* losses, and not the additional US troop casualty figures.
8. Fife, p. 22.
9. ibid.
10. Pershing, vol. 1, p. 318.
11. Latitude 55 degrees, 25 minutes north; longitude 6 degrees, 13 minutes west.
12. Fife, pp. 33–4.
13. ibid., p. 26.
14. Drum diary, 30 January–10 February 1918/Carlisle.
15. Paul H. Clark, vol. 1, letter no. 2/Carlisle. Attached to the French GHQ on the personal orders of Pershing, Clark's job was to act as a conduit between Pershing and the GHQ of the AEF and the highest levels of command of the French army. At the end of each day Clark dictated to a stenographer an account of all the conversations held with, impressions gained from, and views expressed by the senior French officers with whom he came into contact. The

resulting reports were then sent to Pershing, who thus had access to an important intelligence source about French thinking on the direction of the war. Of course, the French officers knew of Clark's work – and came to use him to promote their own views on, for example, the importance of AEF units being amalgamated with French divisions.

16. Thomas, p. 66.

17. Pershing, vol. 2, pp. 32–3.

18. ibid., p. 41.

19. ibid., p. 45.

20. Liggett, p. 50.

21. Pershing, vol. 2, pp. 130–31. Pershing admitted that 8,000 horses a month was hopelessly inadequate and that if the planned 80-division programme was to be implemented the real need was for a minimum of 25,000 horses a month for eight months from August 1918. 'These numbers were never reached and we were always approximately 50 per cent short of our requirements,' he added (p. 132). But he believed the French promise, and curtailed US shipments accordingly.

22. Bullard, *Personalities*, pp. 126–7.

23. Austin/Carlisle.

24. ibid., 17 September 1918.

25. Paul H. Clark, papers, vol. 1, p. 6, note 29/Carlisle.

26. Griscom was a trusted member of the relatively small squad of Pershing admirers; Pershing had served under Griscom, a career diplomat, as military attaché in Tokyo.

27. Griscom/Carlisle.

28. ibid.

29. Yensen/Carlisle.

30. March, Peyton C., pp. 39–40.

31. Millett and Williamson, p. 100.

32. Bullard, *Personalities*, p. 116.

33. Austin, 27 March 1918/Carlisle.

34. Bullard, *Personalities*, p. 193.

35. ibid., pp. 174–5.

36. Stallings, pp. 47–8. ('Among the curiosities of the outfit was a second lieutenant who was awarded the Croix de Guerre by the French, not because he was an excellent interpreter and liaison officer capable of leaping from shell hole to shell hole in times of emergency, but simply because Mr Richard F. Peters was sixty-seven years old', p. 48.)

37. Pershing, vol. 2, p. 16.

38. Dexter/ASEQ/Carlisle.

12. Cantigny and Belleau Wood

1. Stallings, p. 105.
2. The complete divisions were the 1st, 2nd, 3rd, 26th, 32nd, 41st, 42nd and 77th; the incomplete, the 5th, 28th, 35th, 82nd and 93rd.
3. Pershing, vol. 2, pp. 46–7.
4. Stallings, p. 58.
5. 'Truly the mountainous AEF had labored mightily and brought forth a mouse,' according to Smythe (p. 129).
6. All references to Daniel Sargent's view of the battle of Cantigny are taken from his memoir deposited at Carlisle.
7. Austin, 1 June 1918/Carlisle.
8. Smythe, p. 126.
9. Austin, 1 June 1918/Carlisle.
10. Bullard, *Personalities*, pp. 197–8.
11. Austin, 8 June 1918/Carlisle.
12. Smythe, pp. 128–9.
13. Pershing, vol. 2, pp. 65–6.
14. ibid., p. 71.
15. ibid., p. 73.
16. ibid., pp. 78–9.
17. ibid., pp. 80–81.
18. Stallings, p. 86.
19. Francis, diary/Carlisle.
20. Thomason, pp. 4–5.
21. Francis, diary/Carlisle.
22. ibid.
23. Stallings, p. 88. Like most of the other legends, this one has become encrusted with myth. A number of other claimants exist for this memorable statement.
24. Thomason, pp. 27–8.
25. Daly was later wounded at Belleau Wood, but he survived the war and gained a Navy Cross, the Distinguished Service Cross, and the French Médaille Militaire and Croix de Guerre; he later claimed that what he actually said was rather more dull: 'Come one! Do you want to live forever?'
26. Stallings, p. 103.
27. Thomason, pp. 58–9.
28. Aitken/ASEQ/Carlisle.
29. Aitken, letter home dated 28 June/Carlisle.
30. Thomas, p. 96.
31. Bullard, *American Soldiers*, p. 39.

32. Aitken was to fight in almost every other battle of the AEF save that at St-Mihiel in September; but he came through the war without a scratch, except for a bout of blistered feet after a 90-kilometre forced march in September 1918.

33. Aitken, letter dated 15 June/Carlisle.

34. Aitken/ASEQ/Carlisle.

35. Pershing, vol. 2, p. 129.

36. ibid., pp. 107–8.

37. Bullard, *Personalities*, p. 200.

13. July–August 1918

1. 2nd Company Grenadiers Regiment 6, 10th Division, German army. Quoted in Wooldridge, p. 81.

2. John D. Clark, diary, 7 July/Carlisle.

3. Austin, 31 July 1918/Carlisle.

4. Wooldridge, pp. 59, 81.

5. Austin, 31 July 1918/Carlisle.

6. ibid.

7. John D. Clark/ASEQ/Carlisle. Harbord had not the slightest idea because the French had refused to tell him, on the grounds of minimizing the chance of the Germans getting advance warning of the attack!

8. Austin, 31 July 1918/Carlisle.

9. Francis/Carlisle.

10. Austin, 31 July 1918/Carlisle.

11. ibid.

12. John D. Clark/ASEQ/Carlisle.

13. Austin, 31 July 1918/Carlisle.

14. John D. Clark/ASEQ/Carlisle.

15. ibid.

16. Thomas puts the 2nd Division's casualties at 183 officers and 4,742 men.

17. John D. Clark/ASEQ/Carlisle.

18. Pershing, vol. 2, p. 195.

19. Donnelly/Carlisle.

20. For example, in this interregnum the Germans attacked the 77th Division, which was supported by the 32nd's Field Artillery, on 13 August; this attack went on for twenty-four hours during which the 119th Field Artillery Regiment alone fired more than 13,000 rounds, about twenty-five shells per gun per hour, an astonishing rate. (Donnelly/Carlisle.)

21. Pershing, vol. 2, pp. 225–6.

22. Pershing, vol. 2, p. 218.

23. ibid., p. 224.

24. ASEQ/Carlisle. John D. Clark, diary, 31 August/Carlisle.

14. Siberia

1. Hagood/Carlisle. Brigadier-General Johnson Hagood; served as chief-of-staff to Major-General James Harbord of the SOS; he was forty-five when the war ended. Hagood was a gifted writer whose uncle, also Johnson Hagood, was a Confederate brigadier and former governor of South Carolina. He graduated from West Point in 1892 (along with another brigadier-general from the 1917–18 conflict, Dennis Nolan), and gained a well-deserved reputation for impatience with meaningless military form and a direct simplicity of approach in all things.

2. Stewart, p. 133.

3. ibid., p. 123.

4. On 23 December 1917 the SWC had also recommended that all possible support should be given to those Russians who were determined to continue the war against Germany.

5. March, pp. 114–15.

6. Stewart, p. 91.

7. Figure given in *The Illustrated Times History of the War*, vol. 20, p. 151; more conservative estimates range as low as 45,000.

8. Graves, p. 116.

9. Bugbee/Carlisle.

10. Stewart, p. 106.

11. Ahearn/ASEQ/Carlisle.

12. Thompson/Carlisle.

13. Sterling/ASEQ/Carlisle.

14. Rhodes, p. 371.

15. Hagood, pp. 232–3/Carlisle.

16. Only the headquarters staff of the 8th Division ever made it to France, on 10 November 1918.

17. Hagood, p. 233/Carlisle.

18. ibid., p. 234.

19. ibid., p. 235.

20. Stewart, p. 242.

21. ibid., p. 141.

22. Slaughter/Carlisle. Intriguingly enough, Slaughter adds in this paper (which was dated 1934) the following tantalizing anecdote: 'It is a very curious fact that correspondence from Russia, from France, and from England during February and March, 1918, carries the very definite suggestion that Germany

and Japan may ally to divide control of Russia. I am convinced that it is a fact that in October 1917 Japanese and German representatives met in Stockholm and negotiated a treaty of alliance which divided Russia and Asia between them and provided for Japanese intervention on the side of Germany in the summer of 1918. Had the German offensive of July 15 captured Paris the treaty might well have become effective as intended. This purported treaty became known and was published at Hamburg by the German revolutionaries in November 1918, and was immediately republished in the Moscow *Izvestia* on November 22.'

23. Graves, p. 55.
24. Slaughter, p. 26/Carlisle.
25. Graves, p. 55.
26. ibid., p. 108.
27. Mr Sayres, secretary of the American Railway Corps, quoted in Stewart, p. 314.
28. Slaughter, p. 40/Carlisle.
29. Letter from Schuyler to Barrows, 1 March 1919, AEF Siberia/Carlisle.

15. September 1918

1. Marshall, p. 138.
2. Austin, 17 September 1918/Carlisle.
3. Pershing, vol. 2, p. 231.
4. ibid., p. 247.
5. ibid., p. 253.
6. ibid., pp. 254-5
7. Marshall, pp. 137-8.
8. Marshall, p. 138.
9. Devan/Carlisle. Even as late as 21 October Devan was recording that his regiment was undergoing yet another reorganization, with another 'half dozen officers leaving this morning for America', including the regiment's commander. This kind of disruption must have been enormously unsettling, and it is quite evident that there was considerable injustice in many of these sackings.
10. Yensen/Carlisle.
11. Marshall, p. 139. Pershing so appreciated Marshall that he appointed him after the war to help him research and write his memoirs.
12. Bullard, *Personalities*, p. 133.
13. The details of the ruse are given in 'Two Unfought Battles' by Thomas M. Johnson in the May 1927 edition of *Century* magazine.
14. Clark, letter dated 8 September/Carlisle.
15. Thomas, p. 217.

16. Lanza, extracts in the Drum papers/Carlisle. A total of 3.31 million rounds for the twenty-six different calibres were provided, and 842,500 were expended.

17. Figures from Pershing, vol. 2, pp. 260–61.

18. Forderhase, memoir and ASEQ/Carlisle.

19. Forderhase, memoir/Carlisle.

20. Austin, 17 September 1918/Carlisle.

21. Austin, 29 September 1918; and letter from the War Department, Washington DC, dated 20 April 1923, in the Austin file at Carlisle.

22. Marshall, p. 135.

23. Pershing, vol. 2, p. 268.

24. ibid., p. 268.

25. Marshall, p. 146.

26. Pershing, vol. 2, pp. 272–3.

27. Comment by Colonel Paille at the French GHQ to Colonel Paul H. Clark, AEF liaison officer: Paul H. Clark, 'Secret Letters to Pershing', no. 198, dated 13 September/Carlisle.

28. Griscom/Carlisle.

29. Pershing, vol. 2, pp. 256–7.

30. Lanza/Carlisle.

31. Pershing, vol. 2, p. 295.

32. ibid., p. 300.

33. Donnelly/Carlisle.

16. October 1918

1. Liddell Hart, p. 490.

2. Hagood, p. 38/Carlisle.

3. Pershing, vol. 2, p. 321.

4. ibid., pp. 303–4.

5. Stallings, p. 294.

6. Liddell Hart, p. 494.

7. This account of the meeting is taken from Stallings, pp. 326–8.

8. Stallings, p. 270.

9. Copy at Carlisle.

10. Francis, diary/Carlisle.

11. Stallings, p. 285.

12. Francis, diary/Carlisle.

13. Stallings puts the figure rather higher, at 6,300 officers and men.

14. Stallings, p. 287.

15. Pershing, vol. 2, p. 327.

16. Stallings, pp. 274–5.
17. York's diary, Internet web site: http://funnelweb.utcc...du/tildaacyork/ diary.html.
18. ibid.
19. ibid.
20. Numerous articles were written after the war by supporters of Edwards; most ignore the fact that Pershing sacked many other officers for lesser complaints than were made against Edwards, and over a much shorter period.
21. Figures taken from the *Preliminary Report on the Historical Method in Military Forecasting*, by Major Hoffman Nickerson (April 1944), Carlisle.
22. Pershing, vol. 2, pp. 336–7.
23. Ettinger, 'Shamrocks Under the Rainbow'/Carlisle.
24. Pershing, vol. 2, p. 344.
25. Hagood, pp. 40–41/Carlisle.
26. Pershing, vol. 2, pp. 350–51
27. *Memoirs of Marshal Foch*, pp. 504–8.
28. ibid., p. 509.
29. Pershing, vol. 2, p. 357, footnote.
30. Yensen/Carlisle.

17. 11 November 1918

1. Stallings, p. 374.
2. McCullough, p. 123.
3. Pershing, vol. 2, p. 374.
4. Aitken/ASEQ/Carlisle.
5. Donnelly/Carlisle.
6. Pershing, vol. 2, p. 381.
7. ibid., p. 389.
8. Wechmeyer/ASEQ/Carlisle.
9. 'The 1st Battalion, 356th Infantry, 178th Brigade, 89th Division – was definitely notified by 12.20 p.m., and was found to have already ceased fire, probably because of the many armistice rumors then current. [. . .] One reason for the dash with which the 178th brigade was attacking was the hope of finding good billets and bathing facilities in the town of Stenay, the men having been for some time without these greatly desired things.' (Nickerson, *Lessons of the Armistice*, p. 9.)
10. Liggett, p. 234.
11. Jordan/ASEQ/Carlisle.
12. Forderhase/Carlisle.
13. ibid.

14. Wright/Carlisle. The kind of task at hand was described by Clinton Dattel, of the 1st Ammunition Train, 1st Division, after the successful taking of the St-Mihiel salient in September 1918: 'We pushed them out so fast that for about a week the dead was unburied. And I'll tell you something right now, that's the first time I saw maggots crawling in and out of people's eyes. Their heads were twice the size and their skin was like parchment. Then I was on details where they issued you a raincoat, rubber boots, and an axe and a shovel.'

15. Ettinger/Carlisle.

16. Pershing, vol. 2, p. 367.

17. ibid., p. 369.

18. Moore, pp. 130–31.

19. ibid., pp. 130–31.

20. ibid., p. 131.

21. Hagood, p. 58/Carlisle.

22. Devan/Carlisle.

23. Dawes, vol. 1, p. 16.

24. Yensen/Carlisle.

25. In many letters from the archive material, doughboys refer to the Germans as 'Dutch', a bowdlerization of 'Deutsch'.

26. Yensen/Carlisle.

27. Bullard, *Personalities*, pp. 296–8.

28. Barbeau and Henri, pp. 160–63; this number of DSCs was greater than those awarded in each of several white divisions of the AEF, such as the 6th, 35th, 81st and 88th.

18. The Cost

1. Nolan papers/Carlisle.

2. March, p. 48. March claims in his book to have plucked Ayres from his previous post and appointed him to be the War Department's statistical chief.

3. Ayres, *1919*.

4. Ayres, p. 101.

5. ibid., p. 104.

6. ibid., p. 116.

7. ibid., p. 119.

8. As in all statistics concerning the Great War, there is never a consensus. For example, Hunter Liggett (p. 248) said the AEF suffered as follows: 35,556 killed in battle; 15,130 died of battle wounds; 5,660 died as a result of other wounds; 24,786 died of diseases; 179,629 wounded; 1,160 missing; 2,163 taken prisoner.

9. Statistics can be bent in all directions: the AEF's 50,300 battle deaths would of course have been much more easily absorbed (and have done far less damage both emotionally and economically) within the large population of the United States than the 102,000 such deaths suffered by the much smaller population of Belgium.

10. Middlebrook, p. 23.

11. The figures that follow are calculations of my own based on p. 117 of Woytinsky's *Die Welt in Zahlen*, vol. 7, which in turn was based on German government statistics. I am very grateful to Ralph Rotte for drawing my attention to this invaluable source.

12. Clark, pp. 180–82.

13. ibid., p. 182.

14. ibid., p. 185.

15. ibid., p. 216.

16. ibid., pp. 192–3.

17. ibid., p. 194.

18. ibid., p. 191.

19. ibid., p. 181.

20. ibid., p. 196.

21. According to official figures from the US Mint in 1918 the exchange rates were £1=$4.87, 1 French franc=$0.19 (from *The Chicago Daily News War Book for American Soldiers, Sailors and Marines*).

22. March, Peyton C., pp. 88–9

23. Fear/ASEQ/Carlisle.

24. *The New War Encyclopaedia and Dictionary*, pp. 50–51.

25. Millett and Williamson, p. 33.

26. Jeze and Truchy, p. 106.

27. ibid., p. 301.

28. Crowell and Wilson, vol. 6, p. 317.

29. Crowell and Wilson, vol. 4, pp. 603–9.

30. Clark, p. 30.

31. ibid., pp. 137–8.

32. ibid., p. 69.

33. ibid., p. 99.

34. ibid., p. 113.

35. ibid., p. 115.

36. ibid., p. 4.

37. ibid., p. 13.

38. ibid., p. 24.

39. Ellis, p. 384.

40. Salter, p. 84.

41. Clark, p. 149.

42. ibid., p. 263.

43. Bishop/ASEQ/Carlisle.

44. From the June 1917 issue of *Masses*; quoted in Peterson and Fite, p. 98.

45. Moore, p. 151.

46. Peterson and Fite, p. 123.

47. ibid., p. 131.

48. ibid., p. 134.

49. Churchill, vol. 2, p. 1127.

50. Moore, p. 132.

51. Peterson and Fite, p. 11.

52. Quoted in Fiebig-von Hase and Lehmkuhl, p. 191.

53. Fiebig-von Hase and Lehmkuhl, p. 204.

54. Yockelson.

55. No. 1 was at Fort McPherson, four miles from Atlanta, Georgia; No. 2 was at Fort Oglethorpe, Georgia, just across the Tennessee border from Chattanooga, Tennessee; No. 3 was four miles from Salt Lake City, at Fort Douglas, Utah.

56. The Espionage Act was introduced to Congress on 2 April 1917 and was an amalgam of seventeen Bills prepared by the Attorney-General's office. It became law on 25 June 1917.

57. Statutes at Large, Washington DC, 1918, vol. XL, p. 553.

58. Peterson and Fite, p. 36.

59. Quoted in Peterson and Fite, p. 50.

60. McCleary/Carlisle.

61. ibid.

62. Peterson and Fite, pp. 56–8.

63. ibid., p. 240.

64. ibid., p. 90.

65. Garcia/ASEQ/Carlisle.

66. Devan/Carlisle: letter dated 20 August 1918 to his fiancée, Winifrede Richards.

67. July 1918 issue of *Crisis*, the monthly journal of the National Association for the Advancement of Colored People (NAACP).

68. Spingarn worked in a sub-section which dealt entirely with alleged 'negro subversion'; as a white liberal he bizarrely believed that he could best serve the cause of greater emancipation by working from within the establishment which was, needless to say, deeply racist. The director of the Military Intelligence Branch was the wonderfully named Colonel Marlborough Churchill.

69. A thorough discussion of this issue is to be found in Ellis, *Journal of American History*, June 1992.

70. *Crisis*, April 1917.

71. Peterson and Fite, p. 303.

19. Falling Apart in Russia

1. MacMorland, letter dated 29 March 1919/Carlisle.

2. Swihart/Carlisle.

3. Hochee/Carlisle.

4. Thompson/Carlisle.

5. MacMorland, letter dated 27 April 1919/Carlisle.

6. MacMorland, letter dated 24 July 1919/Carlisle.

7. Thompson/Carlisle.

8. Yarborough was wounded by a sniper near Gordievka on 7 July 1919, but recovered and returned to duty. In February 1922 he became a diplomatic courier and was given missions to deliver dispatches to the US consulates in Yokohama, Tokyo, Mukden, Manchuria, Tientsin, Peking, Shanghai and Hong Kong. He studied Russian at the University of California in 1923–4, and retired to Mechanicsville after thirty years in intelligence. He died in 1965.

9. Osborn/Carlisle.

10. Yarborough papers/Carlisle.

11. Slaughter, pp. 35–6/Carlisle.

12. Loughran letter/Carlisle.

13. Rhodes, p. 372.

14. Yarborough, memo dated 27 December 1919/Carlisle. Joseph Loughran, a sergeant with C Company of the 31st Infantry in Vladivostok, recorded that 'the senior sergeant under me (while stationed at Churkin, which is just over the hill from the Golden Horn Bay and the city of Vladivostok) became a user of narcotics in one of its many forms and was subjected to hallucinations'. (Document in Box 5 of AEF, Siberia, Joseph Loughran papers, at Carlisle.)

15. Yarborough, memo dated 14 August 1919/Carlisle.

16. Yarborough/Carlisle.

17. Loughran papers/Carlisle. Sergeant Joseph Loughran of the 31st Infantry recorded the testimony of his fellow 31st Infantry sergeant Almus E. Beck, who was part of the platoon attacked at Romanovka. Beck's figures were 19 killed immediately, 5 dying of wounds later, and 25 wounded. Sergeant Alan Ferguson, of the 31st Infantry's Intelligence section, was not present during the attack but helped prepare the report of Captain Frank A. Paul (regimental Intelligence Officer). The report stated there were 76 Americans in the camp at the time of the attack, 26 were killed and 25 wounded. Colonel Frank Bugbee, who took over command of the 31st from Colonel Frederic Sargent

at the end of September 1919, recorded that there were 75 doughboys at Romanovka, and that 18 died and 35 were wounded.

18. Graves, p. 254.

19. Stewart, p. 283.

20. Graves, quoted in Stewart, p. 287.

21. Yarborough papers/Carlisle.

22. ibid.

23. Thus one capitalist at least had cause to be grateful for the democratic excesses of primitive communism.

24. AEF Siberia/Carlisle. Typed report by Colonel O. P. Robinson, dated 6 August 1919.

25. Gillem papers/Carlisle.

26. *San Francisco Examiner*, Thursday, 8 October 1919. Such sentiments were to linger and colour the way Americans considered the next world war, also seen for a while as a clash of empires and commercial interests.

27. Bugbee, letter to his wife dated 9 November 1919/Carlisle.

28. Opperman, p. 1/Carlisle.

29. From *Hearings before the Select Committee on POW/MIA Affairs*, United States Senate.

30. *New York Times*, 18 April 1921, carried a headline, 'Captives Release Repeatedly Sought'.

31. From *Hearings before the Select Committee on POW/MIA Affairs*, United States Senate, 23 May 1991.

32. Gillem papers/Carlisle.

20. Aftermath

1. Hagood, p. 81/Carlisle.

2. Devan, letter to Fannie M. Devan (his aunt), dated 24 November 1918/Carlisle.

3. Intelligence report from GHQ AEF, no. 286, originally marked 'secret' (since declassified), dated 24 November 1918: Conger papers/Carlisle. The intelligence officer was not named in the report; the trip itself took place on 20–21 November.

4. March, Peyton C., p. 310.

5. Hagood, p. 96/Carlisle.

6. Lea, p. 233.

7. ibid., p. 236.

8. ibid., p. 261.

9. March, Peyton C., pp. 322–3.

10. John D. Clark, letter dated 22 November 1918/Carlisle.

11. Nickerson/Carlisle.

12. Yensen/Carlisle.

13. Document from AMHI, Carlisle.

14. Yensen/Carlisle.

15. *A Study of Anglo-American and Franco-American Relations During World War I*: Part 2, *Franco-American Relations*, Colonel C. H. Goddard, Army War College, 9 October 1943. Appendix, pp. 19–20: letter from Brigadier-General Malin Craig, chief-of-staff, US Third Army, to Brigadier-General Leroy Eltinge, deputy chief-of-staff, GHQ AEF, dated 8 December, 1918, enclosing translation of confidential report submitted by a Major Kann, French liaison officer with the Third Army AEF, to Marshal Foch's chief-of-staff, in which Craig writes, 'We do not like to be spied upon.'

16. ibid., p. 20.

17. Bullard, *Personalities*, p. 57.

18. Goddard/Carlisle.

19. Ashburn, p. 358.

20. Wechmeyer/Carlisle.

21. Yensen/Carlisle.

22. Devan, journal dated 16 November 1918/Carlisle.

23. Hagood/Carlisle, p. 238.

24. ibid., p. 239.

25. MacMorland, letter dated 29 November 1919/Carlisle.

26. MacMorland, letters dated 3 and 4 December 1919/Carlisle.

27. Bandholtz, diary/Carlisle.

28. D'Este, p. 272.

29. Hagood, pp. 244–7/Carlisle.

30. Ely/Carlisle.

31. In Newcastle-upon-Tyne in 1919, Field Marshal Sir Douglas Haig told a roaring crowd: 'It is right to speak of our allies, but it was the British army that won the war. It was old England that bore the brunt of the fighting in the last two years, and I hope everyone at home will realize that fact' (*Daily Express*, 9 July 1919).

32. A study of volunteer enlistments, Army of the United States (1775–1945), by Colonel C. Benson, September 1945, Army War College, Carlisle. The numbers included 502,216 infantry, 70,126 machine-gunners, 60,028 cavalry, 202,162 field artillery, 81,556 engineers, 1,821 chemical warfare, 10,214 tank corps, 21,328 signals, and 34,828 in the air service.

33. Crowell and Wilson, vol. 4, p. 603. In October 1918 the AEF sent word back to the US War Department that by 1 January 1919 the demand for soluble coffee in the trenches would be 25,000 pounds a day, in addition to the already allocated ration of 12,000 pounds a day. The entire US output of

soluble coffee was already taken by the US army – but that was only 6,000 pounds a day.

34. Ayres, p. 131. At the height of the war Britain spent an estimated £5,000,000 a day on its military effort.

35. Glover/ASEQ/Carlisle.

36. Foster/ASEQ/Carlisle.

37. J. M. Keynes, *The Economic Consequences of the Peace* (London, 1920), p. 256.

38. Drum papers/Carlisle.

Index